WITCHCRAFT

The moment you start to think that you know everything about life is the moment your glory will be taken away from you.

– Christopher Todd

WITCHCRAFT

A MAGICAL PATH TO ENLIGHTENMENT

Your Guide to the Craft of the Wise

Christopher Todd

Mandrake

© Christopher Todd 2022, 2023

First Edition

All rights reserved. No part of this work may be reproduced, stored in a retrieval system, or transmitted in any form or by any means, electronic, mechanical, photocopying, recording or otherwise without the prior permission of the publisher.

Published by
Mandrake
PO Box 250
OXFORD
OX1 1AP (UK)

Contents

Introduction	7
Part One: About Witchcraft	11
Chapter One: Witchcraft Past and Present	13
Chapter Two: The Ultimate Deity	37
Chapter Three: The Elements	52
Chapter Four: The Wheel of the Year	64
Chapter Five: Witchcraft Rites	82
Chapter Six: Tools of the Trade	97
Chapter Seven: The Altar and Sacred Space	120
Part Two: Spellcraft	133
Chapter Eight: Casting Spells	134
Chapter Nine: Love Spells	185
Chapter Ten: Money Spells	194
Chapter Eleven: Healing Spells	204

Chapter Twelve:
Success Spells   216

Chapter Thirteen:
Protection Spells   225

Chapter Fourteen:
Fertility Spells   237

Part Three:
Occult Aspects and Correspondences   247

Chapter Fifteen:
Astrology   248

Chapter Sixteen:
Herbal Lore   285

Chapter Seventeen:
Crystals, Stones and Metals   314

Chapter Eighteen:
Animal Kingdom   342

Chapter Nineteen:
Dreams and Dream Work   391

Chapter Twenty:
Divination   426

Bibliography   463

Contents Index   468

Introduction

Welcome to the wonderful, magical and enchanted world of Witchcraft and thank you so much for choosing my book. This book is the result of many years of study and practice on the subject of Witchcraft, the legendary priesthood that has endured throughout the history of humankind. I have officially been a Witch since the autumn of 2007, but in reality all my life. It was only when I reached a certain age of maturity that I felt compelled to make it official with a self-initiation in the autumn equinox of that year. I have actually practised Witchcraft and its many magical practices ever since I was a young boy and this compelled me to write this book in later life. When I began writing this book I had no idea just how difficult it would be, but with the strength of the deities, nature, my partner, some of my close family and my own personal inner fire I managed to get through it. The ability to get through life's challenges is at the heart of the Witchcraft religion and this is something that you need to consider when embarking on its path to enlightenment. Witchcraft can help you to get through some of life's most difficult times and it can help you to enhance and embrace the good things of life, but you also need that inner fire and strength to be able to face your own inner demons and to get the things desired or needed out of life. Witchcraft is about enhancing your life and personality as well as that of other people. It is a priesthood and a spiritual path of personal discovery that only some of us are truly meant to follow.

This book is a very educated look at Witchcraft, magic, spellcraft and some of the other many beliefs and practices that Witches hold dear to their hearts. It can be seen as a tutorial for those who are new to Witchcraft as well as a reference book for those who have more experience. I would suggest that you read the book from beginning to end to get the most out of it if you are truly serious about taking on Witchcraft for yourself. The book is divided into three basic parts:

Part One: Part one deals with historical aspects of Witchcraft as well as Witchcraft in the modern world. It deals with the fundamentals of Witchcraft and the beliefs and practices that it holds in the modern world. Here, you will find out the very basics of Witchcraft as a belief system as your knowledge increases. This part will help you to understand what it is that Witches actually believe in and the religious festivals and rituals that they hold. You can also find information on the special tools and the sacred altar in this part of the book.

Part Two: Part two deals with the subjects of magic and spellcraft. It contains everything you will need to know as you embark on the world of spellcraft to enhance your life and help you deal with your problems. Magic will be clearly explained and defined in this part of the book. Part two will also cover specific aspects of spellcraft, such as love spells, money spells and protection spells. This part of the book also contains spells that I have devised over the years that you can use for yourself. This part of the book basically takes a much deeper look at magic and spellcraft and their many aspects.

Part Three: Part three deals with specific occult aspects and magical correspondences that Witches use in their many workings. Here, you will have the chance to develop your skills and knowledge on the subjects that Witches hold very close to their hearts indeed. Here, you will find subjects such as astrology, herbal lore and divination. This part of the book is designed not only to enhance your knowledge, but also as a reference guide as you devise your own spells, rituals and other magical workings. It contains very useful information for both the would-be Witch and the adept.

There are certain words in Witchcraft that need to be explained before you proceed with the reading of this book. The difficulty with Witchcraft that is often confusing is that people have different ideas as to what words actually mean. This is because, as you will come to understand, Witchcraft is a very personal way of life and each Witch decides for himself or herself what they want to believe certain words, so famous with Witchcraft, actually mean. I can only explain what I personally believe these words mean. My beliefs about what these words mean are shared by many, if not most, Witches. First and foremost I would like to explain that all Witches are Pagans, but not all Pagans are Witches. Witchcraft is a distinct type of Paganism. A Druid is another type of Pagan for example.

Paganism is basically the original religion of humankind. It referred to those who worship, honour and revere nature and the natural world. It is often known as the old religion, but over millennia it has actually developed into many kinds of religions, branches of Paganism if you will, with Witchcraft being one of them. It is derived from the words *pagani* or *paganus* which referred to people who lived in the countryside and did not belong to towns or cities. It meant "dweller of the land", "dweller of the fields" or "country dweller". It basically meant people who did not belong to the organised religions, people who were spiritually and magically tied to the energies of the land and of nature.

Another word that you will come across in Witchcraft that has often caused considerable confusion is Wicca or Wiccan. To me, Wicca is simply another word for Witchcraft and its followers. Some people believe that Wicca is a type of Witchcraft, but I cannot agree with this. Originally, Wicca was the word for Witches and Witchcraft. It referred to people who worked with nature and its natural forces. It was originally never a type of Witchcraft, it simply was Witchcraft. It referred to those people who held a lot of knowledge and wisdom, basically the folk who ordinary people came to for help and advice. Before Christianity got powerful, it was a badge of honour by some of the Pagan folk who had developed their knowledge and wisdom to a certain level. To avoid confusion, I rarely use the words Wicca or Wiccan to describe Witchcraft or Witches in general.

There are even some people who believe that Wicca is a Pagan religion and Witchcraft is a magical practice. They believe that Wicca is a contemporary Pagan religion that derives its beliefs and practices from ancient Pagan religions and the earliest expressions of reverence of nature. Again, I cannot agree with this. To me, Witchcraft is first and foremost a religion that honours the male and female balance and energies of nature. It is a beautiful religion with ancient roots that embraces magical practices (spellcraft, astrology, midwifery, divination, spiritual healing and so on) to enhance our lives and the lives of those around us. To be a Witch is to understand the powers and forces of nature that help us to further understand the magical practices that we embrace.

It is really only for those who are actually strong enough to face up to their own inner demons head-on.

Another word that is frequently used in Witchcraft is supernatural. Now, I dislike this word and will only use it if I have to explain something. But I want to make it clear my beliefs about it before you read the chapters of this book. As a common definition, the word supernatural refers to all things or events that are above, beyond or outside of the laws of nature. How can anything be so, I ask you? Just because something is not yet fully understood does not mean that it is supernatural or above the laws of nature. To me, everything that exists works within the laws of nature, not outside them. The correct word for anything that is unexplained should be paranormal. This word, as a common definition, refers to all things that are not yet understood, defined or labelled by science. So anything that is not fully understood of a mysterious nature that Witches are involved with should be, in my opinion, known as the paranormal. The magical practices of Witchcraft may well be more understood by science in the future. Hypnotism, for example, is an ancient magical practice associated with the paranormal before it was "discovered" and more understood by science in more recent times. Witchcraft is very much open to the discoveries of science, but Witches also understand that not everything can be explained by it as of yet. Some things, such as the true nature of the divine, may never be truly understood.

If you are drawn to Witchcraft and wish to pursue a deeper exploration and understanding of the ancient magical practices you should always remember that Witchcraft is a free religion. You are free to believe and to practise whatever is right for you, so long as you don't cause harm. Never take any book on the subject of Witchcraft as "holy writ", because no such thing truly exists. Only what feels right to you personally is what you should be aiming for. Witchcraft is, after all, a spiritual and magical path to enlightenment that should let each of its followers find their own ways within their practices. It is a spiritual journey of self-discovery and exploration of someone's personal relationship with the divine. Think of any books that you read of a magical or spiritual nature only as guides and not as Bibles that must be followed to the last detail. Your own experiences and revelations concerning the divine are most important to you personally and are just as valid and rational as someone else's. I truly do hope that you will enjoy my book and that you will learn a lot from it. Remember to always follow your heart and just enjoy your experiences and development on your magical path to enlightenment.

Blessings be.

Part One:
About Witchcraft

Chapter One:
Witchcraft Past and Present

Witchcraft is a nature religion which is also known as Wicca, the Craft, Wise Craft and the Craft of the Wise. Its history has long been shrouded in much mystery and secrecy. Dr. Margaret A. Murray (1863-1963), an anthropologist and Professor of Egyptology, had studied the history of Witchcraft in great detail. She argued in her books, including *The Witch Cult in Western Europe* (1921), that Witchcraft was a fully organised Pagan religion of ancient times that had existed centuries before the rise of Christianity. She insisted that it had survived as a secret religion throughout the Pagan persecutions and the infamous Witch hunts. While most scholars and historians have dismissed Murray's claims as wishful thinking, there are many people who believe that there is some truth in much of what she said.

The Ancient Roots of Witchcraft

Around thirty thousand years ago humankind lived in total harmony with nature. The prehistoric tribes constantly observed the changing seasons and how the sun and the moon's power influenced their lives and everything else within the natural world on earth. Our ancestors understood that they had to bow down to the powers of nature since they were dependent on it for survival.

While our Pagan ancestors observed the seasons – spring, summer, autumn and winter – they began to understand that each had a particular importance to all life on earth. For our ancestors, each season had its own significance. The spring and summer were times when the sun's power waxed and peaked, times that our ancestors knew were of great importance for the growth of the plant kingdom, a major food source. As the autumn became apparent, our ancestors began to gather in the bounty of the year's harvest ready for the approaching long and cold nights ahead. In the winter, when the earth rested and became barren, our ancestors knew that they would have no choice but to turn to the animal kingdom as their major food source. The all-important hunt.

Through the changing seasons, our ancestors also began to understand nature's spiritual messages. They understood that the seasons were symbolic to the spiritual and physical changes of life. As the seasons progressed in the cycle of the year, in which the sun's strength waxed and became full in the spring and summer, and waned and went into darkness in the autumn and winter, so too did these basic changes occur within the cycle of their own lives. It was through this understanding that our ancestors sought to understand more about their spiritual connection to nature.

In these ancient times, our ancestors believed in a multitude of deities. It was the gods who were the powerful forces of nature. For our ancestors, it was a god who controlled the thunderstorms, a god who controlled the tidal movements, a god who controlled the rain, a god who controlled the migration of animals…the list is virtually endless.

In the knowledge that these forces were much more powerful than themselves, our ancestors sought to appease the gods by giving them worship and respect. In doing so, our ancestors hoped that the spirits of nature would grant them abundant harvests and successful hunts.

Though our ancestors acknowledged many gods, they also began to understand that there were two deities who were superior over all the others – the God and the Goddess. Our ancestors knew that these two forces were real since everywhere they looked they could see that the natural world was dominated by male and female principles.

The Goddess, as the representative of woman, became associated with the abundant earth, since the earth gave birth to new life through its plant life. This was a time when humans knew nothing of the role that males played in procreation and since life miraculously came from the womb of a woman, our ancestors reasoned that it must be the Goddess who caused life to grow from the earth. Thus, the earth was worshipped as the creative force and the mysteries of the woman's womb (known today as Mother Nature, Mother Earth or Earth Mother). The Goddess, therefore, was predominantly a figure of fertility for our ancient ancestors.

In Lower Austria, in a village near Krems, archaeologists discovered an ancient small statue depicting a very fertile feminine figure – which is estimated by experts to have been created between about 28, 000 and 25, 000 B. C. E. – known as the Venus of Willendorf. The figurine, just over eleven centimetres high, emphasises parts of the female form that are typically associated with childbearing (such as a swollen belly and large breasts). The Venus of Willendorf is just one of many Venus figurines surviving from the Paleolithic period. They are some of the best evidence in existence that show just how important the Goddess was for prehistoric humans.

Hunting was predominately an activity of the males of prehistoric times, since their natural muscular physique seemed more capable of catching animals for food and thus the God, as the representative of man, was identified primarily through his god of the hunt persona in many cultures. The god of the hunt was often envisioned as a horned being, since most of the animals that were hunted were horned, and by worshipping the god of the hunt in this way our ancestors hoped that the God would grant them successful hunts. A bountiful hunt was all-important for our ancestors because not only could it provide food for their peoples in the winter, it also provided skins for warmth/shelter and bones that could be fashioned into tools and weapons. This is why the horned god became a prominent figure throughout the ancient world.

There is indisputable evidence, in fact, that our Pagan ancestors engaged in the worship of the horned god in many cultures all over the world, because of ancient paintings left behind on cave walls. These paintings show primitive man, adorned in the skins and horns of animals, performing ritual observances in honour of the god of the hunt. These were the days when humans knew that by enacting out a successful hunt in a type of sympathetic magical ritual, it would encourage a successful hunt in the physical world. The humans performing these rites were the Shamans, the first humans to combine religious beliefs with magic.

Naturally, our ancestors worshipped the Goddess as supreme deity when the fruits of the land from the plant kingdom were readily available for food. In contrast, it was the God who reigned supreme when barrenness covered the land and humans had to revert to hunting for food. Yet, even though supremacy alternated between the two deities, rarely was one venerated to the exclusion of the other.

While it is true to say that the Goddess was worshipped as the sole creator of all life, most cultures acknowledged the God as equal to her, for it was his power that provided the strength and passion that men needed to hunt for food in the winter, while the women of the tribe stayed home to take care of their young.

Over time, as agriculture grew and humans became more civilised, however, the need for hunting decreased but for many cultures the powerful god of the hunt never ceased to exist. Instead, he became a powerful deity of success and fertility and was called upon for these reasons. Today, he is still a powerful representation of the male principle of nature and is most commonly known as the half-man and half-goat and Greek god of the wild woods Pan or the Celtic god of the hunt and protector of nature Cernunnos.

As time passed on and our Pagan ancestors became more and more in tune with the forces of nature, they became advanced enough to become priests and priestesses of the God and the Goddess. These priests and priestesses, in many cultures all over the world, came together in their rituals and celebrations to represent the natural male and female balance of nature. In doing so, our ancestors brought into their lives the magic and power of the divine. It was our ancient Pagan ancestors who formed the basis for all the religions and all the magical practices – spellcraft, necromancy, astrology, divination, spiritual healing, concocting potions from herbs and so on – of the world today.

The Pagan Persecutions and the Witch Hunts

When the Christian religion began in the first century C. E. there was not the instant mass-conversion that is sometimes assumed. In fact, for the first few centuries of Christianity the old religion was still very prominent throughout all of Europe, as it had always been for thousands of years. The new religion of Christianity – which was essentially a small cult at that time – was not yet powerful enough to uproot the ways that the Pagan folk had practised for thousands of years.

In those early days when Christianity began to slowly spread across Europe, those who were advanced in the old religion – the Pagan priests and priestesses – were the spiritual leaders to whom ordinary people looked for help and advice. They were the healers, the herbalists, the diviners, the astrologers, the power wielders and the experts in magic and spellcraft. To all intents and purposes, the Pagan priests and priestesses were the physicians, the magicians, the counsellors and the spiritual leaders all rolled into one and for this reason they were very much respected by the populace.

Over time, however, Christianity began to gain strength and in 317 C. E. the Emperor Constantine declared it the official religion of the decaying Roman Empire. At a rate of one country at a time, Christianity began to slowly take over Europe and as a result Paganism was increasingly seen as a threat to the supremacy of the Church. All over Europe, the Christians began to persecute the Pagans in an effort to coerce them into converting to Christianity.

One of the most successful attempts at mass-conversion occurred during the pontificate of Pope Gregory the Great (590-604 C. E.). Gregory did much to secure the power of the Church. Thousands of people converted to Christianity during his papacy. He began to realise that it was inevitable that the people would continue to gather in places where they were accustomed to worshipping the old gods. Therefore, he decreed to his clergy that wherever it was possible Pagan idols should be destroyed and Christian churches should be built on sites of the ancient Pagan temples.

But Paganism had a heritage that stemmed back thousands of years. Its beliefs and traditions were not likely to disappear as easily as the Pope had anticipated. When the churches had been built, for instance, many of them were dedicated to the Virgin Mary and were named "The Church of Our Lady" – "Our Lady" being another name that the Pagans had for the Goddess. So even if the people were forced to attend the Christian churches at least they could still worship Mary as an archetypal symbol of the Goddess in them.

As the centuries passed the smear campaign against the Pagans grew stronger and stronger. All over Europe, the Christian authorities began to impose new laws that forbid the worship of the old Pagan deities. Those who were believed to be worshipping the old gods were branded as heretics and were subsequently punished (often by death). Over time, Christianity had gained so much power and control over Europe that Paganism no longer represented the sole religion of the land.

The Christians were aware that it was the horned god in particular who needed to be dethroned in order to really discourage the people from practising the old religion. Therefore, they began to teach that he was, in fact, the Biblical Devil. In other words, the Church was claiming that the Pagans had been Devil worshippers all along. Throughout Europe, the alleged crime of Devil worship would soon be considered to be the most noxious of all crimes since the Devil in Christian beliefs represented all that was evil in the world.

Since Paganism was now associated with Devil worship, a mass-hysteria began to take over Europe and by the fifteenth century any form of pre-Christian, Pagan-related belief or practice was now regarded as Witchcraft (the word "Witch" is derived from the Anglo-Saxon word *"Wicca"* which simply means "wise one". Historically, Wicca was a title that was given to some of the ancient Pagan priests and priestesses). Throughout Europe, it was increasingly believed that Witches had entered into a diabolical pact with Satan and that Christianity was under an apocalyptic battle against Satan and his secret army of evil Witches. Those who were believed to be guilty of the alleged crime of Satanic Witchcraft were interrogated, brutally tortured and murdered.

On December 5th 1484 Pope Innocent VIII issued his papal bull *"Summis Desiderantes Affectibus"*, which essentially put yet more pressure on the Inquisition to root out Witchcraft. The Pontiff issued the bull because he believed that the threat of Witchcraft was not taken seriously enough by the Church's clergy. All over Europe, laymen and women were encouraged to help the Inquisitors of the Church to hunt out Witches. It was because of Innocent's bull that the Witch hunts and murders began to spiral out of control.

Two years after Innocent had issued his bull, a very infamous book was published called the *Malleus Maleficarum* (the Hammer of Witches), which was fully supported by the Pope. This bizarre book – which was written by two German monks called Jakob Sprenger and Heinrich Kramer – explained why Witchcraft was real and why Witches should be exterminated. It laid down the foundations to what Witchcraft was believed to involve and contained detailed instructions on how to find, persecute and punish Witches. Soon the iconic Witch we see at Halloween, flying a broomstick to meet the Devil or casting evil spells over a large bubbling cauldron, was increasingly believed to be a terrifying fact in these superstitious times.

Witches were believed to attend what was known as the *"Witches' Sabbaths"*, here they would meet in groups, perhaps in a nearby woods, and worship the Christian Devil and perform all manner of evil deeds imagined by the Christians. It was at these Sabbaths that Witches were thought to perform a Satanic rite known as the *"Osculum Infame"* – which was believed to be the actual kissing of the Devil's backside. This was a rite that Witches were thought to do to pay homage to Satan and was also a rite that was believed to be required for the initiation of a new Witch. After the initiation of a Witch had taken place, she or he was no longer classed as a human being, but an evil creature of Satan and his demons.

In a time when the patriarchal religion of Christianity had an extremely powerful influence over Europe, women were more likely to be accused of Witchcraft than men because women were classed as the weaker sex and could, therefore, be easily tempted over to the "dark side" of Satan's powers, just as Eve did in the Garden of Eden. Any woman possessing great knowledge, especially of the ancient magical practices, was accused of Witchcraft. In essence, the Church wanted to keep women in their place if they stepped out of line and threatened male supremacy.

As the years passed, the penalties for the crimes of Witchcraft began to stiffen and torture became increasingly accepted as the most effective way of extracting confessions from the accused. Some of the unfortunate victims were forced to stay awake for days on end until they were just too exhausted to protest their innocence, while others were tortured with devices that caused excruciating pain. The Iron Spider, for example, was a device that contained four metal claws that were heated and then used to slowly rip off the breasts, and the Witches' Chair, as another example, was a metal seat with a fire lit below it that the accused were forced to sit on. Inevitably, most of the victims confessed under such extreme methods of torture and those who did were promptly sentenced to death – usually by hanging or burning at the stake.

In some parts of Europe, especially in England and Scotland, if the accused continued to protest their innocence, the authorities would search them for the "Devil's Mark". In the sixteenth and seventeenth centuries, it was commonly believed that when the Devil made a pact with his Witches at the infamous Sabbaths he would leave a permanent mark on them to seal their obedience and service to him. Any unusual birthmark, blemish, mole or wart would be enough to convince the authorities that the person in question was indeed guilty of Witchcraft.

Suspected Witches also had to undergo a test called "Swimming the Witch". Basically, this hideous method involved tying an accused Witch's hands and feet together, or tying them to a chair, and then dunking her in a nearby lake or river – which was usually blessed by the local Christian priest. If she sank then she was proclaimed innocent (but probably died anyhow), but if she floated then she was a Witch, since water was believed to be the pure element of God used in Christian baptism that would, in no uncertain terms, reject the Witch.

Matthew Hopkins, the infamous "Witchfinder General", was well-known in England for his use of this method of identifying the guilt of Witches. He appointed himself as "Witchfinder General", though he was never actually given this title by any authority, because no such title officially existed. He simply assumed the title himself and benefited financially in doing so. He began his work in Manningtree, Essex, in the 1640s, and went from village to village accusing many innocent people of Witchcraft and charging large sums of money to root out what he believed to be the Devil's work. It is estimated that he was responsible for the deaths of up to 300 women between 1644 and 1646. In the end, however, people grew tired of him and he was refused entry into villages. Legend has it that he was thrown into a river and accused of Witchcraft himself when the public found him to float. In reality, however, he returned to Manningtree and died of tuberculosis at the young age of 27. Perhaps he finally received some of his karma!

Although Witches were believed to be Satan's allies, there is little to no hard evidence to suggest that any of the accused actually worshipped the Christian Satan or anyone who used Satan to manifest their evil work (who would be brave enough?). There is some evidence that people did curse each other with the use of Voodoo image magic, for revenge perhaps, but it is unlikely that anyone attempted to do this through powers from Satan.

While some of those people accused of Witchcraft may have indeed been Pagan Witches – those who believed in and practised pre-Christian ways – evidence suggests that many of the accused were actually Christians who combined Pagan beliefs and practices with Christianity. They were people who believed that the ancient spells, charms and herbal remedies, that had been handed down to them through successive generations, actually worked. They were simply respectable healers who were often known as "Wise Folk", "Cunning Folk" or "White Witches".

The late 1600s and early 1700s saw a dramatic decrease in most of Europe's Witch hunts and murders. With the growing understanding of scientific study and research, it was beginning to be understood that there had been a terrible mistake, where those who had been accused of Witchcraft had never been Satanic Witches at all. The so-called crimes that many people had been accused of during the Witch hunts were increasingly seen as crimes that they could simply never have committed. In short, Witches were regarded as less of a threat.

All in all, it is estimated that as many as one million people were put to a terrible death on the charge of Witchcraft throughout the medieval and early modern periods. Though this is just a rough estimate. Some scholars believe that there may have been as many as nine million people put to death during this dark period of Pagan history. Either way these very dark times will go down in history as one of the biggest injustices of all time.

In England, the last three hangings of Witches occurred at Exeter in 1682. Scotland was one of the worst places to be for accused Witches. It is estimated that over 4, 000 people were executed there between 1590 and 1680 – mostly by burning at the stake. The last execution occurred in 1727. The last Witches put to death elsewhere in Europe are varied. In Germany it was 1775, 1745 in France, 1781 in Spain, 1782 in Switzerland, and as late as 1792 in Poland.

In England, the death penalty for Witchcraft was repealed in 1735. The new law on Witchcraft – which remained in effect until 1951 – targeted Witchcraft as a fraudulent practice and made it illegal to pretend to conjure spirits or claim that a human had magical powers. The maximum penalty for these crimes was one year imprisonment. The last person imprisoned under this law was the spiritualist medium Helen Duncan who was sent to London's Holloway prison in 1944.

Since many of the victims were burned during the Witch hunts, modern Witches have adopted a saying *"never again the burning"*, because we never want one of the biggest and most horrific injustices of all time to happen again. Modern Witches are peaceful and earth-centred people who believe that no religion has the right to force their beliefs on others. This kind of attitude should have always been the case and was in ancient Pagan times. Live and let live is a rule that Witches today follow.

The Golden Dawning of a New Era

When the death penalty was repealed in England attitudes towards Paganism and the occult (from the Latin word *"occultus"* meaning "hidden" or "concealed") began to change. The 1800s in particular showed an increase in the public's fascination with the grey area of the occult, magic and the possibility of contact with the spirit world. No longer were people totally controlled by the Christian religion.

In time, movements such as the Hermetic Order of the Golden Dawn and the Spiritualists' National Union further increased the public's awareness of the occult. At last, people had a little more freedom to believe in the old Pagan teachings.

The Hermetic Order of the Golden Dawn was truly influential on the beliefs of modern Witches. The organisation helped Witchcraft to evolve into what it is today. It was formed near the end of the nineteenth century by three Freemasons namely, William Woodman, William Westcott and Samuel MacGregor Mathers. It dealt with understanding many ancient Pagan-related subjects that modern Witchcraft is involved with today including magic, metaphysics, paranormal activity, theurgy, astrology, divination, astral travel and alchemy.

One such man largely responsible for the re-emergence of the old Pagan ways was a man named Dr. Gerald B. Gardner (1884-1964). Gardner, a former British civil servant and Freemason, was heavily involved in such subjects of the Golden Dawn and was deeply fascinated by ancient magical religions. After spending many years studying the occult, he encountered a Traditional British coven of Witches (the New Forest coven) during the late 1930s. In 1939, just before the start of the Second World War, he was initiated into this coven by a woman known as "Old Dorothy" Clutterbuck. Gardner later claimed that this coven came from a long line of Witches going back throughout the ages.

Throughout his experience in the New Forest coven, Gardner became extremely enthusiastic about what he found. He had spent many years studying religious magic and was now a part of it. He became eager to tell the world about his knowledge and experience. But the Witchcraft Act of 1735 prevented him from doing so. After some time, however, Gardner found a way. In 1949 he published a fictional book called *High Magic's Aid* which basically gave clues about the beliefs and practices of modern Witchcraft.

When the last Witchcraft laws were finally repealed in 1951, Gardner was delighted. He was finally able to publish non-fiction books about the Craft. *Witchcraft Today* (1954) and *The Meaning of Witchcraft* (1959) by Gerald Gardner were two of the earliest non-fiction books widely available about the Craft. As a result of his writings and his experience in the New Forest coven, Gardner went on to create one of the most influential forms of Witchcraft that the world has ever seen: the Gardnerian tradition (see below). At last, the knowledge that had been handed down in secret Witchcraft traditions was finally available to all and as a result more and more people began to take on Witchcraft as their religion.

Gardner genuinely believed in the powers of nature and that men and women could tune into it to make positive changes. He also embraced and advocated the use of ancient, long-established rituals that were once the way of the people. According to several anthropologists, his work has three direct links to the ancient Pagan religions: the use of herbs and woods in magic, the use of ceremonial magic, and the use of ancient folk rites and customs to manipulate the forces of nature.

The work that had began with Gerald Gardner was furthered by other notable members of the Craft. Doreen Valiente (1922-1999) actively promoted and defended Witchcraft during the 1960s, and played a leading role in the Witchcraft Research Association and the Pagan Front. Sybil Leek (1919-1982), a respected Hereditary Witch, provided further evidence to support Murray's theories about Witchcraft being an ancient Pagan religion. Alex Sanders (1926-1988), who claimed to have been initiated into the Craft by his grandmother, founded the Alexandrian form of Witchcraft in the 1960s. Leo Martello (1931-2000) spoke up about Italian Witches known as the Strega. Raymond Buckland (1934-2017), who many consider to be the grandfather of modern American Witchcraft, founded the Seax tradition of Witchcraft in the 1970s, and continued to be a significant figure in the modern Craft right up until his death.

At the time of Gardner's writing, Witchcraft was a dying religion with very few members. If it hadn't been for his huge efforts to bring Witchcraft out of the darkness, the religion would have died out completely. So to Gardner we owe a huge debt of gratitude for having had the courage to finally speak up about this ancient religion. It is thanks to Gardner that modern Witches and would-be Witches can appreciate the Craft, in all its beauty, mystery and power, today.

What Then is Modern Witchcraft?

Modern Witchcraft can be described as a life-affirming, earth-based spirituality that seeks to work in harmony with nature. Unlike some of the modern religions of today, Witchcraft celebrates both the spiritual and the physical aspects of life and teaches us how to retain our spiritual closeness with nature in the modern world. Witchcraft is a very joyous and loving religion, one that celebrates and honours all life.

There is no supreme leader or central government in Witchcraft, nor do all Witches share exactly the same beliefs. While our beliefs are very similar,

Witchcraft is an open-minded religion that encourages freedom of thought and personal integrity. Having said that, Witches generally do have a great respect for those who have gained a certain level of spiritual wisdom – whether they are Pagan or of another religious background – and believe that much can be learnt from them.

As with their Pagan ancestors, Witches today generally acknowledge both a God and a Goddess. We believe that the divine is made up of both male and female energies and that these two forces are active throughout the entire universe. Witches link with the God and Goddess, to whom we often refer to as the Lord and the Lady, through the various deities in mythology. The deities represent the God and Goddess in the eyes of Witches.

Witches worship the Goddess and God as the two universal energies that created everything seen and unseen. Together they are the force that connects all life – which we often refer to as the web of life – and it is through our sacred rituals and our various magical practices that we increasingly become aware of the Goddess and God, both within ourselves and in the world around us. Our practices allow us to draw closer to them.

Many Witches also believe that much of reality is unseen. They believe that the physical world is but one of many dimensions. The only difference between the physical world and the spiritual realities is that the physical world is simply denser. Modern-day science is slowly, but surely, beginning to catch up with these ancient beliefs.

As with eastern religions, Witchcraft embraces the ancient doctrine of reincarnation. Most Witches do not see death as the absolute end of life but rather as a transition. The cycle of creation, destruction and re-creation – birth, death and rebirth – is repeated throughout the natural world so most Witches believe that this pattern is also true of the human life. Many Witches believe that between incarnations the soul or consciousness rests in a place called the Summerlands or the Land of the Young. This place of pristine beauty is where we are thought to meet with our loved ones, review all the lessons we have learned from the life we have just completed, until we are ready to reincarnate once again.

Since Witchcraft is an earth religion, many Witches feel a great responsibility towards looking after the health and well-being of our planet. As such, many Witches are heavily involved in the ecological movement. Saving our sacred planet in any way we can from the destruction of humans is a way that we can honour the Goddess and God and is, therefore, an important part of the religion of Witchcraft.

As Witches, we see all of nature as a manifestation of the divine and believe that it is only through nature may we develop a true relationship with the Goddess and God. Additionally, Witches do not see themselves as separate from nature but rather as being a part of it. As a result of these beliefs, Witches are happiest when they are surrounded by the beauty of nature. Their sacred temples are forests, fields, beaches, gardens, deserts, valleys and anywhere else they can feel close to the powers of nature. Unlike those of Christianity, Witches do not feel that the only place they can worship is within the confines of a church.

As followers of the old Pagan ways, the Witches of today are the modern-day priests and priestesses of the Goddess and God, the healers and Shamans of the twenty-first century, and the keepers of the old secrets and lores of nature. They honour the four sacred elements of nature (earth, air, fire and water); celebrate the spiritual significance of the seasons and use the spiritual and healing properties of natural materials (herbs, woods, fossils, crystals, stones, metals, shells, feathers and so on) and astrological energies to strengthen the power of their work. Witches use their various magical practices and continuous development in the Craft to help and to heal themselves and others in any way they can. They understand that healing comes in many forms.

Witchcraft is a world that can open the door to many vistas of learning. It can teach us much more about ourselves and the world around us than we could ever have imagined – trust me. With a little patience and full trust in the powers of nature, you can enter that world and I can guarantee that your life will be filled with the love and harmony of nature.

Witchcraft and Magic

Many people assume that the words Witchcraft and magic are interchangeable but this is simply not the case. Witchcraft is a religion that embraces the practice of magic, but strictly speaking the main purpose of Witchcraft is the worship of the Goddess and God. Still, magic plays an important role within the lives of Witches because it allows us to improve the quality of our lives and to battle our demons (illnesses, depression, fears, addictions, anger and so on).

Magic has been defined as the ability to manipulate energy to bring about a desired change. Creating magic is not like baking a cake – simply following a recipe in order to get a result. Magic requires real emotion. A strong will to succeed and the ability to concentrate are the key components to creating magic. This is why it is so important that you take your time when you decide to cast a spell so that you can really focus all your thoughts and emotions on the intent. As with everything else in life, the more you put into your spells the more you will get out of them. Just believe in yourself.

There are many different forms of magic to explore. Some examples include the following: candle magic, chant magic, crystal magic, hand magic, herb magic, image magic, kitchen magic, knot magic, lunar magic, magnet magic, mirror magic, runic magic, sea magic, sigil magic, solar magic, star magic, sympathetic magic, talismanic magic, weather magic...the list is virtually endless. Simply choose the forms that work best for you and your needs.

Magic is a wonderful way for us to take control of our lives. It can bring some extraordinary results and transform our lives in many, delightful ways. But, as the old saying goes, be very careful what you wish for – you may just get it.

The Wiccan Rede

On a very basic level, the Wiccan Rede (*"Rede"* is a Middle English word meaning "advice" or "counsel") is a set of laws that the majority of modern Witches choose to live by. Many Witches see its teachings as a foundation to their basic beliefs and ethical codes. It truly is a loving poem which is also known as *"the Wiccan Law"*, *"the Wiccan Rune"* or *"the Rede of the Wiccae"*.

Many people assume that the Rede was written by Doreen Valiente, one of Gerald Gardner's high priestesses, but this is not the case. She did, however, write a very special prayer called *"the Charge of the Goddess"*, an important ethical prayer recited by many Witches within their celebrations to help them understand the nature of femininity – the Goddess. The origins of the Rede are actually little understood but the majority of its teachings are based on ancient, European, Pagan, folkloric knowledge.

If you are truly serious about Witchcraft I believe that it is very important that you thoroughly learn the Rede and then try to incorporate its teaching into your life. Never attempt to rush this process. Learning to incorporate the Rede's wise words into your life is not something that can happen overnight. It requires a lifelong commitment as any Witch who follows the Rede will tell you. As you begin following the Rede, however, you will see great changes in your life almost immediately. You will also begin the process of transforming yourself into a wiser, more balanced individual. This is, after all, the goal of any Witch.

Following is a popular version of the Rede which was handed down to a woman known as Lady Gwen Thompson, high priestess of a Welsh tradition of Witchcraft, by her grandmother Adriana Porter who was over 90 years old when she died in 1946. Thompson included this version in a neo-Pagan magazine called *Green Egg* in the spring of 1975. The Rede consists of twenty-six Middle English rhyming lines which, for newcomers, may be difficult to understand. Therefore, I have given a full explanation to each of the steps so that they are easier for you to grasp. Enjoy.

Bide the Wiccan laws ye must, in perfect love an' perfect trust. Keep the laws of the Rede lovingly and with all your trust. If you have full trust in these laws then your life will be filled with harmony and love, and you will have every success in your magical work.

Live an' let live, fairly take an' fairly give. This is a basic understanding of Witchcraft. It basically means that we should be wise enough not to interfere with other people's lives and beliefs, and only give advice when we are asked. As Witches, it is important that we never attempt to force our beliefs on others and we should learn to treat others how we would like to be treated. To earn respect we have to give it. Also, this part of the Rede teaches us to always be fair in the giving and receiving of things.

Cast the circle thrice about, to keep all evil spirits out. When Witches decide to undertake any important magical/spiritual work, they traditionally cast a magic circle. The magic circle is basically an extension of personal power and serves to protect us from any unwanted negative energies that may influence our work. Witches traditionally cast the circle by walking its circumference three times. The number three corresponds to the unity of the mind, body and soul and the moon's waxing, full and waning phases. In Witchcraft, the moon is a symbol of the Goddess.

To bind the spell every time, let the spell be spake in rhyme. When Witches work magic, they often speak their spells in rhyme. Rhyming spells helps to keep the conscious mind focused so that the unconscious mind is able to tap into the energies of nature and thus put the magic to work.

Soft of eye an' light of touch, speak little, listen much. The only way to develop wisdom in this life is to listen and learn, and not think that we have all the answers. Witches are wise enough not to be so narrow-minded as to think they are better than everyone else. We understand that there is always something new to learn from others of all backgrounds because every single one of us has had different experiences in life.

Deosil go by the waxing moon, sing an' dance the Wiccan rune. This refers to the moon when waxing in the sky (increasing in size). The waxing moon is a perfect time to perform magic designed to draw things into your life (such as money for instance). Spells associated with the waxing moon are thought to be extra powerful when we move around the magic circle deosil (clockwise).

Widdershins go when the moon doth wane, an' the werewolf howls by the dread wolfsbane. This refers to the moon when waning in the sky (decreasing in size). The waning moon is a perfect time to perform magic designed to banish things that are negative in your life (such as addictions for instance). Spells associated with the waning moon are thought to be extra powerful when we move around the magic circle widdershins (anti-clockwise).

Wolf's bane is a feared plant because it is highly toxic.

When the Lady's moon is new, kiss the hand to her times two. The new moon is all about changes and new beginnings. It is a fantastic time to let go of the past and to make positive plans for the future, and to perform any spells to do with these. As a mark of respect to the Goddess, many Witches greet the new moon by blowing her two kisses with the index and middle fingers.

When the moon rides at her peak, then your heart's desire seek. The full moon is a time when lunar energies are ripe and potent. It is a time of great power. Thus, any type of spells can be performed at the full moon. The full moon represents the mother aspect of the Goddess. Her maternal instinct is to provide us, her children, anything we need to be happy and content.

Heed the north wind's mighty gale, lock the door and drop the sail. North is the direction where Witches honour the element of earth. The element of earth represents our sacred planet and is associated with the human body, growth, stability and prosperity.

When the wind comes from the south, love will kiss thee on the mouth. South is the direction where Witches honour the element of fire. The element of fire represents the heat we need to survive and is associated with human energy, passion, potential and achievement.

When the wind blows from the east, expect the new and set the feast. East is the direction where Witches honour the element of air. The element of air represents the sacred breath of life and is associated with the human mind, beginnings, swiftness and communication.

When the west wind blows o'er thee, departed spirits restless be. West is the direction where Witches honour the element of water. The element of water represents the fountain of life and is associated with human emotions, fertility, intuition and beauty.

Nine woods in the cauldron go, burn them quick an' burn them slow. Traditionally, there are nine special woods that are burned in a Witch's cauldron during various rituals. Each of these woods naturally has their own specific energies: apple (healing and love), birch (protection and determination), fir (success and wealth), hawthorn (love and fertility), hazel (protection and luck), oak (strength and wisdom), rowan (growth and protection), vine (sensuality and happiness) and willow (psychic power and healing).

Elder be ye Lady's tree, burn it not or cursed ye'll be. The elder tree is sacred to the Goddess and so its wood should never be burned. Many Witches believe that if elder wood is burned then bad luck will surely come. Elder wood is well-known not to make a good firewood anyhow since it burns very quickly with a poor heat output and produces a thick, acrid smoke. Perhaps these are nature's ways of telling us to keep the wood away from fire. The tree also symbolises rebirth, healing and protection.

When the wheel begins to turn, let the Beltane fires burn.

When the wheel has turned a Yule, light the log an' let Pan rule. These last two lines are referring to the eight very ancient Pagan times of power, or Sabbats as they are also known (Beltane and Yule are two of these Sabbats), which occur on certain dates throughout the cycle of the year. These powerful days, which were so important to the pre-Christian agricultural folk, reflect the physical and spiritual changes of nature and are symbolic to the changes within the cycle of our own lives. Witches celebrate them to keep in tune with nature.

Heed ye flower, bush an' tree, by the Lady blessed be. As Witches our aim is to love, honour and respect all nature's life. Our aim is to look after our Mother Earth to the best of our abilities. Even small actions like tree-planting, protecting wildlife, taking litter home and recycling can all help in the eyes of the Earth Mother.

Where the rippling waters go, cast a stone an' truth ye'll know. Witches realise that every action we take in life not only affects our own lives but the lives of those around us. We are wise enough to consider every action we take in life and the consequences these may have. Like the ripples caused by a stone dropping into a pond, our actions start from ourselves and spread out into the web of life affecting everything and everyone around us.

When ye have need, hearken not to other's greed. Witches never take money for nature's sacred gift of magic because it is spiritually wrong. Our aim is to help others through magic so that they can live full and productive lives. Generally, Witches aim to take only what they need in life to survive and be comfortable. As Witches, we should never allow greed to take over our lives because it will eventually lead to self-destruction and imbalance.

With the fool no season spend, or be counted as his friend. In your lifetime, you will meet a lot of different kinds of people, some make great friends, others not so great. It is always wise to avoid destructive people who are unkind to you or wish to emotionally drain you. If you mix with such people then others will associated you with the company you keep. Wise Witches try to spot the signs in people that are idiots and move on.

Merry meet an' merry part, bright the cheeks an' warm the heart. The friends and family who show us unconditional love are extremely important to Witches. We must keep them close to our hearts and realise how important they are and how much joy they bring. Witches always respect them and view them with high regards.

Mind the threefold law ye should, three times bad an' three times good. Whatever you put out in life, good or bad, will return to you threefold. This law of the universe is known as karma (from the Sanskrit word *"karman"* meaning "act" or "action") and its purpose is to teach us lessons in life. It is a spiritual and ethical guideline and serves to keep humanity principled.

When misfortune is enow, wear the blue star on thy brow. Sometimes in life negative things happen that we simply can't avoid. In such cases, many Witches visualise a blue pentagram on their brow to remove negative energy from their lives. It is a way for us to protect ourselves. That said, Witches always try to learn what they can from life's experiences, good and bad, and apply them with wisdom in the future.

True in love ever be, unless thy lover's false to thee. As Witches, we believe that we should always show our loved ones, those who we are intimate with, respect and loyalty. However, if this is not reciprocated then it is wise to move on. Life is for living!

Eight words the Wiccan Rede fulfil, an' it harm none, do what ye will. This sums up the main teaching of the Wiccan Rede. It basically means that we can do whatever we want in life as long as we don't cause harm. Because Witches believe that all life is a manifestation of the divine, they consider the act of causing harm an act against the Goddess and God.

Witchcraft Traditions

Since Gerald Gardner's time, there are many different traditions that have arisen out of the religion of Witchcraft. Over the years, many people have chosen to create their own unique form of Witchcraft to suit their own individual beliefs and personal circumstances. Some of these traditions work exclusively in covens (groups of Witches) while others embrace Solitaries (Witches who work alone). There is usually some form of initiation ceremony required for those who wish to join a coven and many traditions have degrees of initiation. In many covens, there are three levels of initiation, with the third being the highest level of spiritual knowledge and wisdom. Those who choose to be Solitary Witches can hold self-initiation ceremonies if they so wish. I will examine initiation further in chapter five.

Following is some brief discussions on some of the most well-known Witchcraft traditions, beginning with Gerald Gardner's own traditional path:

Gardnerian Witchcraft: Gardnerian Witchcraft is a strict and formal path that is believed to be based on the teachings of the New Forest coven. The Gardnerians work in covens and worship the male aspect of the divine as the Celtic horned god Cernunnos and the female as Aradia, the Italian goddess of the Witches. The tradition has three levels of initiation and each coven is led by a high priestess with the priest of her choice. Each coven also consists of no more than thirteen members. The Gardnerians are very choosy to whom they take on and the covens are very difficult to find. Gender polarity and ritual nudity are very important in this tradition.

Alexandrian Witchcraft: This form of Witchcraft was founded by Alex and Maxine Sanders; it is the newer form of the Gardnerian tradition, but is also strictly followed. Alex Sanders was an original member of a Gardnerian coven from which he developed some of his knowledge. The tradition was developed in Britain in the early 1960s and puts hard emphasis into training each individual member. Alexandrian Witchcraft is named after the ancient occult library of Alexandria, not the founder of the tradition. Gardnerian and Alexandrian Witchcraft are sometimes referred to as British Traditional Witchcraft.

Georgian Witchcraft: This version of Witchcraft began in California in 1970 and has a rather relaxed approach to Witchcraft. It was formed by a man called George Patterson who became known as "Pat" and "Lord Scorpio". The tradition is similar to the Gardnerian and Alexandrian traditions but has a somewhat individualist approach to its teachings. It also works in covens. Georgians have three levels of initiation and often worship in the nude.

Seax or Saxon Witchcraft: Raymond and Rosemary Buckland founded this version of Witchcraft in 1973 and it takes some of its teachings from the Gardnerian tradition since both Raymond and Rosemary were original initiates from Gardner's coven. Seax Witchcraft, however, is less formal than the Gardnerian tradition and allows its members to follow the tradition in covens or as Solitaries. In his book *The Tree: The Complete Book of Saxon Witchcraft* (1974), Buckland describes Seax Witchcraft in great detail.

Feri Witchcraft: Often known as Faery Witchcraft, this tradition was founded by Victor Anderson (along with several other people) in the early 1970s. Followers of this tradition teach that there are male and female attributes in both the God and the Goddess and that much of reality is unseen. There is also a strong emphasis on gender equality and faery magic in this tradition. Feri Witches tend to work alone or in very small covens.

Reclaiming Tradition: A lady known as Starhawk helped to form this version of Witchcraft and it was developed in the late 1970s. Starhawk was an original member of the Feri tradition and is now a major figure in the Reclaiming tradition. The tradition is strongly influenced by the Feri tradition and can be followed as a Solitary or within covens. It offers workshops and classes that anyone considering the path of Witchcraft can follow. It is a much more relaxed form of Witchcraft than some of the more traditional forms outlined above. Entrance into a coven of this tradition is through initiation but this usually only comes after considerable training.

Dianic Witchcraft: This is a very feminist form of Witchcraft that acknowledges the Goddess as the all and rarely puts emphasis on the God. Dianics can work alone or within covens though many exclude men from their rituals altogether. As with all Witches, Dianics celebrate the seasons but only in a very Goddess-orientated way. The tradition is named after the Roman goddess Diana, who is a very feminine and independent goddess. The most well-known form of Dianic Witchcraft was founded by Zsuzsanna Budapest in the early 1970s.

I must admit that in all my years as a practising Witch I have never followed a particular tradition. I have never wanted to either. I prefer to be totally self-taught. I take a very eclectic approach to Witchcraft since it suits my lifestyle, as do many other Witches these days. Eclectic Witchcraft allows us to draw from many traditions what we will so that we can build our own traditions and beliefs. It is a way for us to bring Witchcraft together in a more natural, relaxed and intuitive way. In contemporary Witchcraft, the eclectic approach is becoming increasingly popular among Solitary Witches.

Some Witches of the more formal traditions hold that you can't be a true Witch unless you are initiated into a coven by a high priestess and/or priest. Which means Solitary Witches are simply not recognised as true Witches by them. As a Solitary Witch myself, I strongly disagree. Many Witches, in their various forms and cultures, have existed throughout the ages and have managed quite fine, working alone, while self-teaching themselves and picking up teachings here and there from other practising Pagan-like peoples. Furthermore, you don't have to be a part of a coven to worship the Goddess and God or to practise magic. The old Hedgewitches and Cunning Men, for instance, almost always worked alone.

There is no one true way to practise Witchcraft or to find the Goddess and God. The only way we learn is to study hard and to practise the Craft to the best of our abilities. Witchcraft is about freedom and choices not rigidly and unnaturally following others who claim that their way is the only way. In reality, the Goddess and God are the true deciders to whom they take on as their priests and priestesses.

Chapter Two: The Ultimate Deity

Throughout the history of humankind, religions have taught that there is a supreme higher power, a force that is behind all creation. This great force – what I call the "Ultimate Deity" – is so powerful that it is above and beyond any scientific explanation. It is not some distant being, watching over us from "heaven", but a force that permeates the entire universe. The Ultimate Deity is the immutable soul of formation, the power behind stars and galaxies not yet formed, and the ultimate source of all energy. It is the one universal truth that is not exclusive to any religion.

Since nature is generally divided into male and female polarity, Witches believe that it is only logical that the Ultimate Deity should be identified this way too. We personify this concept as the God and the Goddess. Most Witches simply see the God and Goddess as different aspects of the Ultimate Deity. In personifying the Ultimate Deity in this way, Witches believe they can gain a deeper understanding of its nature as well as draw closer to it.

One of the greatest symbols that depicts the male and female aspects of the Ultimate Deity is the ancient Chinese Yin and Yang symbol, which depicts the dark part (Yin aspect) as the intuitive and receptive feminine mysteries, and the light part (Yang aspect) as the passionate and projective masculine mysteries. On a closer inspection of the Chinese symbol, however, it becomes evident that both the male and female principles are contained within each other, since the dark part contains a white spot and the light part contains a black one. This is a powerful reminder that both the male and female forces are ultimately dependent on each other for the balance and survival of nature. We only have to observe the natural world to understand this concept.

Every single one of us has both male and female attributes. We all have both the Yin and Yang contained within us, as evinced by the male and female hormones within our bodies. We are simply a small product of the great creative male and female energies of the universe. In other words, we are a miniature version of the Ultimate Deity. Even the Swiss psychologist Carl Jung believed that the male psyche contained a female component (which he called the *anima*) and the female psyche contained a male component (which he called the *animus*). The reasons above are why many Witches believe that the human soul itself is androgynous.

To truly progress in the Craft, it is vital that you begin developing a relationship with both the God and the Goddess and that you begin sharpening your knowledge of their mysteries. A deeper understanding of their mysteries will help you to draw closer to the divine and you will begin to understand some of the greatest mysteries of life. Witches are not the kind of people to leave these mysteries up to faith alone, we are naturally inquisitive about the world around us. Indeed, it is only human to have a thirst for knowledge.

There are many ways in which you can begin building a relationship with the Goddess and God: spend time under the sun and moon, observe stars at night, visit forests and fields, visit the seaside or lakes, observe wildlife, meditate, hug trees, plant a garden, study herbalism, feed birds, nurture children, bond with a pet, watch moving clouds, observe thunderstorms and lightning, cast spells in times of need and so on. While you do these types of activities, keep an open mind and consider the great creative male and female roles in the world around you and give thanks for their gifts of life.

The God and the Goddess are always there for us when we need guidance, but they can't help us if we don't ask for their assistance. They will respond to your calls because ultimately they are a part of you. All you have to do is believe in their powers. When you find the Goddess and God invite them into your life, and watch their powers manifesting in the world around you, transforming your life positively.

Although you will find that some Witches tend to focus their worship primarily on the Goddess – a result of hundreds of years of female repression – the ideal is to worship the Goddess and God equally. Neither the God nor Goddess is more deserving of worship than the other in my opinion. Both are omnipresent forces and complete all nature. We should respect them equally for these reasons.

Mysteries of the Goddess

In Witchcraft we associate the Goddess with the fertility of the land, she is the mother of all nature. Her powers are seen in the regeneration, reproduction and growth of the animal and plant kingdoms, this is why Witches see the earth as a powerful symbol of her womb. The Goddess is the power behind the fruits of the earth, the sustenance of all life, she is the abundance of all love, emotion, nurture, compassion, creativity, intuition, healing and wisdom. Her power is the infinity of the universe, she is the ultimate giver of all life. Witches know the Goddess by her many names: Queen of the Land, Queen of Heaven, the Great Goddess, the Universal Lady, the Universal Mother, the Universal Matrix, the Universal Creatrix, Mother of the Gods that Made the Gods and by a whole host of other names.

The earth is a powerful reminder that all life is born of the Goddess's womb, yet all life returns to her upon physical death, symbolised by the seemingly lifeless winter. Just as the Goddess promises death, shown in the life that withdraws into the earth over the winter period, we are also reminded that with death comes the promise of rebirth from her womb, as evinced in the spring when nature bursts to life. The Goddess is the life-giver, she promises the continuation of life. It is her natural law. The cycle of the seasons are simply the Goddess's way of showing us the universal progressions and spiritual changes of all life.

Witches acknowledge our planet as the primal earth goddess Gaia, she is a cohesive living organism and every single one of us is a part of her consciousness. We understand that humans, as well as the animal and plant kingdoms, are her nervous system and it is through the many life forms on earth that Gaia becomes aware of herself. All life forms (as we know them on earth) are divine entities and are directly evolved from the powers of Gaia.

In the field of parapsychology, even some scientists believe that the earth has some kind of life force within it, similar to that of humans. It has been widely accepted that the human body has energy points or lines of energy (also known as meridians) that can be utilised for healing in alternative therapies, such as acupuncture for instance. Now some scientists believe that the earth has similar lines of power. This would certainly be a start to explaining why many ancient and sacred structures, which are believed to be built on ley lines (lines of mystical earth power), such as Stonehenge for instance, seem to have the most paranormal activity to that of other areas on earth. It has also been theorised that the earth's natural magnetic field is interconnected with the biospheres of living creatures and plants. Perhaps this can explain the ancient Pagan belief that all life is connected through energy; the web and thread of life. Scientists have named this the Gaia Principle and believe that this theory could be a start to unravelling some of the earth's greatest mysteries.

Witches also, as we have seen, acknowledge the moon as a powerful symbol of the Goddess. She chose it to remind us of her power and glory. There is indisputable evidence, in fact, that our ancestors worshipped the Goddess through the moon because there are many ancient structures, in evidence, that were created in her honour, as well as many moon myths and legends. All types of Pagan folk, in many cultures and traditions all over the world, have worshipped the moon as the Goddess and have channelled her power in order to build their relationships with the feminine divine, in the knowledge that this will improve their lives.

One of the reasons Witches see the power of the Goddess in the moon is because it is associated with the coolness and darkness of the night, the time when the conscious mind slows down and the unconscious mind is awakened (when we dream for example). This is the magical part of the brain that basically holds those traits that we traditionally associate with femininity, such as intuition and psychic sensitivity for instance.

As Witches we see the monthly cycle of the moon's waxing, full and waning as symbolic to the three aspects of the Goddess: maiden, mother and crone. The three aspects of the Goddess reflect the three ages of women. In her maiden aspect, the Goddess becomes eager to explore the world, she is the Goddess of freshness and potential. In her mother aspect, she is the Goddess of fullness and childbirth, and becomes eager to express her maternal power. In her crone aspect, the Goddess becomes the patroness of wisdom and prophecy, and becomes eager to share this wisdom with her children.

As the moon journeys around the earth during the lunar cycle, she also controls the ebb and flow of the ocean tides, the sap in plants and the waters and emotions within ourselves. Thus, the Goddess's power is heavily connected with the fertile and emotional element of water, the very element that surrounds us within the wombs of our mothers. The theory of evolution now accepts that all life slowly evolved, over billions of years, from the sea. Perhaps this is one of the greatest reminders that all life is a product of the Goddess's eternal womb.

Mysteries of the God

Witches do not believe that the God is the omnipotent, overpowering, demanding "Father God" of some religions of today, we simply see him as the force that works in unity with the Goddess in the work of creation.

The God, for many Witches, is the Sky Father who unites with the Earth Mother through the wild weather that descends upon her. His power can be seen in the stars of the heavens and in the blazing sun that shines down and fertilises the womb of the Goddess, like the sperm that fertilises the ovum within a woman's reproductive system. Without the power of the God the earth would be cold, dark and desolate.

The sun, as the God's symbol, is the source of life on Mother Earth, the force that brings vitality to the seeds in the spring after the cold and bitter winter. It is the life of the fields, the spirit of the life-sustaining corn, and of freshly baked bread. It has the power to uplift our spirits and heal away the darkness of illness and depression, just as it heals away the darkness of winter. It is the power of the conscious mind and the passion and drive within us all to move forward in life. It represents the spirit in the flesh and our most basic physical and sexual needs – thus the sun imbues us with the God's lusty and courageous appetite that ensures our survival.

The sun has been worshipped as a symbol of the God, in many cultures and civilisations, for eons. There are many major male deities held sacred to it. The ancients perceived in the sun's brilliance those qualities that are traditionally attributed to the perfection of man. The ancient Greeks, for instance, held the powerful god Apollo sacred to the sun (though the ancient Romans eventually took on this Greek deity as well). His arrows symbolised the sun's healing rays, striking humanity with the sun's powers of clarity, rational thought, inspiration and enlightenment. He was the god who brought hope and good fortune to the ill and downhearted, just as the sun does.

The ancient Celts in Britain, as another example, held the god Belenos sacred to the sun. His name is given to the ancient fire festival of Beltane (see chapter four) – which literally means "the fire of the god Bel" – a time when the Pagan folk celebrate the rise of the sun and the beginning of summer. Such was the importance of Belenos to the Celts in Britain that he is often named "the British Apollo".

Since the God's symbol is the sun, there are sun legends throughout the cycle of the year that are parallel to the changes of life. At the beginning of the year the God is born of the Goddess's womb and as the days pass into the spring season he begins to grow in strength and impregnates the Goddess. In the summer, when the sun's power is at its height and nature is full of life, he is at his full strength. In the autumn, as the sun's power declines, however, he ages but with this comes his endless wisdom and his ability to provide through the harvests that sustain us. Finally, in the winter, he dies and completes his life cycle when life returns to the earth, the womb of the Goddess.

These legends form our understanding of the endless cycles that govern our lives, seen within nature all around us as the year progresses. We too are born of our mothers' wombs, strengthen with each passing day, become potential or actual parents, age and become wise, and finally return to the Goddess's womb when we die. However, with death comes the promise of the next cycle and life renewed once again (reincarnation), symbolised by the God's birth and by the life that emerges from the earth in the following spring.

Just as we see the three aspects of the Goddess in the lunar month, we also see the three aspects of the God in the cycle of the solar year. During the spring season he is the young God and full of potential, during the summer season he is the warrior, provider and protector (an image associated with fatherhood), finally he is the sage during the waning of the sun and becomes full of the wisdom of life. These aspects of the God can also be seen in the rising, noon and setting of the sun – another powerful reminder that we are governed by the cycles of nature.

The God's lusty and courageous nature means that Witches still worship him as the ancient horned god of the hunt (he is often nicknamed "Old Hornie"). The horns are a powerful symbol of virility, fertility and the most basic animal instincts that ensure our survival – the God's connection to the wild beasts of nature (nothing to do with the Christian Devil).

The Green Man

If Gaia is a representation of Mother Nature then her opposite, and equal, partner is the Green Man. In Pagan religions the Green Man is a symbol of the spirit of nature and the changing seasons. Often known as Jack in the Green, Robin Hood or the Wild Man, the Green Man is our Father Nature and is an archetypal symbol of the male principle of nature; he is a powerful reminder to Witches of the importance of the God's role in the regeneration and growth of the land. He is the champion of environmentalism and a powerful symbol of the survival instincts of nature. He truly is a symbol of earth power and wisdom.

Although the origins of the Green Man are little understood, he certainly is ancient. He has been found on many ancient structures (especially around the British Isles) and has even been found carved on some of the early Christian churches, though nobody knows for sure why this is because the Green Man has always been a Pagan symbol of fertility. One theory is that it was an attempt to bring the Pagan folk into the churches to help convert them into Christianity, since the early Christians were well-known to incorporate the old Pagan beliefs and practices into theirs.

Though the Green Man can be associated with all the seasons, he is typically associated with the spring period and is often depicted with a vibrant leafy green face with vegetation emerging from his mouth. In contemporary Witchcraft this is a symbol of the fertility of the land, representing the cycle of renewed growth once again (and the ancient belief in reincarnation), that we associate with the springtime. During the May Day celebrations (see chapter four), when the sexual force of nature is coming towards its height, many Witches honour the Green Man as the King of the May alongside the Goddess, his Queen of the May. The Green Man's strong association with fertility is the reason why he is believed to have evolved from the ancient horned god of the hunting times.

There is a tradition in contemporary Witchcraft in which the Green Man is seen as two different personas, alter egos or twins. These are the Oak King and the Holly King. In the dark half of the year (after the summer solstice), the Green Man manifests himself as the Holly King and in the light half of the year (after the winter solstice), he manifests as the Oak King.

The Holly King is the lord of the waning sun, the god of maturity, and a powerful reminder that over the winter the earth is only sleeping and that life will return with the coming of the next cycle. This is symbolised by the holly that makes up the Green Man's face during the dark half of the year, an evergreen to remind us that the earth will be green once again after winter. The Oak King, in contrast, is the lord of the waxing sun and an adversary of the Holly King, whose face is traditionally made up of trees that symbolise the light half of the year, such as hawthorn and oak for instance. With the Earth Mother, the Oak King is the power behind the fruits of creation and the greening of the land.

This legend has spiritual messages behind it and helps modern Witches to make sense of the year's division. It helps us to understand just how important the balance of the dark and light halves of the year are for the continuation of life. The Holly King symbolises rest and retreat and the Oak King symbolises fullness and wholeness. This is a powerful reminder to Witches that if we are to achieve the fullness and completeness of life – as well as keep in tune with nature – then we too must keep as balanced as possible.

Gods and Goddesses

Witchcraft is, as we have seen, a polytheistic religion. There is the worship of the Goddess and God and also many pantheons of gods and goddesses from many different religions and cultures, all over the world. In Witchcraft we believe that the male and female deities are simply aspects of the Ultimate Deity. In other words, every goddess deity is a face of the Goddess herself and every god deity is a face of the God himself. They are merely faces of the divine – hence the phrase "God has many faces". If you find this concept difficult to understand, consider a diamond with many sides to it and imagine that each side is a different deity, flashing out a different truth from the one great source.

Witches do not believe that the deities existed before our ancestors acknowledged them. However, the specific powers behind each of them did exist, they were the forces of nature itself. Early worshippers simply identified with these forces as well as personify and name them in an attempt to understand them. The deities are simply the creative forces that permeate the entire universe. They reflect the complex thought forms of the human psyche.

When Witches work magic, they may call upon the deities to ask for assistance. Each deity has their own qualities that can be useful for specific types of spells. Essentially, this strengthens the power of our spells and helps us to channel energy more efficiently. The deities simply aid the power of the mind. Calling upon the deities for spells can create extremely powerful outcomes.

One of the best ways to know the deities (apart from working with them personally) is to study their stories in mythology. There is much wisdom in this. Studying mythology is time well spent and you will soon discover much about yourself and the world around you. There are many different cultures to choose from (Celtic, Greek, Norse, Egyptian, Roman, Hindu and so on), simply choose the deities and cultures that you are inspired by.

What is really interesting is that the stories of the deities, from culture to culture, are all very similar. Ultimately, they relate to the human experiences of life. This is a powerful reminder that no matter what culture or religion we belong to, we all share a common experience. The stories of all religions (and even the stories in the Bible) are simply designed to help us understand the human connection to the divine. They help us identify with its complex energies.

Over the next few pages I have presented you with just some of the deities from around the world that a Witch may call upon for assistance. I have only intended the following notes to be a simple introduction to each deity, a more rounded look to each, however, will require more research.

Aphrodite: A Greek goddess of love and erotic sexuality, Aphrodite is a very sensual goddess and is often pictured emerging from the sea on a scallop shell.

Aphrodite epitomises the essence of beauty, fertility and emotion. She has a great love of all finery and luxury. Her Roman equivalent is the goddess Venus.

Apollo: Often portrayed as a handsome youth, Apollo is the Greek god of the sun who symbolises inspiration, creativity, healing, music, comfort, joy and youth. He is also a god of prophecy and in ancient times bay leaves were burned in his temples to induce his prophetic powers.

Aries: A Greek god of war, Aries is the fiery god of protection and defence. In mythology he is often portrayed as a very bad-tempered and volatile deity but he had the power to bring much-needed change and transformation. He is very similar to the Roman god of war Mars, though Mars is also a god of agriculture.

Athena: A Greek goddess of justice and victory, Athena is often called upon when we need help in making important decisions during difficult situations. She is often seen with an owl, a bird of wisdom that can see in the dark with ease, implying Athena's clarity of vision. Her Roman counterpart is Minerva.

Bast: Also known as Bastet (meaning "She of Beast"), Bast is the Egyptian cat-headed goddess of joy, music, dancing, love and laughter. Cats are held sacred to her and symbolise her femininity.

Bes: A protector and friend of children, Bes is the Egyptian god that was often seen as a deity who helped women to give birth. He is often depicted as an ugly, dwarf-like creature (often pulling faces with his tongue out) that could easily scare away demons and dangerous animals. His image was often placed in the home for his protective powers.

Brigit: Often seen as the midwife of spring, Brigit is the Celtic solar goddess of healing, poetry, inspiration, creativity and smithcraft. In mythology she brought life back to the earth after the cold and bitter winter. She is also worshipped as the protector of women, children, the home and newborn animals (especially sheep and cattle). Brigit was often said to be a member of a trio of goddesses (all named Brigit) who were known for their prophetic skills. Brigit's festival is held on February 1st-2nd, the time when the first signs of spring are beginning to show.

Cernunnos: The Celtic god Cernunnos (meaning "Horned One") is typically depicted as a young god with the horns of a stag on his head. He is a powerful god of hunting, regeneration, wisdom, maturity, fertility and male authority. He is worshipped as the protector of nature and the provider of food. Many modern Witches use his image as a representation of the male principle of nature. He is also often known as "Herne the Hunter". His image is found all over Europe.

Cerridwen: Often associated with the crone aspect of the Goddess, Cerridwen is the Celtic goddess of earth wisdom, transformation, death and rebirth. Her sacred cauldron of wisdom held the brew of bardic inspiration. She is a favourite in contemporary Witchcraft and is often worshipped as the death sow and as a goddess associated with the moon. She is also the patroness of magic and shape-shifting.

Demeter: An earth goddess of fertility and agriculture, Demeter was an extremely important goddess of ancient Greece who was worshipped as the provider of the harvests. She is a powerful symbol of the Earth Mother and is the mother of Persephone, goddess of spring and the underworld (see below). Her Roman equivalent is the goddess Ceres.

Diana: Diana is the Roman goddess of hunting and the moon. She is often portrayed as a very virginal, maiden goddess. She is also associated with women-only groups and anciently men were forbidden from entering her temples. In ancient Italy she was often associated with sacred forests. Originally, Diana was the goddess of childbirth but today she is portrayed as a very independent and self-reliant goddess. Her Greek equivalent is the goddess Artemis.

Dionysus: A Greek god of wine and ecstasy, Dionysus embodies the physical pleasures of life and fertility. Dionysus is honoured by Witches as the mysterious god who rules "divine madness" and those impulses within us to leap into the unknown without giving much thought to the consequences. Though such impulses may be dangerous, Dionysus is a reminder that risks may have to be taken in life to make way for positive change. He symbolises those animal instincts within us that are ecstatic and disobedient. His Roman equivalent is Bacchus.

Epona: A Celtic horse deity, Epona is the goddess of travel, speed, change and protection. She is often called upon for protection against hostile spirits during the Samhain celebrations, the time when the veil between the physical and spiritual worlds is said to be at its thinnest (see chapter four). Epona is often associated with the Welsh goddess Rhiannon, though Rhiannon is also a sea goddess who is linked to natural justice.

Freya: An earth goddess of fertility and growth, Freya is the Nordic goddess of love, female sexuality, beauty and divination. She is often seen on a chariot drawn by cats. She also wears the brisingamen necklace which represents the source of all life.

Hades: is the much-feared Greek god of the underworld (which the Greeks called the "Kingdom of Hades"), the unseen realm to which souls were believed to go after physical death. He is considered a very shadowy and somewhat gloomy deity who symbolises the mysteries of death, the afterlife and the darkness of winter. In the tarot deck he is symbolised by the Death card, which symbolises the end of one cycle and the beginning of the next. His Roman equivalent is Pluto.

Hecate: A famous crone and moon goddess, Hecate is the Greek goddess of music, enchantment, arcane knowledge, herbal knowledge, Witchcraft and night-time. Hecate is also the ruler of crossroads, and guides those making important decisions in life. Like the goddess Freya, she is often seen on a chariot drawn by cats but she is also famous for her love of all nocturnal creatures. Hecate is a favourite in contemporary Witchcraft.

Hermes: Known as a trickster, magician and a bringer of sudden good luck, Hermes is the Greek god of speed, communication, intellect, wit, divination, medicine, merchants, health and healing. He is often depicted holding a staff with two snakes entwined around it, symbolising the power of opposites such as good and evil or light and dark. He is said to be a trusted messenger of the gods and a guide to the souls of the underworld. His Roman equivalent is the god Mercury.

Horus: is the falcon-headed Egyptian sun god who is worshipped as the child of light who brings forth hope and promise in the midwinter celebrations of Yule, the time of the returning sun (see chapter four). Ancient depictions of Horus show him feeding from his divine mother's breasts, an image which was later depicted in the Christian faith with the Madonna and Child. The eye of Horus is said to be extremely protective and is often utilised in protection magic.

Inanna: An ancient deity of the moon, Inanna is an Asian goddess of love, fertility, wisdom and knowledge. She is often seen as a goddess of the underworld who symbolises the time of rest in the darkness of winter. She is also associated with change and transformation.

Isis: is the mother of the sun god Horus. She symbolises the Great Goddess, mother of all creation. She is a healing Egyptian goddess of magic and transformation and symbolises the mysteries of death and rebirth, the endless cycles of life that we see in the seasons. She is very powerful in protection magic.

Juno: is the Roman equivalent of the Greek goddess Hera, the great mother. Often associated with marriage and love, Juno is the goddess of the hearth and home and is often called upon for protection (especially of newborn babies) and fertility. She is a wise counsellor and defender of the home and is often associated with peacocks, the birds of love and inner wisdom.

Lakshmi: Portrayed as a beautiful woman, Lakshmi is the Indian goddess of health, healing, marriage, family and wealth. She is a very joyous deity of fate and fortune who brings happiness to the downhearted. She brings much luck to those who call upon her power and is often associated with the lotus plant, a plant that symbolises fertility and spiritual perfection.

Lugh: A powerful solar deity, Lugh is the Celtic god of success, skills, strength, vitality, health and healing. His relation to the sun makes him a powerful god of truth and clarity. His radiant power is celebrated during the harvest festival celebrations, the time when we celebrate the sun's power in the life of the fields.

Medusa: is a dark Greek deity who is part of a trio of gorgons (the others being Euryale and Stheno). In myth, her eyes were so powerful that anyone who looked at her was instantly turned into stone – a powerful reminder of staring death in the face. She is portrayed as a serpent deity because she has snakes emerging from her head.

Nuada: Often portrayed as a great king and hero, Nuada is a Norse god of the sun, protection, defence, valour, light, regeneration and healing.

Odin: A very complex deity, Odin is the Norse god of eloquence, magic, war, poetry, knowledge, wisdom and spiritual growth. He is said to be the master of runes – an ancient set of magical symbols. He is also known as a shape-shifter who oversees the connections between sky and earth. His Anglo-Saxon name is Woden.

Pan: is the personification of the God's sexual nature. While Cernunnos is the Celtic version of the ancient horned god of the hunting times, Pan is the Greek version. Half-man and half-goat, Pan is the lord of the wild woods and a very earthy figure. When trouble beckons, he represents that basic animal instinct within us: fight or flight. His name is often associated with the word panic.

Persephone: Greek goddess of spring and the underworld, is the daughter of Demeter. She rules the underworld with Hades over the winter period as the earth sleeps and waits for her return in the spring when the earth bursts to life. Her Roman equivalent is the goddess Proserpina.

Poseidon: is the Greek god of the sea and is often called upon to calm tensions in relationships and to ensure safe journeys. He is often seen as a bearded man who holds a trident, which symbolises his great power over the seas. Atlantis, a mysterious city that some people believe had sank below the Atlantic Ocean millennia ago due to a volcanic eruption, was said to be under Poseidon's domain. The Roman equivalent of Poseidon is Neptune.

Thor: An often feared deity, Thor is the Norse god of thunder, industry, strength and justice. Although he is a very humorous deity, he is also very ill-tempered when he sees injustice. He is often depicted with a red beard and a fearsome hammer which he uses to dispatch his enemies.

Thoth: An Egyptian god of the occult and medicine, Thoth is a very wise deity who can be called upon when we need assistance in putting our thoughts into words. He is the patron of knowledge and writing (especially of music) and is also a lunar god.

Zeus: Often seen as a divine father aspect of the God, Zeus is the Greek god of thunder, lightning, rain, freedom, joy, hospitality, generosity, good fortune, charity, mercy, compassion and wisdom. He was one of the most important deities of ancient Greece who was honoured for his great power and sexual appetite. The planet of Jupiter, the planet of great luck, is named after the Roman equivalent of Zeus.

Chapter Three: The Elements

In ancient Greece, long before the rise of Christianity, our Pagan ancestors believed that the universe was composed of four basic elements. They were earth, air, fire and water. For our ancestors, these elements were more than merely sun, soil, wind and sea. They were the four creative powers of the universe. This belief, which was incorporated into many ancient religions, is a one that is still held in Witchcraft and Paganism to this day.

As followers of a religion that celebrates life, Witches naturally honour these elements because we understand that each has their own specific roles to play in the work of creation. They are the four sacred powers that work in harmony to sustain the natural order of our universe. Without just one of these powers, our planet would be lifeless.

Having a basic understanding of the spiritual significance and the workings of each element is an essential part of any Witch's development. Elemental awareness strengthens our relationship with the Goddess and God (who are the primal forces behind the elements) and helps us to understand just how closely connected we are to the powers and cycles of nature. Working closely with the elements is a way that Witches can bring the harmony of nature into their everyday lives.

In fact, such is the importance of the elements to Witches that almost everything we use within our occult practices relates to the elements in some way. In the ancient practice of astrology, for instance, the twelve signs of the zodiac are divided into four groups of three signs each, with each group belonging to one of the four elements. Aries, Leo and Sagittarius, for example, belong to the element of fire. The people born under these signs are said to be energetic and enthusiastic, which are some of the qualities that are traditionally associated with fire.

Of course, the elemental powers are also an important part of magic. When we cast a magic circle for a spell we call upon the powers of each element at their associated cardinal points – north/earth, east/air, south/fire and west/water – to complete the circle. When we invite the elements to join us they become our protectors who watch over our work. They also aid us, guide us, strengthen us and create harmony within our magic. Inviting the elements to join us is another way that we can honour them as well as establish a connection with the forces of nature.

Over the next few pages I have presented you with some brief discussions on each of the elements as well as some of their magical information that you can use in your quest to further your understanding on them. Always bear in mind, however, that the best way to become aware of the elemental powers is to work with them directly.

Note: In reading the below information, keep in mind that each element naturally has its own specific uses in spellcraft.

Element of Earth

The earth element can be seen in the fertile and nurturing green of the land, it is the power behind the life-sustaining crops and the herbs that we use as medicine and to flavour our food. Everything we need, and have, originates from the realm of this element. It is the power of physicality – both on our planet and within the universe itself – and the very foundation of the other three elements. Through the element of earth we see the abundance of stability, prosperity, constancy, certainty and truth. It is the power behind the results we get from our spellcraft.

Since our bodies are made from the molecules of our planet – molecules that originate from the universe – we are reminded that the earth element represents our spiritual connection to the Great Goddess, mother of all creation. It is the element that symbolises the spirit of creation and the great powers of Gaia.

Here is some magical information for this most basic element:

Basic Nature: Cold, dry, emotional, feminine, fertile, grounding, heavy, melancholic, nurturing, passive, receptive, stabilising. Gravity is an example manifestation of this element.

Symbol: Downward-pointing triangle with a horizontal line through it.

Planets: Earth, Jupiter, Saturn, Venus.

Time: Midnight (the time of darkness and earth wisdom).

Day: Friday.

Season: Winter (when life returns to the earth).

Cardinal Point: North (the direction of greatest darkness and coldness).

Point in Life: Advanced age (the time of greatest potential wisdom).

Sense: Touch.

Traditional Magical Tool: Pentacle.

Places: Basements, canyons, caves, farmlands, fields, forests, gardens, groves, hills, holes, kitchens, mines, mountains, museums, parks, plant nurseries, rocky places, sand pits, standing stones, the home, under trees, valleys.

Zodiac Signs: Capricorn (cardinal earth), Taurus (fixed earth), Virgo (mutable earth).

Colours: Black, brown, green, grey, white, yellow.

Incense: Benzoin, fumitory, patchouli, storax.

Plants/Trees: Adonis, alfalfa, asphodel, barley, beet, bistort, buckwheat, cinquefoil, comfrey, corn, cotton, cypress, fern, fumitory, honesty, honeysuckle, hops, horehound, horsetail, indiangrass, ivy, jalap root, jasmine, knotweed, loosestrife, millet, moss, mugwort, nut-bearing trees, oak, oats, oleander, pea, patchouli, pennyroyal, plantain, potato, primrose, quince, rhubarb, rice, sagebrush, tulip, turnip, vervain, vetivert, white bryony, wood sorrel. Generally low-growing plants and root vegetables.

Crystals/Stones: Agate, amazonite, apache tear, aventurine, azurite, black tourmaline, bloodstone, carnelian, diamond, emerald, fluorite, jade, jasper, jet, lodestone, malachite, olivine, onyx, orange calcite, peridot, ruby, salt, serpentine, smoky quartz, sugilite, tiger's eye, turquoise, unakite. Generally heavy or opaque stones.

Metals: Iron, lead, mercury (quicksilver).

Creatures: Ant, bear, beetle, bison, bull, chicken, cow, coyote, dog, earth-dwelling snakes, earthworm, goat, gopher, horse, mole, mouse, stag, tortoise, wolf. Generally burrowing animals.

Mythical Beast: Unicorn.

Archangel: Uriel.

Governs: Abundance, agriculture, animals, binding from harm, birth, bones, business matters, control, conservation, creativity, death, dedication, dependence, determination, ecology, employment, evolution, fertility, food, fruition, garden magic, growth, healing, honesty, household magic, image magic, industry, investments, justice, karmic forces, law, learning from the past, life, manifestations, material abundance, minerals, money, nature, nourishment, peace, perseverance, physicality, possessions, practicality, progress, prosperity, protection, reason, rebirth, recuperation, reliability, secrets, security, sensuality, shelter, silence, solitude, stability, strength, support, sustenance, the feminine principle, the first astral plane, the womb, uncovering mysteries, wisdom.

Element of Air

Air is the only element that cannot be seen. It is the invisible, yet very real, gases that move around us all the time. As such, air has its roots in the world of spirit. It represents the non-physical dimensions that many of us are unaware of these days.

The power of air can be seen in the bright blue sky that surrounds our Mother Earth – the sky is limitless, and thus air fills us with the inspiration we need to aim high in life.

Traditionally, air also represents the power of the human mind. It is the wisdom that comes with both study and knowledge. It is the realm of intelligence and communication; of movement and action; of clarity and rational thought; of poetry and artistic talent; of hope and freedom; and of freshness and new beginnings. It is the inner child within us that yearns to explore and discover the big wide world.

Air is also the kingdom of intuition and psychic awareness. It represents the potential ability to sense the energies that move around us all the time, just as we sense the wind moving around our bodies. According to folklore, from various cultures, a sudden cool breeze in an area of a calm room could be an indication that a spirit wants to communicate.

Here is some magical information for this very creative element:

Basic Nature: Active, contemplative, creative, flying, fresh, hot, intelligent, light, masculine, moist, moving, projective, sanguine, suspending. Sound and fragrances are example manifestations of this element.

Symbol: An upward-pointing triangle with a horizontal line through it.

Planets: Jupiter, Mercury, Neptune.

Time: Dawn (the time that symbolises beginnings).

Day: Wednesday.

Season: Spring (the season that brings freshness and potential).

Cardinal Point: East (the direction where the sun rises, symbolising beginnings).

Point in Life: Childhood (the time of learning and discovering).

Sense: Hearing, smell.

Traditional Magical Tool: Wand (some traditions sword).

Places: Airports, colleges, foggy places, high towers, hilltops, libraries, mountaintops, places where moving clouds can be seen, psychologists' or psychiatrists' offices, schools, travel agencies, universities, windy places.

Zodiac Signs: Aquarius (fixed air), Gemini (mutable air), Libra (cardinal air).

Colours: Bright yellow, clear, crimson, light green, pastels, pink, sky blue.

Incense: Frankincense, fumitory, galbanum, myrrh.

Plants/Trees: Acacia, agaric, agrimony, almond, anemone, anise, aspen, bean, banyan, benzoin, bergamot, birch, bistort, bittersweet, bodhi tree, borage, bracken, Brazil nut, broom, caraway, cedar elm, chicory, citron, clover, comfrey, cypress, dandelion, dill, dock, fenugreek, fern, hazel, hops, lavender, lemongrass, lily of the valley, maple, marjoram, meadowsweet, mint, mistletoe, mulberry, palm, parsley, pansy, pecan, pine, pistachio, poplar, primrose, rice, sage, senna, slippery elm, vervain, violet, wall fern, yarrow. Generally plants with a strong scent.

Crystals/Stones: Alexandrite, amethyst, azurite, beryl, blue lace agate, blue tourmaline, carnelian, chrysoprase, citrine, diamond, fluorite, mica, moldavite, opal, pearl, pumice, rainbow stone, sapphire, snow quartz, sodalite, topaz, turquoise. Generally light or transparent stones.

Metals: Aluminium, copper, tin.

Creatures: Ant, bat, bee, butterfly, dragonfly, eagle, most birds, spider, wolf. Generally winged creatures.

Mythical Beast: Winged horse.

Archangel: Raphael.

Governs: Adventures, artistic talent, ascetic spirituality, astral travel, clarity, communication, creativity, divination, expedition, faith, freedom, group work, happiness, harmony, healing of ears, healing of lungs, humour, ideas, inspiration, instructions, intellect, intuition, joy, knowledge, language, laughter, learning, legal matters, memory, mental power, messages, movement, new beginnings, organisation, poetry, projects, psychic power, reason, schooling, secrets of the dead, study, success, teaching, telepathy, tests, the abstract, the connection between the earth and the heavens, the masculine principle, the mental plane, the recovery of lost or stolen items, theories, thoughts, travel, truths, visions, visualisation, wisdom, writing.

Element of Fire

The most volatile of all the elements is obviously fire. The power of fire can be seen in the passion that shines down from the sun, the moon and the stars. It is the only element that needs other substances to fuel it. When fire burns it has the ability to transform substances into new forms: smoke, ash, light and heat. As such, fire is the realm of change and transformation. It is both the destroyer and the creator. It clears away the old and allows room for rebirth and renewal – the rising of the phoenix from its own ashes is a powerful symbol of this.

Fire represents the undying spirit within every single one of us. It is the confidence and passion that lies behind both survival and progress. It is the spark of light in the dark that drives away outside influences that may threaten our willpower to move forward in life and achieve our goals. It is the element of strength and victory; of vengeance and war; of encouragement and enthusiasm; of ruthlessness and courageousness; and of purpose and achievement. Watch fire burn and you will soon begin to understand these concepts.

Here is some magical information for this very stimulating element:

Basic Nature: Active, ascending, choleric, cleansing, creative, destructive, dry, energetic, forceful, hot, light, masculine, projective, purifying, sexual, stimulating. Heat and lightning are example manifestations of this element.

Symbol: An upward-pointing triangle.

Planets: Jupiter, Mars, Sun.

Time: Noon (the time when the sun is at its height in the sky).

Day: Sunday.

Season: Summer (the season of heat and passion).

Cardinal Point: South (the direction closest to the earth's equator, the place of heat).

Point in Life: Youth (the time when we become aware of our responsibilities).

Sense: Sight.

Traditional Magical Tool: Sword (some traditions wand).

Places: Bedrooms (for sex), bonfire displays, deserts, firework displays, hot springs, ovens, saunas, sport fields, starry places, stormy places, the hearth, volcanoes, weightlifting rooms.

Zodiac Signs: Aries (cardinal fire), Leo (fixed fire), Sagittarius (mutable fire).

Colours: Crimson, gold, orange, red, rusty colours, white (symbolising white-hot fury), yellow.

Incense: Copal, frankincense, olibanum, rose.

Plants/Trees: Alder, allspice, almond tree in bloom, anemone, angelica, ash, basil, bay, betony, cacti, carnation, cashew, cedar, chrysanthemum, cinnamon, clove, coffee beans, coriander, curry, dill, dittany, dragon's blood, flame tree, frankincense, garlic, ginger, hawthorn, holly, hot peppers, juniper, lime, lovage, mandrake, marigold, mustard, nettle, nutmeg, oak, onion, orange, pomegranate, rosemary, rowan, saffron, sunflower, thistle, tobacco, walnut, witch hazel, wormwood. Generally spicy, stinging or thorny plants.

Crystals/Stones: Amber, amethyst, beryl, bloodstone, carnelian, chrysolite, citrine, coal, diamond, fire agate, fire garnet, fire opal, geodes, gold calcite, jasper, lava, obsidian, peridot, pyrite, rhodochrosite, ruby, smoky quartz, sunstone, yellow topaz. Generally red or fiery stones.

Metals: Brass, gold, steel.

Creatures: Ant, bear, bearded dragon, bee, beetle, cat, coyote, cricket, fox, horse, ladybird, lion, lizard, praying mantis, salamander, scorpion, shark, snake, stag, tiger, wolf. Generally stinging or volatile creatures.

Mythical Beast: Dragon.

Archangel: Michael.

Governs: Achievement, activity, ambition, anger, authority, banishment, body heat, challenges, change, combustions, comfort, competitions, confidence, conflicts, contests, courage, courtrooms, creativity, desires, destruction, electricity, encouragement, energy, enlightenment, enthusiasm, eruptions, excitement, exorcism, freedom, hard work, healing (fire destroys disease), health, hope, illumination, inspiration, law, lust, motivation, passion, perceptions, personal power, protection, purification, purpose, rapid growth, reactions, responsibilities, sexual potency, solar power, stimulation, strength, success, the masculine principle, transformation, trust, vitality, war, willpower.

Element of Water

Water is the element of emotion, purification, healing and psychic sensitivity. It releases our emotions when we cry, restores life in us when we are dehydrated, revitalises us when we take a morning shower and heals away the stresses of the day when we take an evening bath. It is nature's precious gift and symbolises the fountain of life.

Water is also a timeless symbol of love. It is the need within us to love and to feel loved. It is the element that represents the universal love of the Goddess's womb and her power to nurture and sustain all life. Water is the ultimate reminder that everything we do should be out of love.

One of the physical gifts of water is the sea. The depths of the ocean represent the mysteries behind life. Water is the mysteries that reside deep within the unconscious mind. It is the depths of the human soul and its connection to the spirit world. It is the unquenchable thirst within us to understand the meanings behind both life and death. It is the land of arcane knowledge.

Here is some magical information for this very mysterious element:

Basic Nature: Cleansing, cold, dreamy, emotional, feminine, fertile, flowing, healing, heavy, intuitive, loving, moist, mysterious, nurturing, passive, phlegmatic, purifying, receptive, sensitive, soothing. Rain is an example manifestation of this element.

Symbol: Downward-pointing triangle.

Planets: Moon, Neptune, Saturn, Venus.

Time: Dusk (the time of reflection).

Day: Monday.

Season: Autumn (the season of the harvest, symbolising that which we have nurtured).

Cardinal Point: West (the direction of the setting sun).

Point in Life: Adulthood (the reproductive years).

Sense: Taste.

Traditional Magical Tool: Chalice/cup.

Places: Bathrooms, beaches, bedrooms (for dreams), brooks, fountains, health spas, lakes, lighthouses, oceans, ponds, rivers, sea life centres, springs, steam rooms, swimming pools, waterfalls, wells.

Zodiac Signs: Cancer (cardinal water), Pisces (mutable water), Scorpio (fixed water).

Colours: Aqua, black, blue, green, grey, indigo, silver, transparent.

Incense: Aromatic rush roots, lotus, myrrh.

Plants/Trees: Aloe, apple, aster, birch, blackberry, burdock, cabbage, camellia, caper, cardamom, catnip, chamomile, chickweed, coconut, coltsfoot, columbine, cowslip, cucumber, daffodil, daisy, elder, eucalyptus, feverfew, foxglove, fungi, geranium, grape, hazel, heather, hemlock, hibiscus, hyacinth, lilac, mallow, morning glory, myrrh, orchid, pansy, passionflower, peach, plum, pondweed, potato, rose, sandalwood, seaweed, tansy, thyme, tomato, valerian, violet, water lily, wax myrtle, willow, wolf's bane, yarrow, yew. Generally flowers and those plants with a high water content.

Crystals/Stones: Amethyst, aquamarine, beryl, calcite, chalcedony, clear quartz, coral, diamond, emerald, jade, kunzite, lapis lazuli, limestone, magnetite, malachite, moonstone, obsidian, onyx, opal, pearl, peridot, rose quartz, selenite, sodalite, sugilite, tourmaline, turquoise, zircon. Generally transparent or translucent stones.

Metals: Copper, mercury (quicksilver), silver.

Creatures: Cat, crab, crocodile, dolphin, frog, otter, seabirds, seal, shellfish, swan, turtle, water snake, whale. Generally aquatic creatures.

Mythical Beast: Sea serpent.

Archangel: Gabriel.

Governs: Affection, ancestors, artistic talent, balance, beauty, change, charity, childbirth, compassion, contract negotiations, clairvoyance, courage, cycles, daring, death, dependence, dreams, ecstasy, emotions, empathy, family, fertility, fidelity, forgiveness, friendship, happiness, healing, intuition, life, love, lunar power, marriage, medicine, meditation, modesty, motherhood, mysteries, peace, pleasure, psychic sensitivity, purification, rebirth, recuperation, reflection, research, rest, sensitivity, sensuality, sleep, sorrow, spirituality, the feminine principle, the subconscious mind, the unconscious mind, the womb, transformation, unions of every kind, universal wisdom.

Elemental Spirits

Have you ever been transfixed by the dancing flames of an open fire? Or have you ever stood at the edge of a ship and had the sudden inexplicable urge to jump in the sea? If so, you have experienced just a fraction of the power of the elemental spirits. In the occult, each element has its own particular class of spirits that exist as part of, and in support of, the element. Each elemental race vibrates at their own unique rate of existence and are the personification of their element. When the elemental powers are asked to join us to aid and guide our magic, it is these spirits that Witches call forward.

In ancient Greece, elemental spirits became known as *daimons* (Latin *daemons*), though the Christians later changed this word to demons. According to the Christians, demons were angels who had rebelled against their creator. They were dangerous beings who were associated with Satan and evil. Of course, this teaching was yet another attempt by the Church to dissuade the people away from Pagan beliefs. In reality, the elementals are simply the forces behind nature and are neither good nor evil. They're neutral, like nature is as a whole. Elemental spirits are extremely powerful beings – they should be respected at all times.

Following is some brief discussions on each elemental race:

Earth Elementals: are traditionally known as gnomes, which is derived from the Greek word *"gnoma"*, meaning "knowledge". These dwarf-like creatures are thought to vibrate at a rate closest to that of humans and are ruled by a being called Boreas, who is associated with the north wind.

Air Elementals: are traditionally known as sylphs, which is derived from the Greek word *"silphe"*, meaning "butterfly". These winged creatures are thought to dwell in a world of the highest vibratory rate and are ruled by a being called Eurius, who is associated with the east wind.

Fire Elementals: are traditionally known as salamanders, which is derived from the Greek word *"salambe"*, meaning "fireplace". These legendary fiery creatures are the most intense of all the elemental spirits and are ruled by a being called Notus, who is associated with the south wind.

Water Elementals: complete the primal foursome of elemental spirits and are traditionally known as undines, which is derived from the Latin word *"unda"*, meaning "wave". These very emotional beings are the forces behind the ebb and flow of the earth's waters and are ruled by a being called Zephyrus, who is associated with the west wind.

Chapter Four: The Wheel of the Year

One of the greatest ways to develop a deeper relationship with the Goddess and God is to celebrate the spiritual significance of the seasons. Witches envision the year as an ever-turning wheel with eight spokes (the eight-spoked wheel is often associated with Fortuna, the Roman goddess of chance and fate). Each spoke is a Witches' festival or holiday known as a Sabbat (thought to be from the Hebrew word *"Shabbath"* meaning "sacred time" or "holy time"). These Sabbats represent the seasonal changes of nature and reflect the ever-changing relationship between the Goddess and God. They also give shape to the meanings of life and represent the mysteries behind birth, death and rebirth. In celebrating the Sabbats, the ancient agricultural days of our Pagan ancestors, we are reminded that life constantly changes and evolves. At each Sabbat, a different energy flows through the land which Witches use to empower their lives and to improve their connection to nature.

The Witches' festivals are divided into four Lesser Sabbats and four Greater Sabbats. The four Lesser Sabbats are often known as the quarter festivals and are related to the astronomical events produced by the earth's tilt. They are Yule (the winter solstice), Eostar (the spring equinox), Litha (the summer solstice) and Mabon (the autumn equinox). The four Greater Sabbats, which are thought to be older than the Lesser Sabbats, are often known as the cross-quarter festivals and these occur halfway between the solstices and the equinoxes. They are Imbolc, Beltane, Lughnasadh and Samhain. The names of the Sabbats are Celtic and Nordic in origin and relate specifically to the natural farming cycle of the year which includes the planting and harvesting of crops. All eight Sabbats have spiritual influences from many different cultures.

The Sabbats are basically times of feasting for Witches. They are times to celebrate our joyous connection to nature – to the Goddess and God. In celebrating the Sabbats, we are walking the paths of our ancient, pre-Christian, Pagan ancestors to remember just how much we depend on nature for survival.

Without the constant turning of the seasons, humankind would simply not exist. Following is some information on each of the Sabbats and some of the many ways in which they are celebrated. While there are many different versions of the Wheel of the Year myth between the Goddess and God, the one below is the one I follow and is quite common in contemporary Witchcraft.

Note: The dates for the Sabbats below are those that are followed in the Northern Hemisphere. Witches who live in the Southern Hemisphere, however, celebrate the Sabbats in reverse because they have opposite seasons. Yule, for example, is celebrated towards the end of December in the Northern Hemisphere but in the Southern Hemisphere it is celebrated towards the end of June.

Yule: December 20th-23rd

Yule (pronounced *yool*) brings the midwinter celebrations and is sometimes seen as the first Sabbat to grace the Witches' calendar. Also known as Saturnalia, Longest Night and the winter solstice, Yule marks the time when the sun's power is at its weakest – it is the time when we experience the shortest day of the year, yet it also marks the coming of the longer days. This is the time to celebrate the return of the sun, whose power will increase with every passing day.

In myth, the Goddess goes into labour and then gives birth to the God (the sun); he is the Star Child and the Child of Promise who brings forth hope in the dead of winter. He represents the spark of light that emerges from the greatest darkness, symbolising rebirth and renewal from the Goddess's eternal womb. As such, Yule is a very special time for many Witches for without the return of the sun there would be no future harvests to sustain us.

In the year 273 C. E., the ancient story of the God's birth at Yule was adopted by the Christian faith in their story of the Nativity (the Christians had no fixed date for the birth of Jesus before this time). In placing Jesus's birth around the time of Yule, which had long been associated with divine births, the Christians were able to mystically connect Jesus with the sun. This was one of their many efforts to help with the conversion process of the Pagans during the early centuries of Christianity. In ancient Egyptian art, some of the depictions of Isis and Horus, who symbolise the story of the Goddess and God at Yule, are almost identical to the images of the Madonna and Child in early Christian art.

Yule is also a time to remember the story of the Oak and Holly Kings. At Yule, they symbolically go into battle. The Oak King triumphs over the Holly King and reigns supreme until Litha when they symbolically go into battle yet again (see below). Thus, the Oak King represents the return of the sun's power and the greening of the land. He is the lord of the waxing sun, the god of the light half of the year, who represents the fullness and joy of nature in the months to come.

Since Yule is a time to celebrate the coming of the light half of the year, Witches decorate their homes with evergreens – such as holly, mistletoe, rosemary, bay leaves and ivy – to remind themselves that the earth will be green once again. We gather with friends and family by the hearth (which is symbolic of the sun's power) to cheer our hearts in the cold grip of winter. Yule is a time to sing and dance, and to celebrate the bonds we share with our nearest and dearest. It is a time for the giving of gifts to remind our loved ones of just how much they mean to us.

As a time of rebirth and renewal, Yule is also the perfect time to let go of the past and to make positive plans for the future. The increasing strength of the sun's power from this time onward gives our hopes and dreams the power they need to manifest into reality. Know that with the sun's positive energy you have the power to make great changes in your life. It was at a Yule celebration when I decided to write this book!

Traditionally, Witches also decorate a Yule tree during the midwinter celebrations. This age-old Pagan custom is extremely entertaining and is a good excuse to bring the family together. Many Witches decorate their Yule trees with items that remind them of the sun's power, such as cinnamon sticks and gold-painted baubles for instance. The star at the top of a Yule tree is a powerful symbol of the sun for many Witches. The sun is, after all, our closest star. The Yule tree is also a very powerful symbol of the Yggdrasil, the Tree of the World, where the Norse god Odin hung for nine days and nights in the ordeal that won him the magical symbols of the runes. Incidentally, this god, the white-bearded, gift-giver of the ancient Yule celebrations, is thought to be the origin of Santa Claus.

Many Witches also decorate their Yule trees with clear quartz crystals to imitate icicles. These beautiful crystals can be wrapped up with shiny wire and then hung on the branches of your Yule tree. Clear quartz crystals are excellent for clearing away negative energy from our lives and are thus perfect for the Yuletide celebrations.

Another Pagan custom involves the burning of a Yule log in a ritual fire (today's Yule log chocolate cake is a remnant of this old Pagan custom). Traditionally, the Yule log is cut from a sacred tree, such as oak, ash or fir, and then carved with sun symbols to remind us of the God's birth. At sundown, the Yule log is then lit and kept alight until sunrise. It is then appropriate to thank the Goddess for the return of the sun and the promise of the spring to come.

Foods appropriate to Yule include apples, oranges, pears, nuts, pork and cookies. Spicy drinks, such as mulled wine and ginger tea, are also perfect for the Yuletide celebrations.

Imbolc: February 1st-2nd

Imbolc (pronounced *im-bolk* or *im-bolg*), also known as Candlemas, Oimelc and the Festival of Waxing Light, marks the halfway point between the winter solstice and the spring equinox. It is the time of the year when life begins to stir under the frozen earth and there are already early signs of spring. This is a time when Witches celebrate the waxing of the sun, a time when they say farewell to the winter as they look forward to the months of spring and the warmer days to come. In myth, the Goddess recovers from giving birth and her divine child, the God, begins to mature as the sun strengthens with every passing day. With the Goddess, he will bring renewed life to the earth in the months to come.

Imbolc is also a fire festival, a festival of lights, that is sacred to the ancient solar healing goddess Brigit, the female patron of Ireland and the midwife of spring. In myth, her fiery breath brought life back to the earth after the barren time of winter. Such was the importance of Brigit to the ancient

Pagans that the Christians were unable to eradicate her completely – eventually they canonised her a saint. The Christians actually made little effort to hide the fact that they had Christianised a clearly Pagan deity. The fascinating story of St. Brigit (or Brigid) being the midwife to Mary in Christian mythology reflects the deity's fierce role as protector and defender of women and children.

In ancient times, Imbolc was a time of hardship for our Pagan ancestors. It was a time when food stores were running low and the earth was still quite barren before spring became more apparent. As such, many modern Witches use Imbolc to remember those who are less fortunate than themselves. We involve ourselves in charity work and work towards bettering the lives of others. We take unneeded clothes, toys and extra food to the homeless in the hope that we can bring some joy and make the world a better place. Imbolc is also a great time to take care of those animals that are in need of help.

Since Imbolc is a time when the sun's power is waxing in strength, many Witches light a candle in every room of their homes (these are usually white or yellow candles) in honour of the young God as he begins to grow to his fullness. The candles represent the spark of light in the dark that brings forth the promise of spring after the long months of winter. The candles can also symbolise the spark of fire within ourselves that gives us the confidence and passion we need to move forward in life and achieve the things that we so desire. As the candles are lit, Witches focus on those areas of their lives that they wish to improve on. Many Witches also plant seeds and bulbs to represent the things within their lives that they wish to nurture and grow.

Imbolc is also a time of purification. It is a time when Witches clean their homes from top to bottom. This cleansing is symbolic for Imbolc is a time to clear away the clutter of winter as we prepare for the season of renewed growth. It is a time not only for physical cleansing but also spiritual and mental cleansing for it is only when our minds and hearts are clear that we can really focus on our goals in life. Some Witches like to burn sage in every room of their homes at this Sabbat to aid the purification process.

Since Brigit is the goddess of poetry, inspiration and creativity, you may like to write some poems that reflect any goals or desires that you wish to achieve over the coming year. This can be highly entertaining and is a good excuse to really focus your mind on the things that you wish to achieve. It is a good idea to place these poems on your bedside table so that you can read them before you retire. Your dreams will give clues of how to achieve your goals. Know that these dreams are Brigit's gifts of inspiration and creativity, and don't forget to thank her for these gifts (see chapter nineteen for more information on dreams).

Foods traditional to this Sabbat include peppers, onions, garlic, leeks, shallots, seeds and all spicy dishes (in honour of the young God). Many Witches also eat dairy products in honour of the sheep that are lactating at this time of the year. Herbal teas that have a purifying effect on the body are also highly appropriate for Imbolc.

Eostar: March 20th-23rd

The next Sabbat to grace the Witches' calendar is Eostar (pronounced *o-star*). Also known as Rites of Spring, Ostara and the spring equinox, Eostar is a time when day and night become equal in length. It is a time of balance and harmony. At Eostar, we are reminded that the length of daylight will exceed the length of darkness with every passing day and that the earth will become greener as the months progress into the summer. This is a time when winter is becoming a distant memory, a time when Witches celebrate the fact that the sun's power is more apparent upon the earth. It is a time when we celebrate fertility, rebirth and renewal as the earth wakes up from its long slumber.

In myth, the Goddess becomes fertile at Eostar and the young God begins to realise his potential to become a father as he grows towards maturity. The Goddess bursts to life throughout the land and the God becomes her lover. The result of their union is rebirth and renewal. They dance in courtship and this is symbolised by the creatures of the earth that dance in order to attract a mate at this time of the year. The previously barren soil covers itself with green splendour and the birds sing and rejoice in the warmth of the sun. At Eostar, the Goddess and God delight in the abundance of the natural world.

The Christianised version of Eostar is Easter (notice how similar that word sounds to the Pagan version). In Christian mythology, Jesus, the son of God, willingly gave up his life by being crucified in order to save the world from sin and to reconcile humankind with the Christian God. After three days, however, Jesus rose from the dead and eventually ascended into heaven. The Pagans had always celebrated the rebirth and renewal of the earth at Eostar so the Christians simply adopted the story of Jesus's "rebirth" from the dead in order to bring the people into the Christian churches.

Eostar is actually named after the German goddess of spring whose animal totem is the hare. You may have heard the saying "mad as a March hare". Around the time of Eostar, the hare's mating behaviour seems to be ecstatic and unpredictable. They appear to "box" and leap about in the fields as if they are completely crazy. In reality, however, hares are no more ecstatic in their behaviour in March than at any other time of the year. It's simply the short grass in March that makes their behaviour more visible to us. Hares are especially linked to the moon. They are, therefore, strongly associated with fertility and female mysteries. They represent the fertility of the earth. There are many goddesses of fertility to whom hares are held sacred. Today's Easter Bunny is a remnant of the hare's ancient, Pagan, fertility symbolism.

One of the greatest ways to celebrate Eostar is to decorate hard-boiled eggs. Eggs, which are abundant among birds and many other animals at Eostar, are especially sacred in Witchcraft because they represent fertility, rebirth and new life. For Witches who believe in reincarnation, eggs represent the return of a soul to a life of physicality. Decorating eggs is an ancient Pagan custom and is an extremely entertaining activity to do with children. Your decorated eggs can be placed around your home to bring forth good health, wealth and prosperity.

Another traditional activity to do at Eostar involves the picking of random wildflowers when out on a walk through forests and other natural green places (or you can simply buy wildflowers from a florist or a garden centre if you so wish). Chosen wildflowers can then be used to decorate the home, to bring in the spring energies, and to divine with. Many Witches use books and their intuition to interpret the spiritual meanings of the wildflowers that they have chosen. Divining with wildflowers is an excellent way to reveal deep secrets about our lives and inner emotions.

Many Witches also like to plant seeds at Eostar. The seeds can represent the goals you had set at your Yuletide and Imbolc celebrations. As the seeds come to life and grow to fullness, see also your goals and dreams come to life and to fullness. See your young plants in your mind's eye as a symbol of your ability to let go of the past and to really bring your wishes to fruition. Know that with the powers of nature you have the ability to make positive things happen in your life providing your will is strong enough. If you have been meaning to start a new project, such as a course of study, Eostar is the perfect time to do so.

Another Pagan custom of Eostar involves the baking of a silver coin in sweet bread. Once the bread is baked, it is traditionally shared out among the family or coven members and whoever receives the piece with the silver coin in it will be especially blessed by the Lord and the Lady of spring. The person who receives the coin should expect excellent luck throughout the coming year.

Foods in tune with Eostar include seeds, nuts, eggs, fish, sweet breads, chocolate, honey cake, dairy products, edible flowers, leafy green vegetables and seasonal fruits.

Beltane: April 30th to May 1st

Also known as May Day, Bealtaine and Walpurgis Night, Beltane (pronounced *bel-tayn* or *bell-tain*) is thought to be the oldest holiday in the world. At Beltane, Witches celebrate the rise of the sun and the beginning of summer. It is the time of the year when Witches honour the fertility of the earth as well as life in its many forms. Plants and trees begin to blossom and the height of summer is not too far away. The land fills us with powerful energies as we look forward to the summer months to come.

In myth, the Goddess is pregnant with the Star Child by now and she unites with the God in marriage and love. Their sexual chemistry and loving energies are evident all around us within the natural world at this time. This is a time to celebrate the sacred bond between the Goddess and God. It is a time of great festivity, for outdoor feasting, and for lovers to enact the Great Rite (this is a celebration of sacred sexuality, see chapter five). In ancient times,

Pagans often made love in fields as this was thought to boost the growth of crops and the fertility of livestock. Unsurprisingly, Beltane is a time when many Witches choose to hold handfasting rites (Witches' marriage ceremonies, see chapter five) or to renew their vows of love.

Beltane is another fire festival that is sacred to the Celtic sun god Belenos who was dubbed "the British Apollo" by the ancient Romans. Belenos, god of sunlight, healing and health, was honoured by our ancestors by lighting fires on hilltops at Beltane. This was done to celebrate Belenos's victory over the darkness of winter. It was also thought to strengthen the sun's power as it rose in the sky and to bring fertility to the earth after the ashes were sprinkled upon crops. Often, sacred herbs were sprinkled on these ritual fires so that the smoke would purify livestock. Couples were also encouraged to jump over the fires to bring forth good luck and fertility within their unions. Fires burned at Beltane were also thought to ward away evil or negative influences.

Since Beltane is a powerful time of fertility, many Witches honour the Green Man in his Oak King aspect. At Beltane, he becomes King of the May and the Goddess becomes his Queen of the May. Their union symbolises the increasing fullness and joy of nature at this very sacred time of the year. With the Earth Mother, the Green Man stretches his fertile power over the land to ensure that life can continue. At Beltane, he is coming towards his height and is, therefore, the protector of nature. He is the ancient god of the greenwood who is tender of wild animals and livestock. If we call upon his power, he will ensure that our future harvests are bountiful and that our garden plants will prosper.

One of the most traditional ways to celebrate Beltane is to erect a Maypole to dance around. The Maypole is a tall pole stuck into the ground and represents the supreme phallic symbol of the God. It represents his power within the natural world and is associated with sexuality, fertility, birth and creativity. Traditionally, the Maypole is decorated with seasonal flowers and green branches to represent the fertility of the Goddess wrapped around the phallic symbol of the God. Ribbons or streamers are then attached at the top and allowed to flow down far enough for participants to comfortably grasp the ends. It is then appropriate for men and women to dance around the Maypole in a fashion that involves much meeting and kissing. Traditionally, this involves men dancing in one direction and women in the other. This joyous activity is done to represent the natural male and female balance of nature.

In ancient times, Beltane celebrations would continue way into the night and often until dawn. It was at dawn that many young ladies would then wash their faces with the first dew of May. It was thought that this tradition would encourage the young women to achieve fullness and fertility over the coming months ahead even as the crops matured to their ripeness. This custom was also thought to encourage beauty – both inside and out. Many young lady Witches of our modern times still do it for all these reasons. The first dew of May is a wonderful substance that can be very useful in spellcraft as well as many other magical practices.

Foods traditional to Beltane include dairy products, oat cakes, sweets, honey, salad and seasonal fruits.

Litha: June 20th-23rd

Litha (pronounced *lith-ah*), also known as St. John's Day and the summer solstice, brings the midsummer celebrations and marks the time when the sun's power is at its strongest – it is the time when we experience the longest day of the year, yet it also marks the coming of the shorter days. All around us, the fruits of the earth are more apparent than the previous months of the year and the earth is teeming with life and green splendour. This is a time to honour the God who is at his greatest stature and to celebrate the sacred union of the divine Goddess and God whose combined powers are evident all around us within the natural world. However, nothing in nature will be as good again. When the sun shines at its fullest glory it casts the deepest shadows as we look towards the dark half of the year to come.

Of course, Litha is also a time to remember the story of the Holly King's triumph over the Oak King. At Litha, when the sun has strengthened as much as it possibly can, the Oak and Holly Kings symbolically go into battle once again. Inevitably, the Holly King, whose evergreen holly face symbolises the darkness of winter, wins because the Oak King is unable to retain his strength as the sun weakens and the days progress into the dark half of the year. Thus, the Holly King rules until the sun is able to begin strengthening once again at Yule.

There are many paired hero-figures in legend who are believed to be variants of this myth between the Oak and Holly Kings. Some examples include Lleu Llaw Gyffes and Gronw Pebr, Gwyn and Gwythr, Lugh and Balan, the robin and the wren, and even Jesus and John the Baptist. In the Christian story, St. John (who symbolises the Oak King) baptised many people in the River Jordan and preached repentance until he was imprisoned by Herod Antipas. His role as preacher and redeemer was then given to Jesus (who symbolises the Holly King).

The theme of Litha is very similar to Beltane. Like Beltane, the ancient festivals of Litha were wild, passionate and filled with joy. There would have been much feasting before ritual bonfires to celebrate the sun's power. Herds of farm animals were often paraded between these bonfires for blessings and protection. It was also thought to remove any curses and sicknesses. The thunderstorms and lightning that occurred in many places each year at Litha were another reason why fire rituals were so important for our ancient ancestors.

One traditional way to celebrate Litha is to make love wreaths. These are constructed from ribbons and summer flowers, and are then exchanged by friends and family members to symbolise the bonds they share. It is a way for the Pagan folk to spread their love among their nearest and dearest at this very loving time of the year.

Since nature is at its full strength at Litha, it is a very powerful time indeed to perform magic of any kind. Spells of healing, love, fertility, protection and success are particularly powerful. You may also like to gather any herbs that you wish to use in your spellcraft since their energies will be extra potent at this time. It is also a good idea to dry herbs picked at Litha before a ritual fire so that you can store them for future magical workings. You may also like to leap your ritual fire to encourage purification, renewed energy, fertility, good health and success. It is said that fires kept alight until midnight on the exact date of the longest day of the year will bring good luck and blessings.

Since Litha is a time when thunderstorms and lightning are more likely, you may want to take some measures to protect your home from their ill effects. One of the more traditional ways to do this is to decorate your home with St. John's wort. Simply cut some of the flowers and stalks from the plant and hang them around your home or alternatively place them in jars and then hang these jars near windows. Not only will this guard your home against the ill effects of thunderstorms and lightning, it will also protect your property and all those who live within against negativity of all kinds, especially illnesses such as colds and fevers.

Litha is also an excellent time to take long walks through your local forest so that you can really be at one with nature. You can use this time to talk to the Goddess and God about any problems that you may have in your life. Use their strength at this very powerful time of the year to help you overcome these problems and know that the Goddess and God are always there for you. All you need to do is ask for their assistance. Incidentally, these walks can be a really good excuse for you to gather the herbs that you may need for your future spells and other magical workings.

Foods and drinks in tune with Litha include fruits and vegetables of all kinds, honey, bread, ale and mead.

Lughnasadh: July 31st to August 1st

The next Sabbat in the cycle of the Witches' year is Lughnasadh (pronounced *loo-nuh-sa* or *loo-nah-sah*), the time of the first harvest. Also known as Lammas (this is the Christianised name for this ancient festival, which means "loaf mass"), Lunasdal and Lunasa, Lughnasadh is the time when the plants of the earth begin to wither, and fruits and seeds drop to the ground so that we humans, as well as the animal kingdom, can be sustained over the long winter to come. It is a time when Witches traditionally begin to gather in the bounty of the year's harvest as they prepare for the cold nights of winter. It is a time of thanksgiving and a time to celebrate not only the harvests of the land, but also the harvests in the spiritual aspects of life. It is a time to celebrate that which we have nurtured over the year so far, a time to focus on all our achievements – both physically and spiritually.

In myth, the Goddess is heavy with the Star Child. The God grows old as the sun's power decreases with every passing day, but with this comes his endless wisdom. The Goddess feels a sadness in her heart because she knows that the God, her husband, is living out his final days. Yet, she also feels joy in her heart because she knows that the God lives on within her womb of transformation and that he will be reborn as her child once again at Yule. Witches celebrate the power of the God's symbol, the sun, in the life of fields. The ripe corn, which is abundant in the fields at Lughnasadh, is often made into bread to represent the God's power and strength to nurture and sustain us, his children, as we look towards the darker nights to come.

In ancient times, Lughnasadh was a very mysterious time indeed for our Pagan ancestors. The cereal crops that dropped to the earth represented death and decay, yet they also represented rebirth and renewal. For our ancestors, the grain that lay on the ground waiting for the spring to become apparent in the following year represented the rest that the soul takes between incarnations before it is reborn into a life of physicality. It represented the natural cycle of life – birth, death, rest and then rebirth. In fact, carvings that indicate both the physical and spiritual significance of grain can be found in many ancient burial sites.

As a time to celebrate the power of our closest star in the life of the fields, Witches often use Lughnasadh to remember their connection to the other stars of the heavens as well. All life on this planet is a product of the stars. We are literally made of "star stuff" and are thus very much connected to the powers of the universe. We are born of the stars and one day our bodies will return to them. The stars are our oldest ancestors and have a direct influence on all life on earth. They are a powerful reminder that all life is a product of the combined powers of the Goddess and God – the universe itself. For all these reasons, star-watching is a favourite pastime for many Witches at this very sacred time of the year.

Another activity of Lughnasadh involves the making of corn dollies or kirn babies. These represent the spirit of the corn and are traditionally suspended around the home to bring forth protection and good fortune over the autumn and winter. Once spring finally graces the land, they are traditionally buried with the new seeds so that the corn spirit is released back to the Earth Mother.

Foods traditional to Lughnasadh include bread, berries, crab apples, all grains, cakes, nuts and all vegetables and fruits. Drinks of wine, beer and cider (to symbolise the power of the fields) are also highly appropriate for Lughnasadh.

Mabon: September 20th-23rd

Towards the end of September the land is visited by Mabon (pronounced *may-bun* or *may-bon*), the time of the second harvest. Also known as Modron, Harvest Home and the autumn equinox, Mabon is a time of balance and harmony, like Eostar. It is a time when day and night become equal in length. Unlike Eostar, however, the darkness dominates our lives and everything else throughout the land. All around us, nature declines as the sun's power continues to fade. The earth prepares for its time of rest and leaves fall to the ground to ensure that the soil has sufficient nutrients for the plant life in the following spring. At Mabon, Witches reflect on the transience of life as the end of the harvest season draws near.

Mystically, the Goddess goes into mourning for the God, her husband, whose strength continues to weaken as the nights become longer with each day that passes. However, she feels the God's presence even as the sun wanes because he lives and burns on within her womb. The God prepares to leave his physical body and awaits his journey into the Summerlands where he will rest until he is reborn once again at Yule. At Mabon, the dark aspect of the God is becoming increasingly apparent.

One of the greatest symbols of Mabon is the apple. Apples, which are ready to be picked at Mabon, are said to be fruits of the underworld and represent the immortality of the soul. They are a powerful reminder that even as we age and then die the seed of life within us all lives on. Also, if you cut an apple through the centre you will find one of the most powerful symbols of the Witch – the pentagram, a five-pointed star, that represents the four sacred elements of nature plus a fifth element, that of spirit, the very element that binds the other four together in the work of creation (see chapter six for more information on the pentagram). The apple has been an especially spiritual symbol for eons and the apple tree in particular is said to mark a boundary between the worlds.

Since Mabon is a time of balance, many Witches focus on balancing their own lives. We work towards removing negativity from our lives, such as stress and hatred, and focus on those areas that we need to improve on. It is also a good time to reflect on what we have learned in the Craft so far and to finish up any projects. When Witches talk of a good harvest, they often mean it symbolically. In other words, the things that we want out of life can only be bountiful if we have put the hard work in. This is always good to remember when we focus on any goals that we wish to achieve over the coming year at the Yuletide celebrations (and indeed within life in general).

One of the favourite pastimes of Mabon, for many Witches, is to take long walks through wild places, such as fields and forests for instance. Often, Witches gather autumnal items, such as seeds, pods and dried plants, to decorate their homes (to bring in the autumn energies) and for future magical workings. If you choose to take such an autumnal walk then I would strongly encourage you to take a note of any animals that you happen to see. Animals are usually quite active at Mabon because they are preparing for their long rest over the winter period. The animals that you come across can reveal deep secrets about your inner thoughts and emotions or even possible future events. If you happen to come across a deer, for instance, it could be an indication that you are a very sensitive soul and are aware of the feelings of others even before they are. Deers can also indicate that you are about to embark on an exciting adventure that will lead to many possibilities (see chapter eighteen for more information on the spiritual meanings of animals).

Foods in tune with Mabon include bread, apples, pomegranates, root vegetables, grains, beans and baked squash. Beer and cider are also very traditional drinks for Mabon as with Lughnasadh.

Samhain: October 31st to November 1st

Samhain (pronounced *sow-in* or *sow-en*), also known as Halloween, Ancestor Night and the Feast of the Dead, is the dark counterpart of Beltane. Many Witches see Samhain as the start of their new year, though other Witches, myself included, see Yule as the true start of the new year given the fact that the birth of the God (the sun) is celebrated at that time. At Samhain, however, the onset of winter is initiated and the last of the leaves fall from the trees. According to folklore, from various cultures, catching thirteen leaves will guarantee love, luck and joy to flourish over the coming year. It is also said that all harvests must be picked by Samhain as Pooka, a shape-shifting nature spirit from Celtic folklore who delighted in tormenting people, will contaminate any produce that is left in the fields. Pooka's favourite disguise is said to be that of an ugly black horse.

Samhain is a celebration of death basically and is a very solemn time for Witches indeed. It is also the time when the veil between our world and the world of spirit is said to be at its thinnest. Witches, therefore, may attempt to contact their departed loved ones at this very mysterious time of the year. The Christian version of this ancient festival is All Saints' Day, a time when the Christian folk commemorate, and commune with, the deceased heroes of the Christian religion.

In myth, the God departs from the physical world and then rests in the Summerlands where he will also remember and review all his achievements over the spring, summer and autumn until he is ready to return once again at Yule and begin his life cycle all over again. The Goddess deeply mourns the death of the God and becomes the keeper of the mysteries of life and death. She also enters her period of sleeping and dreaming as she prepares for the rebirth of her Star Child.

In ancient times, Samhain was a time of sacrifice. It was a time when our Pagan ancestors slaughtered animals to ensure that there would be enough food throughout the cold depths of winter. The God, who was identified with the wild beasts of nature, fell too so that the tribes could continue. Although this part of Samhain symbolism probably won't be appreciated by vegetarian Witches, the sacrifice of animals at Samhain was once a very traditional farming practice. Early Pagans sacrificed animals out of necessity (the animals that were sacrificed were usually the weakest who had little chance of survival throughout the winter anyhow). Of course, Witches don't sacrifice animals within their rituals. We wouldn't dream of it. The ritual sacrifice of any living creature would be the ultimate way to violate the Witches' rule of harm none.

Since Samhain is a celebration of death, many Witches hold a dumb supper to commemorate their departed loved ones and other ancestors. This is a special dinner held in total silence. Traditionally, an extra space is set at the dinner table and a meal of pork, bread and apples is placed there as an offering to the souls of the dead. Some Witches like to place items that remind them of their deceased loved ones at the dinner table too, such as photographs and jewellery. Once the meal is over, many Witches place the plate of food that was set out in honour of the departed on their back doorsteps for woodland creatures who will be looking for extra food to store in their places of hibernation for the long winter ahead. The apples can also be buried in the garden to "nourish" the souls of the dead.

Since Samhain is a time when the Goddess enters her dreamy, psychic period, many Witches consider it a perfect time to do some form of divination. For reasons not yet understood to science, there is a substantial increase in paranormal activity and psychic phenomena at Samhain and Witches use this profound energy shift to increase their psychic awareness. Tools such as tarot cards and crystal balls are often utilised to gain insight into inner emotions and the year ahead. Scrying in particular is said to be extremely powerful at Samhain (see chapter twenty for more information on divination).

Samhain is also a perfect time for introspection – a time to examine all that has occurred over the previous months. Witches consider Samhain a time to think about all the projects that have been successful and the ones that have not. We re-evaluate them all at Samhain and consider where we have gone wrong in life and where we have been more successful. We focus on what is important in life, clarify any priorities and consider any projects that we wish to accomplish over the year ahead in order for our lives to be more productive. We may also use Samhain to break any bad habits or addictions (such as smoking) and as a time for healing any mental or physical illnesses.

Of course, Samhain is also the traditional time for dressing up, carving pumpkins or turnips, trick or treating and all other fun games that involve bonfires and fireworks. Although all these activities have become very popular in more recent times, they do have their origins in ancient Pagan times. Our ancestors knew that the winter ahead would be a time of hardship (there was no electricity in homes or shops to buy food in ancient times) so they would lighten the mood with fun and games. Bonfires were lit to honour the death of the God (the sun) and to ward off evil. The bonfires were also thought to light the path of the souls of the dead to the other side. Turnip or pumpkin carving at Samhain is actually thought to originate from Ireland and many Witches of our modern times still do it as part of their religious practices. Often, eerie faces or sacred symbols are carved into the turnips or pumpkins and candles are then placed inside them. These are then placed around the home to repel negative energy or evil spirits.

As the year continues to draw to a close around the time of Samhain, many Witches often find themselves thinking deeply about the natural process of reincarnation. Witches who accept this ancient doctrine understand that with death comes the promise of rebirth, symbolised by the ouroboros snake consuming its own tail and indeed the rebirth of the God at Yule. The tomb becomes the womb as I always say. If there was no death nothing in life would ever progress forward. The purpose of reincarnation is to evolve the soul. Each time we live out an incarnation we learn a new set of karmic lessons and thus we gain wisdom. Once the soul has gained sufficient wisdom, over many lifetimes, it will reach a state of perfection, at which point it may choose to give up the physical world completely and return to the divine source from which it originated. All life within the natural world evolves and adapts – and this same principle applies to the immortal soul.

Foods traditional to this festival include beets, gourds, squashes, cakes, spices, garlic, turnips, pumpkins (pumpkin soup is very traditional at Samhain), apples, nuts, corn, gingerbread and all meats. Drinks of cider and mulled wine are also highly appropriate for Samhain.

Chapter Five: Witchcraft Rites

Rituals are the essence and the heart of the Witchcraft religion. Through rituals, we are able to commune with our deep spiritual selves, the powers of the earth and the ultimate higher power that is the Goddess and God. Rituals, which can be performed alone or within groups, are a way for Witches to celebrate and to strengthen their relationships with the deities. By performing rituals on a regular basis, a Witch is able to honour the Goddess and God and to nourish the mind, the heart, the body and the soul.

So what exactly is a Witchcraft ritual? Well, within Witchcraft a ritual is a religious or spiritual ceremony that a Witch (or group of Witches) performs for a specific purpose. Rituals, which can be elaborate or simple, are practical procedures that can be employed for any number of reasons. A ritual may be employed to celebrate a Sabbat; to celebrate a particular phase of the moon, or to mark a certain milestone within life, as a few examples. Rituals can be employed for an almost unlimited range of reasons. What is important within Witchcraft, however, is that the main purpose of ritual is to commune with, understand and experience the powers of the Goddess and God.

Some of the most famous rituals within Witchcraft today are known as rites of passage. These are very personal rituals that mark certain milestones within a person's life. Initiation and marriage are two classic examples. These rites of passage are often marked with beautiful, elaborate rituals to reflect the most significant changes of life – the transition of one stage of life to another. Just as Witches celebrate the changing phases of nature within the world around them, they also celebrate the changing phases within the cycle of the human life.

Within many religions of the world today, many rituals are obligatory. The Holy Eucharist (the consuming of the body and blood of Christ) within Catholicism, for example, is deemed an essential part of a Catholic's spiritual life. In Witchcraft, however, a Witch will only hold a ritual if he or she feels the need to do so. The rituals of Witchcraft are not obligatory. No Witch (or would-be Witch) should ever feel obliged to hold a ritual. Witchcraft is a free religion that allows us to hold rituals when we feel moved to do so. The most effective rituals anyhow are those that are performed when we are emotionally ready to hold them.

Following is some information on some of the most well-known Witchcraft rituals. The rituals of Witchcraft may be performed in public or private depending on the circumstances. Within the coven, the high priest and priestess traditionally take the leading roles within rituals. Rituals may be handed down from a particular tradition or they can be newly written for future occasions. Some Witches simply use books about Witchcraft to guide them through their rituals. What is important, however, is that rituals are performed with sincerity and an open heart.

Naming or Wiccaning Rites

These are rituals held to name new babies and to place them under the protection of the Goddess and God and the four sacred elements of nature. Unlike Catholics, who have the doctrine of the Original Sin of Adam and Eve, Witches do not feel that there is a need for a spiritual cleansing when a child is born. There is no washing away of sin when Witches perform naming ceremonies on children. They are simply a way for Witches to welcome new babies into the world of physicality. In addition, the great majority of Witches do not see a naming ceremony as a formal initiation of a child into the religion of Witchcraft. Witches generally do not believe that such a commitment should be forced on to a child. In earlier times, the blessing of a baby at birth was the job of the midwife who was usually also known as the local Wise Woman or White Witch. She would bless the baby before the local priest of the orthodox religion baptised the baby into the Christian faith. In modern times, there are many Witches and other Pagans who are highly trained in naming ceremonies and they are very much in demand.

There is much debate among Witches over whether or not children should be taught some aspects of the Craft before they reach a certain age. Some Witches believe that no teaching should be given at all. They believe that children should be given freedom and should not be asked to make any choices until they are mature enough to do so. In my opinion, children should be able to explore all religions before they make a balanced decision on which one to follow. There is some truth in all religions and each one can help us to develop in one way or another. Some children may not want to follow any religion whatsoever and again this should be their own choice. Religion is not for some of us and this should be respected – especially by followers of the open-minded religion of Witchcraft.

Naming ceremonies are truly joyous occasions. They are times to thank the Goddess and God for the beautiful gift of receiving children (whether by adoption or by natural birth). Children help to shape the future in generations to come. They should, therefore, be greatly respected. We must do everything in our power to ensure that they are brought up well with love and care. They come to love us, to teach us and to help us grow as people. There is a great deal of wisdom within the minds of children. They can be difficult at times, but this only helps us to spiritually develop as people as well as Witches. Often, natal astrology charts are given to couples who have been blessed with new children to assist them in the bringing up of their offspring or adopted children. Talismans, amulets and other magical items are also highly appropriate gifts for naming ceremonies.

Coming of Age Rites

Coming of age rites mark the transition of young people from childhood to manhood or womanhood. They are usually held when young people reach puberty. As with the rest of society, many Witches who are parents are not completely comfortable with their children reaching sexual maturity and so coming of age rituals are not a universal practice within Witchcraft. In addition, some teenagers may not feel comfortable in holding such rituals because they may feel too embarrassed or too shy by their changing bodies. Nonetheless, some Witches feel that rituals that mark puberty are of great importance. They deem puberty an important time of a young person's life when he or she has great potential to learn much about how the world works. For a female, a coming of age ritual is traditionally held when she has her first menstruation cycle. A male will usually have his when his voice deepens and he develops body hair.

Coming of age rituals are far more common among females, however, and many Witches place a great emphasis on rituals that mark the first cycle of menstruation. Often, female Witches whose daughters have reached this milestone will organise coming of age rituals where only females are allowed to attend. These rituals are designed to help the attendants to celebrate the female body and to remove any negativity that has become attached to the female form due to the erroneous teachings of other religions. Menstruation is a beautiful thing and is not a curse or punishment for evil regardless of what the Christians have taught over the years.

As with naming ceremonies, coming of age rituals are generally not seen as formal initiations. Many Witches feel that the age that people reach puberty is far too young to make such a huge commitment as initiation. They believe that initiation should come later when some wisdom about life and religion has been gained (the minimum age for initiation is usually 18). Coming of age rituals, for many Witches, are simply a way to welcome young people into adulthood. Often, advice about pride and responsibility is given to young people by adults. Coming of age rituals may also involve the parting of something from childhood. The young people are then given magical gifts by adults to symbolically mark the transition into adulthood. These can include tarot cards, crystal balls, wands, chalices and symbols of the clan or community. For some Witchcraft traditions/covens, coming of age rituals mark the time when young people get their very first ritual tools.

Initiation

Anyone who wishes to practise the Witchcraft religion full-time should understand that the title of Witch should never be taken lightly. To take on the title of Witch is to set yourself apart from most other humans. It is a binding contract to serve the earth, the elements and the Goddess and God. It is only for those who are actually strong enough to face up to their own inner demons. When you take on the title of Witch you become a priest or priestess for life – through the good times and the bad. As a priest or priestess, your job is to serve the deities as well as to look after the health and well-being of the earth and all its creatures and plants. There are only certain people who can take on this kind of responsibility. Those who can have what it takes to be Witches, the priests and priestesses of the ancient ways.

Many Witchcraft covens (though certainly not all) insist that some form of initiation (*"initiation"* means "to enter in" or "to begin") ceremony be gone through for individuals who wish to join them. The reason for this primarily lies in the fact that a coven is like a close-knit family unit and an initiation rite is like a formal introduction of a new Witch into the family of Witches. As with any close-knit family, members of a coven are loving and supportive towards one another (though they are also often in conflict) and an initiation rite is a way of introducing a new Witch into the ways of a coven in question. In many covens, there are three levels of initiation: first degree, second degree and third degree.

First Degree: is basically an initiation of the personality. It is a ritual that marks the beginning of someone's life as an anointed Witch. It is the start of a Witch's life on the path of the Craft of the Wise. It is the onset of learning and discovering. It is symbolised by a downward-pointing triangle. At first degree initiation, a woman becomes the Goddess and a man becomes the God. First degree initiates are expected to make a promise to keep the secrecy of the Craft and of the coven. Some covens have some kind of "ordeal" that must be carried out during a first degree initiation. This indicates the fact that Witchcraft is a difficult and brave path – nobody should feel too comfortable when embarking on this path. Some Witches never feel the need to move beyond their first degree. They feel that it was enough that they became Witches in the first place and do not feel the need to progress up the ranks. Many covens require a period of a year and a day of intense study before a first degree initiation can take place.

Second Degree: is an initiation of the spirit and marks the time when the true hard work begins. It is a ritual that marks the time when the initiate begins to learn how to teach others. The Goddess and God can only be found and experienced within and are no longer to be found "out there". Second degree initiation is truly a challenging time for Witches and has to be experienced to be fully understood. It is often described as the dark night of the soul and as a journey to the underworld where certainties vanish. It is symbolised by a downward-pointing pentagram. Some Witches experience a devastating loss of faith after their second degree initiation but in the long run this only strengthens them as priests and priestesses.

Third Degree: is considered the highest level of spiritual knowledge and wisdom. It is symbolised by an upward-pointing pentagram piercing an upward-pointing triangle. The Witch who reaches this level has emerged from the dark uncertainties of the underworld and is now stronger as a person as well as a Witch. Third degree basically returns a Witch to the everyday world. Witchcraft now becomes as natural as eating and breathing. Faith is strong and the Goddess and God are once again there. There is, however, a much deeper understanding of them. At third degree initiation, a woman understands the God more and a man understands the Goddess more. Third degree initiates are now able to take on the responsibility of running their own covens. They are high priests and priestesses of the Goddess and God.

If you desire to join a coven you will have to look for one – few covens advertise for new members because there is often a big emphasis on secrecy. Most Witches believe that their religion should be kept private from the outside world. They believe that their Witchcraft is between them and the Goddess and God only. The internet is a good place to look for Witchcraft groups and you can subscribe to your local Pagan magazines to improve your chances of finding a coven. The magazines will introduce you to your local Witchcraft or Pagan scene. You will find that one thing will lead to another. Be patient and persevere. If the Goddess and God want you to join a coven they will guide you to one.

Self-Initiation

A self-initiation is basically a ritual that someone does to mark the onset of his or her life as a Solitary practitioner of the Craft (few Solitary Witches follow a degree system). The Witch who has chosen the Solitary priesthood is on the path of the Hermit in the tarot deck. His lantern symbolises his great wisdom and the Star of Hope and Desire that casts light in dark and lonely places. The Solitary Witch has been chosen by the old gods of nature and is answerable to them alone. He or she will work towards bettering the lives of others without the support and guidance of a coven. Solitary Witches are sometimes referred to as Hedgewitches, though strictly speaking a Hedgewitch is someone who serves their local community. He or she will have a vast amount of knowledge about the magical powers of herbs and traditional healing. So Hedgewitches can belong to covens as well.

Some people who choose the Solitary path, however, never feel the need for a self-initiation ritual. One of the beauties of choosing the Solitary priesthood is that you only have yourself to answer to. You have complete freedom to choose what is right for you and what is not. Not having a self-initiation ceremony will not make you any less of a Witch. I personally believe that you are entitled to call yourself a Witch from the moment you feel that the time is right. If you feel the need for an initiation ceremony, however, simply have one but there is no obligation. Those who have chosen to be Solitary Witches can hold self-initiation rites of their own devising if they so wish.

There are many reasons why some individuals would choose the Solitary priesthood. Some people, for example, may feel drawn to the Craft but are not too keen on the idea of having to answer to others. It may be that some people simply have a personal preference to communicating with the Goddess and God in private. Others might have problems finding covens and simply choose the Solitary priesthood as a substitute until they find suitable covens. Many covens will only consider those who have some knowledge and experience of the Craft.

There are some Witches who would have us believe that you can't possibly practise Witchcraft alone. They believe that only a high priest and/or priestess can truly make a Witch and that the Goddess and God won't listen to those who practise alone. This, however, is narrow-minded nonsense. We have to ask the question: who initiated the very first Witch? There was no high priests and priestesses when Witchcraft very first came into being. As I explained in chapter one, you do not have to be a part of a coven to worship the Goddess and God. The deities do not turn their backs away from anyone seeking to practise the ancient ways regardless of whether we belong to a coven or not. During the persecution times of Witches, it was far more likely that most serious practitioners of the Craft were Solitary anyhow so as not to draw attention to themselves from the superstitious Witch hunters. It is likely that covens were popular before Christianity got powerful but I suspect that covens have only become popular once again in more recent times.

True initiation is not a ritual conducted on one human being by another. Initiation, which can be gradual or instantaneous, is a natural process whereby a person becomes attuned with the energies of the Goddess and God. When you are able to sense the changing seasons; to feel the energies that stream down from the sun and moon; to hear the language of birds; to feel the heartbeat of the Earth Mother; and to feel the energies within plants and stones (as a few examples), you will know that true initiation has taken place and that the Goddess and God has accepted you as their priest or priestess. Initiation is a very personal thing and should never be thought of as something that only a high priest or priestess can do. While any high priest or priestess should be respected, only the Goddess and God have the true power to make a Witch.

If you feel drawn to the Solitary priesthood for whatever reason you may want to hold a self-initiation ceremony to formalise your life within the Craft of the Wise. This can be a ritual of your own devising but before you hold your ritual please be sure to set yourself enough time to study the Craft in great detail. Read fifteen serious books about the Craft and mythology. Study magical systems and the magic of herbs and stones. Learn how to meditate as well as some form of divination to strengthen your psychic powers. Get involved with ecology and work towards bettering the environment. Keep a written record of all that you have learned in a blank book/ring binder file and use this as a basis for your own personal magical book or Book of Shadows (see chapter six for information on the Book of Shadows). Once you feel that you have acquired enough knowledge and are satisfied with your work you may feel ready to call yourself a Witch and hold your self-initiation rite to affirm your relationship with the Goddess and God.

A self-initiation rite does not have to be complicated. You could, for example, simply stand before a mirror during the time of a full or new moon with a purple candle (purple heightens psychic powers and deepens our spiritual awareness of the Goddess and God) in front of you while saying these or similar words:

> *O Mother Goddess and Father God,*
> *Lady of the silver moon and Lord of the golden sun,*
> *I ask you to accept me as your priest/priestess.*
> *I open up my mind, body and soul to your essence.*
> *Grant me the power to see your presence in all things.*
> *On this day/night I am truly transformed.*
> *I breathe in the energies of my Mother Goddess*
> *and my Father God.*
> *I feel at one with nature and ready to walk*
> *the path of the Craft of the Wise.*
> *I will use the powers given to me wisely*
> *and I promise that I will not wish any harm.*
> *I ask my Mother Goddess and my Father God for their love*
> *and guidance in everything I do.*
> *I promise that I will do my best to serve you well*
> *as your priest/priestess.*
> *Teach me all that I need to know as I walk your path of love*
> *and light.*
> *I now stand before my Goddess and God who know me well*
> *and do declare:*
> *I am a Witch!*
> *I am a Witch!*
> *I am a Witch!*

Craft Names

Many people choose a Craft name when they become Witches. This is a magical or spirit name and is optional unless you choose to follow a tradition/coven that requires you to assume a new name. Your magical name should say something about your personality or perhaps something about what you hope for in the future. Names of deities, plants, trees, crystals, stones, animals and mythical creatures are very common in Witchcraft. A woman who is looking for a little more love in her life, for example, may choose Aphrodite as her spirit name, while a man who wishes to enhance his courageous nature may choose Wolf as his spirit name. This is a free planet so you can call yourself anything you like.

As Witches develop in the Craft and they acquire new skills and knowledge, they may choose to change their Craft names. Choosing to change a Craft name does not mean that a Witch is discarding a previous identity. It rather means that everything that the Witch has learned while having the old name is now absorbed into his or her personality and it is now time to move on in the Craft with a new name. Our old names are always a part of us because they marked our development and progression within the Craft. Choosing a new name is also an excellent way for Witches to change their luck or direction within life in general.

Although any name can be chosen I would strongly encourage those who are new to the Craft not to assume titles like "Lord" or "Lady" or "Sir". Such titles should be earned and not assumed. They should only be reserved for those who have had many years of experience within the Craft.

Handfasting Rites

Handfasting is a ritual joining of two people (whether different- or same-sex) in marriage and love before the Goddess and God and the elemental powers. It is called handfasting because the wrists of the two people who are to be married are bound together with a ribbon or a cord to symbolise their union. This is traditionally done before the couple jump over a fire, a candle or a broomstick (the broomstick is usually held by witnesses). You may have heard the old song "Let's Jump the Broomstick". It comes from an ancient fertility rite that was performed by couples who were married outside of Christianity. It was thought that this act would encourage good luck, blessings and fertility for those who were handfasted (see chapter six for information on the broomstick).

Some couples choose only to have their religious handfasting rites, while other couples may take steps to make their unions legal. A couple who wishes to make their union legal must follow necessary legal procedures set by their civil government. The vows of a handfasting rite are usually written by the couple who are to be married. These vows or oaths are traditionally set for "as long as love lasts". This takes into account that people continue to change after they have fallen in love and marriage may not reflect this. Rings are sometimes exchanged as a way of showing a long-term commitment and many couples incorporate songs, readings and prayers during their handfasting rites.

Severing or divorce ceremonies can be employed by couples who are unable to stand the test of time. When a couple grows apart or have simply fallen out of love, severing is a way of breaking the spiritual bond between the two people involved. Although endings can be very painful and traumatic, it is important that a couple who wish to sever treat each other with the respect they had promised at their handfasting rite. All affairs and differences should be sorted out in a civilised manner during the process of ending a marriage. Within Witchcraft, it is hoped that severing rituals are as peaceful as possible. Traditionally, a couple who wish to sever are bound together with the ribbon or cord that was used at their handfasting rite. They are then expected to jump over a fire, a candle or a broomstick backwards and the ribbon or cord is then severed or untied. This is why severing rites are also known as handparting rites. Rings may be taken off and then thrown into the sea (or other body of water) or perhaps given to a goldsmith to melt down. This further symbolises the undoing of the magic of joining. A cake may also be cut at a severing rite as another indication of parting.

In addition to the rule of "as long as love lasts" there are three other forms of handfasting rites that should not be overlooked:

- Handfasting rites that last for a period of a year and a day. Again this takes into account that people continue to change after they have fallen in love and marriage may not reflect this. Once the period of a year and a day is over, a handfasted couple can go their separate ways or re-handfast if they still love each other.
- Handfasting rites that last for the rest of this life. These types of handfasting rites can only end at death.
- Handfasting rites that last for the rest of this life and all other future

incarnations. These types of handfasting rites are rare in Witchcraft. Once a couple has chosen to be bound together for eternity they cannot ever be severed. A couple who chooses to be handfasted together for eternity will always find each other in future incarnations.

The Great Rite

The Great Rite is basically sexual union. It is a celebration of sacred sexuality within the magic circle. It is the union of the lance and the grail. It represents the combined powers of the Goddess and God and their ability to create and sustain all life. The Goddess is invoked into the female Witch and this is known as "drawing down the moon". When this occurs, the female Witch becomes the Goddess incarnate. The God is then invoked into the male Witch and this is known as "drawing down the sun". When this occurs, the male Witch becomes the God incarnate. Traditionally, the Great Rite will involve the Fivefold Kiss. This is the Witches' ritual salute – woman-to-man or man-to-woman – and is the kissing of the feet, knees, lower belly, breasts and lips. The act of sex is only symbolic when performed in front of other coven members. It is actual, however, when celebrated in private. As we have seen in chapter two, there is male and female within every single one of us so there should be no reason why gay men and lesbians cannot celebrate the Great Rite with rituals of their own devising.

Elderhood Rites

The beauty of ageing is celebrated, honoured and respected within Witchcraft. When we enter into elderhood it marks the time when we have spent a number of years on the planet and have grown wiser and more knowledgable. Witches, therefore, may mark it with rituals to celebrate the final stage of their lives. For women, an elderhood rite is known as croning. The decision to hold elderhood rites may be based on many factors. Traditionally, female Witches will hold their elderhood rituals at the beginning or end of menopause. Men may simply hold theirs when they have reached a certain age of maturity (usually in their late 50s) when they have gained much knowledge and wisdom about life's experiences. Other reasons why Witches would choose to hold elderhood rites can include the following: retirement from work, an astrological milestone and the time when the last son or daughter has left home. Some Witches hold rituals to mark elderhood simply because they feel that the time is right.

Witches generally have a great respect for the elderly (I have personally always enjoyed the company of the elderly). We do not see them as unproductive members of the community. We rather believe that they have much to offer society with all their knowledge and wisdom about life. Without them, there wouldn't be many people to turn to for help and advice about our lives. It is always good advice to make friends with as many trusted members of the older community as possible. The Witch's values go far back to earlier times when the elderly were cherished and respected as much as everyone else.

Elderhood rituals should be very joyous occasions. They are times to honour older members of the Craft who have gained wisdom, knowledge, skill and experience. They are times of great celebration and recognition. The past achievements are acknowledged and respected, and it is now time for the Witches who have entered elderhood to look forward to the rest of their lives. Some Witchcraft traditions/covens also crown elders to further symbolise their entry into elderhood. Guests may also be invited to speak about the lives of the elders at elderhood rites and the elders may receive gifts as marks of respect. It should be understood that the term crone for female Witches is never seen as derogatory within Witchcraft. It relates to the third aspect of the Goddess and is, therefore, a title of great honour.

Death Rites

These are rituals that mark the passing of people from the world of physicality. As we have seen, Witches generally do not see death as the absolute end of life. It is simply a transition of our energy into another form. Even some scientists agree that some form of consciousness survives after death and there have been many studies to support this. Energy cannot be destroyed it can only change its form. Our physical bodies are simply the vehicles that we travel around in until we wear them out or perhaps there is nothing more to learn in this particular lifetime. The Celtic sea goddess Rhiannon is often seen as the deity who midwifes the dying into the spirit world.

The purpose of death rites is to celebrate the lives of the deceased. They are both solemn and joyous. Death rites are times to say farewell to our departed loved ones and to help them to move on to the next level of existence. They help to dispel any earthly ties and to safely deliver the departed souls to the other side. A death rite may also be performed when an earth-bound spirit is haunting a place and Witches wish to help it to move on to the Summerlands. The process makes it easier for the spirit to move on to the next level of existence.

The death of a much-loved family member or friend is always a sad time for anyone but the death rites within Witchcraft are more about the celebration of the life that has been rather than the sad and gloomy funerals of other religions. Some Witches find it a great comfort to erect shrines of remembrance in their homes to honour their deceased loved ones. A shrine of remembrance can be no more than a small table with a few items placed upon it: photographs, jewellery, a candle, some fresh or dried herbs (rosemary and meadowsweet are excellent for remembrance shrines), some burning incense and so on.

Following is a very beautiful poem written by a very beautiful person – my aunt, Louisa M. Stokoe, who was a very gifted artist. The poem was recited at my grandmother's funeral (my aunt's mother) who I was very close to. The poem is called *Beautiful Spring* and was written because of my aunt's love of the springtime. As you will be aware by now, the spring represents the continuation of life and the rebirth of the soul into a world of physicality. I have found this poem a great comfort whenever I have wished to take a few moments to think about those I love who are in the spirit world. I hope that you find some comfort from it too when you want to think about your deceased loved ones. Enjoy.

> **Bud break at last!**
> **The long, cold fast of winter**
> **Is broken;**
> **Renewal has begun;**
> **Warmed by the light**

Of the glorious sun,
While the warm sou' westerly breeze,
Gently rocks the trees
And shimmies the leaves
Of the still clad evergreen bushes.
Oh beautiful spring!
Herald of lighter nights,
Long days of useful activity;
Warm rain gently falling
Washing winter's grip away,
Softening the earth, and promoting,
Floral reactivity.
Blossom waxing on my trees
At the waning of the freeze
And flowers in my garden;
Little faces turned upwards to the light
To my delight.

Chapter Six:
Tools of the Trade

In common with the majority of the religions of the world today, there are certain tools that are utilised in Witchcraft for ritual and magic. In Witchcraft, these magical furnishings are designed to help us to expand our awareness of the male and female mysteries of nature – the Goddess and God. They also help us to channel and attract certain energies through the power of the mind. They are implements that help us to access the specific energies that we are wanting to work with. They effectively help us to change the vibrational energies around us so that we can get the most out of our work. Although some tools (the broomstick, the cauldron, the wand and so on) have become closely associated with Witches and magic, many people do not understand the power behind them and their inner symbolism within the religion of Witchcraft.

Although the tools that we use in Witchcraft today are associated with particular characteristics and specific energies, it is important to point out that the tools themselves do not necessarily contain the true power. They rather absorb the energies we give to them through our touch and intent. They can still be powerful symbols, yes, but only because of the complex energies that they represent. The tools, however, are really nothing more than tools without their owners for the true power lies within ourselves. Sure, the materials that make up certain tools will have their own specific spiritual properties – but those properties are completely useless without ourselves. You have to have a belief in those properties to truly activate them. When a Witch performs a ritual, he or she is doing so to primarily expand his or her awareness of the divine. When a Witch works magic, he or she is doing so to bring about a specific change. In either case, it is the power of the mind that does the real work, but certain tools give the brain a magical boost by triggering certain responses. In other words, they help to expand the mind's power to act.

In earlier times, Witches simply used items that they could find in their homes. The broomstick (see below), for example, was used to clear away dirt from the home. But the Witch also used it symbolically. She knew that by symbolically moving her broomstick back and forth throughout her home that she could sweep away negativity or blocked energy. She knew that her broomstick would help her mind to focus on this symbolic cleansing. She knew that the symbolic cleansing began in her mind, within her very soul, but she also knew that her broomstick sparked the potential. She knew that her broomstick helped her to access the true power.

To practise the Witchcraft religion, you may want to obtain at least some of the special tools that are closely associated with Witchcraft. You can find them, receive them as gifts (my partner has kindly gave me many of my tools over the years as presents for special occasions), purchase them (perhaps through the internet or from special occult supply stores) or simply make them. The choice is yours. Each Witch decides for himself or herself. Many Witches believe that the most magically potent tools are those that are crafted by hand and I agree with this. Though tools are not absolutely necessary to practise Witchcraft, they do enhance and enrich our work. They are, therefore, well worth the effort to obtain them – especially by those who are new to the Craft.

Over the next few pages we will look at some of the tools that are utilised within Witchcraft – but first, we will look at some of the superstitions.

Superstitions

Throughout the years, there are superstitions that have arisen with regards to the magical tools that are used in Witchcraft. You should accept or disregard these superstitions as seems right to you as an individual. If a superstition does not feel right, simply don't follow it. There are no rules with regards to the superstitions – only what feels right to you. So without further ado, here are some of the most well-known, though often-conflicting in nature, superstitions:

- The best tools are those that are crafted by hand from raw materials. This is a superstition that I fully support. Our ritual tools are for personal use and are very personal in nature. When someone constructs a tool by hand, it is truly imbued with that person's own energies. It is a creative extension of its owner. This truly makes it a very effective magical tool.

- Tools should be formally consecrated before they are used in sacred work. Consecrating tools makes them fit for ritual use. It removes any negative energies that may have become attached to them. It also transmits power into them and makes them dedicated to the Goddess and God. I will show you how I consecrate my tools in chapter eight.

- Tools should only ever be used for ritual work. The tools of Witchcraft are sacred. Many Witches, therefore, believe that they should only be reserved for sacred work and should never be used for mundane activities.

- Tools should only be handled by their owners. A Witch's tools are, with regular use, imbued with his or her own energies. Many Witches, therefore, believe that if someone else handles them it will disturb their energies and thus make them less effective.

- Tools should never be haggled over when they are purchased. Tools are items that will be dedicated to the Goddess and God. Haggling over them cheapens their worth and thus makes them less effective in ritual, according to many Witches.

- Athames and swords (see below) are symbolic weapons – they are not actual weapons. It should be obvious by now that violence is not a part of Witchcraft. Athames and swords should only ever be used to protect on a spiritual level. Many Witches believe that athames and swords that have been used to draw blood are ineffective in ritual.

- Tools should be purchased brand-new. Some Witches believe that tools that are purchased brand-new are pure enough to absorb the energies given to them by their owners. It is thought that a tool that is purchased brand-new is untainted by others and can thus truly become an extension of its owner.

- Tools should be purchased from an antique store, flea market or an estate sale. Some Witches are of the opinion that tools that are "old" are the most magically potent because they have already absorbed enough energies over the years to take on a life and power of their own.

Athame

The athame (usually pronounced *ath-uh-may*), magical knife, or ritual dagger, is a ceremonial knife that is used for directing, cutting, banishing, summoning and commanding energies. It may, for example, be used to symbolically "cut" the sacred space (see chapter seven for information on the sacred space) in which to conduct magical workings or to call upon the God, the Goddess and the elemental powers. It is considered a Witch's magical weapon because of its protective associations. This is why many Witches consider it a very important tool to own. As with all phallic symbols, the athame is magically linked with the God. It also corresponds to the element of fire (though, in some traditions, it corresponds to the element of air) and to the war and action planet of Mars.

Most often, the athame has a double-edged blade and the handle is usually black, since black is well-known to absorb energy. The black handle symbolises darkness and the sharp blade symbolises the path to illumination. Traditionally, the blade is made from metal, because metal is a good conductor of energy (think of electricity), though some Witches prefer to have the blades of their athames made from other natural materials, such as flint or crystal. The handle should also be made from natural substances, generally wood, and never plastic. The size of the athame is up to the Witch but many Witches prefer to have a blade of at least four inches. Some Witches also like to inscribe their athames with magical symbols to make them more personal.

Bell

The bell, when rung, can be very useful in magical workings. It has the ability, for instance, to help us to conjure spirits since it has an enormous effect on the mind and the vibrations within the sacred space in which we have chosen to work. Merely ringing a bell when casting a magic circle can signify that we are about to create a space between the worlds and are ready to work magically. Likewise, ringing a bell at the end of magical work can also signify that we are ready to return to the mundane world so that the spirits that we have summoned for help can return to their realms.

The bell is traditionally a feminine symbol and so it is sacred to the Goddess. Any type of bell can be used for magical workings. The bell is also considered to be a highly protective tool and so it can be rung to ward off evil entities, to halt storms and to banish negative energies of all kinds. It is also excellent for evoking good energies. Hung on doorways or around the necks of our pets, bells are also said to guard against the evil eye.

Bolline

The bolline (usually pronounced *bow-leen*) is simply a knife that is used for more practical reasons. While the athame is used for cutting energy, the bolline is only utilised for cutting physical objects. It may, for example, be used for harvesting herbs, cutting candles and other magical tools or to inscribe magical symbols on things. These example uses for the bolline are usually activities done before Witches conduct their main magical workings. The handle of the bolline is usually white to ensure that it does not get confused with the black-handled athame because both carry very different energies. The primal use for the bolline is to harvest herbs and so many Witches have bollines that look very much like hand sickles.

Book of Shadows

The Book of Shadows, Witch's workbook, or grimoire (widely believed to come from an Old French word meaning "grammar"), is a magical book that is usually constructed by its owner. It is often considered to be a Witch's most important attribute. A Witch's Book of Shadows may contain things like the Wiccan Rede, rituals and ritual patterns, spells, tools, magical correspondences (crystals, stones, herbs, animals, deities, planets, zodiac signs and so on), the elements, the history of Witchcraft, Witchcraft traditions, psychic exercises, magical or spiritual experiences, divination records (tarot readings for instance), herbal recipes and cures, the Sabbats and so on. A Book of Shadows should contain anything that the Witch deems important for his or her spiritual growth and development. It is his or her personal book for learning and reflecting.

Occult grimoires have a very long history. Some were created thousands of years ago when our ancestors became intelligent enough to be able to commune through writing about their spiritual beliefs and practices. Some of the occult grimoires that were found are believed to be at least five thousand years old – many of which originate from Egypt, the land where much of the occult knowledge that we understand today originates from. This means that the occult grimoires that Witches write today are based on knowledge that predates all of the organised religions of the world today.

Surprisingly, occult grimoires were quite popular during medieval Europe, not just among the Pagan folk, but other people as well (even Pope Sylvester II, who occupied the papal throne from 999 to 1003, was said to have owned one). As Christianity became increasingly powerful, however, the Church became hell-bent on destroying them. The Christians began to teach that occult grimoires were the work of the Devil and his demons. In reality, however, they were simply books based on ancient knowledge designed to help people to tap into, and understand more about, the other higher realms beyond the physical world. They were simply books that contained magical information to help with life's problems. Anyone found to own an occult grimoire, however, would be accused of Witchcraft and would, therefore, have to face the death penalty.

To create your own personal Book of Shadows, all you need to do is obtain a fairly large blank book or perhaps a ring binder file with paper placed inside it. These can be obtained from arts and crafts stores. You can then use your blank book or file to record any magical or spiritual knowledge that you consider important for your spiritual development. Let it contain all the information that you feel is natural to you personally. This can be information that you have composed yourself or perhaps information that you have found elsewhere, perhaps from other books about Witchcraft, Paganism and mythology.

You can organise your grimoire into chapters, if you like, or perhaps place all your information in alphabetical order. It's your book so have it exactly how you would like it. It is also a good idea to decorate the cover of your grimoire to your own individual taste, perhaps with magical symbols and signs. The more personal and original your grimoire is, the more meaningful it will become to you.

Today, a grimoire can be typed at the Witch's convenience, but the most magically potent grimoires are said to be those that are written by hand, since these are truly imbued with their owners' energies. Always keep your grimoire in a safe place when it is not in use and treat it with the respect it deserves.

Bowls

Most magical procedures involve the use of salt and water. These are used in a variety of different ways in Witchcraft. They are primarily, however, used to consecrate our tools. As such, you may want to keep two special bowls for the purpose of consecration – one for the salt and one for the water. Natural sea salt and spring water are always best for ritual use. If you cannot obtain these, however, simply use table salt and tap water. These can be placed in your special bowls and you can then ask the Goddess and God to return them to purity. This is best done under the light of the sun or a full moon. Salt is a powerful representation of the element of earth, while water is obviously a powerful representation of the element of water. Some Witches also have an additional bowl to make offerings to the deities. Fruits and flowers are examples of offerings that are often placed in an offering bowl.

Broomstick

Many people may be surprised to learn that modern Witches do often possess broomsticks. Broomsticks, however, have never been used by Witches as implements for flying through the air. Witches flying on broomsticks is purely an invention of the Christian Church. All magic is natural not supernatural. It works within the laws of nature – not outside them – and flying on a broomstick would be considered a supernatural act because it is physically impossible. Today, broomsticks are utilised in Witchcraft rituals because of what they powerfully symbolise. The broomstick, or besom, in a Witch's mind, is a symbol of the combination of the male and female energies of the universe – the Yin and Yang of being. The handle is the phallic shape that Witches associate with the God and the brush, in which the handle is tied into, is the feminine genitals of the Goddess. The handle and brush come together to create one of the most powerful symbols of sexuality and fertility. In many Witchcraft traditions, however, the broomstick is primarily a symbol of the God.

During the persecution times, it was thought that Witches would murder babies and children and then reduce their fat and bones into a gooey substance with a pestle and a mortar. Witches were then thought to spread this substance on their broomsticks. This act was thought to activate the broomsticks so that Witches could use them to fly through the air in order to be able to attend the infamous Witches' Sabbaths. Though this was complete nonsense, it is another reason why broomsticks have become closely associated with Witches.

The link of Witches with broomsticks, however, is actually far older than the persecution times. There is an ancient, Mexican, Witch-like deity, for example, called Tlazelteotl who became associated with flying through the night skies on her broomstick. She was a deity closely associated with snakes and owls and was called upon to clear away negativity and illnesses. In fact, there are many deities closely associated with broomsticks from all over the world, since the broomstick has long been associated with sacred and magical workings.

Other tales of Witches flying broomsticks most likely came about because Witches have used them in fertility rites for centuries. Witches were known to run into the fields, in the nude, while riding their broomsticks hobby-horse style. They would then leap into the air as high as they could while asking nature to grant them abundant harvests. The higher they jumped, the taller the crops would become later in the year at the harvest festival celebrations. This type of sympathetic magic was also performed to help clear away the old crops and to make way for the new.

Today, the modern Witch may use the broomstick in a variety of different ways during magical workings. The primal use of the broomstick, however, is to "sweep" away astral clutter or negativity in preparation for sacred activities. The broomstick simply helps us to focus on this symbolic cleansing. By "sweeping" away astral clutter, a Witch is able to create a "clear" doorway for the energies that he or she wishes to invite into the sacred space.

As we have seen in chapter five, a couple may also traditionally "jump" the broomstick at their handfasting rite to encourage good luck, blessings and fertility within their union. The act is thought to grant a couple the abundance of nature. This ancient fertility rite is also done to symbolise a couple "jumping" into a new life together. Traditionally, broomsticks are kept near doorways or windows to guard the home from hostility, given the fact that the broomstick also has ancient protective associations. The best, most magically potent broomsticks are said to be those that have been composed by their owners. Any type of wood can be used to construct a broomstick.

Candles

Candles are so well-known in many religious and magical rites and have adorned many religious temples for at least five thousand years given their spiritual significance. The candle flame symbolises the power of spiritual light and illumination and the triumph over darkness and ignorance. In Witchcraft, candles can be used in a variety of different ways in magical workings which is why many Witches consider them to be an essential part of any Witch's magical pantry. When lit, candles help to still and calm our minds so that we can focus on more sacred activities. They ultimately help to trigger changes in consciousness and help us to slip into a more ritual frame of mind so that we are able to focus on our goals.

Candles obviously symbolise the element of fire. They are, therefore, very useful in magical workings that specifically involve dramatic change and transformation. Since night or twilight are considered the most magically potent times to get psychic results, illumination is needed and this is where candles come in very handy indeed. Many Witches prefer the soft glow of candlelight to that of artificial illumination. Artificial illumination can be somewhat distracting. Midnight, which is often known as the "Witching hour", is a powerful time because it represents the time of the element of earth. It represents the end of one cycle and the beginning of the next. Witches often burn their candles at midnight for these reasons. Almost all rituals and spells utilise candles.

Candles can be very affordable and they come in many different shapes and sizes, though it is always a good idea to use small candles in spellcraft because many spells may require you to leave your candles to burn out to symbolise the completion of your work. Large pillar candles will simply take too long to burn out. Tealight and taper candles are ideal for spellcraft. Any type of wax candles can be used for magical workings, though the best are those that are made from natural vegetable wax or beeswax. Always keep the candles that you aim to use in your sacred work separate from any candles that you simply aim to use as decoration in your home.

Incidentally, it is considered bad luck to blow your candles out in sacred work because your breath represents the sacred breath of life, while the candle flame represents the divine life force. Thus, I would advise you to let your candles burn out of their own accord when conducting magical workings, or to simply snuff them out with a candle snuffer, depending on the requirements of your magical workings. Always use fresh candles for sacred work, never candles that have already been used because these will hold different energies. Also, it is best to use matches to light your candles rather than a lighter because the fuel from the lighter may influence the energy of your work.

Many Witches use specific candle colours too within their magical workings. Each colour has specific spiritual vibrations that can be useful in rituals and spellcraft. Colours speak to the mind and are very useful for attracting specific energies into our lives. Green, for example, represents the growth of plants. Thus, green candles can be very useful in all magical procedures involving prosperity and fertility. Generally, white candles can symbolise any colour, because the colour white symbolises all the colours of the light spectrum. When lit at the bottom, a white candle can symbolise black in magical workings (see the end of chapter seven for a guide to colours).

Cauldron

The iron cauldron, like the broomstick and the wand (see below), is one of the most powerful symbols of the Witch. The feminine shape of the cauldron links it firmly with Mother Nature – the Goddess. It represents the cosmic mysteries of her womb of regeneration and transformation. The cauldron, as a powerful symbol of Mother Nature, is a reminder to Witches that all life is a creation of the Goddess's womb. This is why the cauldron has become a very powerful symbol of the Holy Grail (the idea of the Holy Grail is far older than Christianity). The magical symbolism of the cauldron goes way back into ancient times. The word cauldron is believed to come from the Latin word *"caldarium"* meaning a "hot bath". Although the cauldron is a feminine symbol of the Goddess, there are male deities who are associated with the cauldron. The Celtic god the Dagda, for example, is associated with an enormous cauldron that provides enough nourishment to feed a whole army. The Gundestrup cauldron, from the second century B. C. E., has the Dagda on it.

The fact that inedible foods can be transformed into something delicious within the cauldron with the aid of fire is another reason why the cauldron is such a powerful magical symbol. Records suggest that the cauldron has been utilised in magical workings for way over two thousand years in Europe. Such was the importance of the cauldron to the Celts that they held it sacred to the goddess Cerridwen, the keeper of the cauldron of inspiration, knowledge and regeneration. Cerridwen's legends have had a very powerful impact on contemporary Witchcraft. Her sacred cauldron of wisdom was the Holy Grail of immortality. It is said that Cerridwen's name is simply an old word that was used to indicate a cauldron. In the mystical country of Egypt, the goddess Mut is associated with three cauldrons. In ancient Egyptian hieroglyphics, the sign that indicated women in general was a cauldron, a pot. This further indicates the cauldron's ancient link with women and female mysteries.

William Shakespeare's play *Macbeth* is always something that comes to the minds of many people whenever they think of the cauldron. This is primarily because of the famous Witch-scene that depicts the three Witches moving around a large cauldron while reciting incantations. Because Witches were regarded as evil during the infamous Witch hunts, many actors consider *Macbeth* to be an unlucky or uncanny play. This is why many of them refuse to say the word *Macbeth* in a theatre. *Macbeth* was always my favourite play to learn about at school and I achieved very high grades in exams and projects to do with it. This would not at all come as a surprise to those around me who know me well!

During the persecution times of Witches, the Wise Women were well-known to brew up their lotions and potions with the aid of the cauldron. This is another reason why the cauldron has become so closely connected with Witches. Some of these women were very receptive to the strange images that appeared on the surfaces of their bubbling cauldrons and they used these images to be able to see possible future events or events that were happening far away. The cauldron was, therefore, considered a very useful tool for divination. Many people often went to these Wise Women for advice about the future. Unsurprisingly, the cauldron is still used today by Witches for divination.

The cauldron's link with the Goddess's womb makes it primarily a symbol of the element of water. It can, however, symbolise all four of the sacred elements of nature when it is in action: the iron pot itself and the herbs within to symbolise earth; the flames below it to symbolise fire; the boiling liquid to symbolise water; and the fragrant steam that arises from it to symbolise air. Resting upon three legs, the cauldron can also symbolise the three aspects of the Goddess: maiden, mother and crone.

There are many uses for the cauldron in magical workings in contemporary Witchcraft. It may be used to brew up herbs and potions; to reflect the moon during lunar rites; to perform divination (scrying); and to safely burn things, as a few examples. The cauldron's link with transformation makes it a very useful tool for wishes of all types. Some Witches, for instance, like to write their wishes on pieces of paper and then throw these wishes into their flaming cauldrons. The ashes are then traditionally sprinkled in a garden or into a moving body of water. This act is thought to transfer our wishes into our lives. I have personally had much success with this type of magic.

The cauldron has also been utilised in fertility rites for centuries given the cauldron's link with the Goddess's womb. Many modern Witches and other Pagans may, for instance, honour the fertility of nature by leaping over their flaming cauldrons at certain seasonal celebrations. The fire within represents the sun, the God's symbol. Thus, the fire and the cauldron come together to represent the natural male and female balance of nature. At Yule, Witches often light a fire or a candle within the cauldron to represent the God within the Goddess's womb. The fire or candle within the cauldron at Yule can represent the returning heat and light of the sun and the promise of the spring to come.

Censer

The censer, or thurible as it is otherwise known, is an incense burner that is usually made from brass, copper or clay. The censer may be elaborate, like the censers found swinging in the churches of the Catholic faith, or simple, such as a seashell for example. The censer is simply a vessel that Witches use to hold the smouldering incense for magical procedures. The incense that is used in the censer will usually correspond to the type of work that the Witch is performing. It may, for example, reflect a particular seasonal celebration or a spell.

When incense is burned within the censer, the particular aromas release specific energy vibrations that reside within the incense. This can have a profound effect on the mind and can help us to open higher states of consciousness. In other words, the incense works on the olfactory organs to help us to activate the magical part of the brain. Merely watching the smoke rise above us while focusing on our breathing can also help us to slip into a more ritual frame of mind. Many Witches see the rising smoke as a way of carrying their intents and desires up to the divine. The censer is a powerful symbol of both the elements of air and fire and has been used in purification rites for centuries.

If you do not have a specialised censer, do not worry – you can always make one. Simply find a fireproof bowl (I simply use my small cauldron for this), fill it about halfway with sand or salt (to absorb the heat), heat some lumps of charcoal with tongs until the charcoal glows and then place them in your makeshift censer. You can then sprinkle the incense – herbs, spices, resins, seeds, gums and so on – that you want to use over the charcoal. Alternatively, simply push incense sticks, cones or blocks into the sand or salt and then light them. Please be very careful with your censer as it can become very hot indeed – even with sand or salt in it. It is always a good idea to place your censer on a fireproof surface.

Chalice

The chalice, or cup, basically has all the spiritual symbolism of the cauldron. It is, therefore, another powerful symbol of the Holy Grail. It can be made from many substances – wood, silver, stone, bronze, brass, crystal, glass and so on – though it is always best to avoid substances that break easily. The chalice truly is a symbol of love, as expressed in the Minor Arcana of the tarot deck, and is traditionally given to a Witch for this reason. The chalice and the athame together represent the sexual union of the Goddess and God, the Great Rite. Both are utilised at many fertility rites within Witchcraft, especially at Beltane when the sexual force of nature is coming towards its height.

Traditionally, some wine or some other drink is poured into the chalice near the end of a magical procedure. This is then consumed, along with ritual food, such as cakes for example, to symbolise completion. This is known as "earthing the power" and involves the blessing of the food and wine (or other drink) followed by feasting. It is considered by many Witches to be an important part of ritual when we toast the Goddess and God while we eat, drink and be merry (see chapter eight for more information on this).

The chalice can also be utilised for mixing herbal infusions (herbal teas); for mixing salt and water; for evoking the power of emotions; for healing work; and for making offerings to the Goddess and God. When the chalice is full, it can symbolise the many gifts and blessings that we have in life. Filled with rosewater, the chalice is excellent in all types of love spells and is a perfect offering to the goddesses Aphrodite, Venus and Isis.

Cords

A cord is sometimes known as a cingulum within Witchcraft. Cords can often play a special role in various forms of ritual and magic. Their uses in magical procedures are becoming increasingly popular. In magical work, a cord can be knotted in order to store energy so that it can be released later. A cord can also be used in binding magic – spells that bind people from doing harm, either to themselves or others. Many Witches also wear cords with their robes (see chapter eight for information on robes). The best cords are obviously those that are made from natural materials, such as silk or cotton. Some Witchcraft traditions use different coloured cords to denote specific degrees of initiation. Red, white and blue, for example, are the traditional colours for first degree initiates in some covens. Initiates are, in some cases, expected to create their own cords.

There are some traditions that actually tie novices up during initiations. Sometimes in the nude. This is supposed to be a symbolic, solemn and religious act and probably has ancient origins. But I personally see it as somewhat dark and sexual. There could be potential for abuse of some kind in this type of ritual work. Personally, I would never allow anyone to tie me up. There are some strange people out there who may not be all that they seem to be.

Witches and magicians during the persecution times were sometimes accused of carrying magical cords. Presumably, this was because cords have probably been used in ritual and magic since ancient times. Even Joan of Arc (who is believed by many to have been a Witch) and the Knights Templars were accused of owning magical cords. And yet, Christianity has used cords probably since it was created. Monks have worn cords around their waists for centuries. The traditional Christian monk's cord has three knots to denote his three vows of poverty, chastity and obedience. If I were to wear a cord around my waist with three knots in it for magical work it would symbolise the three aspects of the Goddess and the three aspects of the God: maiden/young God, mother/warrior and crone/sage.

Crystal Ball

The crystal ball, crystal sphere, or orbuculum, is a divination tool *par excellence*. It is considered a tool of the Goddess because its spheroid shape and cool temperature links it firmly with the moon, the Goddess's symbol. Often, the crystal ball is utilised as a "facilitator" during certain lunar rituals or divination exercises so that we can still the conscious mind in order to be able to make contact with the psychic mind (unconscious mind). This allows us to become aware of the energies around us. This is truly a powerful way for us to make contact with the Goddess so that she can assist us in our sacred work and guide our lives. The above reasons are why the crystal ball may be the central focus during rituals that honour the moon, especially the full moon. Some Witches, however, prefer the cauldron for the above reasons.

The best crystal balls are those that are made of clear quartz or obsidian and those that are periodically exposed to the light of the full moon. Many Witches also like to wash their crystal balls with an infusion of mugwort. The herb mugwort is well-known to help us to awaken psychic powers.

Deity Images

When Witches arrange the tools on their altars (see chapter seven for information on the altar), they often place deity images or figurines to represent the God (sun base) and the Goddess (moon base). This is obviously entirely optional but it does make the altar very pleasing to the eye indeed and helps us to focus on the male and female balance of nature more effectively so that we can get the most out of our work. Some Witches choose figurines of their favourite deities from a specific culture. Others may choose deities that specifically relate to the type of work that they are doing. The choice is yours. Figurines of Isis and Horus, for example, would be excellent for spells involving protection. Other Witches simply place symbols of the sun and moon to represent the God and Goddess.

Necklace

Traditionally, priestesses wear special necklaces within the magic circle. These necklaces represent the Goddess and the natural cycle of life: birth, death, rest and then rebirth. Beads of amber and jet are the necklaces of choice among many high priestesses. Jet represents the moon (especially the dark aspect of the moon) and amber represents the sun, so reflecting the male and female energies of the universe. Wearing a necklace within the magic circle is a way for the high priestesses of Witchcraft to honour the Goddess and her many aspects. There are many ancient goddesses who are depicted wearing necklaces. The ancient Egyptian goddess Hathor, for example, wore a sacred necklace which she shook as a musical instrument. The Nordic goddess Freya, as another example, wore the brisingamen necklace which represents the source of all life. The use of necklaces, however, shouldn't only be restricted to women in Witchcraft. Men can wear necklaces if they wish as well. Both men and women can wear whatever necklaces that have meaning to them. Some Witches like to wear necklaces with symbols and signs that relate to their astrological birth signs. This can be a very empowering thing to do. Witches who are Scorpios, for example, may wear scorpions to represent their powerful and intense personalities. Other Witches may wear specific runes to help them to bring forth specific energies. The choices are virtually endless. I personally usually wear my Yin and Yang necklace that my partner gave me as a Yule present for sacred work simply to honour the Goddess and God.

Pentacle

The pentacle is one of the most powerful symbols of the Witch and is very sacred within the Witchcraft religion. It is the pentagram, or five-pointed star, with a circle around it. The five points of the pentacle represent the four sacred elements of nature plus a fifth element, that of spirit. The circle of the pentacle represents unity, infinity and the connection of all the elements. The pentacle, however, is primarily a symbol of the element of earth given the fact that the earth element represents a meeting place for all five of the elements. The five-pointed star has been utilised in sacred activities for thousands of years. It is considered one of the most sacred symbols of ancient times. It is usually pointed upwards with the top point representing the element of spirit. Starting at the top point and moving in a clockwise direction, many traditions portray the elements in this way:

- Spirit, water, earth, air and fire.

In other traditions, however, the elements may be portrayed in these ways:

- Spirit, air, water, earth and fire.
- Spirit, water, fire, earth and air.

The top point represents the ultimate source of all the other four elements. It represents the very element that binds the other four elements together in the work of creation. It represents the Ultimate Deity and the male and female principles of nature. When a Witch works magic, the top point represents the higher self and his or her ultimate goals in life. It represents that for magic to work it has to start from the power of the mind before it can manifest on a physical level. When it is utilised in magical procedures, the star helps us to bring the powers of all the elements into our work. It is used to invoke their powers.

The five-pointed star can also symbolise other important aspects of life. Here are a few examples:

- Taste, touch, smell, sound and sight.
- Birth, life, initiation, marriage and death (and thus rebirth).
- Perception, cognition, action, evolution and volition.
- Sex, self, passion, pride and power.

The five-pointed star may also symbolise the head, hands and feet of the Witch. This is the symbol of the microcosm which represents the human connection to the elements and the cosmos. Christianity also once regarded the star as a sacred symbol. It symbolised the Five Wounds of Christ. It is, for this reason, sometimes found in Church architecture. There is a wonderful form of the five-pointed star in one of the windows of the cathedral in Exeter, Britain, for example.

Our ancestors most likely saw the five-pointed star as a spiritual symbol because it is found naturally throughout nature (in the centre of apples for instance). In addition, through retrograde motions Venus, the planet of love, traces the star over a certain period of time. Perhaps this is a message from the heavens of just how important the elements are for the continuation of life and for all occult understanding.

Although the pentagram is traditionally found pointing upwards in Witchcraft rituals, there are times when it can be found pointing downwards. When the five-pointed star is reversed it is used in banishing and binding magic. Reversed pentagrams have long been used in spells that banish and bind. Some traditions may also insist that second degree initiates wear inverted pentagrams because second degree is a time to overcome the negatives of life, those that stop us from progressing forward spiritually.

Some traditions, however, avoid the reversed pentagram at all costs because of its association with Satanism and the dark arts. To a large degree, I can understand why some Witches would choose to do this because of the stigma that Witches have been given as a result of Christianity. Of ancient origin, however, the pentagram, reversed or not, has never had any association with Satan or black magic in genuine Paganism. The association of the pentagram with evil eventually came along with the Christian religion. The creation of the Church of Satan by Anton S. LaVey in 1966 also did not help the pentagram's supposed association with evil.

Although the five-pointed star is only used for positive purposes in Witchcraft, the Christians have taught for centuries that any practice that is not Christian-orientated must be the work of Satan and his demons. This is simply not true. We have to remind ourselves that the tools themselves simply serve as symbols. They help the power of the mind to focus on the energies that we wish to work with. The tools themselves are neither good nor evil – it is only the intents of our minds that can be good or evil, not the tools themselves. This is why I see no reason why Witches should not use an inverted five-pointed star for banishing and binding magic.

The five-pointed star can be made from many substances for sacred work – twigs, metal, stone, wax, clay, glass and so on – but most often it appears fashioned on a copper or wooden disc and is typically placed in the centre of the altar. Additional tools that rituals and spells may require – herbs, woods, crystals, stones, paper, ink and so on – may then be placed on the disc. The five-pointed star is associated with the fertility of Mother Nature and so it is primarily a feminine symbol. It represents the need for all the elements in order for life to exist. When the star is placed on the altar, it represents the connection between the physical and spiritual realms. It is also a very powerful symbol of money and financial issues, as expressed in the Minor Arcana of the tarot deck. It is, therefore, very useful in all spells of money and prosperity.

Scourge

The scourge is a symbol of authority. It is not typically used by Solitary Witches. Many of the more formal traditions of Witchcraft use the scourge. It is a many-tailed whip that is sometimes made of silk. Covens traditionally use the scourge for purification, enlightenment, initiation rites, domination, severity, gaining the sight and prophecy. In magical procedures, flagellation, or light scourging (traditionally forty lashes), brings blood away from the body's vital organs. This can create a "high" and can thus help the mind to activate different states of consciousness. This can create extremely powerful outcomes in all types of spellcraft. In other words, it helps the mind to raise power. Flagellation is an ancient practice. Even the Christians have used it for centuries as a form of punishment for sins. It was thought that flagellation would help to purify the soul and thus bring the Christian closer to his or her God. Even in Witchcraft today there are some hierarchical traditions that use scourging as a form of punishment for coven members. Again, this seems a little dark and sexual to me personally and more like S&M than Witchcraft. But each Witch to their own I suppose. Fasting is another popular way to activate different states of consciousness in Witchcraft.

Sword

The sword is used for the same purposes as the athame in Witchcraft. It is, however, considered more formal and authoritative than the athame. It corresponds to the element of fire (though, in some traditions, it corresponds to the element of air) and to the war and action planet of Mars. Its phallic nature links it firmly with the God. The use of the sword in contemporary Witchcraft probably derives from Freemasonry and ancient ceremonial magic. Swords have also played a special, magical role in Chinese, Japanese, Jewish and Persian cultures and traditions. Like the athame, the sword is a ritual weapon. It is used to protect the Witch or coven of Witches against any unwanted negative energies.

As a symbol of authority, the sword is traditionally passed between high priest and priestess within the coven at certain times of the year as leadership changes. When the fruits of the land are readily apparent, the Goddess reigns supreme and so the high priestess, as her earthly representative, holds the sword. When barrenness covers the land (the traditional time of hunting for our ancient ancestors), the God reigns supreme and so the high priest, as his earthly representative, holds the sword. In some traditions, however, when a female Witch straps a sword to herself she is regarded as masculine in the context of ritual until she removes it from herself.

When Joan of Arc took the sword she not only did so for personal defence but also in defence of France. Thus, the sword has ancient authoritative associations. It adds enormous weight to very solemn occasions. When a high priest or priestess has a particularly important announcement to make to the rest of the coven, he or she may well take the sword in order to draw the attention of the rest of the coven. "With this in my hands, I am the ruler of the circle" is what is often found in many Witches' Books of Shadows with regards to the sword. As with the athame, the sword is never actually used to cut anything physical – the only exception of this rule is that the athame or sword may be used to cut handfasting or handparting cakes.

Swords can be very dangerous tools to own. As a young boy, my mother and father had two swords that hung on one of the walls of our home at the time. I remember being unable to take my eyes off them. If I had been able to reach them, I would have found them irresistible to play with. Most young boys feel this way about swords because the male psyche has more of the warrior God in him than what the female psyche does (with the exception of transgender females who were born in the wrong genders). Thus, if you choose to own a sword please be very careful with it. Keep it well out of sight if you have young children living in your home. The wand is a much safer alternative.

Wand

The wand is a very magical and creative symbol. It has been utilised, in many cultures and traditions, for millennia. It is aligned with the element of air (though, in some traditions, to fire). As with the athame and sword, the wand is a phallic masculine symbol and so it is sacred to the God. In some traditions, however, the gender of the wand is not specifically expressed. Like the athame and sword, the wand can be used to conduct, direct, banish and summon energies. It has, however, a much more inviting and gentler nature than the athame and sword. This is why many Witches prefer the use of the wand over the athame and the sword. The wand can also be a good substitute when the athame or sword is inappropriate.

The word "wand" is derived from the Gothic word *"windan"* meaning "wind" or "to bind". When Witches work magic, the wand is used symbolically to bind the energies of the spell together. The wand's excellent directing ability makes it perfect for magic-making. It evokes the power of the intents of our spells and can help the mind to channel energies in the direction in which the wand is pointed. This is a form of transforming our spells into physical reality. The wand is simply seen as an extension of willpower. It is a psychological aid for directing energies – a magic finger if you will.

The wand can be made from many substances – metal, glass, stone, crystal and so forth – but many Witches prefer woods. As you will be aware by now, Witches work closely with the spiritual properties of nature's materials and different types of woods can be very useful as wands for the magical energies that are locked inside them. Popular woods that are used as wands include the following: apple (healing and love), bay (psychic power and healing), birch (protection and determination), cherry (love and divination), elder (healing and protection), fir (success and wealth), hawthorn (love and fertility), hazel (protection and luck), hickory (law and justice), holly (wisdom and protection), juniper (love and protection), maple (love and finance), oak (strength and wisdom), peach (love and exorcism), pear (love and harmony), rowan (growth and protection), vine (sensuality and happiness), walnut (health and healing) and willow (psychic power and healing). Any wood, however, can be used to construct a wand. If you do decide to take wood from a tree please ask for the tree's permission first and then leave it an offering as a mark of respect, such as an apple or a feather. Many Witches prefer to use a fallen branch rather than cut from a live tree.

Traditionally, the wand is cut to match the distance of its owner's elbow to his or her fingertips, though this is not a necessity. It is also said that wands should be cut with one single stroke from one-year-old trees at sunrise on a Wednesday, the day of the Greek god Hermes who is a magician. Many Witches favour adorning their wands with materials to make them look special and more pleasing to their eyes: ribbons, cords, feathers, shells and so on. Others may also inscribe them with magical symbols. Decorating a wand, however, is a matter of personal preference. If you choose to have a wand simply have it how you would like it. I personally like to leave the majority of my wands natural as they come from nature. Some Witches also like to attach crystals or stones at the tops of their wands. These crystals or stones can relate to specific magical goals. A rose quartz, for example, can be attached at the end of a wand for spells involving love and fertility. A tiger's eye, as another example, can be attached at the top of a wand to aid spells involving justice and protection (see chapter seventeen for more information on crystals and stones).

Chapter Seven: The Altar and Sacred Space

When you consider becoming a practitioner of Witchcraft and magic, it is an excellent idea to familiarise yourself with the altar, a Witch's place of worship and communion. The altar (meaning "on high" in Latin), or shrine as it is otherwise known, has ancient origins and is primarily a place where Witches focus their attention on the Goddess and God and their many deities. It is a convenient and practical place for Witches to work magic and to attune themselves to the rhythms and cycles of nature. Many Witches may also use their altars to practise various forms of divination or other psychic work. The altar, for the reasons above, can be seen as a "gateway" between the physical world and the spiritual realities, a place where there is potentially infinite knowledge and wisdom available to us. Ultimately, the altar can allow a closer connection between deity and human. Thus, the altar can be viewed as the central focal point of Witchcraft rituals and other magical practices. It is a place where most of the action takes place.

The altar, as a place dedicated to the Goddess and God, is also a place where we arrange our tools for rituals and other magical procedures. You should erect an altar if you can for all of the above reasons. Many Witches also use the altar as a place to put other simpler tools, such as flowers, stones and fruits, as offerings to the Goddess and God or their deities. You should always be aware that your own altar should be treated as a sacred place where you pay homage to the Goddess and God and their various deities, a place where you will honour their powers. Thus, you must take good care of it. Your altar should be treated with the respect that it deserves. However, before you decide on what you are actually going to use as your altar, perhaps it is a good idea to first choose an area in which to work – a sacred space.

Sacred Space

The sacred space, or temple as it is otherwise known, is an area set apart where Witches choose to conduct their magical and ritual work. It can be a permanent place or a temporary one. It is a space in which the altar stands. This should be a private place where you are able to feel comfortable enough to conduct whatever work that you wish to accomplish. A place where you can honour the Goddess and God in peace and quiet. Some Witches are lucky enough to have a spare room or perhaps a particular area of a garden specifically set aside for sacred work but many of us have to find a space in which to create a temple. The area in which Witches choose to work can change according to personal circumstances.

The best places for Witches to work are secluded places outdoors, in local woodland or by the sea perhaps, places where we can feel and hear nature speak to us. Indeed, the pre-Christian Pagan folk were well-known to have held their ceremonies outdoors where they could be close to the natural elements, before their practices were outlawed by the increasingly powerful Christian Church during the early centuries of its existence. To see the Pagan folk in action, within their sacred stone circles for example, would have been the norm for the people of pre-Christian Europe. Through no fault of their own, the Pagan folk were forced to take their practices indoors, under the cover of darkness, shutting them away from the true powers of the natural world.

Unfortunately, indoor rites are a legacy that has carried on to this day for many of the Pagan folk. No longer do we feel totally comfortable in practising our religious activities outside amongst the beauty and powers of nature because even today many people do not understand the ways of such an ancient and natural way of life. Witches and other Pagans are surprisingly still persecuted. Thus, many of the Pagan folk today have adapted to worshipping the old gods in the safety and privacy of their own homes. All of their practices are shut away from the true powers of the Goddess and God. If you are lucky enough, however, to find a place outdoors, such as a garden or a grove, then all the more powerful and profound your sacred activities will be. But always make sure that the place in which you have chosen to work is as private as possible, ideally far away from the haunts of other people. Make it your mission to draw as little attention to yourself as possible. There are some very judgemental people out there who may be unkind to you.

If you do not have a place to practise outdoors, or perhaps you do not feel comfortable practising outdoors (weather can also obviously be a problem), then please do not worry. Indoor rooms can be transformed into beautiful temples. They can be adorned with seasonal flowers and greenery, for example, or perhaps decorated with pictures of trees or the seaside, or even figurines or pictures of favourite deities. Adorning chosen temples in this way can help us to bring the powers of nature indoors and into our lives. How you have your own personal sacred space is a matter of individual taste and personal choice. Simply use your intuition when creating an indoor sacred space. The sacred activities that take place within it will then make it a wonderful temple of the Goddess and God.

Altar Types

Once you have decided on the place in which you want to work, you need to consider what you are actually going to use as your altar frame itself. Altars come in many different shapes and sizes but in reality they can be anything that has a strong, flat and steady surface. There are no particular rules as to what can be used as an altar. They can be elaborate or simple. The choice is, as always, yours. Indoor altars, as a few examples, can be no more than a simple coffee table, a bedside table, a bookshelf or a mantelpiece (the fire below a mantelpiece is a very powerful symbol), while outdoor altars can simply be a large flat rock or a tree stump. The altar itself plays an important role for many Witches but it does not have to be anything special – so long as you are comfortable with the frame that you have chosen. Simply use your imagination and intuition. An area on the floor will serve as an altar if all else fails. As a young boy, my first ever altar was simply my windowsill in my bedroom, which was excellent because beyond my altar and tools I could see the movements of the sun, moon and stars. This helped me to feel a real connection to the powers of nature when I conducted my rituals and other magical work. It also intensified the experiences of my magical workings. I had many spiritual experiences in my old bedroom that I simply can't explain. All of them in the comfort of my own home.

Some Witches may also like to choose a particular wood or metal for their altar frames that may be useful for the types of magical workings that they wish to carry out and again this is entirely up to you. Oak wood, for example, is excellent for magical workings that involve strength and wisdom, while copper (which is linked to the love planet of Venus) is excellent for all magical workings that involve fertility, love and beauty. Your altar frame can also be any shape. My altar is simply rectangle (it is a stand that I once used to rest my fish tank on), with each of the four corners representing the four cardinal points and the elements. Round altars, on the other hand, are also excellent. They represent the earth, the cycles of nature and the infinity of spirit.

You may also decide to keep a temporary altar or a permanent one. You may decide, for example, to keep a permanent altar in your home and temporary altars for magical procedures conducted outdoors. When I conduct my magical work outdoors, I simply go in search for a suitable altar frame. If, after some time, I can't find one I simply find a secluded place to work and arrange my tools on the ground and then simply clean up after myself when my work is complete. Having an altar on the ground is an excellent way to connect with the natural energies of the earth – to the great powers of Gaia. Whether you decide to keep a permanent altar, a temporary one or both is once again entirely up to you and your personal circumstances. Permanent altars must be carefully maintained, however, because dust and clutter shows a lack of respect and can attract negative energies.

Placing the Altar

On deciding the sacred space in which you want to work and the type of altar that you want to use, you may want to now consider where to place your altar within the sacred space. This is where a compass comes in very handy indeed. Some Witches, for instance, like to place their altars in the east in honour of the place where the sun and moon rise. Many religions are known to place their altars in the east. Since the sun rises in the east, the direction symbolises the spiritual origin of all creation. The east, therefore, is a place of freshness and new beginnings – those energies that are typically associated with the element of air.

Ideally, however, the altar is best placed in the centre and facing north. The centre is the place of spirit. It represents the self and our needs and goals. North is a powerful direction because it is the place of the element of earth. Earth represents the end of one cycle and the beginning of the next. It is stability and truth. When Witches place their altars facing north, it represents a connection between physical and spiritual matters. Witchcraft is, after all, an earth-based spirituality that celebrates both the physical and spiritual realities of existence.

Ancient civilisations were well-known to place their altars facing the north because it is the realm of midnight and Witchery, the direction from which enormous power naturally flows. It represents the path from darkness and into light. Altars placed facing north are well-known to have the best results from magical workings. All four directions have their own specific powers, however, and many Witches simply place the altar facing the direction that relates to the type of work that they are conducting. West, for example, is the place of the element of water and would be excellent for love and friendship spells, while south, the place of fire, would be excellent for magical workings involving success and confidence.

Do not worry if you are unable to place your altar in the centre facing north (fixed structures, such as windowsills, can certainly be a problem), simply place your altar anywhere in your sacred space and imagine that it is facing north. The most important element in any type of magical working is, after all, the self.

Arranging the Tools on the Altar

Although the assembling of the tools on the altar may vary from tradition to tradition, coven to coven, Solitary Witch to Solitary Witch, there are some general rules that are usually shared by the majority of Witches. As long as these are understood, the way in which you design your altar is entirely up to you. It is a matter of individual taste and personal preference.

Traditionally, an altar is first covered with a suitable altar cloth but again this is entirely up to you. Any material can be used as an altar cloth, though natural materials, such as cotton, are preferred by many Witches. Also, many Witches like to use specific colours for their altar cloths that are perhaps useful for the types of workings that they are aiming to fulfil. As we have seen in chapter six, colours speak to the mind and have specific spiritual vibrations that help us to attract specific energies into our lives. As indicated, I will give you a guide to colours at the end of this chapter. Incidentally, it is an excellent idea to wrap some of your smaller tools in your chosen altar cloths when they are not in use. They can then be placed in a safe place, such as a magical pantry, as a gesture of respect to the Goddess and God.

Once you have covered your altar with a suitable cloth (if you choose to have an altar cloth), the next thing to consider, before the tools are actually placed on the altar, is that the altar itself represents balance and polarity. It represents the natural balance of the male and female mysteries of nature that Witches personify as the Goddess and God. The left-hand side is dedicated to the Goddess. This area of the altar represents the female mysteries of nature. It is the place of intuition, childbirth, fertility, psychic sensitivity and lunar power. It represents the female psyche and the *anima* in the male psyche. Thus, all the tools that are dedicated to the Goddess – bell, cauldron, crystal ball, chalice and so on – are generally placed in that area of the altar. To the right-hand side of the altar, the emphasis is placed on the God. This area of the altar represents the male mysteries of nature. It is the place of enlightenment, sexual potency, courage, virility and solar power. It represents the male psyche and the *animus* in the female psyche. Thus, all the tools that are dedicated to the God – athame, broomstick, sword, wand and so on – are generally placed in that area of the altar.

The left and right sides of the altar help us to visualise the existence of the male and female powers of nature – of the universe. The powers that actually reside within ourselves – both physically and spiritually. The middle of the altar represents the combination of both the God and the Goddess. It represents the Ultimate Deity and the sexual force of nature. In a Witch's mind, the middle of the altar symbolises the ultimate spirit of creation. It is a prominent place of magic and mystery. Thus, this is the place where the Book of Shadows, the pentacle and any additional spell or ritual materials – herbs, woods, crystals, stones, paper, ink and so on – are generally placed. The censer may also be placed here to represent our goals and desires rising up to the divine through the smoke.

To honour the Goddess and God, Witches also traditionally place a candle to either side of the altar. It is traditional to place candle colours that suit the Goddess and God. Silver, for example, is a traditional colour of the moon (the Goddess's symbol) and so a silver candle can be placed to the top left of the altar, while gold is a traditional colour of the sun (the God's symbol) and so a gold candle can be placed to the top right of the altar. As well as the candles, you can also place figurines of the Goddess and God or symbols of the moon and sun to the appropriate places on the altar.

Of course, Witches also work with the four sacred elements of nature and the cardinal points that they represent – north/earth, east/air, south/fire and west/water – and so these areas of the altar have pride of place too. To help us honour the four sacred elements of nature, Witches generally place items that are associated with their directions on the altar. Following are some example items that can be placed to each area of the altar to represent the elements:

North: Acorns, bowl of salt, coins, fossils, garden gnomes, grains, green candle, images of forest creatures, plants, pottery, rocks, roots, sand, stones, woods.

East: Airborne seeds, bright yellow candle, carved birds or sylphs, feathers, incense, scented herbs (such as lavender), wind chimes, windmills.

South: Carved dragons or salamanders, dish of oil with a wick in it, lamps, lava, matches, red candle, spices and gums (such as frankincense), sunstones.

West: Blue candle, bowl of water, carved undines or mermaids, dried pond or sea life (such as starfish), moonstones, watery plants (such as aloe).

Note: If you find that some of the tools that you acquire are too large, simply place them near to your altar. The sword, for example, can simply be placed on the ground near to the right-hand side of your altar. As with the sacred space, the altar itself can be decorated to your own individual taste with whatever you feel is appropriate. It's your altar so have it exactly how you would like it. Be creative and experiment with it. Fashion it in ways that are pleasing to you personally. Good luck.

A Guide to Colours

Here, we will look at a guide to colours that you can use if you decide to have an altar cloth. Obviously, this guide can be used for any types of materials that you use in your magical workings, such as candles, ribbons and cords. Knowledge of colours is essential for any Witch's development. Colours are used in many different types of rituals, spells, psychic work, potions, powders, invocations, worship, candle magic, altar decoration and so on. Although there is traditional colour lore in which certain colours are associated with specific spiritual vibrations, you should trust your intuition when working with colours. If a specific spell requires only the use of green materials, for example, but you feel that blue would be a more appropriate colour simply use blue.

Colours are everywhere throughout the natural world. They permeate every single moment of our lives and each has their own unique spiritual vibrations that can have a profound effect on our minds. They have psychological, spiritual and therapeutic effects on us that can be useful for all kinds of magical workings. At the centre of everything is light which is an interaction of magnetism and electrical energy. Colours are simply the various wavelengths that create light. The human aura, an energy field that surrounds the body, itself is made up of colours. These colours are electrical emanations from our bodies. People who are psychic can often see auras. Even some scientists agree that the brain emits thoughts that can be measured as colours. These colours can be used by psychics to determine a person's physical health, beliefs, experiences, emotional state and spiritual development.

Black: Contrary to popular belief, black is not the hue of sheer evil. In Witchcraft, it simply represents the rest that the soul takes between incarnations. It is a protective hue that represents the dark sacred night, the blackness and darkness of the universe and the lack of falsehood. It represents the ultimate source of divine power. This is why it is favoured by many Witches in their magical workings. Black is sacred to the crone aspect of the Goddess and her many crone deities. It is also linked to the protective planet of Saturn and to the zodiac signs of Capricorn and Aquarius. There are many moon goddesses associated with black. Use black for protection, banishing, binding, legal matters, exorcism, coping with death, all issues to do with the elderly, limitations, bringing periods of rest, meditation, psychic development, divination, restricting someone or something, crone magic and all occult matters.

Blue: is the healing colour associated with the Goddess. It represents the various sea goddesses of mythology. It is also related to the philosophical planet of Jupiter and to the zodiac signs of Sagittarius and Pisces. Use blue for healing, purification, dream work, truth, emotions, enhancing the power of the unconscious mind, harmony, instincts, getting in touch with your inner child qualities, sleep, spirituality, happiness, guidance, religious issues, communication, peace, psychic development, organisation, repelling negativity, serenity, tranquillity, administration, blessing a new home, hope, making a safe space, meditation, patience and creativity. Sky blue is said to be sacred to the Egyptian goddess Isis and is excellent for magic particularly involving the element of air. Dark blue enhances workings of fertility.

Brown: is one of my favourite colours. My own robes that my partner gave me as a Yule present are brown. It is the colour of the earth and its many creatures and plants. It is the colour of the lover of animals. It is for those who work closely with animal energies and animal spirit totems. It is for those who wish to draw close to the great powers of Gaia. It is a neutral and gentle colour associated with the wild woods and the wilderness. Use brown for material matters, prosperity, fertility, balance, level-headedness, telepathy, recovering lost or stolen items, stopping people from harming you without cutting them out of your life completely, animal magic, healing pets and herbs, decision-making, dependence, wisdom, attuning with the powers of the earth, honesty, keeping grounded, peace, stability and security.

Gold: is the colour associated with the sun and the element of fire. It is, therefore, an archetypal symbol of the God and his many deities – especially his solar or fiery deities. It is the colour of masculinity. It is associated with the zodiac sign of Leo. It has ancient associations with wealth, prosperity and winning. Use gold for success, fertility, protection, authority, solar work, longevity, vitality, youth, wisdom, comfort, strength, purity, truth, legal matters, happiness, health, healing, averting depression, financial issues, influencing cosmic forces and the astral planes, stimulating the life force and fulfilment. In the ancient practice of alchemy, gold is said to bring spiritual attainment.

Green: is the wonderful colour of the Earth Mother and the Green Man. It is the colour that strengthens the power of the herbalist and the magical ecologist. It symbolises new life, fertility, harmony, youth, vegetation, regeneration and growth. It is also related to the love planet of Venus and it is said that gardens are under the protection of this planet. In Irish folklore, green is associated with great luck. In feng shui, green is the colour of prosperity. Use green for working with the powers of the earth, growth, finance, fertility, love, material matters, employment, beauty, youth, garden or herb magic, good luck, prosperity, success, courage, renewal, acceptance, instinct, faery magic, working with your inner child, making a safe space, healing, health, intuition, faith and harmony. Dark green is said to help us to counter greed and jealousy and aqua, a mixture of green and blue, represents the depths of the ocean and is thus good for all types of sea magic.

Grey: is another colour of neutrality and is sacred to the crone aspect of the Goddess and her many crone deities. It is also associated with the three gorgons of Greek mythology – Medusa, Euryale and Stheno. Use grey for balance, neutralising negativity, sorrow, crone magic, moving on, avoiding loneliness, legal matters, formality and all issues to do with the elderly.

Orange: is a secondary colour of the sun. It is also associated with the element of fire and the communication planet of Mercury. It is often seen as a somewhat adaptable colour that is associated with many things. Primarily, however, it is the colour of ambition and the business world. Use orange for confidence, health, travel, communication, legal issues, justice, artistic talent, enhancing power, wisdom, intellectual pursuits, fertility, attracting love or romance, healing, building empathy, pride, strength, getting noticed, success, balance, stimulation, strong results, solar work, business matters and protection.

Pastels: are soft, gentle and delicate colours that relate to the element of air. They generally symbolise freshness, new beginnings, freedom, clarity, happiness, creativity, artistic talent and harmony.

Pink: The poet William Blake called pink an angelic colour. It is sacred to both Aphrodite and Venus, the goddesses of love and fertility. It is also connected with the zodiac signs of Libra and Taurus. Use pink for romance, love, enhancing female power, good will, peace, marriage, reconciliation, youth, friendships, relationships, beauty, affection, joy, happiness, leisure, gentleness, attraction, devotion, fertility, female health, working with angels, harmony, averting depression and all emotional workings.

Purple: This is another one of my favourite colours. Purple is the colour of royalty and is connected to Jupiter, the planet of royalty. Monarchs throughout history have worn purple to show their divine appointments to their thrones. It is also associated with the zodiac signs of Gemini and Virgo. Purple is a pure divine colour that deepens our spiritual awareness of the Goddess and God. Use purple for psychic development, working with divine power, healing, committing, success, justice, generosity, independence, wisdom, riches, spiritual contact, ambition, divination, astral travel, prophecy, self-assurance, uncovering mysteries and transformation. Violet, a bluish purple colour, is excellent for matters of spirituality, insight, intuition, psychic development, gay love and gay sex magic.

Rainbow: is obviously not a specific colour but all the colours of the light spectrum. In the west, the rainbow has become a symbol of gay pride and is thus excellent for magical workings that involve gay love and sexuality. It is also sacred to Iris, Greek messenger goddess of the rainbow who is beloved by the gods because of her kind and loving personality. Iris is the feminine counterpart of Hermes, the magician. Use the rainbow for overcoming negativity, working with divine power, psychic development, hope, unity, contact with ancestors and understanding the connection between physical and spiritual matters.

Red: is the colour of blood and so it represents the life force within us. It is a passionate and fiery colour that is related to the God. It symbolises the male, electric principle. It represents those fast action and driving forces within us. It is also associated with the war and action planet of Mars and with the zodiac signs of Aries and Scorpio. The cardinals of the Catholic Church have worn red throughout history to symbolise that they would spill their blood in the name of the Church. In ancient Greece and Britain, red foods – lobsters, red berries, red meats, red apples and so on – were only eaten at feasts that specifically honour the souls of the dead. Many scientific studies have shown that those involved with sports are more competitive when they wear red. Use red for high energy, courage, fertility, enhancing willpower, overcoming obstacles, health, healing, passion, passionate love, exorcism, motivation, ambition, success, mercy, protection, finding love, keeping love, magnetism, enhancing sexual energy, endurance, vitality, moving forward in life, repelling negativity, strength, romance and working with the male principle. Wearing red is said to avert evil. Scarlet, a vivid red colour tinged with orange, is a particularly good colour for women who wish to enhance their sexual potency. It is sacred to Aphrodite and Venus.

Silver: is the colour associated with the moon and the element of water. It is, however, particularly associated with the new moon. It symbolises life in death and is sacred to the Goddess and all her many deities – especially her moon deities. It is also related to the zodiac sign of Cancer – the most mothering sign out of all of the zodiac signs. It is strongly associated with psychic abilities, intuition and all things that are feminine. Use silver for lunar work, psychic development, divination, success, fertility, health, healing, protection, money, banishing negativity, stability, working with the Goddess, female sexuality, motherhood issues, menstrual issues, wishes, good luck, love, relationships, sleep, peace, intuition and attuning with the rhythms and cycles of nature.

White: represents all the colours of the light spectrum. It can symbolise any colour. It represents the Goddess in her purest form. It symbolises motherhood, childhood and love in their purest forms. It is also particularly associated with the maiden aspect of the Goddess. It represents innocence, peace, sincerity, the higher self and truth. William Blake referred to this hue as the "white light of reason". Use white for lunar work, purification, working with angels, intuition, issues to do with children, spiritual matters, fertility, calming atmospheres, weather magic, relationships, love, celebrations, artistic talent, truth, health, healing, innocence, conjuring spirits, meditation, creativity, sleep, motherhood issues, empathy, sympathy, positivity, repelling negativity, ecstasy, reason, enlightenment, protection, psychic development and creating a sacred space. Wearing white is good for working with many goddess deities, especially Isis.

Yellow: is another secondary colour of the sun. It is associated with the nervous system, confidence, charm, persuasion and imagination. It is also associated with the communication planet of Mercury and with the goddess Athena. Yellow was once associated with death to the Mayans. It was also associated with Judas and the Spanish Inquisition. Use yellow for mind and memory issues, success, fertility, health, healing, concentration, intellectual pursuits, communication, travel, moving on in life, wisdom, enhancing power, attraction, bonding, happiness, learning new ideas and theories, creativity, psychic development, confidence, joy, speeding up matters, enhancing the power of persuasion, making a safe space, activating any magical working, philosophical matters, new beginnings and solar work.

Part Two:
Spellcraft

Chapter Eight: Casting Spells

Spellcraft is a very personal, creative and individual thing. There are probably no two Witches who cast spells in exactly the same ways. No matter how many Witches you ask about how to cast a spell, you will probably always get different answers. Some Witches prefer candle or knot magic, while others like to work with image or runic magic. There is simply no right or wrong way to cast a spell – only what is right for you as an individual. Each Witch has to find their own way through trial and error – what works best and what does not work so well. The more times a Witch uses spellcraft, the more he or she will come to understand this. Some Witches learn how to cast successful spells rather quickly, while others may take a long time to become an adept. Knowledge is the true power and so successful spell-casting comes with experience, practice, effort, inner work and time. Spells require a deep understanding of the self and the energies that are within and around us. They also require an ability to be able to control and focus those energies. The more you cast spells and the more you put into them, the more you will get out of them. It really is that simple.

Later in this chapter, I will show you how I typically perform a major spell. Of course, this does not mean that my way is the best way for you to work. You will have to practise and experiment and over time you will find your own way and your own unique style. Always bear in mind that creativity is of great importance when it comes to spellcraft. This is one of the beauties of the Witchcraft religion – it is an open-minded, creative and free religion that lets us find our own ways within our magical practices. When you decide to cast a spell, allow your mind, body and soul to be open to the energies of the universe. Don't just believe that your spell will work – know that it will work. Have no doubt in your mind. This will allow you to effectively log in your wish and so the universe will hear your wish clearly and will, therefore, be able to manifest it for you. Simply believe in yourself and be open to receive. Your thoughts are the most powerful things available to you as any reputable Witch will tell you. You create magic simply by focusing those thoughts and this is the big secret of successful spellcraft.

The word "spell" is believed to come from the Gothic word *"spill"*, which means a story, a saying, a narrative or a particular item of news. This is where the word "gospel" comes from that we see in the Bible and the literal translation of the word gospel is "the narrative of God" or "God's news". So even the word "spell" has ancient associations with the divine. A spell is very similar to the belief in the power of prayer in many of the orthodox religions of the world today. However, Witches are of the belief that it is our personal intervention that creates the change, not necessarily the whim of a superior being. Sure, Witches may well call upon the deities to ask for assistance, but without our personal intervention, our desired changes would simply not manifest. As superior beings, however, the deities will lean down and help us if we call upon their powers. They can help us to strengthen and empower our work.

Low Magic and High Magic

Many Witches see magic as being two basic types. These are low magic and high magic. Low magic, which is often referred to as practical magic, is practised in many parts of the world and was surprisingly popular during medieval times. It combines the art of spellcraft with everyday, commonplace items. It may not even require any of the special tools outlined in chapter six. It may involve the use of Voodoo image magic and/or the use of herbs, crystals, stones, metals, shells, feathers, amulets, talismans and other simple items combined with visualisation and incantations (otherwise known as "words of power") to achieve the desired change. It is a simple form of magic that is also often known as folk magic. In many developed parts of the world, it is the beautiful magic of many spell-casters.

High magic, which is often known as ceremonial magic, is utilised to bring about a union with the divine. It is religious magic in its purest form and is the most effective type of magic. Low magic can still be very effective providing your will is strong enough and that you are properly focused on your goals. High magic, however, can help us to develop a special relationship with the divine – with the Goddess and God. It combines the use of willpower with external forces or spirits – deities, elemental spirits, angels and so on. It may also involve the use of everyday items and magical correspondences, but it is more formal than low magic. It includes the casting of the magic circle, the invocation of the elements, the invocation of the Goddess and God or their specific deities and so forth. Practised in many parts of the world since very ancient times, high magic is for those who wish to seek mystical power, self-empowerment and enlightenment.

Contrary to what many people would have us believe, magic is not a supernatural practice. It is simply a harmonious movement of energy to produce our desired changes. It is the process of rousing up energies through the power of the mind, giving those energies a purpose, and then releasing them towards our intended goals. It is the ability and knowledge to work with, and manipulate, the energies of the natural world. The mind is an amazing thing and science is only just beginning to understand just how powerful it is. Things like hypnotism, precognition, extrasensory perception, acupuncture and so on would have been dismissed as wishful thinking by science only a hundred or so years ago, but modern-day science is now starting to accept these things as valid. Is it, then, so surprising that the mind can create change in the world around us just through the power of thoughts? Though science has come very far in understanding much about how the world works, it does not yet have the necessary tools to understand, define or label magic.

Even in modern-day quantum physics it's understood that we can affect the movement of particles simply by concentrating on them. That is to say that we can actually affect or alter something just by focusing our attention. This is how magic works. The simple fact of the matter is that you do have personal power and you can make things happen. No one who practises magic really knows for sure how it works, even the most experienced and advanced of Witches and magicians, we just know that it does work. I'm no expert in how computers or laptops work, but I can sit here in front of my laptop and type this book! All it takes for magic to be effective is a little patience, preparation, concentration, willpower and energy. The more you practise magic, the more you will come to realise just how real it is. But in doing so, you must learn to let go of any thoughts of it being supernatural. Don't believe that it somehow works outside of the laws of nature.

White Magic and Black Magic

Magic in itself is neutral. It reflects both the dark and light aspects of nature. It can be used to smash or to build, much like a hammer. It is coloured by our intents. In other words, magic can be created for helpful, constructive purposes as well as harmful, destructive purposes. As Witches, however, who choose to be bound to the law of harm none, we only utilise magic for the greater good of ourselves and others. We see magic as a sacred gift of nature that should never be misused or abused. We call upon magic to help ourselves and others through the dark times of life since this is important for our health and well-being.

The type of magic Witches work is often referred to as "white magic" or "the right-handed path" – magic designed to bring about harmonious positivity within our lives. This involves the use of positive spells – healing, love, success, protection, fertility and so forth. That is to say that as long as we don't cause harm, we may use magic to follow our own true will. Achieving true will is not a selfish act or against all that is deemed spiritual by the way, it is the very reason we are here. If we work towards our true will we are able to achieve the fullness and completeness of life and thus become physically, psychologically and spiritually well enough to help and to heal others to our optimum. This is extremely important for Witches.

Destructive or harmful magic – curses, jinxes or hexes – is often referred to as "black magic" or "the left-handed path". This type of magic has no place in Witchcraft because it violates our basic ethical law – harm none. Black magic is not a part of genuine Witchcraft or Paganism, nor has it ever been. Indeed, Witchcraft is about the positive side of life. It is about understanding the self and others and working towards betterment. If others foolishly use magic to harm us (or generally abuse us in other ways), we don't retaliate by using black magic against them (two wrongs don't make a right), we simply use magic to protect ourselves, perhaps by using banishing and binding magic. That is to say that Witches choose to defend and deflect rather than attack.

Those who do practise destructive magic are involving themselves in forces way beyond their control and understanding and eventually these people will lead to their own destruction as Scott Cunningham tells us in his book *Cunningham's Encyclopedia of Magical Herbs* (1985):

> *The moment anger or hatred tinges your magic you have crossed the border into a dangerous world, one that will ultimately consume you.*

The term "grey magic" is often used as a representation of spells cast on others without their consent, but also for their benefit. As Witches, we avoid this type of magic at all costs too because we should be familiar with the term "live and let live". None of us have the right to influence others without their knowledge (except in certain forms of protection magic) because this is influencing free will. This could be potentially harmful because we may not have all the facts about the people's lives who we wish to influence. Thus, this type of magic has the potential to blur into the left-handed path. Many Witches may make an exception of this rule, however, in the case of healing magic – when the people who we wish to heal are unable to give us their specific consent as a result of their illness.

The Witches' Pyramid

When performing magic, it is wise to keep the Witches' Pyramid in mind. Also known as the Four Powers of the Sphinx, the Four Powers of the Magus and the Four Words of the Magus, the Witches' Pyramid represents the mind-set necessary for successful spell-casting. Many Witches consider it to be an important guide for successful magic-making. At the base of the Witches' Pyramid are the four actions of a spell. These represent the four sacred elements of nature, and at the top is the goal of the spell and this represents the fifth element of spirit. Witches traditionally interpret the Witches' Pyramid in this way:

To Know: This represents the element of air. It means that for magic to work you must know in your heart that it will work. In other words, you must have no doubt in your mind. It represents that the actions of your spell are the result of intelligence and study. When you perform a spell, this part of the Witches' Pyramid represents that you must be clear in your mind and heart about the outcome of your spell.

To Dare: This represents the element of water. It is thus all to do with emotions. It means that you must be willing to take a risk when performing a spell and that you are persistent in your efforts to achieve your desires. You must have the courage to seek your goals and the consequences of your spells.

To Will: This part of the Witches' Pyramid symbolises the element of fire. It represents strength of character. It represents your willpower to achieve your goal when performing a spell. For successful spell-casting, you must be strong in your desire to achieve your goals. In other words, be confident that your magic will work when performing a spell. When performing a spell, this part of the Witches' Pyramid represents that you must carry out your spell through to the end regardless of inner fears and outward obstacles.

To Keep Silent: This part of the Witches' Pyramid represents the element of earth. It means that once you have cast the spell you should keep silent about it. In other words, you should consider the matter closed. As such, you should not talk about your effort to work magic after you have performed a particular spell. If you do talk about your magic you run the risk of dissipating the energy of your spell and thus it makes your spell less likely to work. Talking about spells after they are cast also gives others the chance to will you to fail or to give you persecution. Witches may only discuss their spells once they have fully come to fruition.

The Goal: This represents the element of spirit. It is the tip of the Witches' Pyramid. It represents the ultimate goal of a particular spell. This part of the Witches' Pyramid represents that you should walk away with knowledge, conviction and empowerment once you have cast a spell. It represents that you should have calm assurance that the energy of your spell will create your desired change and that the result will be the best possible outcome. This part of the Witches' Pyramid can really only be achieved when all the other four actions outlined above are carried out.

Meditation

Meditation is a basic Witch's magical skill. In my opinion, every Witch should learn how to successfully meditate. Meditation teaches self-discipline and is very calming on the mind. Meditation can help us to awaken psychic powers, but it must be practised on a regular basis for it to be effective. For successful magic-making, you must be centred, balanced and properly focused and this is where meditation comes in very handy indeed. You should practise meditation for at least ten minutes each day to get the most out of it. Meditation is like a prelude to working with magic. It will support any inner work you do and will help you to properly focus on your needs and goals. Meditation is considered to be excellent for the mind and body. It reduces stress levels, reduces depression, reduces anger, lowers blood pressure, relieves pain and thus helps us to live longer. Many studies have shown that people who meditate can have younger and healthier minds. Meditation is a welcome relief from the cares and frustrations of everyday life. This is particularly important for magic-making.

The best time to practise meditation, in my opinion, is on a late afternoon or an evening just before, during or just after sundown. This is the time of reflection when we can really focus on our needs and goals. To perform meditation, I would recommend that you find a private and comfortable place where you won't be disturbed. This can be a place filled with meditation devices if you wish: candles, incense, recordings of nature sounds, recordings of drumming and so forth. Turn off any disturbing electrical equipment such as televisions, telephones and so on. Then sit in an upright position with your legs crossed and your hands resting on them and your palms facing upwards. If this is uncomfortable for you, however, you can simply lie on your back, perhaps on a bed, with your hands crossed over your chest or placed on your belly. Then allow yourself to enter into a deep state of relaxation, one step away from sleep if you will. You can do this by completely clearing your mind and then allowing it to wander wherever it will. Wherever your mind wanders can actually tell you much about yourself. You can then try flexing and relaxing every muscle in your body, from your head to your toes. You may do this until you feel no tension in your body at all.

The next step is to focus on your breathing. You should slow down your breathing while deeply focusing on it. By doing this, you will actually slow down your brain activity. This will further help you to enter into a deep state of relaxation. You may then breathe in for five seconds, hold your breath for five seconds and then breathe out for five seconds. You should repeat this until you are completely relaxed and focused. After some time, you may find that your mind enters into a state of complete blackness and non-thought. This is what you should be aiming to eventually achieve. Don't worry if you fall asleep during the process of meditation, you probably needed the sleep anyhow, but by repeating the above you will train yourself not to fall asleep and condition your mind to enter into a wonderful and blissful state of meditation.

Visualisation

Visualisation is another basic Witch's magical skill. Yet, it is also the most advanced technique called for successful magic-making. In spellcraft, visualisation is the process of forming the goal of the spell in the mind. It is the art of controlled imagination. This process allows us to move the energy of the spell in the intended direction. Meditation is one way to help us to achieve the ability to visualise. It helps us to gently push away any distracting thoughts that may inhibit our ability to see in our minds our needs and goals. There have been many books written on the art of visualisation and this is because many people who wish to practise magic find it a very hard thing to do. The ability to successfully visualise is usually present in all of us but many people are hindered by the stresses and strains of life. This is why I believe that meditation is essential for those who wish to learn the art of visualisation for magic.

Can you at this very moment picture your favourite actor, actress or vocalist? Can you picture your mother's or partner's face? What about your favourite animals, flowers and trees perhaps? If you can do these things, then you have the ability to successfully visualise. In magic-making, visualisation is employed simply to help us to move power. If you desire something to be in your life, visualise yourself having it. Bring forward any feelings you will have when you achieve your desire. By forming a picture of your goal – love, money, a car, employment and so on – and bringing forward any positive emotions to do with it, you are actually telling the energy of your spell where to go through the power of the mind. This is the most effective way for you to focus all your thoughts on the intent of a particular spell.

Visualisation in magic-making requires us to see our goals as if we have already obtained them. It is the ability to see our needs and goals as if they have already come to fruition. It requires us to use our creativity. One simple way to begin practising visualisation techniques is to picture all the colours of the light spectrum – one by one. This can help you to build upon your visualisation skills. As with everything else in life, the more you put into your visualisation the more effective you will become at it. Practice will make perfection as my grandmother always used to say. It takes time to become an adept. Don't worry if at first you find visualisation extremely hard to master. You're certainly not alone. But with patience, practice and concentration you will eventually learn how to master the ancient and wonderful art of visualisation. Good luck.

Spells and the Moon

Many Witches work their spells religiously with the monthly cycle of the moon. The moon has enormous power and Witches harness this power to get the most out of their spellcraft. Traditionally, celebrations and magical workings based on the cycle of the moon are known as the "Esbats". This word comes from an Old French word *"esbattre"* meaning "to frolic and amuse oneself". As we have seen, Witchcraft is a very joyous religion that celebrates life and the word "Esbat" embraces the essence of this. Because the moon governs our emotions, rituals and spells based on the phases of the moon can have an enormous effect on ourselves and our work. There is a great deal of wisdom in working with the cycle of the moon. It is one of the most powerful representations of the Goddess ever known to humankind. Of course, there are lunar male deities but the moon has always been mostly regarded as feminine. The moon is changing woman, constantly in a state of transformation and metamorphosis, as are all women. It is considered to be the most important heavenly body when working spellcraft. The best way to keep track of the moon's phases is to buy a good astrological calendar or an almanac. There are basically four phases that the moon goes through during its 29.5-day cycle around the earth. Each has specific energies that are very useful in spellcraft and we will explore them here:

Dark or New Moon: is considered to be the first phase of the moon. It symbolises both death and rebirth and is a time when Witches traditionally welcome the return of the Goddess. It represents the promise of the things in life to come – just like the springtime. This is a time of banishing the old and making way for the new. It is an excellent time to banish any negativity that may be burdening your life. It is a time to banish any negative influences so that you can sow the seeds for future success. All spells to do with new beginnings and projects are best cast at this phase of the moon.

Waxing Moon: is a powerful time of the maiden aspect of the Goddess. This is the time when the moon is growing in the sky as the days pass towards the full moon. Power is said to increase as the moon waxes. The waxing moon is best for spells involving accumulation, motivation, luck, courage, health, healing, beauty, fertility, psychic awareness, growth, expansion, money, increase, productivity, invitation, encouragement, prosperity, inspiration and attraction. The waxing moon stimulates the heart and is a powerful time for invocation or summoning desired energies.

Full Moon: is a powerful time of the mother aspect of the Goddess. It is the most powerful phase of the entire lunar cycle. It is an extremely powerful time to perform magic of any kind. At the full moon there seems to be a psychic power surge. Witches tend to be more receptive to this. Even those who are not magically inclined will notice that there is something strange about the time of the full moon. People may act totally different when the moon is full. They may be irritable, argumentative, ecstatic, irrational, overly enthusiastic and so on. For many people, the power of the full moon can manifest as nervous tension. Whatever is happening in your life, good or bad, will most likely come to a head at the full moon. The fact that the emergency services have to ask more staff to come on duty at the full moon is a reminder of just how powerful it can be. The mysterious effects of the full moon are sometimes known as the *Transylvania Effect* and the root of *lunacy*, an old word used to describe insanity, is derived from *luna* which is the Latin word for moon. Although the full moon is excellent for any type of spellcraft, it is particularly powerful for spells involving achievement, conclusions, fulfilment, fertility, love, romance, motivation, self-development, completion, health, healing, issues to do with children, family, legal matters, culmination, protection, purification, money, travel, knowledge and prosperity.

Waning Moon: is associated with the crone aspect of the Goddess. It occurs any time between the full moon and the new moon. This is the time when the moon is decreasing in size. Power is said to decrease or calm down as the moon wanes in the sky. It is a time to reflect on what has occurred over the waxing moon and the full moon. It is a symbolic time to reflect on what we have achieved – both physically and spiritually. It represents a time of harvest. The waning moon is appropriate for spells involving banishing, binding, decrease, discovering inner secrets, healing, issues to do with the elderly, repelling negative thoughts, releasing jealousy or guilt, retreat, reversal and cleansing. The waning moon helps us to balance the mind, body and soul so that we can move forward in life more easily. Incidentally, it is also a very useful time for divination and other psychic work given the fact that it is associated with the wisdom of the crone aspect of the Goddess. So this is the time to contact the crone aspect of the Goddess with the use of divination tools – tarot cards, crystal balls, runes and so on – to seek her guidance for any issues that you may have in your life.

Spells and the Sun

Many Witches consider the sun to be the second most important heavenly body for magical workings. While the moon generally affects us in a more personal, spiritual and emotional way, the sun generally affects us in a more physical and practical way. It generally represents things that are external – things that we can actually see with our eyes in the everyday mundane world.

Thus, all spells that represent the mundane things in the world around you are said to be strongly governed by the sun. The phases of the sun in a given day can be very useful in spellcraft. Be aware, however, that the energies of the sun can be overbearing, domineering and somewhat arrogant. Here are the phases of the sun and their particular energies that Witches use in their spellcraft:

Sunrise: is a symbolic time of the birth of the God. As a new day begins, light stretches over the eastern horizon. The air fills us with the excitement of a new day. Use the time of sunrise for spells involving employment, success (especially in business), breaking addictions, travel, releasing jealousy or guilt, healing, study, purification and all issues to do with the conscious mind.

Noon: symbolises the father aspect of the God. It is considered to be a powerful time of the day by many Witches. The sun shines as strong as it possibly can in the south. Use the noon of the sun for all spells associated with the sunrise as well as physical energy, strength, protection, courage and money. The noon of the sun is considered to be a very powerful time to work with all spells that involve the element of fire. It adds enormous strength and magical power to spells.

Dusk: symbolises the sage aspect of the God as the sun slips below the western horizon. It is a time to work spells that break addictions and bad habits. It is also good for spells involving banishing misery and pain. It is a powerful time of transformation.

Night: the sun is out of sight but this doesn't mean that we can't work with its powerful energies. Night symbolises the time when the God rests in the Summerlands for many Witches. It is a very drowsy time and a time that symbolises winter. It is a time to work specifically with the spiritual aspect of the sun. Use night for spells involving beauty, psychic awareness, psychic dreams, love, friendship, healing, releasing stress and guilt, purification, peace, tranquillity and all spiritual matters.

Spells and the Zodiac

Many Witches also work with the sun or moon's visits to the signs of the zodiac. Each sign of the zodiac has specific energies that are useful when working with spellcraft. Astrology tells us that the positions of the sun and moon in particular at birth can have an enormous effect on our personalities. It comes as no surprise to Witches, then, that their positions can also have a huge effect on our spellcraft. Once again, a good astrological calendar or an almanac can tell you the sun and moon's visits to the signs of the zodiac in a given year. Here, I have presented you with each sign of the zodiac and the types of spells that are best cast during the sun or moon's visits to each:

Aries: Aries is associated with the war and action planet of Mars. The effects of the sun or moon in this sign generates fiery energy. Work spells involving protection, defence, assertiveness, dramatic change, transformation and battle.

Taurus: is associated with the love planet of Venus. The effects of the sun or moon in this sign are very positive and cheerful. Work spells involving love, fertility, money, material matters, beauty and sex magic.

Gemini: is associated with the communication planet of Mercury. The effects of the sun or moon in this sign are all to do with communication. Work spells involving enhancing communication skills, travel, writing and projects. It is said that writers often find that they can write better during the sun or moon's visits to this sign of the zodiac. I can very much support this.

Cancer: is associated with the moon which is one of the most powerful symbols of the Goddess. The effects of the sun or moon in this sign are very caring and mothering. Work spells involving the home, family, fertility, protection, friendship, emotional matters, motherhood, psychic work and lunar power.

Leo: is associated with the sun which is one of the most powerful symbols of the God. The effects of the sun or moon in this sign are positive and ambitious. Work spells involving leadership, solar power, success, wealth, recognition, ambition, generosity, fatherhood, health and healing.

Virgo: is another sign associated with the communication planet of Mercury. The effects of the sun or moon in this sign are analytical and creative. Work spells involving intellect, employment, wealth, health, purification and modesty. It is said that the sun or moon in Virgo encourages an abundant harvest.

Libra: is another sign associated with the love planet of Venus. The effects of the sun or moon in this sign are all to do with balance and harmony. Work spells involving friendship, love, fertility, law, justice and peace.

Scorpio: is a very powerful sign associated with the mysterious planet of Pluto. The effects of the sun or moon in this sign are all to do with transformation. Work spells involving sex, challenges, dramatic change, transformation, healing and determination.

Sagittarius: is associated with Jupiter, the planet of great luck. The effects of the sun or moon in this sign are authoritative and sympathetic. Work spells involving travel, wisdom, wealth, success, transcendence, getting the truth of a matter, honesty, expansion, searching for someone or something and all philosophical matters.

Capricorn: is associated with the systematic planet of Saturn. The effects of the sun or moon in this sign are all to do with overcoming obstacles. Work spells involving ambition, wealth, self-control, success, responsibility and climbing up the career ladder.

Aquarius: is associated with the eccentric and ecstatic planet of Uranus. The effects of the sun or moon in this sign promotes mental health, intellect and higher thoughts. Work spells involving health, healing, intelligence, humanitarianism, friendships, independence, increasing personal freedom, creative expression and animal magic. Aquarius is strongly associated with the welfare of animals.

Pisces: is associated with the watery planet of Neptune. The effects of the sun or moon in this sign are compassionate and emotional. Work spells involving dream work, psychic work, endings, issues to do with children and artistic talent.

Spells and the Seasons

Another way to really enhance our spellcraft is to work with the four seasons of nature. Each season can have an enormous psychological effect on the mind. Each can thus have a powerful effect on specific types of spellcraft. Following are each of the seasons and the types of spells that are best cast during each:

Spring: is a wonderful time of rebirth and renewal. Birds sing and rejoice as the sun shines stronger with each day that passes and the earth becomes greener. Use spring for spells involving healing, fertility, purification (spring cleaning is a remnant of this), garden or herb magic, finance, psychic awareness and air magic. The two Sabbats for this season are Imbolc and Eostar.

Summer: is a time to celebrate the heightened strength of the sun. It is a time of great power when the fruits of the land are readily apparent. Use summer for spells involving love, healing, fertility, success, marriage, beauty, friendship, courage, protection, physical energy, strength and fire magic. Summer is said to add enormous magical power to spells. The two Sabbats for this season are Beltane and Litha.

Autumn: is a time of decline when leaves drop to the ground and animals prepare for their long rest over the winter. Summer is gone and we gather in the bounty of the year's harvest. Use autumn for spells involving money, new possessions, employment, beauty, healing, love, tranquillity, fertility and water magic. The two Sabbats for this season are Lughnasadh and Mabon.

Winter: is a time of death and destruction. It is the time when life returns to the earth, the symbolic womb of the Goddess, to rest in preparation for the following spring. Use winter for spells involving banishment, healing, recognition, breaking addictions, seeking past lives, stability, determination and earth magic. Winter is a time to put to death any burdens so that we can prepare for the coming of spring. The two Sabbats for this season are Samhain and Yule.

Spells and the Four Winds

Some Witches also like to work with the four winds. Since ancient times many magical peoples have thought of the wind as being four basic types. These are the north wind, the east wind, the south wind and the west wind. These winds are associated with the four sacred elements of nature and each has specific magical virtues that are very useful for specific types of spells. You can use a compass to find out where the wind is blowing from at a given time. Following are the four winds and the spells best cast during each:

North Wind: The north wind is associated with the element of earth. It is known as the wind of death and transformation because of its association with winter. All spells are said to be empowered when the wind is blowing from the north. However, it is particularly powerful for spells that release depression, anxiety, envy, anger, jealousy and additions. The north wind is also very useful for all types of healing spells. It is strongly associated with the time of midnight.

East Wind: is associated with the element of air. It is the wind associated with spring and with freshness, new beginnings and intellect. It represents the increasing heat of the sun and the spark of potential and creation. Use it in all spells that involve dramatic improvement and changes for the better. Spells involving fertility, growth and purification are ideal when the wind blows from the east. The east wind is strongly associated with the time of dawn.

South Wind: is a hot and fiery one associated with the summer. It is the wind associated with light, illumination and enlightenment. All spells are said to be empowered when the wind is blowing from the south. It can give spells an enormous jolt of magical power. Spells involving courage, healing, strength, protection and physical energy are said to be particularly powerful during the time of a south wind. The south wind is strongly associated with the time of noon.

West Wind: is associated with the element of water. It is a cool, loving and moist wind associated with autumn. When the wind blows from the west it brings forward the gentle energies of that cardinal point. It is excellent for all spells involving love, tranquillity, reflection, money, employment, new possessions, religious magic, healing and fertility. The west wind can be a welcome relief after the dry and hot wind from the south. It is strongly associated with the time of dusk.

Spells and Correspondences

Magical correspondences are like lists of ingredients for our spellcraft. This is the best way to think of them. This book is full of information on magical correspondences. Knowledge of magical correspondences is the basis for successful spellcraft and is important for any Witch's development. Magical correspondences – herbs, crystals, stones, planets, metals, colours, animals and so on – enhance and empower our spellcraft. Each has unique, spiritual and magical associations that can give our spells a magical boost. By working with magical correspondences, a Witch is able to feel the presence of the Goddess and God and the life force of the universe. Magical correspondences help Witches to draw closer to the natural powers of the earth and that of the universe.

So how exactly would a Witch work with magical correspondences? Let's say, for example, you had a job interview and you wanted to be successful in it. That being the case, a spell that specifically asks for success would be in order. Some example correspondences for success include the following: the planet of Jupiter, a rose quartz crystal, the colour green and the herbs of rowan, hawthorn, lemon balm and ginger. Using this information you would first need to find or write a suitable spell (I will give you some examples of spells throughout part two of this book) and then you could do the following:

- Cast your spell on Jupiter's sacred day (Thursday).
- Wear a necklace with a rose quartz crystal on it during the casting of your spell.
- Fill a green sachet with the leaves of rowan, hawthorn and lemon balm and place this sachet under your pillow once your spell is complete.
- Create a ginger infusion to drink during the casting of your spell.

The possibilities of working with magical correspondences are virtually endless. Simply experiment with them and in this way you will gain a deeper knowledge and understanding of them for your magical workings.

Spells and Herbs

Herbs can be very useful in our spellcraft. Peoples of all religions and cultures have used herbs in magical or spiritual work since very ancient times. In Witchcraft, we generally associate the word "herbs" with all plants and trees that are known to have medicinal or magical uses. Knowledge of the medicinal and magical uses of herbs should be, in my opinion, a priority for any Witch's development. Most Witches are drawn to herbalism because Witchcraft is a nature-based religion that seeks to work with the natural powers of Gaia. It helps us to work with her on all levels. Herbs are wonderful manifestations of divine power.

To develop a knowledge of herbs, you will have to study herbalism. You can also grow your own herbs; plant a herb garden; visit garden centres or plant nurseries; and identify herbs that grow near your home and study their specific folklore. Always remember that some herbs are toxic and so caution should be taken when working with herbs. Don't ingest any herbs that are not meant to be consumed. Be reasonable when working with any herbs that you are unsure of as some can cause adverse reactions in certain circumstances, such as during pregnancy, breastfeeding or when on certain medications. In addition, some herbs may be harmful when used for long periods of time. Some may also be harmful to children. Following are some of the ways in which Witches use herbs within their practices (always bear in mind, however, that fresh herbs are best since these have the most potent energies):

Incense: The creation of incense is an art in and of itself. In spellcraft and other magical work, incense is burned to release the specific vibrational energies within the herbs that are used. These herbs usually correspond to the type of work that the Witch, or group of Witches, is performing. Incense is created by combining herb materials and often with oils. The incense is then burned or smouldered on charcoal.

Infusions: are simply herbal teas. I adore using them within my practices. They are the origin of the "potions" that are so related to Witchcraft and are very useful in many types of spells and other magical workings. As well as being special drinks for medicinal and magical purposes, they are sometimes added to purification baths in preparation for sacred and magical work. They are also very simple to create. I would suggest one teaspoon of dried herb or herbs to every mug of water. Generally, to create a herbal infusion place the dried herb or herbs directly into a mug and pour on hot (but not boiling) water. Let the infusion steep for nine to thirteen minutes before straining. The tea will then be ready to use.

Oils: The uses of oils in magical work are varied. They can be worn on the body, dabbed on magical tools, added to ritual baths, smeared on roots, added to creams, burned on charcoal and so on. You can buy oils from shops but please be aware that these may be synthetic. If they smell good, however, they will still be effective in magical workings. Oils are usually created using a complex distillation process. Oils are very useful in spells and other magical work that utilise candles. Anointing candles with an oil that relates to your goal is a simple process. If you are wanting to draw something to you, anoint your candle from the base and work your way to the middle. If you are wanting to draw away energy, anoint your candle from the middle and work your way to the base of it. When handling essential oils, it is best to mix them with a carrier oil, such as almond or sunflower oil.

Ointments: The uses of herbs as ointments are an ancient form of magic and medicine. An ointment is simply a mixture of any fatty substance along with herb materials and/or oils. Vegetable shortening is better as a base, however, than lard. It also smells much better than lard. In spellcraft, ointments are usually created simply by placing the fatty substance into a cup along with the herb or herbs and/or oils. This substance is then pounded or smashed together while using visualisation. It can then be placed into an airtight container to store.

Sachets: When herbs are carried or used in the home it is best to place them into sachets. A herbal sachet is a small bag or piece of cloth in which herbs are contained. In Voodoo, a herbal sachet is known as a "charm bag" or a "root bag". They are incredibly simple to create. To use them in magical workings, take a small amount of cloth material. This can be square, triangular or round. The colour of the cloth material should relate to the type of work you are wanting to carry out. Place the herbs, dried or fresh, into the centre of this cloth material. Then gather the ends of the cloth material together and tie it up, making sure that no herbs escape, with a cord or yarn of an appropriate colour.

Tinctures: are used in very much the same ways as herbal infusions. They are created for future magical workings because, unlike herbal infusions, they have a shelf life of at least two years. Tinctures involve the use of alcohol to make a much more concentrated extract than herbal infusions. To create a tincture use a clean glass jar with a tight fitting lid. Then grind the herb or herbs into a fine powder with a pestle and a mortar. Add this to the jar and cover it with alcohol. Vodka is fine. Put the lid on the jar and secure it tight and then shake the mixture up. The mixture should then be stored in a cool, dark place until the alcohol takes on the colour of the herb or herbs. You should then strain your tincture through a cheesecloth into another clean glass jar with a tight fitting lid. Your tincture is then ready for use.

Spells and Runic Magic

One way to really propel your spells along is with the use of the runes. I adore using runes in my magical workings. Runes are traditionally used for divination but they are also highly useful in spellcraft and other magical workings. When they are drawn, painted, carved, traced, worn, carried or visualised they can help us to release specific powers towards our needs and goals. They are a set of magical symbols from the Old Norse or Germanic cultures and have been used in magical practices for millennia. It is believed that they were created before 200 B. C. E. as an alphabet used to keep records. The word *"rune"* means "mystery" or "secret" and this is because the runes are very mysterious symbols that represent hidden knowledge, wisdom, power and spirituality. As we have seen, the runes are associated with the Norse god Odin who won the runes after his ordeal hanging from the Yggdrasil, the Tree of the World. Once this mysterious god had won the runes he achieved enlightenment, power and wisdom. He then gave his runes to the people as a magical gift. In divination, runes are usually shaken in a bag and then a specific number is drawn for interpretation. This form of divination (along with many other forms) is known as casting lots and is once again gaining popularity.

Today, Witches may buy their own runes or simply make them. There are many bookstores today that have sets of runes available for purchase. The internet is also a good place to look for runic sets. Witches who create their own runes may simply paint them on materials, perhaps on chips of wood or on pebbles collected from beaches. Some Witches may also simply buy some glass pebbles that florists use in vases and simply paint the runes on them. Many of these pebbles come in beautiful colours. Following are the twenty-four runes and their uses in magic and spellcraft:

Fehu: This rune describes value. It speaks of the need to defend, protect and appreciate whatever you hold dear. Use it in spells that involve money, wealth, possessions, projects, food, prosperity, redistribution and strength. It is also good for spells that protect these things.

Uruz: This rune is all to do with the strength, courage and mental or physical stamina needed to face problems or obstacles. It represents the responsibility we have to take for our actions. Use it in spells involving challenges, overcoming problems, courage, strength, health, transformation and dramatic change.

Thurisaz: This rune describes the turbulences of life that act as catalysts for positive or constructive change. In divination it warns that difficulties and problems may arise without warning. Use it in spells involving breakthroughs, dramatic change, defence, protection, generosity, overcoming difficult situations and opposition.

Ansuz: This rune is all to do with communication in its many and varied forms. It represents contact with family, friends and associates who are respected and admired. It is associated with the need within us to understand others as well as ourselves. Use it in spells involving inspiration, communication (especially with other people), movement, progress, passing tests, speech, wisdom and eloquence.

Raidho: This rune is associated with journeys of every description. It also represents the ability to rise above any problems and to put our decisions into action. Use it in spells involving travel, good fortune, negotiations, luck, getting something to move ahead and astral travel.

Kenaz: This is a very positive rune that is all to do with energy and enthusiasm. But it also describes the need to channel this positivity in the right directions in life. It represents the light shed on areas of life that have been dark and destructive. Use it in spells involving creativity, banishment, illumination, enlightenment, wisdom, healing, recovery, proposals and fire magic.

Gebo: This rune speaks of love, talents and gifts. It describes the receiving or giving of love and working for higher purposes. It also speaks of the rewards we receive from the sacrifices we take in life. Use it in spells involving healing, bonding with others, partnerships, gifts, love, creating balance and good will.

Wunjo: This rune is associated with happiness, contentment and laughter. It also warns us to be careful what we wish for in life. Use it in spells involving success, binding groups together in a positive way, companionship, happiness, strong results and relationships.

Hagalaz: This rune is all about learning from personal experiences. It speaks of the positivity, wisdom and knowledge that will come from these experiences. Use it in spells involving transformation, dramatic change, balance, unification, reconciliation, overcoming obstacles, banishment, blessings and defence.

Nauthiz: This rune speaks of the need to sort out any priorities. It represents the need to face the facts of life in order to improve negative situations and to move forward in life. Use it in spells involving adversity, patience, necessities, seeking freedom, finding liberation, repelling negative people and turning bad situations into good ones.

Isa: This rune speaks of those situations of life that are in a state of limbo or are frozen in some way. It represents the resistance of necessary change. Use it in spells involving freezing a situation, finding clarity, binding magic, blocking negative thoughts or energies, isolation, rest and recuperation.

Jera: This rune symbolises both death and rebirth. It represents the end of one cycle and the beginning of the next. It speaks of the state of being in a period of transition. It is also a very nostalgic rune associated with living in the past. Use it in spells involving completions, strong results, harvesting what you have done, bringing rewards that you have worked for, improving situations, transformation and dramatic change.

Eihwaz: This rune links with our ancestors and ancient wisdom. It also represents that we must show endurance when facing the problems that life throws at us. It speaks of the need to keep on keeping on no matter what our problems are. Use it in spells involving averting disaster, flexibility, contact with ancestors, wisdom, finishing projects, achievement and closure.

Perthro: This rune is all about looking beyond the surface of life in order to gain knowledge and inner wisdom. It also speaks of the need to take note of our dreams to discover inner secrets about our deep spiritual selves. This rune also symbolises birth in all its forms – both symbolically and literally. Use it in spells involving good luck, good fortune, the recovery of things feared or lost, joy, gaining understanding, fertility, fresh ideas and growth.

Algiz: This rune speaks of the need to find your spiritual path. It is a protective rune that represents the need to seek spiritual awareness. Use it in spells involving psychic development, protection, luck, defence, peace, banishment, personal and spiritual change, evolution of the self and friendship.

Sowilo: This is an optimistic rune that tells us to remain enthusiastic even through the difficult times. It speaks of success regardless of the hard times we face. This is a good rune for those who are involved with music or poetry. Use it in spells involving health, healing, success, victory, making wise choices and guidance.

Tiwaz: This rune speaks of bravery and relates to the battles that are fought for the common good. Use it in spells that involve competitiveness, victory, strength, justice, success and courage. This rune will help you to add strength and high energy to spells.

Berkano: This rune speaks of fertility in all its forms as well as secrets that have yet to be discovered. It is favoured by those who wish to enhance their creative projects. Use it in spells involving growth, expansion, fertility of any kind, discipline, interpersonal skills, fairness, patience, projects, motherhood issues and purification.

Ehwaz: This rune represents any form of travel and the benefits of a harmonious and fruitful partnership. It also describes the need for communication, cooperation and flexibility. Use it in spells involving travel, gradual changes, growth, communication, hard work, new places, partnerships, overcoming obstacles within group work and psychic development with others.

Mannaz: This rune describes the need to use intelligence and objectivity regarding difficult situations. It also describes the need to use consideration with regards to other people. Use it in spells involving justice, dignity, self-esteem, issues to do with the mind, intelligence, career, employment, school work and all issues to do with humanitarianism.

Laguz: This rune speaks of the need to tune into intuition and to strengthen psychic powers. It also describes women's cycles and that something is coming slowly but surely. Use it in spells involving female magic, pregnancy, conduits, psychic sensitivity, travel, seeking balance and glamour.

Ingwaz: This rune represents the onset of projects, friendships and relationships. It speaks of the times when they are beginning to develop and to strengthen. It also encourages us to appreciate life despite any adversity. Use it in spells involving fertility, beginnings, friendships, relationships, family issues, consolidation, domestic property and seeking opportunities.

Othala: This rune represents the things that are passed on from one generation to another. It speaks of those things that are passed down – money, possessions, character traits and so on. Use it in spells involving inheritance, separation, material and spiritual legacy, preservation of customs and laws, prosperity, finding fortunate influences and family issues.

Dagaz: This rune is all to do with fresh starts and new beginnings – whether physical, mental, emotional or spiritual. When life becomes difficult this rune represents that things are about to improve. Use it in spells involving dramatic change, finding the truth of matters, beauty, finding balance and harmony, clarity and transformation.

Note: Some Witches have runic sets that include a blank rune. This rune, however, is not a part of the original set of runes that our ancestors worked with. It is supposed to mean fate or destiny and it is entirely up to you if you want to work with a blank rune in your magical procedures.

Spells and Poppets

All spells need to be properly directed in order for them to work and one very effective way to do this is with the use of poppets. These are simple, magical dolls that have been used in magic and spellcraft in many cultures and civilisations for eons – at least four thousand years. They are also often known as "Voodoo dolls". The ancient Greeks used these dolls to protect themselves against evil spirits or to bind two lovers together. West African slaves often used them as protective devices. Around the British Isles, these little figures were referred to as mommets and this term was used to describe figures of both sexes. Some Witches nowadays use the term poppet for a male doll and the term mommet for a female doll. Though other modern Witches, myself included, simply use the term poppet for dolls of both sexes.

A poppet is a humanoid figure that can be made of cloth, wax, paper, clay, wood, roots, lead, bark or any other material. It can even be a chess piece, a puppet, a Barbie or Ken doll, a piece of twisted wire, a piece of twisted cord or anything else. It really doesn't matter as long as it has a basic humanoid shape. The poppet is then used to represent a particular person in spellcraft. In other words, your poppet can represent yourself or anyone else who you wish to influence. Poppets can be used in all forms of magic – love, luck, prosperity, fertility, protection, healing and so forth. When a poppet is made of cloth it can be stuffed with items that represent the magical goal. In the case of a healing spell, for example, healing herbs and stones can be stuffed into the doll. The poppet's stuffing may also involve the hair and fingernail clippings of the person that it represents. Alternatively, these items can be placed around the doll if it is something else that can't be stuffed.

A poppet is very simple to activate during spellcraft. Simply bring forward in your mind any thoughts and feelings you have about the person that the poppet represents. If the poppet represents yourself, simply think of your personality traits. Then hold your hands over the poppet until you feel a tingling sensation in them and say these or similar words:

O poppet made of cloth I now name you...

Then simply say the name of the person who the poppet represents. If you have a photograph of the person that you're wishing to influence then all the better. His or her face can be affixed to the poppet to help you to visualise the person more efficiently. After you have cast the spell, the poppet should then be safeguarded until the spell fully takes effect. Once the spell has worked simply see the poppet as nothing more than a doll with no connection to the person that it was used to cast the spell on. Then you can perhaps pick it apart or smash it and bury the remains in a garden or local woodland. Alternatively, simply throw them in the sea or other body of water. Only do these, however, if the remains of your poppet are biodegradable or environmentally friendly. If they are not, simply throw them in a recycling bin.

Spells and Witch-Bottles

The creation of Witch-bottles are another magical activity that I adore doing during my spellcraft. They are fun and easy to create. Whenever I think of Witch-bottles I think of the Witch-bottle I created for protection some time ago because the effects were so powerful. Me and my partner were having trouble with youths outside our home. They were ganging up outside and making a lot of noise, calling me and my partner names, throwing things at the house, pulling my plants out of the garden and so on. So I decided to do a spell of protection that involved the making of a Witch-bottle. Once my bottle of protection was created I buried it in my garden near the front door next to my rosemary plant (which is also protective). As of this writing, me and my partner have had no problems with youths causing trouble for over ten years. I also planted hawthorns in my garden to aid the effects of my spell of protection.

You don't necessarily need special bottles to create Witch-bottles – you can simply use clean glass jars. If you do have pretty bottles, however, you can decorate them and make them an interesting feature in your home. Today, Witch-bottles are very similar in structure to those of historical times. Witch-bottles can be created for many purposes – financial gain, health, healing, attracting artistic creativity, fertility, success and so on – but they are most commonly created for protective purposes. A Witch-bottle of protection is said to capture negativity that is targeted at the Witch, his or her family or property and then transform this negativity into positivity. This positivity is then released into the surrounding area.

A Witch-bottle is basically any container, usually a clean glass bottle or jar, in which material objects are placed. These magical objects should relate to the type of spellcraft that the Witch is aiming to carry out. These magical objects are magically charged with the intent of the spell. It is said that Witch-bottles will continue to work for years or even possibly centuries as long as they do not become broken. A Witch-bottle may contain anything that the Witch deems important for the type of work he or she is doing – herbs, crystals, stones, woods, nails, sand or different coloured sands, knotted cords or threads, spices, gums, resins, incense, salt, vinegar, coins, ashes, votive candles or anything else. In actuality, anything that is used in "normal spells" can be used in this bottled version of spellcraft. Old Witch-bottles called for bodily fluids, hair and fingernail clippings. Witches today may or may not use these types of things. This is entirely up to you if you choose to work with Witch-bottles.

Spells, Amulets and Talismans

Amulets and talismans are special, magical objects that are incorporated into our spellcraft. Although some people confuse amulets with talismans, there are differences between the two. Amulets are generally objects that are used for protective purposes. They help Witches and magicians to remove and repel evil or negativity. Talismans, on the other hand, are objects that attract specific energies to Witches and magicians. They are magical charms that attract wealth, prosperity, happiness, success, good health and so on.

Talismans are created for a specific purpose whereas amulets serve a general protective purpose. Amulets and talismans are magically charged with the intents of spells and are then worn, carried or placed somewhere special in the home. They can be anything really as long as they relate to your goals. They can be pieces of wood with special symbols carved on them (such as the runes), pieces of herb materials, crystals or stones, dried flowers, coins, bracelets, metals and so on.

The use of talismans in particular is ancient – dating back thousands of years. The ancient Egyptians, for instance, used these special, magical charms in many of their magical workings. They also used them in their death rites to help to safely deliver the souls of the dead to the other side of the threshold of death. Some Witches believe that a talisman will only hold the magical intent of the spell for a year and a day, while others believe that it will hold it for up to nine years. When talismans have served their purposes, however, many Witches bury them in the earth or throw them in the sea or other body of water as a gesture of respect to nature and the Earth Mother.

Spell Materials and a Magical Pantry

Never frustrate yourself trying to obtain special, exotic objects when you come to performing your spellcraft. Simply use whatever you have to hand. Remember that spellcraft requires you to use your creativity. Thoroughly learn magical correspondences and over time you can use substitutes for spells that require something that you don't have. If you need to cast a spell just gather together whatever you can. In the meantime, you can begin creating a special, magical pantry. This can be any spare kitchen cupboard where you can place all your special tools as well as your magical correspondences. Over time, you can build up on your collection. A magical pantry is a very handy thing to have in your home. It can be a convenient place where you can always find your spell and ritual materials.

Robes or Skyclad?

The other thing that you may want to consider is how you are actually going to present yourself when you decide to perform spellcraft. Some Witches like to wear robes, while others like to perform their spells skyclad (naked), though neither way is essential. You can actually present yourself in any way you like. I personally usually wear my brown robes for spellcraft and other magical workings that my partner gave me as a Yule gift. Witches may wear robes for a variety of different reasons. One of the most common reasons is that wearing robes specifically set aside for magical procedures helps us to slip into a more ritual frame of mind. It creates a mystical atmosphere and shifts our awareness on to the magical workings ahead. It, therefore, helps us to promote ritual consciousness. Some Witches wear robes that are also hooded. It is believed that robes with hoods can help us to shut off outside interferences so that we can truly concentrate. It is thought to control sensory stimulation during magical workings. Other Witches, however, don't like to be hooded because they believe that it shuts us too far away from the true energies of the natural world. I personally believe that robes with hoods are excellent for meditation when we really do have to focus our attention on our inner selves. You can buy robes or simply make them but it is best to use natural materials, such as cotton or silk.

Skyclad is favoured by many Witches – especially those of the more formal traditions of Witchcraft. The reason for this primarily lies in the fact that Witches see the human body as a sacred manifestation of divine power. There is nothing wrong, evil or shameful about the naked human body. Ritual nudity was practised in many ancient magical religions. Unfortunately, the Christian religion did much to instil negative associations with regards to the naked body and these distorted, unnatural emotions still exist to this day within the minds of many people. When Witches perform their magical workings naked it represents that we are willing to stand before the Goddess and God the way we came into the world. It represents that we are willing to stand before the Goddess and God, mother and father of all nature, the way nature originally intended us to be. It symbolises honesty, innocence and openness. It is considered a blessed and whole state and is a way of promoting reverence for nature and the physical world. When a Witch is naked it is believed that nothing can come between him or her and the powers of the universe. Remember that Witchcraft is a nature religion that seeks to celebrate both its physical and spiritual aspects. Some Witches believe that a clothed body can't emit as much power during magical workings as effectively as the naked body can. Though other Witches believe that clothing is no barrier to the transference of magical power. How you personally present yourself in your spellcraft is entirely up to you.

Performing High Magic

Although there is no right or wrong way to cast a spell, there are basically thirteen components that are considered to be of central importance to the performing of high magic by many Witches. Each of these steps plays a special, magical role in guaranteeing the success of your spellcraft in formal magic. These components are:

- General preparation.
- Purification of self.
- Consecration of the altar and tools.
- Purification of the sacred space.
- Casting of the magic circle.
- Invocation of the elements.
- Invocation of deities.
- Raising the power.
- Fulfilment of purpose.
- Earthing the power.
- Thanksgiving and farewell to deities.
- Thanksgiving and farewell to the elements.
- Breaking the magic circle.

Each of these components will be delineated for the remainder of this chapter. My hope is that you will gain inspiration from the way I have explained these steps so that you can find your own unique style when performing high magic. Good luck.

General Preparation

To begin preparing for a spell, you must first be clear on the intention. Your intention focuses your mind and effectively channels your absolute will to succeed. A spell will simply not work properly unless you learn how to properly focus your willpower. So your intention must be crystal clear or you may have unintended results. I would suggest that you study your spell carefully before you actually carry it out so that you know exactly what it is that you need to do. Spells are best done when they build up inside us before we actually carry them out. Once you are focused on the intention of your spell you can then begin to assemble your tools and magical correspondences on your altar as well as prepare your sacred space for the magical workings ahead. This is important because it will help you to focus your willpower as you gather your special tools, herbs, ink, paper, pens, matches, oils, candles, incense, crystals, stones, feathers, metals, runes and so on. Remember that knowledge of correspondences is essential for this so that you know for sure the items that are in tune with your spell.

The area in which you have chosen to work should also be tidy. Clutter attracts negative energy and shows a lack of respect for spiritual work. In essence, it clutters the mind and distracts our attention from the magical workings ahead. If you are working indoors, you should vacuum, brush and/or mop the floor. If your temple does not have a carpet, you can mop the floor with a purification infusion. An infusion of hyssop is excellent for this. The physical cleansing of your temple will help you to centre and clear your mind. This is important for magical procedures. If you are performing your spell outdoors, simply make sure your chosen sacred space is litter free. All of the above preparation is actually the very beginnings of your spell.

Purification of Self

The next step that you may want to take for formal magic is the purification of the self. Many Witches consider this part of high magic to be essential. Purification of the self is another way of helping us to focus on the intention of the spell. It also helps us to remove any negativity that may be dwelling inside us. The most effective way to purify the self, in my opinion, is to take a ritual bath. Water is the ultimate element of purification and taking a ritual bath allows us to spiritually connect with it. Having a ritual bath is a very spiritual thing to do. It cleanses the body of any physical dirt and thus removes negativity from the mind, body and soul. In short, it prepares us physically and spiritually for the magical workings ahead. Having a ritual bath heals away the stresses and strains of life so that we can really focus on the spell. It is a way for us to let go of the mundane activities of the everyday physical world; to centre the mind; and to shift our awareness on to more spiritual and magical matters.

Have you ever noticed how differently you feel when you are bathed and how differently you perceive things? You will probably feel a lot lighter and that your stress levels are reduced. Well, it is these feelings that will help you to get the most out of your spellcraft. It is these feelings that will help you to draw closer to the Goddess and God. This is exactly what a purification bath is designed for. "Cleanliness is next to Godliness" as the old saying goes. Negative emotions simply distract our attention from the divine and our needs and goals. They stop us from focusing on spiritual and magical matters and a purification bath is one excellent way for us to prevent these negative emotions from happening during magical workings.

To prepare a purification bath, add some salt (sea salt is best) to the running water. Then add some purification herbs as well as herbal oils and/or infusions. The best herbs for purification include rosemary, sage, lavender, chamomile and jasmine. You may also like to burn purification herbs as incense in the bathroom to aid the purification process. While you bathe, you may like to place a purification crystal on your third eye chakra such as a clear quartz crystal. The third eye chakra is located between your eyebrows. This will help you to open up your spiritual awareness because the third eye chakra is an energy point which allows us to "see" the spiritual or magical realms. The purification crystal will help you to activate it. While you are in the process of taking your purification bath visualise the stresses and strains of the day washing away from your body.

If you can't take a ritual bath, however, a ritual shower can be very effective as well. Simply place some purification herbs in the centre of a small, clean cloth and secure them in this cloth with a cord or yarn. You can then use this to wash your body. While you do this visualise any negativity washing away from your body and going down the plughole. When you emerge from your purification bath or shower pat yourself dry and lie on your bed for a few moments to gather your thoughts for the magical workings of your spell and know that your body has been purified and freed of the stresses and strains of the day.

Of course, there are other methods of purifying yourself that can also be very effective. Purification is really any activity that allows us to shift our awareness away from everyday mundane activities and on to more spiritual matters. Some Witches, for example, simply like to observe oncoming thunderstorms and lightning. These are dramatic times of intense magical power that can really propel our magical workings along. They are times that clear the air and are thus very effective for purifying the mind, body and soul.

Other ways in which Witches may purify themselves include sitting under the healing rays of the sun for a few moments, observing the full moon at night and skinny-dipping in the sea or other body of water. All of these example purification activities in this paragraph are particularly excellent for spellcraft conducted far away from the home – places where a purification bath or shower are not possible. Simply find the methods of purification that work best for you and your circumstances.

Consecration of the Altar and Tools

The next stage of high magic that you may want to consider is the consecration of your altar and tools. This process essentially activates your altar and all the tools on and around it spiritually. It also removes any negative vibrations that may have become attached to them, charges them with your personal power, asks for the blessings of the Goddess and God to be placed upon them and makes them fit for ritual and magical use. The consecration process makes your altar and tools effective for their proper use within the magic circle. If your altar frame itself is an item of furniture that you use in your home then it will have the potential to pick up negative vibrations from others that you live with or even yourself depending on what is going on in your life and so it is always best to carry out this process for high magic.

To carry out the consecration process, you can simply mix a small amount of salt into a bowl of water. Then bunch together some purification herbs – such as bay, chamomile, lavender, parsley, rosemary, sage and thyme – with a white cord or ribbon and place this in the centre of your altar. Then light the Goddess and God candles and if you are using candles/incense to represent the four elements of nature, light these also. Then hold your representation of the element of earth over your altar and circle it three times deosil (clockwise) and say these or similar words:

In the presence of spirit all around me,
I circle this symbol of the element of earth,
To cleanse and purify my altar and tools of negativity.
Spiritually my altar and tools are consecrated,
And endowed with the virtues of the sacred element of earth,
And fit for ritual and magical use.
Blessings be.

Then see in your mind's eye negative energy dissipating from your altar and tools and place your representation of earth back to its appropriate place on the altar. Then when you are ready, hold your representation of the element of air over your altar and circle it three times deosil and say these or similar words:

In the presence of spirit all around me,
I circle this symbol of the element of air,
To cleanse and purify my altar and tools of negativity.
Spiritually my altar and tools are consecrated,
And endowed with the virtues of the sacred element of air,
And fit for ritual and magical use.
Blessings be.

Then see in your mind's eye negative energy dissipating from your altar and tools and place your representation of air back to its appropriate place on the altar. Then when you are ready, hold your representation of the element of fire over your altar and circle it three times deosil and say these or similar words:

In the presence of spirit all around me,

> *I circle this symbol of the element of fire,*
> *To cleanse and purify my altar and tools of negativity.*
> *Spiritually my altar and tools are consecrated,*
> *And endowed with the virtues of the sacred element of fire,*
> *And fit for ritual and magical use.*
> *Blessings be.*

Then see in your mind's eye negative energy dissipating from your altar and tools and place your representation of fire back to its appropriate place on the altar. Then when you are ready, hold your representation of the element of water over your altar and circle it three times deosil and say these or similar words:

> *In the presence of spirit all around me,*
> *I circle this symbol of the element of water,*
> *To cleanse and purify my altar and tools of negativity.*
> *Spiritually my altar and tools are consecrated,*
> *And endowed with the virtues of the sacred element of water,*
> *And fit for ritual and magical use.*
> *Blessings be.*

Then see in your mind's eye negative energy dissipating from your altar and tools and place your representation of water back to its appropriate place on the altar. Then when you are ready, dip your bunched purification herbs in the consecration water and gently splash (this is known as asperging) your altar and tools and then see in your mind's eye them glowing with an electric blue colour. You can also trace a pentagram over your altar and tools with your index finger while saying these or similar words:

> *O Mother Goddess and Father God,*
> *Lady and Lord of all nature,*
> *I humbly ask for your all-powerful blessings to be placed*
> *on my altar and tools.*
> *May they be consecrated and empowered with your virtues,*
> *And fit for ritual and magical use in your honour.*
> *So mote it be.*

Purification of the Sacred Space

The next stage of high magic usually involves the purification of the sacred space itself. This process rids the sacred space of any astral clutter or negativity and makes it fit for ritual and magical workings. One of the best ways to do this is with the broomstick. Simply take a hold of your broomstick and stand in the centre of your sacred space, facing north. Then begin by giving long and brisk sweeps from the centre of your sacred space to the boundaries of it. Continue doing this in a deosil fashion all the way around your chosen sacred space. The bristles do not actually have to touch the floor for this. While you are sweeping, see in your mind's eye any blocked energy or negativity dissipating from the sacred space. I usually do this three times. With this done, you may then take a hold of your representation of the element of earth and then walk once around your sacred space with it and say these or similar words:

In the presence of spirit all around me,
I walk the sacred space with my representation
of the element of earth,
To cleanse and purify my temple of negativity.
Spiritually my sacred space is consecrated,
And endowed with the virtues of the sacred element of earth,
And fit for ritual and magical use.
Blessings be.

Then see in your mind's eye negative energy dissipating from your sacred space and place your representation of earth back to its appropriate place on the altar. Then when you are ready, hold your representation of the element of air and then walk once around your sacred space with it and say these or similar words:

In the presence of spirit all around me,
I walk the sacred space with my representation
of the element of air,
To cleanse and purify my temple of negativity.
Spiritually my sacred space is consecrated,
And endowed with the virtues of the sacred element of air,

And fit for ritual and magical use.
Blessings be.

Then see in your mind's eye negative energy dissipating from your sacred space and place your representation of air back to its appropriate place on the altar. Then when you are ready, hold your representation of the element of fire and then walk once around your sacred space with it and say these or similar words:

In the presence of spirit all around me,
I walk the sacred space with my representation
of the element of fire,
To cleanse and purify my temple of negativity.
Spiritually my sacred space is consecrated,
And endowed with the virtues of the sacred element of fire,
And fit for ritual and magical use.
Blessings be.

Then see in your mind's eye negative energy dissipating from your sacred space and place your representation of fire back to its appropriate place on the altar. Then when you are ready, hold your representation of the element of water and then walk once around your sacred space with it and say these or similar words:

In the presence of spirit all around me,
I walk the sacred space with my representation
of the element of water,
To cleanse and purify my temple of negativity.
Spiritually my sacred space is consecrated,
And endowed with the virtues of the sacred element of water,
And fit for ritual and magical use.
Blessings be.

Then see in your mind's eye negative energy dissipating from your sacred space and place your representation of water back to its appropriate place on the altar. Then when you are ready, dip the bunched purification herbs in your consecration water and gently splash your sacred space and say these or similar words:

O Mother Goddess and Father God,
Lady and Lord of all nature,
I humbly ask for your all-powerful blessings to be placed
on my sacred space.
May it be consecrated and empowered with your virtues,
And fit for ritual and magical use in your honour.
So mote it be.

Casting of the Magic Circle

This part of high magic is essential. The magic circle is a non-physical, though well-defined, sphere of personal power in which magical workings take place. It is a non-physical temple of the Goddess and God. I always imagine the circle inside a square during my magical workings, with the four points representing the four cardinal directions and the elements that they represent. The magic circle has truly ancient origins. There were forms of it in Old Babylonian ceremonial magic. Indian tribes and ceremonial magicians in medieval times and the Renaissance also utilised them. In Britain, not too far from where I live, there are two example structures that indicate just how important the magic circle was for our ancient ancestors. These are Stonehenge and the Avebury Stones, which are said to be astronomical clocks and cosmic calculators that follow the cyclical movements of the sun, moon and planets. There is said to be much paranormal activity around these sites. The fact that most animals curl up in a circle to sleep and that birds instinctively build their nests in a circular shape are other indications of the magic circle's natural protective and sacred associations.

In magical workings, the magic circle serves as a sphere of protection. It keeps out any unwanted, negative, astral energies or entities that may be attracted to the energy of our work. Witches also cast a magic circle because it contains and amplifies the power that we raise. In major magical workings, there is a lot of energy that is raised and the magic circle stops this energy from escaping or dissipating. The circle puts good use to the energy that is raised. The circle is also a place where we meet the Goddess and God or their specific deities. One day, science may be able to explain the physics behind the magic circle, but Witches know, through experience, that the laws of physics operate somewhat differently within the magic circle. Time, for one thing, seems to operate differently – what can feel like twenty minutes can actually turn out to be an hour or more. Fire seems to burn differently within the magic circle and things that don't usually explode are more likely to do so.

Although the circle is a non-physical sphere of energy, many Witches like to make it also a physical reality. This can be done simply by placing objects or substances in a circular shape around the boundaries of your sacred space. To create a circle of power, it has to be seen in the mind's eye to bring it alive and so placing objects or substances in a circular shape is a very effective way to help you to visualise the magic circle. You can place anything that appeals to you around the boundaries of your sacred space to help you to visualise the magic circle – sand, shells, stones, crystals, glitter, herbs, woods, candles and so on. It's whatever you are comfortable with really. You can even use chalk to draw a circle on the ground around the boundaries of your sacred space. It's your circle so have it exactly how you would like it.

To create a magic circle, walk the boundaries of your sacred space three times deosil. You can begin at the north and end at the north each time if you wish, as I always do. See in your mind's eye a sphere of pure, white light encapsulating your sacred space with the top half of it above the ground and the bottom half of it below the ground. You may also like to point your index finger, wand, athame or sword out as you walk your magic circle. As you walk around your sacred space, say these or similar words:

> *I conjure you great circle,*
> *By the powers of the four sacred elements of nature*
> *and of the Goddess and God,*
> *A mighty sphere of protection now stands around me.*
> *This is a positive and protective shield,*
> *A powerful force field,*
> *Cast with harmony and love.*
> *By the powers of the land and sea,*
> *Of the moon and sun,*
> *And of the wind and rain,*

This circle is now activated.
It is a boundary line between gods,
elemental spirits and humankind,
A place where infinite knowledge
and magical power are now available to me.
The magical workings that take place herein
will be amplified by the Lord and the Lady,
And by the four sacred elements of nature.
May their blessings be ever upon me
and my work here within my sacred circle of power and protection.
So mote it be.

Invocation of the Elements

Invocation of the elements is a formal calling upon their powers – the elemental spirits. The elemental powers are actually ever-present forces all around us but the invocation of their powers allows us to experience them on a much deeper and more spiritual level. When Witches call upon the elemental powers at each of the four cardinal directions, it completes the magic circle and unifies all aspects of the self and that of the natural world. When the elemental powers are asked to join us they aid us, guide us, strengthen us and create harmony within our magical practices. They also become our protectors who watch over our work and heighten our awareness of the powers of the Goddess and God. Depending on the tradition, these elemental spirits may be known as the mighty ones, the guardians of the watchtowers or simply the guardians. Some traditions may salute the elemental powers with their athames or wands, others may trace pentagrams at each point, while others may simply let their words of power suffice. I usually hold my representations of each element up to their associated cardinal points while reciting some words of power.

To call upon the elemental spirits, you may want to begin at the north, as I always do. Then hold your representation of the element of earth up to the cardinal point and say these or similar words:

O come great spirits of the northern quarter,

> *I do summon, stir and call you up great children of the north whose ruler is Boreas.*
> *O guardians of the north, primal beings of earth and stability, hear my plea.*
> *I welcome you within the boundaries of my magic circle,*
> *To aid and guard my spell this day/night.*
> *Hail and welcome.*
> ***Blessings be.***

Then give a little bow and place your representation of earth back to its appropriate place on the altar. Then when you are ready, hold your representation of the element of air up to the east and say these or similar words:

> *O come great spirits of the eastern quarter,*
> *I do summon, stir and call you up great children of the east whose ruler is Eurius.*
> *O guardians of the east, primal beings of air and intelligence, hear my plea.*
> *I welcome you within the boundaries of my magic circle,*
> *To aid and guard my spell this day/night.*
> *Hail and welcome.*
> ***Blessings be.***

Then give a little bow and place your representation of air back to its appropriate place on the altar. Then when you are ready, hold your representation of the element of fire up to the south and say these or similar words:

> *O come great spirits of the southern quarter,*
> *I do summon, stir and call you up great children of the south whose ruler is Notus.*
> *O guardians of the south, primal beings of fire and strength, hear my plea.*
> *I welcome you within the boundaries of my magic circle,*
> *To aid and guard my spell this day/night.*
> *Hail and welcome.*

Blessings be.

Then give a little bow and place your representation of fire back to its appropriate place on the altar. Then when you are ready, hold your representation of the element of water up to the west and say these or similar words:

O come great spirits of the western quarter,
I do summon, stir and call you up great children of the west whose ruler is Zephyrus.
O guardians of the west, primal beings of water and emotion, hear my plea.
I welcome you within the boundaries of my magic circle,
To aid and guard my spell this day/night.
Hail and welcome.
Blessings be.

Then give a little bow and place your representation of water back to its appropriate place on the altar. The elemental spirits are now called into your circle and you will now have established a deep connection with the forces of nature. As with the Goddess and God and their specific deities, remember to always show respect to the elemental spirits – they are extremely powerful beings.

Invocation of Deities

This part of high magic is essential. It is this part of the spell that will truly make your spell religious magic. When Witches work high magic, they call upon the Goddess and God or their specific deities to ask for assistance. Invocation is a formal calling upon them. It allows us to experience their powers more effectively within our rituals and spellcraft. As you will be aware by now, Witches work closely with the male and female energies of the universe – the Yin and Yang of being. The balance or tension between these two forces is the true source of all magical power. An invocation to the Goddess and God does not have to be complicated. Simply stand in the centre of your magic circle, the place of spirit, raise your hands up to the heavens and say these or similar words:

O Mother Goddess and Father God,
Great Lord and Lady of the sun and moon and the entire universe,
I humbly ask you to attend my circle this day/night,
To aid and guide the spell with your almighty powers.
Help me to achieve the best possible outcome of this magic that I do.
O Mother and Father Nature, come to me, speak to me,
I bid you to witness and bless my spell this day/night,
Held in the beautiful realms of your eternal powers.
Hail and welcome.
Blessings be.

If, however, you would prefer to work with specific deities from certain cultures then you can perhaps take the time to write invocations for them prior to your spellcraft. You should focus on their qualities to do this and what you would like them to bring to your magic circle to aid your magical work. Calling upon specific deities is a wonderful thing to do because it allows us to strike specific desired energy vibrations within the universe. Specific deities are keys that open the correct doors in intended directions in magical workings. The names of specific deities are human creations that help us to call upon specific powers that have existed since the dawn of time. For example, Aphrodite governs love, Apollo governs healing, Cernunnos governs fertility, Lugh governs success and so forth. Let's say, for example, you wanted to call upon Aphrodite for a love spell. You could say these or similar words while raising your hands up to the heavens in the centre of your magic circle:

O Aphrodite, beautiful star of the salty seas, come to me.
Great mistress of love and erotic sexuality,
You who are the breaker of the hearts of gods
and the wedding of the seas and shores,
I humbly ask you to attend my circle this day/night,
To aid and guide the spell with your almighty powers.
Help me to achieve the best possible outcome of this magic that I do.
O Aphrodite, come to me, speak to me,

I bid you to witness and bless my spell this day/night,
Held in the beautiful realms of your eternal powers.
Hail and welcome.
Blessings be.

Raising the Power

Once the above actions are carried out the next stage to think about is raising power for your spell. This is the process that is usually carried out just before whatever main actions of a specific spell in high magic are carried out. It is one of the greatest ways to really propel a spell along. The raising of energy for a spell is simply a release of personal power. It is the release of the inner fire and passion that lies within us all. As I explained, the circle will protect the energy you raise from dissipating and will also amplify your raised energy. Every single one of us has natural power that originates from the universe. This is released when we do any types of physical activities, such as sex, and replenished when we eat, drink and breathe. In magical work, we channel this power through our bodies towards our intended needs and goals. Our bodies are simply conduits for the natural powers of the universe. You create magic in your spellcraft through your willpower. Spells, tools, magical correspondences, invocations and so on are simply props that help us to channel energy more efficiently. They help us to channel energy in our intended directions. The true power, however, lies within ourselves. This is very similar to what the Good Witch of the North told Dorothy in the 1939 American musical fantasy film *The Wizard of Oz*.

There are many ways to raise power within the magic circle. Some examples include the following: astral travel, chanting, clapping, dancing, drumming, flagellation, flexing muscles, masturbation, meditation or concentration, reciting poetry, singing and so on. Simply use the methods that you are most comfortable with. To gain an understanding of just how real the power is within your body, try this little experiment: rub your hands together for around thirty seconds. Then slowly pull your hands apart. What you should feel is a tingling or pulsating sensation. Your hands may feel as if they are pulling each other together or retracting in some way like the force of two magnets. What you are feeling is pure energy and that's the stuff that you will need to raise for your spells. In magical workings, energy is raised and then given a purpose. Remember that whatever method of energy raising you choose you should always be focusing on the intent of your spell. It is this that will give the raised energy its purpose. As you raise power in your magic circle, it will take the form of a cone. This is known as the "cone of power" with the circle becoming the base of this cone. The top point of the cone is the ultimate goal of the spell. It is said that the cone of power represents the traditional Witch's pointed hat that we see children wearing at Halloween for trick or treating.

Following is a very beautiful song written by Paul Giovanni for the 1973 British folk horror film *The Wicker Man* (which is one of my favourite films). It is based on an old folk song written by Robert Burns in the eighteenth century. The song is called *Corn Rigs* and I adore singing or chanting it when I raise power for my spellcraft (it is also excellent for celebrations based on Lughnasadh). I have had much success with its use. I'm sure you will too if you choose to use it for raising power. Enjoy.

> *It was upon a Lammas night,*
> *When corn rigs are bonnie,*
> *Beneath the moon's unclouded light,*
> *I held awhile to Annie.*
> *The time went by with careless heed,*
> *Till 'tween the late and early,*
> *With small persuasion she agreed,*
> *To see me through the barley.*
> *Corn rigs and barley rigs,*
> *And corn rigs are bonnie,*
> *I'll not forget that happy night,*
> *Among the rigs with Annie.*
> *The sky was blue, the wind was still,*
> *The moon was shinning clearly.*
> *I sat her down with right good will,*
> *Among the rigs o' barley.*

I kent her heart, was all my own.
I loved her most sincerely.
I kissed her o'er and o'er again,
Among the rigs of barley.
Corn rigs and barley rigs,
And corn rigs are bonnie,
I'll not forget that happy night,
Among the rigs with Annie.

Fulfilment of Purpose

Once you feel that you have raised enough energy, now is the time to address the purpose of the spell itself. In other words, now is the time to carry out whatever main actions your spell requires. In low magic, this part is really the only thing that is required in spellcraft (obviously, apart from any general preparation). The words of your spell should be recited aloud in a clear and commanding voice. Make sure also that you word your spell correctly with no room for misinterpretation so that the universe is able to hear and understand exactly what it is that you are asking for. In addition, spells usually include the words "an' it harm none, so mote it be". In Witchcraft this ensures that the outcome of our spells will not cause any harm in any way, shape or form. "So mote it be" is like the Witches' version of "amen" within the orthodox religions. "Mote" is an Old English word meaning "must" so the whole expression is basically saying "as I will, it must be done".

Chants work very well for spells as does rhyming them. Chants can be long or short in spellcraft. A short chant can always be recited over and over again until you feel that your spell is beginning to take effect. Rhyming carries great magical power (it also helps us to remember spells more efficiently) in spellcraft because it helps the conscious mind to focus on the intents of our spells while the unconscious mind puts the magic to work. As I explained, I will give you some examples of spells throughout part two of this book. There are also plenty of other books out there that contain spells and there are also spells on the internet. I personally, however, think that the spells that you create for yourself will be the most powerful for you since these will be personalised to your own specific needs and goals. Spells written by other people will inspire you to eventually create your own. For now, however, you can use spells composed by other people as you develop your own style. You can simply tweak them a little, if you like, to make them more personal. Good luck.

Earthing the Power

Now that you have carried out the main actions of the spell, it is now time to earth the power. Essentially, this will help you to return to the everyday mundane world. It also symbolises the beginning of the end of your work so that the energy of your spell can work its magic. Earthing the power will effectively allow you to tell the mind that your spell is coming to an end so that it can begin to manifest in the near future. Residual energy will still exist within your magic circle and this should be properly earthed or reprogrammed so that everything can return to normal. If you do not properly earth this power, you are likely to experience headache or dizziness.

One of the best ways to earth the power is with ritual food and drink. Ritual food and drink is traditionally blessed and consumed. Any type of food and drink can be used. I personally like fruits or cakes and wine or beer. It is always best to use food and drink that are as natural as possible. The ritual food and drink are very symbolic of the Great Rite – because without the sexual force between the Goddess and God there would be no food and drink whatsoever. The use of ritual food and drink in magical work is a way for Witches to honour the powers of the Goddess and God. It is a form of true communion. The chosen food can be placed on a special plate or dish and the wine (or other drink) can obviously be poured into the chalice. You can place the plate or dish of food and the bottle of drink somewhere in your sacred space as part of the general preparation until they are ready for use on your altar.

To carry out a rite of earthing the power with food and drink, hold them up to the heavens and focus on the many blessings of life that come from the Goddess and God. Then when you are ready, say these or similar words:

O Mother Goddess and Father God,

Lady and Lord of all nature,
I acknowledge that this food and drink
could not be without your combined powers.
I ask for your blessings to be placed upon them,
And I give thanks for your life-sustaining gifts.
Help me now to gently return to the everyday mundane world.
Blessings be.

Then place the food and drink on the altar. You may also want to trace pentagrams over them at this point. Then when you are ready, you may want to dip your athame or wand into the chalice of drink while focusing on the bond between the Goddess and God. You may then eat and drink in the knowledge that you are earthing the power. This is the time for you to be merry and to toast the Goddess and God. While you are in this process, see in your mind's eye any residual energy sinking into the ground and returning back to the earth. At the same time, think of an activity that you would do in the everyday mundane world.

Thanksgiving and Farewell to Deities

This part of spellcraft is about thanking the Goddess and God or their specific deities for their attendance and assistance in our magical work. It is a time to say farewell to them. It further symbolises that the spell is coming to an end so that the Goddess and God or specific deities can play their roles in helping us to manifest our magic in the near future. Some Witches think of this as dismissing the deities but I think this is very inaccurate. The deities are ever-present forces, both within ourselves and within the natural world, and never truly leave our lives. This part of the spell simply allows the energies to calm down. It also further shifts our awareness on to the everyday mundane world. In other words, it helps us to return to "normality". We can then simply allow the spell to work its magic. To thank the Goddess and God or specific deities, you can simply stand in the centre of your sacred space and say these or similar words:

Gracious Lord and Lady (or specific deity names),
I humbly thank you for your presence and assistance in this spell,

I now bid you farewell as I return to the mundane world,
Filled with the love, harmony and peace of nature.
Blessings be.

Thanksgiving and Farewell to the Elements

The next part of your spellcraft should involve the thanking of the elemental spirits for their attendance and assistance in your magical work. It is a time to say farewell to them and to honour their realms. As with the thanksgiving and farewell to deities, this further symbolises that the spell is coming to an end so that the elemental spirits can play their roles in manifesting your magic in the near future. It will allow energies to calm down and will further help you to shift your awareness on to the everyday mundane world. You can then simply allow the spell to do its work. To thank the elemental spirits, you may want to begin at the north and raise your hands above your head and say these or similar words:

O guardian spirits of the northern quarter,
Primal beings of earth and stability,
I humbly thank you for your presence and assistance in this spell,
I now bid you farewell as I return to the mundane world,
Filled with the love, harmony and peace of nature.
Blessings be.

Then give a little bow. Then when you are ready, face the east and raise your hands above your head and say these or similar words:

O guardian spirits of the eastern quarter,
Primal beings of air and intelligence,
I humbly thank you for your presence and assistance in this spell,
I now bid you farewell as I return to the mundane world,
Filled with the love, harmony and peace of nature.
Blessings be.

Then give a little bow. Then when you are ready, face the south and raise your hands above your head and say these or similar words:

O guardian spirits of the southern quarter,
Primal beings of fire and strength,

I humbly thank you for your presence and assistance in this spell,
I now bid you farewell as I return to the mundane world,
Filled with the love, harmony and peace of nature.
Blessings be.

Then give a little bow. Then when you are ready, face the west and raise your hands above your head and say these or similar words:

O guardian spirits of the western quarter,
Primal beings of water and emotion,
I humbly thank you for your presence and assistance in this spell,
I now bid you farewell as I return to the mundane world,
Filled with the love, harmony and peace of nature.
Blessings be.

Then give a little bow. You have now thanked all the elemental spirits and shown them respect. They can now assist in the manifestation of your spell in the near future.

Breaking the Magic Circle

The final stage of your spell should involve the breaking of the magic circle or the releasing of the magic circle. This will truly and effectively allow you to tell the mind that the magical workings of your spell are now complete so that you can allow the spell to come to fruition in the near future. To break the magic circle, simply stand in the centre of your sacred space and visualise the circle fading away slowly or sinking into the ground. Then when you are ready, say these or similar words:

O great and mystical circle,
You who are the mysteries of the Goddess's
sacred and eternal womb,
The magical workings of this spell are now done,
And so the circle has now served its purpose.
Ever mindful of the Rede of the Wiccae,
The magic has now been freed,
And so I make the circle undone,
As I now return to the mundane world,

Filled with the love, harmony and peace of nature.
Blessings be.
Blessings be.
Blessings be.

At this point, you should then clean up after yourself and carry out any after-spell requirements. You can then relax in the knowledge that your spell will come to fruition in the near future. Remember to always believe in yourself. Then enjoy the fruits of your labour. I truly do wish you every success in your spellcraft.

Chapter Nine: Love Spells

Love is the universal law of the Goddess. It is the sacred bond that unites her with the God. When we experience love, it pleases her very deeply. Love truly is the way of the Goddess as evinced throughout the natural world. It is love that makes the world go round. Without it, we wouldn't be able to bond with others and the world would go into chaos. To understand the nature of love magic is to understand the loving nature of the Goddess and her many loving deities – Aphrodite, Venus, Freya and so on. The loving nature of the Goddess is very beautiful, but it can also be very cruel and vicious. The loving nature of the Goddess has both a dark side and a light side as with all nature. We only have to think of those animals that will fiercely protect their young at all costs to understand this. Love is an endless quest for companionship, sexual contact, emotional fulfilment, warmth and someone to share an evening meal with after a hard day at work. Love spells can provide us with all of these types of things, but there is one very important ethic in Witchcraft that should be considered very carefully.

You should never direct a love spell at a specific person. This is influencing free will and violates the Wiccan Rede. Love spells that ask for a specific person can backfire on you and disastrously so. When you cast a love spell on someone, you are binding him or her to you against their will. You are also binding yourself to your desired person. This can cause a lot of pain and can really complicate things for you. I learnt this the hard way. Many years ago (before I really took on the Witchcraft religion) I cast a love spell on someone who I had split up with. Within days after casting the spell, he was constantly texting my mobile phone basically saying that he had to be with me. We got back together but he was obsessive with me which was totally out of character and eventually the relationship broke down. I then suffered guilt for weeks after and we had no contact at all. So I got my desire but at a huge price. I have never repeated the same mistake again. All a love spell does that asks for a specific person is confuse the victim's emotions. It manipulates a free soul.

You have to ask yourself the question: how would I feel if someone directed a love spell towards me? If you cast a spell to get a specific person all you are encouraging is emotional slavery and are actually performing dark and destructive magic. Witchcraft is about the evolution of the soul for the better and a love spell that entraps another person does the opposite to this.

Love magic should be of this basic type only: that which attracts an unspecified person. A love spell that doesn't ask for a specific person will put you in situations where you will unwittingly communicate that you are ready for love and to settle down with someone. Those of the same frame of mind will be naturally attracted to you. A love spell will, if necessary, help you to overcome any shyness. A love spell that is cast properly will extend its gentle, loving and emotional energies far and wide as your search for love continues. As with any type of magic, you must be open to receive. When you cast a love spell, you need to really want love. After the love spell that I cast to get my ex-partner, I did another love spell some time later that was very powerful. Obviously, this was not directed at a specific person. I simply asked for love to come into my life. It worked within a month. I got my wonderful partner in 2006 and we have been together ever since. As with any romantic relationship, we have had our fair share of ups and downs but we are still deeply in love. We have been in a civil partnership since 2007 but we have had to work hard to make it a successful one.

This leads me to another fundamental point: when you cast a love spell you must also consider that you will get everything that goes with it – good and bad. Everybody has both positive and negative aspects. So when your love spell works you need to expect that your partner will have parts to his or her personality that may irritate and annoy you. He or she may have a very needy personality and need a lot of attention. He or she may have a dark past that will need addressing for the relationship to be fruitful. But at the end of the day, we are all here to learn from each other and every person that we meet can help us to spiritually grow. This is especially true with the people who we wish to settle down with in romantic relationships.

Love magic works on a totally subconscious level. It will help you to release the loving energies that are locked inside you. There is no one out there who is going to walk up to you and say "oh hello there, I've just noticed that you are releasing a lot of loving energies and I would like to enter into a romantic relationship with you". No – this isn't how love magic works. What love magic will do is introduce you to loving people. From these people, you will most likely find someone who really appeals to you, someone who you would like to settle down with. A love spell will begin with a deep attraction to someone and, over time, true love will hopefully grow. Don't expect love to be instantaneous for true love is a mellowed product of time.

Correspondences for Love Spells

Best Symbols: Cauldron, chalice, cup, heart, love-associated runes, love chaplet, love wreath, mermaid (for the bitter-sweetness of love), pair of hearts, ring, undine.

Planets: Earth, Mercury, Moon (especially when it is full), Venus.

Elements: Earth, fire, water.

Cardinal Points: North, south, west.

Best Days: Friday, Monday.

Numbers: 2, 3, 5, 6, 7, 9 (for impersonal love).

Colours: Green, orange (for attraction), pink, rainbow (for gay love), red (for passionate love), rose, silver, violet (for gay love), white (for love in its purest form).

Incense: Aromatic rush roots, benzoin, cinnamon, civet, copal, dragon's blood, ginseng, jasmine, lavender, lotus, musk, myrrh, myrtle, orris, patchouli, rose, spikenard, vanilla, violet.

Plants/Trees: Acacia flowers, almond, apple, apricot, aster, autumn crocus, avens, avocado, bachelor's buttons, balm of Gilead, barley, basil, bay, bean, beet, betony, birch, bleeding heart, bloodroot, Brazil nut, cannabis, caper, cardamom, carnation, cassia, catnip, chamomile, cherry, chestnut, chickweed, chilli pepper, cinnamon, clove, clover, coltsfoot, columbine, coriander, cuckoo flower, cupid's dart, daffodil, daisy, damiana, dill, dogbane, dragon's blood, elderberries, elecampane, elm, feverfew, fig, fuzzy weed, gardenia, gentian, geranium, ginger, ginseng, hawthorn, henbane, hibiscus, hollyhock, hyacinth, jalap root, jasmine, juniper, lady's mantle, lavender, lemon, lemon balm, lettuce, lime, lotus, lovage, love grass, love seed, Madonna lily, maidenhair fern, male fern, mandrake, maple, marjoram, marsh mallow, meadowsweet, mimosa, mint, mistletoe, moonwort, myrtle, oleander, orange, orchid, orris, pansy, patchouli, pea, peach, pear, pennyroyal, peppermint, periwinkle, plum, poppy, primrose, purslane, quince, raspberry, rose, rosemary, rye, saffron, sea holly, skullcap, sorrel, southernwood, spiderwort, strawberry, tansy, thyme, tomato, tuberose, valerian, vanilla, Venus' flytrap, verbena, vervain, violet, willow, wormwood, yarrow, ylang-ylang. Generally flowers that are sweetly scented.

Crystals/Stones: Amazonite, amber, amethyst, ametrine, blue tourmaline, coral, diamond, emerald, garnet, green agate, jade, lapis lazuli, lodestone, malachite, moonstone, opal, pearl, peridot, pink tourmaline, rhodonite, rose quartz, ruby, rutilated quartz, sapphire, turquoise. Pairs of lodestones are excellent for love spells.

Metals: Copper, silver.

Creatures: Butterfly, cockatoo, deer, dog, dove, horse, hummingbird, kiwi, lynx, pairs of birds, partridge, peacock, penguin, rabbit, snow leopard, sparrow, swallow, wolf, wryneck. Peacock feathers are excellent for love spells.

Deities: Adonis, Aegea, Aine, Alalahe, Amor, Anahita, Anath, Angus, Anteros, Aonghus, Aphrodite, Artemis, Asherah, Ashtoreth, Astarte, Atargatis, Attis, Bast, Benzaiten, Blathnat, Branwen, Cernunnos, Cupid, Cytherea, Damuzi, Diana, Dulha Deo, Eostar, Erato, Eros, Erzulie, Evander, Faunus, Freya, Frigg, Gaia, Galatea, Goda, Guinevere, Haddad, Hathor, Hera, Hermes, Hulda, Hymen, Inanna, Io, Iris, Ishtar, Isis, Juno, Kadesh, Kama, Krishna, Kwan-Yin, Lakshmi, Maia, Mercury, Mithras, Myrrha, Neith, Olwen, Oshun, Pan, Phanes, Pothos, Rauni, Rhea, Rosamund, Sarah, Semiramis, Shakti, Shekinah, Shiva, Soma Shakarabru, Syria Dea, Tammuz, Tane, the Green Man, Turan, Uma, Venus, Vishnu, Yarillo, Yemaya.

Magical Ways to Attract Love

Here, we will look at some of my favourite magical ways to attract love that I have picked up over the years as a priest of the Witchcraft religion. These simple ways can help you to enhance and amplify your love magic. They are very effective on their own but they can also be done in addition to love spells (or as parts of them) to really get the most out of them. As you will be aware by now, the more you put into your magic the more effective it will be. These simple ways can also help to inspire you when creating your own love spells – whether these created love spells are for yourself or for others who seek your help.

One very simple way to attract love is to erect a love shrine in your home. This can simply be a small table covered with a pink or red cloth and decorated with a few items of love. You can, perhaps, place upon it a picture or figurine of your favourite deity of love. You can then place a candle of an appropriate colour in the centre and place heart-shaped rose petals at the base of it. The candle can also be inscribed with a magical love symbol and anointed with an oil that relates to your goal. A ring of love crystals can also be placed around the base of your candle. You can also burn some incense of love on your shrine to help you to release loving energies into your home. Placed in the west, a love shrine can be very effective for attracting love. If you are already romantically involved with someone, a love shrine can help to strengthen the bond that you both share.

To create a special love incense, mix together lavender, rose petals, orris, dragon's blood and myrtle in a small bowl. Then add three drops each of musk and patchouli oils. Do this on a Friday, the day of the love planet Venus, and then leave the dish of herbs and oils somewhere to dry out for a week. On the following Friday, place the incense in a clean glass jar with a cork lid. Use two to three spoonfuls when needed. This is said to be a very potent love incense blend that can really enhance and empower love magic.

Another way to attract love involves the use of love potions or infusions. One of my favourites involves the infusion of rose petals, dried lavender buds and the seeds of a vanilla pod. This potion can be added to a love bath or drank before a date or during the casting of a love spell. It is best to drink your love potion from a pink or green cup on a Friday evening. Obviously, any love potion you make should only be drank by yourself to help you to attract a lover. Giving a love potion to someone else who you desire as a romantic partner is not in keeping with the Witches' policy of harm none and is akin to spiking someone's drink if you ask me. Those who are already romantically involved with others, however, can give their partners love potions if their partners have knowledge of these potions. A love potion shared between two lovers can really strengthen their relationship.

Another way to enhance love magic involves the use of love bath salts. Blend together three teaspoons of Epsom salts with the dried herbs of rose petals, lavender and jasmine flowers. You can then add the blend to your bath water. Alternatively, blend together the oils of absolute rose, lavender, ylang-ylang and rosewood with three teaspoons of Epsom salts and add this to your bath water. You can soak in your bath for as long as you like while focusing on bringing love into your life. You can also place amber resin or heart-shaped rose quartz crystals in the bathroom to infuse it with the beautiful scent of love. Your loving bath will also be excellent for increasing your love for yourself. You do, after all, need to learn how to love yourself before anyone else can truly fall in love with you.

Some Witches also like to work with love sachets. To attract a gentleman into your life, add a bay leaf to a sachet of an appropriate loving colour along with lavender, dried bachelor's buttons and a small amount of valerian root. To attract a lady into your life, add patchouli, cinnamon and henbane to a sachet of an appropriate loving colour. It is traditional for a man who wants to attract a woman into his life to gather these herbs on a morning while standing in the nude on one foot. A whole orris root and other loving herbs placed in a green silk sachet are said to be very effective for attracting a loved one.

Another favourite way of mine to attract love involves fire. A blazing fire is very useful for attracting love because of its association with passion. It is said that if dragon's blood, rosemary and rose petals are thrown into a blazing fire then love will surely come if the Witch or magician is looking for love to come into his or her life. Incidentally, vervain thrown into the fire is said to dispel the pangs of unrequited love. Five shiny pennies placed near the main doorway of your home, perhaps beneath the front porch, will also attract love into your life. Alternatively, your five pennies can be buried at the base of a loving tree, such as a cherry tree, perhaps in your garden or near your home.

Another way to attract love is to plant a love garden. Plant as many loving herbs as you can to do this. Some of my personal favourites include carnation, catnip, chamomile, lavender, mint, rose, rosemary, thyme, tomato, jasmine and yarrow. If space is no problem in your garden, you can also plant loving trees such as cherry, peach, pear, willow and apple. A water feature can also be a wonderful addition to a love garden since water is a timeless symbol of love. A crescent-shaped pond circling away from the home is said to be excellent for attracting both love and prosperity. Such pools are quite popular in China and the east. If, however, you don't have a garden simply plant some loving herbs in pots and place your potted herbs around your home.

Valentine's Day (February 14th) has long been associated with love (it is also the date that me and my partner entered into a civil partnership) and is thus a perfect time to carry out magical workings of love. It is traditional in many places to plant peas and lettuce in the garden on this date to attract love. It is also traditional on Valentine's Day to light seven pink candles and a sweet floral incense. This is a very effective way of attracting the beautiful scent of love to flow throughout your home.

Another simple way to attract love involves the sea, an apple and some cloves. On a Friday evening, go to the seaside and simply stud your apple with the cloves into the shape of a loving symbol, such as the Gebo rune, three times. Then throw the studded apple as far out away from yourself into the sea as possible while focusing on loving energies. This is a very effective way of attracting love into your life. Apples have long been used to attract love since the apple tree itself is magically linked to the love planet of Venus. Cutting an apple and sharing it with your loved one will also ensure that you both remain happy together according to folklore. Apple wood is excellent for wands that are utilised for love magic. The blossoms of the apple tree are also added to love incenses, infusions and sachets. The blossoms can also be added to pink or green wax, then strained out, to make very effective candles that attract love. These candles are very useful in all types of love spells.

A Full Moon Love Spell

This love spell utilises the power of the full moon to attract love. It is loosely based on the spell I cast to get my partner back in 2006. It is suitable for those who are ready for love to come into their lives. It is a signal to nature that someone is at a place within their life where a loving relationship is their desire and their goal. It is most effective if it is carried out by the person who wants a loving relationship but it can also be cast on behalf of someone else (with a little tweaking) as long as you feel that the person who wants love is truly ready for love and is open to receive it. The person who wants love must also be prepared to put their trust into the spiritual powers of nature.

Ingredients required for this spell:
- Taper red candle.
- Matches.
- Two small lodestones.
- Chalice or wine glass.
- 125ml of water.
- Small piece of red cloth.
- Green or silver cord.
- Red rose.
- Small piece of clean white paper.
- Pen with red ink.
- Jasmine or rose oil.

Casting the spell:

On a night of a full moon, light the red candle with a match and place the rose next to it while visualising yourself in a romantic relationship. Bring forward any positive thoughts of how you will feel when love comes into your life. Spend at least ten minutes doing this. Then put the lodestones in the chalice or wine glass and pour on the water. If possible, allow the full moon to reflect on the surface of the water for a few moments. Visualise the loving energies of the water and that of the moon absorbing into the lodestones, giving them an extra jolt of loving power. Then pick out the lodestones and hold one of them in one hand and the other in the other hand. Slowly bring your hands together. When your hands meet, cup them together with the two lodestones in the centre. This represents you meeting with your ideal lover. Then by the candlelight, write down the main qualities that you desire in your ideal partner while still focusing on your loving positive thoughts. When you are finished doing this and are ready, allow three drops of the oil to fall on to the paper. Then pick off two heart-shaped petals from the rose and place them in the centre of the paper. Hold the paper up to the candlelight with the two petals secured in place together with your thumb and say these or similar words:

Gracious Lady, passionate woman of the silver moon,
I ask that my love be drawn to me very soon.
Red rose petals, petals of nature's true love's flower,
Lend me your loving power.
As these hearts glow in this beautiful candlelight,
I draw my love to me on this full moon night.
Gone are the lonely days of the past,
As this spell draws my love to me thick and fast.
By the powers of earth and water, of air and fire,
May the powers of nature bring the gift of love that I so desire.
O gracious love Goddess of the mysterious moon above,
Bring me my one true love.
An' it harm none, so mote it be.

If possible, leave the lodestones under the light of the moon for a few moments. You can then use this time to focus on your visualisation and the bringing forward of loving thoughts. Then fold the paper three times and place it, along with the lodestones and the rose petals, in the centre of the cloth and secure it tight with the cord to create a small bag and allow the candle to burn out or simply snuff it out. You can then wear this small bag around your neck and place it under your pillow each night when you retire. You can repeat this until you find love. You may be very surprised by what will happen by the time of the next full moon. I certainly was. I wish you every success in your quest to find love.

Chapter Ten: Money Spells

Money spells are one of the most common reasons that people turn to magic. One of my earliest spells in life involved a money spell and I was very surprised at the result. In fact, it was one of the reasons I became so interested in magic and Witchcraft. Most of us face some form of financial issue at some point within our lives and magic that attracts money is one way to help us to overcome any financial issue that life throws at us. Money and prosperity spells are not always limited to the receiving of some extra cash. They may also involve ridding our lives of debts and creating the right atmosphere to encourage a positive financial flow into your life, home and/or business. But there are some things that you need to consider when it comes to the casting of money spells.

One of the most important facts that you need to face when it comes to financial spells is that you need to be realistic. Over the years, I've often been asked the question: if you're a Witch, why aren't you rich? If I had a hundred pounds for every time that someone asked me that question I certainly would be on my way to becoming rich. When I'm asked this question it often frustrates me because many people do not understand the true nature of money magic – that it is all about balance. The simple fact of the matter is that when you cast a money spell you will probably only get the money that is necessary to get you out of any financial problems that you may have.

It is frequently said in Witchcraft that magic responds better to need rather than want and this is true. So you need to be realistic and reasonable. Don't expect to win the jackpot on the lottery when you perform a spell that attracts money and prosperity. Money spells will respond better if you do what it takes to encourage a good financial flow into your life. In other words, you need to work hard in life in addition to casting money spells. Witches who become greedy are usually frustrated and dissatisfied with their lives and are actually encouraging imbalance. This is not what Witchcraft is about.

Money spells are not about creating money out of thin air. They are utilised to basically increase someone's financial scene. They may manifest as unexpected gifts from family or friends; as a raise in pay or promotion at work; as a sudden increase in extra tips at work; as protection from unfair competition in business; as an unexpected tax rebate; as a loan suddenly being repaid to you; as a good investment; as a win at the bingo or on a scratch card and so on. They may even manifest as you finding money in odd places. In my experience, money spells often manifest in the most strange and unexpected ways.

People actually don't necessarily need money itself and we certainly can't take it with us when we move on to the Summerlands when we die. What people actually need is what money can buy and what money can do to get us out of any financial problems. What money can buy and do for us are important for our health and well-being. So money spells are frequently necessary. Money and prosperity spells help us to achieve peace of mind so that we can just get on with life. When you have financial problems, visualise them disappearing and you emerging free of any worry and stress. This is not you being greedy. This is you doing what is necessary to live a full and productive life. This is, after all, what Witchcraft is about. Give your money spells the magical power they need and they will flow into your life perfectly.

Another fundamental point: magic is never for sale. Witchcraft is a calling for certain people and should never be thought of as an occupation. Magic is a sacred gift of nature and no reputable or ethical Witch would ever accept money for casting a spell. Those who turn to Witchcraft because they think it will give them an easier life or make them rich are actually in the religion for the wrong reasons. Such people are not true Witches in my opinion. However, it is perfectly ethical and acceptable for Witches to sell things like wands, astrological birth charts, books, psychic readings, tarot readings, palm readings, runic readings, deity images, candles, broomsticks, pentacles, herbs, stones, crystals, incense, runic sets and so on. Witches who run websites, festivals and fairs can also do so as a business and as a service to the Pagan community. As with everyone else, Witches have the right to make a living from their skills, knowledge, wisdom and experience. But in doing so they should always remember what the Rede teaches us: fairly take an' fairly give.

Correspondences for Money Spells

Best Symbols: Ankh, Chinese prosperity dragon, corn dolly or kirn baby, cornucopia (the horn of plenty), eagle claw (to grasp and keep a hold of money), egg, eight-spoked wheel, four-leaf clover, gnome, gold box, gold coins, horseshoe, money-associated runes, money bag, money tree, pentacle, seashell, silver coins.

Planets: Earth, Jupiter, Mercury, Pluto, Sun.

Elements: Air, earth, water (water is particularly great for contract negotiations).

Cardinal Points: East, north, west.

Best Days: Sunday, Thursday, Wednesday.

Numbers: 1, 3, 4, 5, 7, 8.

Colours: Brown, gold, green, orange, purple, silver.

Incense: Cedar, cinnamon, cinquefoil, frankincense, fumitory, lavender, mastic, nutmeg, patchouli, pine, sassafras, storax.

Plants/Trees: Alfalfa, allspice, almond, balm, basil, bay, blackberry, bladderwrack, blue flag, borage, bromeliad, buckwheat, calamus, camellia, cascara sagrada, cashew, cedar, chamomile, cinnamon, cinquefoil, clove, clover, comfrey, corn, cowslip, dill, dock, elder, fenugreek, fern, fir, flax, frankincense, fumitory, galangal, ginger, goldenrod, golden seal, gorse, grains of paradise, grape, heliotrope, honeysuckle, horse chestnut, Irish moss, jalap root, jasmine, lavender, lemon balm, lucky hand, mandrake, maple, marjoram, mint, moneywort, moonwort, moss, nutmeg, oak leaves, oats, onion, orange, patchouli, pea, pecan, periwinkle, pine, pineapple, pomegranate, poplar, poppy, rattlesnake root, rice, saffron, sage, sarsaparilla, sassafras, sesame, snakeroot, snapdragon, St. John's wort, sunflower seeds, valerian, vervain, white bryony, wintergreen, woodruff.

Crystals/Stones: Amber, aventurine, bloodstone, brown agate, carnelian, citrine, emerald, fire opal, green tourmaline, jacinth, jade, malachite, moss agate, obsidian, pearl, peridot, sapphire, smoky quartz, tiger's eye, topaz, tree agate. Generally green stones.

Metals: Copper, gold, silver.

Creatures: Buffalo, camel, cow, crane, elephant, elk, frog, gnu, grey kangaroo, jaguar, kingfisher, ladybird, lion, pig, puffin, rat, salmon, seal, swallow, turkey, turtle, walrus, whale, white-tailed deer, woodpecker.

Deities: Abundantia, Aditi, Agathe Tyche, Agathodaemon, Anu, Athena, Bacchus, Belenos, Bona Eventus, Bonus Eventus, Brahma, Ceres, Cernunnos, Chango Macho, Demeter, Dionysus, Dis, Dyaus, Ellil, Epona, Fortuna, Freya, Gaia, Ganesha, Ganga, Gauri, Habondia, Hades, Hecate, Hera, Hercules, Hermes, Inanna, Juno, Jupiter, Kubera, Lakshmi, Lugh, Lupa, Mammon, Mercury, Minerva, Olokun, Olwin, Ops, Oshun, Pan, Pluto, Rosmerta, Sarasvati, Sucellos, the Dagda, the Green Man, Ushas, Volos, Zeus. Generally earthy deities.

Magical Ways to Attract Money

In this part of this chapter we will look at some interesting and magical ways to attract money. Although there are many ways to attract money, these are my personal favourites. These simple ways can really boost any form of money and prosperity magic. They are very effective on their own but they can also be done in addition to money and prosperity spells (or as parts of them) to really enhance and empower them. They will invite prosperous energy into your life that will surround you with good fortune. You can use them also to inspire you when creating your own money and prosperity spells.

One of my ultimate favourite ways to attract money involves something called cosmic ordering. Cosmic ordering can be used to ask for many things but I usually use them when I need some extra financial help – at Yule, for example, the time when I know I will need some financial help to buy presents for my loved ones. I have had much success with this – in fact, I can't think of a single time when I haven't gotten something out of a cosmic order that asked for financial help. A cosmic order is simply a small piece of paper with the need or goal written down on it. This is then attached somewhere special, such as on a main kitchen wall or inside a Book of Shadows, until the need or goal manifests. You could, for example, use a small piece of paper of a colour that relates to money, such as green, and then write down these or similar words during the time of a waxing moon:

> *With the power of the waxing moon,*
> *Extra money will come soon.*
> *An' it harm none, so mote it be.*

In addition to your chosen words you may also want to trace magical symbols that relate to money and prosperity. I personally usually trace a pentacle and a money-associated rune to the bottom left and right sides of the paper. Also, you may want to add a drop of an oil that relates to money and prosperity (such as patchouli oil) to each of the four corners of the paper (the number four is strongly associated with finance). As long as you truly do need financial help, you may be surprised by what will happen in the coming weeks when you create a cosmic order for money and prosperity.

One of the most common ways that Witches do to attract money and prosperity is with the use of symbols, signs and figurines. You can, for example, place figurines of money-associated animals in prominent places in your home for this. Some of the most popular include frogs, pigs and lions. Frogs, which are beautiful creatures that I have always adored, are particularly associated with plenty and abundance. Because pigs are strongly associated with wealth and prosperity, you may want to keep piggy banks in your home that you can use to save money. Seashells can also be placed around the home to attract prosperous energy since they were once used as money. Figurines of Ganesha and Lakshmi placed around the home are also said to be very useful ways to help us to attract money and prosperity. Also, hanging a horseshoe above a main door with the points upwards is said to bring great fortune and prosperous energy. I have one hanging above my back door especially for this.

Another way to encourage a positive financial flow into your life involves the creation of a special prosperity incense. The incense blend that I personally favour involves cinquefoil, patchouli, nutmeg and frankincense. You can burn this incense blend during the casting of money and prosperity spells or simply to encourage prosperous energy in the place where the incense blend is burned. Another prosperous incense blend involves sassafras, cinnamon and nutmeg. This incense blend is said to be particularly useful in times when financial help is urgent. If you are applying for a loan or want to ask someone for money, then this is the incense blend to create and to burn.

If you enjoy working with oils, then why not create a special prosperity oil? One of my personal favourites involves the oils of almond, patchouli, cedar and cinquefoil. This is a general prosperity oil that can really help you to attract a continuous, positive, financial flow into your life. Another prosperity oil involves almond, cinquefoil, cedar and cinnamon. This oil is particularly good for times when you want a quick money fix to get you out of any financial problems. These oils are excellent when they are added to aromatherapy lamps to infuse the area with prosperous energy. They can also be used to anoint candles during spells that attract money. Alternatively, they can be added to water and then used to spray around the home or other places where you wish to attract money.

Another way to attract money into your life involves prosperity infusions or potions. One of my favourite infusions involves a blend of dried orange peel, lemon balm, cinnamon, cloves, nutmeg and valerian. Drink this potion on a Wednesday, Thursday or Sunday during the casting of a money spell, or when negotiating a contract or when filling out a loan application. The potion will help the power of your mind to attract a good financial flow.

Some Witches also like to work with prosperity lotions. To create a special prosperity lotion, add to an unscented lotion (about 250ml) fourteen drops of orange oil, two drops of cinnamon oil and six drops of cinquefoil oil. Apply this lotion to the skin whenever you want to invite prosperous energy into your life, but before you do so, test a small amount on the back of your hand to ensure that you will not have any adverse reactions.

Another way to attract money involves carpets and rugs. Traditionally, Witches ground together herb materials that relate to their money goals into a fine powder and then place the powder under rugs and carpets to attract prosperous energy. You can use any money-associated herbs for this but one of my personal favourites involves Irish moss. Irish moss comes from the sea and is strongly associated with money, prosperity, luck and protection. So if you want to attract and protect money then Irish moss ground into a fine powder and placed under carpets and rugs are the things to consider doing. Incidently, a jar with Irish moss and whiskey in it placed on a sunny windowsill is another way to attract prosperous energy. This jar should be shaken on a daily basis.

Herbal powders can also be placed wherever you wish to attract money, such as your purse or wallet. Prosperous powders are also excellent for attracting prosperity when loaded into candles, stuffed into poppets and sachets, placed around doorways and added to prosperity baths. Incidently, bathing at Yule or Beltane with a penny wrapped in a cloth, perhaps in a green cloth, will bring great fortune and prosperity. You can also imagine that the bath water is churning with money notes to invite prosperous energy.

Another favourite way of mine to attract money involves the herb alfalfa. This is a very earthy herb that is strongly associated with money and prosperity. Keep the herb in a small jar and then place this jar in your magical pantry or other cupboard to attract money and prosperity and to protect yourself from poverty and hunger. Alfalfa can also be burned and then the ashes can be sprinkled around your home or business for the above purposes. Alfalfa, which is also known as buffalo herb, has been used in money magic for centuries. Another herb that I have worked with for money magic is buckwheat which is also very earthy. Because the herb is also protective, it can be ground into a powder and then used to create a magic circle especially for a money spell.

Another way to attract money involves mirrors. Mirrors have long been associated with good luck. It is said that mirrors help us to deflect evil or negativity and attract good energy or positivity. It is also said that having many mirrors in the home will invite good fortune, luck and prosperity. Placing a mirror in the kitchen or dining room will invite great prosperous energy, according to folklore from many cultures. Doing this will also ensure that food will come in abundance.

Another thing you may want to consider is the position in which to sleep at night to attract money. It should be obvious by now that north is the most powerful direction. It is the direction associated with great power because of its association with the element of earth. Earth represents stability, growth and, of course, money and prosperity. So if you want to attract prosperous energy into your life, sleep with your head pointing towards the north. Not only will this help you to attract prosperous energy, it will also promote calmness and healing.

A Runic Money Spell

This money spell utilises the Fehu rune which is strongly associated with money, prosperity, possessions and wealth. Today, many people associate the word "wealth" with having more money than you could ever spend in a lifetime. For our Pagan ancestors, however, wealth meant something quite different, something that many people should learn from in our modern times. It meant having what is necessary for your needs. It came from the word "weal" which referred to the yield of the land that accumulated to the person who cultivated it and worked hard in the fields to get an abundant harvest. So the word wealth, or weal, referred to the material things that are needed to ensure survival. It meant the capacity needed to ensure them. I, therefore, believe that you should only cast this spell if financial help is something that you truly do need at this time in your life. Don't allow greed to take over your life. Be reasonable when dealing with money spells and stay humble.

Ingredients required for this spell:
- Taper green candle with the Fehu rune carved on it.
- Matches.
- Small green pouch.
- Gold or silver cord.
- Prosperity oil (such as the ones suggested above).
- Seven gold coins.
- Small piece of clean green paper.
- Pen with gold or silver ink.

- A mixture of money-associated herbs, such as allspice, cinnamon, alfalfa, cloves, nutmeg, cinquefoil, orange peel and so on.

Casting the spell:

On a night of a waxing or full moon, preferably on a Thursday which is ruled by the generous planet Jupiter, anoint the candle with some of the oil towards yourself and then light it with a match while visualising yourself with some extra money and free of any financial worry. Then, when you are ready, trace the Fehu rune on the piece of paper with the pen while focusing on the rune's association with money and prosperity. Then place this paper, the coins and the herbs into the green pouch. Add four drops of the oil to the pouch. Then secure the pouch shut with a knot with one of the ends of the cord. Place the pouch in the centre of a flat surface, such as your altar, with the length of the cord towards yourself. Remember that you should always be utilising your visualisation. Then slowly pull the pouch towards yourself with the length of the cord and say these or similar words:

> *O gracious Lady of the silver moon and courageous*
> *Lord of the golden sun,*
> *As I pull this pouch I draw prosperity into my life and be it done.*
> *May money and prosperous energy flow ever in my way,*
> *Not just now, but every other day.*
> *May these coins of gold,*
> *Help me to bring money and prosperity*
> *before the moon grows really old.*
> *Sun, moon and stars that passionately shine,*
> *Bring me wealth and be it mine.*
> *Father of the sun and the stars and Mother of the moon*
> *and the sea,*
> *I ask you please to help me to bring forth prosperity.*
> *O Mother Goddess and Father God I do ask this hour,*
> *For prosperous energy on me to shower.*
> *By your powers and that of the elements*
> *I do banish financial worry and strife,*

And bring prosperous energy into my life.
An' it harm none, so mote it be.

If possible, leave the pouch under the light of the moon for a few moments. You can then use this time to focus on your visualisation. Visualise all your financial worries draining away from your life and you emerging free of any worry and stress with some extra money. Remember that you have the power to overcome any negativity in your life providing your will is strong enough. You can then simply allow the candle to burn out or you can simply snuff it out. You can then carry the pouch with you wherever you go and place it under your pillow each night when you retire. Alternatively, you can hang it over a main doorway to bless your home with prosperous power and this blessing will be extended to you each time you depart from your home. May your life be free of any financial worry and strife and filled with good fortune and prosperity. Good luck.

Chapter Eleven: Healing Spells

In the past, Witches were accused of many evil deeds imagined by the Christians. They were accused of causing misfortune, illness and even death when, in actuality, all they ever wanted to do was to help and to heal others to the best of their abilities. They used their vast amount of knowledge and wisdom to help others through the dark times that life often throws at us. It is important to Witches in the modern Craft, as with their Pagan ancestors, to use their skills, knowledge and wisdom in positive ways. Healing — whether of people, plants, trees, animals, nature or negative situations — is an excellent and wonderful use of our skills and knowledge. Throughout history, physicians have sworn by the Hippocratic Oath which is an oath to Apollo, who is a physician, to do no harm to others in any way, shape or form. This is very much akin to the promise that Witches make to the Goddess and God. Healing is another common reason why many people turn to magic. It is why many people turn to Witches for help and is something that Witches do very well indeed.

Healing spells can be used for almost anything — from healing a broken heart to healing a physical or mental ailment. They are basically utilised to relieve suffering in whatever form this may come in. They basically aid and speed up the healing process of the mind, body and soul. However, healing magic alone is not the answer to every single problem. As with all positive magic, healing magic must be backed up with appropriate actions in the physical world. So Witches must never hesitate but to refer people to the appropriate professional care — doctors, psychologists, counsellors, 12-Step Programs and so on. Common sense plays a vital role when it comes to healing. So you must be reasonable. If someone has broken their leg, for example, the first thing you should do is take him or her to the nearest hospital before you even think of doing a healing spell to speed up the healing process of their broken limb. You can't expect healing magic to work to its full potential unless you also seek the correct professional help. Magic works best when we do everything in our power to make our hopes and dreams happen. Never forget this.

When people come to you and ask you for a healing spell, always make it your mission to make them understand that they truly do need to want to be healed. Many people actually enjoy the luxuries of being unwell: the days away from their jobs and other responsibilities; being the centre of attention and enjoying being cared for by their loved ones; not having to answer to others and so on. If people are ill and secretly wish to continue being sick, then no professional care, drugs or healing spells will ever truly cure them. Positive thinking and wanting to be cured play vital roles in the healing process. Even doctors, psychologists and other similar professionals agree with this. So if people truly want and need to be healed, then they probably will be.

In earlier times, illness was believed to be caused by curses or evil spirits. If someone who was ill had the curse removed or the evil spirits exorcised using the correct ritual procedures, he or she made a miraculous recovery. Although curses and evil spirits may well be the cause of illness (though this is very rare), generally illness is caused by the stresses and strains put on the body due to imbalance. Indulging too much in smoking, alcohol, drugs, work, unhealthy foods as well as neglecting adequate physical activity can all weaken the body's immune system and thus reduce the body's natural defences against illness. By reducing or banishing negative habits, eating the right foods and getting plenty of exercise, a person is able to reduce their chances of becoming ill. In short, maintaining good health is one of the best ways to aid the natural healing processes of the body and to prevent illness. In Witchcraft, we should be aiming to be as healthy as possible anyhow – an unhealthy tree bears little fruit!

Another fundamental point: when you aim to heal someone with magic, never allow negative thoughts to cloud your mind. Remember that there should be no place for negative thinking in any form of positive magic. When we are trying to heal someone we can often focus too much on their illness and get sad because of it. You must learn to not let this happen. Instead, focus on the person becoming well and see him or her happy with great health in their everyday life. This is something I learnt many years ago with healing magic.

My grandmother, who I was very close to, became very ill with cancer. So I decided to do a healing spell. It worked very quickly with the help of the doctors. She managed to live an additional ten years after my spell and I truly do believe that she would have died if I hadn't have cast the healing spell. I also repeated a similar healing spell for my mother, who I am also very close to, when she had an intestinal abscess and had to go to hospital. She made a rapid recovery after my healing spell. I believe that my dear love for them and my positive thinking for them gave them the best chances of recovery. Such emotions, I believe, can truly create miracles.

Having a basic knowledge of herbalism, physiology, psychology and astrology can all help a Witch to heal others. If you are serious about Witchcraft, this knowledge will accumulate over time. Throughout history, doctors have used astrology to help them to understand the ailments that their patients were likely to have. It helped the doctors to understand how to best treat their patients. So it is an excellent idea to study astrology and to construct birth charts to help you to heal yourself and others. You can then find appropriate herbs, spells and other healing methods for yourself and those who come to you for healing help. Being a Witch is very much like being a doctor – a spiritual doctor if you will. Hippocrates (460-370 B. C. E.), the father of modern medicine, believed that a knowledge of astrology was a fundamental part of being a physician. To a large degree, I can very much agree with this.

Correspondences for Healing Spells

Best Symbols: Abracadabra triangle, ankh, caduceus, cauldron, chalice, cup, djed pillar, egg, eye of Horus, faery healing symbol, feather wreath, fishtail, healing-associated runes, horseshoe, knots, mermaid, naoratna (nine wisdoms), padlock, pentacle, radiant lotus, sacred flame, salamander, sclepius wand, snake curled around the moon, solar cross, spiral sun, triple moon, undine.

Planets: Earth, Jupiter, Mercury, Moon, Neptune, Sun, Uranus.

Elements: Air, earth, fire (to destroy disease), water.

Cardinal Points: East, north, south, west.

Best Days: Monday, Sunday, Thursday, Wednesday.

Numbers: 1, 3, 7, 9.

Colours: Blue (especially good for healing wounds), gold, green, orange, pink (for female health), purple, red, silver, white, yellow (especially good for healing the mind and memory).

Incense: Cedar, cinnamon, eucalyptus, frankincense, ginseng, myrrh, nutmeg, pine, rose, rosemary, saffron, sage, sandalwood.

Plants/Trees: Adder's tongue, amaranth, anemone, angelica, apple, balm, balm of Gilead, barley, bay, blackberry, burdock, calamus, cannabis, carnation, cedar, chamomile, cinnamon, cowslip, cucumber, cypress, daffodil, dandelion root, dock, echinacea, elder, eucalyptus, fennel, fir, flax, frankincense, gardenia, garlic, geranium, ginseng, hazel, lavender, lemon balm, lemongrass, lime, lotus, mandrake, milk thistle, milkweed, mint, mistletoe, mugwort, myrrh, nettle, nutmeg, oak, onion, orange, passionflower, peppermint, pine, plantain, plum, potato, rose, rosemary, rowan, rue, saffron, sage, sandalwood, sassafras, thyme, vanilla, verbena, vervain, vine, violet, walnut, willow, wintergreen, wood sorrel.

Crystals/Stones: Amber, amethyst, aquamarine, aventurine, banded agate, beryl, bloodstone, carnelian, coral, diamond, emerald, garnet, green agate, hematite, jade, jasper, jet, lapis lazuli, lodestone, moonstone, pearl, peridot, pyrite, ruby, sapphire, sodalite, sunstone, topaz, turquoise.

Metals: Gold, silver.

Creatures: Badger, bear, canary, cat, chinchilla, cow, crow, dog, falcon, fish, flamingo, hummingbird, iguana (especially good for healing skin problems), kinkajou, leopard, macaw, manatee, mole, muskrat, octopus, osprey, otter, parrot, platypus, raven, salamander, sea horse, sloth, snake (especially rattlesnake), tiger, turtle, walrus, wolf, wombat.

Deities: Adonis, Anu, Apollo, Artemis, Asclepius, Athena, Baal, Babalu-Aye, Belenos, Brigit, Caelus, Carmenta, Chiron the Centaur, Dian Cecht, Gaia, Govannon, Hercules, Hermes, Horus, Hygeia, Inanna, Ishtar, Isis, Jupiter, Kadesh, Khonsu, Kulpala, Lakshmi, Lugh, Marduk, Marqod, Meditrina, Mercury, Minerva, Neptune, Nuada, Paeon, Panacea, Poseidon, Sarasvati, Sekhmet, Shakaburu, Spes, Sulis, Tara, the Green Man, Thoth, Tlazelteotl,

Uranus, Vishnu, Zeus. Generally earthy, solar or lunar deities.

Magical Ways to Promote Healing

Here, we will look at some of the most famous ways to promote healing in Witchcraft. These are my personal favourites that can really help you to boost healing magic. These simple healing ways are excellent on their own but they can also be done in addition to healing spells (or as parts of them) to really get the most out of them. They will surround you or your loved ones with the healing powers of nature to relieve any suffering and to speed up recovery. You can also use them to inspire you when creating your own healing spells – whether for yourself or for others who you wish to heal.

One very simple way to promote healing is with healing teas or potions. One of the simplest is a tea of rosemary and bay. Both of these herbs are very healing and can uplift the spirits and help us to feel better when we are unwell. This is the tea I often give to my partner when he is unwell and I have noticed that he often recovers quickly when I give him this tea. Another tea that is very healing involves chamomile, vervain and passionflower. This is a good healing tea to drink to help you to stay calm or before bed to help induce sleep. Most of the body's healing processes occur during sleep. It is the time when the body does much of its repair work. The healing powers of the herbs and their ability to help to induce sleep can really help the body to heal. Healing teas are something I would always recommend to anyone who is burdened with illness.

A cup of healing tea offered by a Witch to someone who is unwell should always be accepted. When Witches offer herbal teas to those who are ill, they pour their own healing energies into the teas with the intention of helping others. Sitting with others who are unwell and giving them your complete support and sympathy while the teas are sipped are very healing things for you to do as a Witch or would-be Witch. Letting people vent out their anger because of their illness while really listening to them without any judgement or comment and giving them your full attention can make them feel so much better and can really aid the healing process. Hugging someone or giving him or her a nice massage with healing oils or lotions are other forms of healing gestures. Touch is an amazing thing and almost everyone responds positively to it when they are unwell. Merely holding or hugging others while they vent out and have a good cry is one of the simplest, yet most effective, healing methods that a Witch can do. Nobody should ever underestimate the power of tea and sympathy in my opinion.

One area of healing that many Witches take a real interest in is crystal healing. Crystals and stones are the very bones of the Earth Mother and each has unique energies that can really boost healing magic. In ancient times, it was believed that crystals and stones had fallen from the heavens as sacred gifts from the old gods and ancestors. This is not so far from the truth as you might expect. Crystals and stones are actually made up of molecules that once originated from the old stars of the universe. Crystals and stones can be carried; worn on the body (on a necklace or bracelet for example); placed somewhere special in the home; placed on a healing altar; held over an affected area of the body (such as a broken limb for example) and so on. Following are some of my favourite healing crystals and stones that I have worked with the most over the years and their specific healing uses:

- Amethyst for overcoming additions, compulsive behaviour, sleeplessness and harsh emotions.
- Aquamarine for boosting the immune system, clearing negative emotions, encouraging optimism and soothing the heart.
- Bloodstone for stimulating the physical systems of the body (especially blood circulation), providing motivation and encouragement and promoting strength and good health.
- Carnelian for reducing stress, anxiety and trauma.
- Emerald for speeding up the cleansing and purifying processes of the body and banishing hidden fears and anxieties.
- Jasper for encouraging enthusiasm and drive, nurturing damaged areas of the body to aid a fast recovery and gently grounding the mind and body.
- Moonstone for balancing blood and lymph systems, encouraging empathy, stabilising emotions and relieving stress, anxiety, tension, stress-

related indigestion, menstrual cramps and other female issues.

- Pearl for regulating glandular function, balancing emotions, encouraging emotional clarity, increasing tolerance and reducing worry, anxiety and frustration.
- Peridot for balancing the mind and body, reducing toxins, banishing negative thoughts and emotions, letting go of the past and strengthening personal identity.
- Pyrite for encouraging vitality, reducing anxiety, depression and frustration, strengthening logical thinking and protecting from pollutants and negativity.
- Ruby for balancing the heart, healing an unhealthy relationship with a father and encouraging good health, confidence, security, enthusiasm and self-esteem.
- Sodalite for physical healing, enhancing the immune system, stabilising emotions, clarifying perception and encouraging calmness, peace and contentment.
- Sunstone for general healing, vitality, strength and all male issues.

Another way to promote healing is with the use of a healing bath or shower. This is one of the most effective ways to heal the mind, body and soul since water is very healing and purifying and can help you to release any negativity. This negativity can be visualised as being washed away from the body and going down the plughole. You can place healing crystals and stones in the bathroom, if you like, as well as healing incense and candles of colours that relate to healing, such as blue and yellow. You can also create a healing body wash. One of my favourites involves the oils of rosemary, sandalwood and lavender which are added to an unscented body wash. Use this with a cloth or bath puff to cleanse the body of negativity and to help the mind to promote healing. If you decide to have a healing bath, add salt to the water (sea salt is best). Salt is very purifying and neutralises and eliminates negativity. It will strengthen the healing process of the body. If you bathe or shower on a Sunday when ill, health will be strengthened and restored very quickly.

After your bath or shower, you can perhaps apply a healing lotion to the skin as well. One of my personal favourites involves the oils of chamomile, lavender and vanilla which are added to an unscented body lotion. This lotion is very calming and is excellent for healing when we are angry, irritated, frustrated or just at our wits' end. It is excellent for those who suffer from nervous tension. If you are feeling run down and need a good energy boost, add the oils of orange, peppermint and lemongrass to an unscented body lotion and apply this to the skin. This can really boost your energy levels and promote your body's natural ability to heal itself. Always first test any body washes or lotions on the back of the hand before use to avoid any adverse reactions.

To create a special incense for healing magic, mix together myrrh, rose buds, sage and saffron in a small bowl. Then add three drops each of rosemary, thyme and sandalwood oils. Do this on a Sunday, the day of the sun which is very healing, and then leave the herbs and oils to dry out for one week. On the following Sunday, place the incense in a clean glass jar with a cork lid. You can then use two to three spoonfuls when needed. This is an incense blend that can be very effective for healing magic of any kind.

Some Witches also like to burn special healing oils in aromatherapy lamps. If you feel that the area in which you live is filled with negativity and that this negativity may be the root of your illness, you can add the oils of rosemary, thyme and lemongrass to a carrier oil, such as almond oil, and then burn this in your lamp. If you simply can't relax and let go of stress, the oils of lemon balm, lavender, passionflower and rose can be added to a carrier oil and burned in your lamp. Relaxation is important when we wish to heal because stress and tension causes imbalance and reduces the body's ability to heal.

Another way to promote healing is with the use of healing wands. Healing wands can involve the use of dried herbs bound together with a cord or yarn in a long shape which are then burned to release the smoke. A sage wand, for example, is very effective for healing magic. Simply bundle the herb or herbs together with the stems even at the bottom. Then, starting at the base, wrap the cord or yarn around the herb or herbs tightly. When you reach the top of your wand, tie a knot to secure the herb or herbs together. Then hang the wand up somewhere special for a week or two to dry out. You can then trim the ends flat, perhaps with your bolline. Then when it is ready, light the end until it glows. Then blow the end gently so that the smoke can be released to aid any healing magic that you wish to carry out or generally to infuse the area with healing powers.

Another way to encourage healing magic is to work with ritual fires. Fire destroys disease and is excellent for promoting healing. The types of woods that are burned in fires can affect magical workings of healing immensely. Oak wood, for example, is a very healing wood to burn according to folklore from many cultures. It is a wood of the sun and of strength that is burned in the fireplace or cauldron when someone within the home has become very sick. Burning oak wood is said to promote good health and to banish the illness and aid recovery. It is also said that burning this wood will prevent anyone else within the home from contracting the illness. Incidentally, the acorn from the oak tree is said to be an excellent charm for protection against illness and pain.

Since sleep is the ideal time to heal the mind and body, there are some curious methods to do with it that are said to aid healing. Sleeping with the head pointing towards the west is said to aid sleep and healing since this is the direction associated with water – the element that strongly governs sleep and healing. Sleeping with an onion tied to the bedpost is said to be very effective for speeding up the recovery of any number of ills. It is also said to protect those who live within the household from future sickness. Placing a horseshoe under the mattress is said to heal toothache and a champagne or wine cork placed there is said to heal back problems. Magnets, especially those that are shaped like a horseshoe, are said to relieve aches and pains when placed in the bed. Purists use lodestones, which are natural magnets, for these problems. Fir branches hung over the bed are also said to speed up healing and to protect against future sickness. A wreath made of feathers and placed under the pillow will also speed up healing.

One of the most effective ways to heal is to work with the healing powers of the sun. The sun has long been associated with healing and Witches and other Pagans have harnessed its healing powers for millennia. If you have become burdened with illness, merely sitting relaxed in a sunny spot and then imagining the sun's healing rays penetrating your body and driving out the darkness of illness and depression can be enough to get the body's healing process going. It will strengthen your body and encourage vitality. If you do this during the summer and on a Sunday, then all the more powerful this simple healing method will be. Please be very careful when sitting under the sun. Too much of it, as with everything else, can be harmful. Remember to use creams to protect yourself from any sun damage.

Another way to promote healing is to work with the healing energies of the earth itself. Simply lie on some fresh, uncovered soil and visualise the illness sinking into the ground. Feel any anxiety, pain, depression, anguish and any other negative association running into the earth and away from you. Feel the powers of the earth and the heartbeat of the Earth Mother. If you are doing this properly, her heartbeat should become in tune with yours. Then feel her cool, soft, gentle and healing energies raising up through your body, healing away the illness. You can then rub the afflicted area of the body with an apple or potato and visualise the problem absorbing into it. Then bury it into the soil. Then raise from the ground and dust yourself off. You should immediately feel better. If you are bedridden and can't do the above, simply have a potted healing plant in your sickroom. The healing powers of the plant and soil will help to speed up your recovery.

One method of healing that I have found very effective is to work with the element of water. Take a stick that will float and carve it with words, symbols or pictures associated with any problems that you have to do with your illness. Visualise all the problems absorbing into the stick. Then go to a river and set it afloat on the water. Then turn around and walk home without looking back. As the stick floats away, so too will your problems as long as your will to heal is strong enough. Let the water, the great healer and cleanser, release your problems and bring you great healing.

A Water Healing Spell

This healing spell utilises the power of the element of water to bring healing. It is loosely based on the healing spells I did for my grandmother and mother. It is suitable for those who need healing and wish to become well. Although healing spells can have remarkable results and can even create miracles, most often healing spells cannot cure terminal illness. Remember that Witches work with the flow of nature and not against it. However, if someone is suffering from a terminal illness, he or she can still benefit from a healing spell. The spell can bring forth strength, comfort, calmness and tranquillity. If nothing else, the healing spell will make the rest of their days more bearable. As Witches, all we can really do is hope for the best for those who are terminally ill.

Ingredients required for this spell:

- Taper blue candle.
- Matches.
- Fine paintbrush.
- Small piece of clean white paper.
- Dot of red watercolour paint.
- Small bowl or cauldron of water.
- Sandalwood oil.
- Small bowl of a mixture of healing-associated herbs, such as lavender, rosemary, mint, thyme, bay, carnation, mugwort and so on.

Casting the spell:

On a night of a waning moon (to banish disease, misery and pain), preferably on a Sunday which is the traditional time of healing, place all the spell ingredients on a flat surface, such as your altar, with the candle in the centre. Light the candle with a match and add seven drops of the oil to the bowl of healing herbs. Mix the herbs and the oil together with your hands and focus on bringing forward healing powers to yourself or whoever else you are wanting to heal. Then sprinkle the herbs around the base of the candle. Paint an "x" in the centre of the paper with the paintbrush and the red paint. Add seven drops of the oil to the bowl or cauldron of water. Visualise any negative associations of the illness absorbing into the "x" on the paper. Then emerge the paper in the bowl or cauldron of water and move the paper around with your hands so that the paint begins to slowly fade. Strongly visualise the negative afflictions fading away also. Then when you are ready, say these or similar words:

As I emerge this paper in this cleansing element of water healing shall flow,
In the name of the Goddess and God the offence of this pain and anxiety shall go.
By the powers of the earth and the heavens, of the land and sea, of the moon and sun,
Sickness and pain depart and be it done.
Healing powers of nature that I now request,
Please let healing be so that (say the name of the person) can be at his/her best.
Sickness you are an offence and nobody needs you to stay,
And so I ask the powers of nature to make you go away.
By the healing powers of this water I ask you to depart,
So that (say the name of the person) can truly be in a better place and heart.
Body please be healthy and please be strong,
As I chant this healing song.
By the powers of my Mother Goddess and my Father God healing health I do restore,
And may it be so evermore.
An' it harm none, so mote it be.

If possible, leave the bowl or cauldron of water under the light of the waning moon for a few moments. You can then use this time to visualise on the bringing forward of healing energies to the person. You can then simply allow the candle to burn out or you can simply snuff it out. You may be very surprised by what will happen by the time that the moon wanes once again in the coming month. I truly do wish you every success in your healing magic. May you and your loved ones be blessed with good health and healing.

Chapter Twelve: Success Spells

When we consider spells that specifically ask for success we think of things like new employment or promotion in an already existing job, the publication of a new book, a fruitful business, good results in exams and so on. Success is necessary for us all. Wanting to be successful in life is not selfish. It gives us the feelings of self-worth, self-confidence and gives us a reason to get up in the morning. This boost is emotionally and physically important for our health and well-being. Nobody should feel guilty about wanting to be successful in life. Magic can be utilised to bring us the success we need to help us to move forward in life. In one way or another, all of us need success.

Whenever I think of success spells, I often think of the spell I cast for my partner. For some time, he was out of employment and was desperate for a job because he is a natural worker and money-maker being a Virgo man. At Beltane one year, I decided to cast a spell to get him his dream. He has been a professional hairstylist, something he is very skilled at, for over ten years as of this writing after I cast a success spell for him but he has had to work hard to maintain his position and this leads me to a fundamental point. As with all positive magic, you have to work hard in life in addition to casting spells that specifically ask for success.

People who believe that they are "unlucky" can truly benefit from casting success spells. Success spells can put us in situations where we are in the right place at the right time, are able to say the right things at the right time and are able to act positively through instinct. If you desire to be "lucky" in life then you can call upon magic to create the right positive atmosphere for this. Generally, people who consider themselves to be "unlucky" have created this for themselves because of their belief in this. This belief can be hard to change and magic that specifically asks for success can be a wonderful way for us to change our attitude. It can reverse the negative energies around us and fill our lives with positivity. The spell that I have created at the end of this chapter is the one I have utilised to help me to get this book published!

Naturally, we all have the power to change our misfortune, but many of us don't know how to do this properly. It all boils down to the power of our emotions. The word "emotion" comes from the Latin word *"emovere"* meaning "to move". The "e" in this word basically means "to emit the motion" or "to send forth the motion". So to be "emotionless" means "to be blocked from motion". In other words, it means that we can't put our emotions into action. Many people are "unlucky" because they have blocked their emotions and, therefore, can't bring forth the success that they truly want. To be successful in life and to cast spells that ask for success, you need to learn to unblock your emotions to create the right positive atmosphere in your life. Remember that you have the power inside you to be able to do this. Learning to take control of your feelings can reverse the negative energies around you immensely. Just have faith and believe in yourself. Take charge of your life and believe that you can be successful in it. That's all you need to do really.

The heavenly bodies that strongly govern success are Jupiter, the planet of great luck, and the sun. Imagine the rays of the sun cutting through the veil of confusion that stops you from moving forward in life. Visualise its positive rays penetrating your soul and helping you to bring forth the success that you truly want. Imagine its fiery energies giving you the strength that you need to achieve your goals. Don't let anyone or anything get in the way of your success. The powers of the sun and the element of fire can affect success spells immensely.

Correspondences for Success Spells

Best Symbols: Ankh, athame, axe, corn dolly or kirn baby, cornucopia (the horn of plenty), eagle claw, four-leaf clover, hag stone, horns (especially ram's horns), horseshoe, miniature champagne bottles, naoratna (nine wisdoms), pentacle, salamander, solar cross, spiral sun, success-associated runes, sword, sylph, triangle.

Planets: Earth, Jupiter, Sun.

Elements: Air, earth, fire, water (water is particularly great for contract negotiations).

Cardinal Points: East, north, south, west.

Best Days: Sunday, Thursday.

Numbers: 1, 2, 3, 4, 5, 6, 7, 8, 9.

Colours: Gold, green, orange, purple, red, silver, yellow.

Incense: Cedar, cinnamon, cinquefoil, dragon's blood, frankincense, lemon verbena, marigold petals, myrrh, nutmeg, orange, patchouli, sandalwood.

Plants/Trees: Allspice, almond, aloe, balm, bamboo, banyan, be-still, bluebell, cabbage, calamus, cedar, chamomile, China berry, cinchona, cinnamon, cinquefoil, clover, corn, cotton, daffodil, dragon's blood, fern, fir, frankincense, ginger, grains of paradise, hawthorn, hazel, heather, holly, houseleek, huckleberry, Irish moss, jalap root, job's tears, lavender, lemon balm, lemongrass, lemon verbena, linden, lucky hand, male fern, marigold, moss, myrrh, nutmeg, oak, orange, patchouli, persimmon, pineapple, pomegranate, poppy, purslane, rowan, rose, sandalwood, snakeroot, star anise, strawberry, sumbul, sunflower, violet, wahoo, wild rose, winter bark.

Crystals/Stones: Amber, apache tear, aventurine, black agate, carnelian, chrysoprase, citrine, emerald, garnet, green tourmaline, hematite, jade, jasper, lodestone, magnetite, malachite, moonstone, opal, pearl, pyrite, rose quartz, ruby, sapphire, sunstone, tiger's eye, topaz, turquoise.

Metals: Gold, silver.

Creatures: Ant, badger, bear, bee, blue jay, bull, cassowary, chipmunk, cockatoo, cormorant, cougar, crane, donkey, eagle, egret, elephant, elk, gibbon, giraffe, gnu, goat, gopher, hyena, jaguar, kangaroo, kingfisher, kookaburra, lion, llama, mongoose, monkey, moose, musk ox, osprey, otter, owl, peacock, pigeon, ram, rat, raven, robin, salamander, salmon, seal, shark, skunk, sparrow, squirrel, stag, swan, tiger, toad, walrus, weasel, wolf, wolverine, wombat, zebra.

Deities: Abundantia, Agathodaemon, Al Yazid, Al Yusif, Apollo, Athena, Belenos, Benzaiten, Bes, Bona Eventus, Bonus Eventus, Caerus, Cernunnos, Ebisu, Felicitas, Fortuna, Gad, Gaia, Ganesha, Ikenga, Jupiter, Krishna, Kubera, Lakshmi, Leib-Olmai, Lugh, Manibhadra, Minerva, Nortia, Nuada,

Pan, Renenutet, Rod, Rundas, Sa'd, Sors, the Green Man, Thor, Tyche, Vishnu, Zeus.

Magical Ways to Attract Success

In this part of this chapter, we will look at some of my favourite ways to attract success. These simple, magical ways can really give your success magic a boost. They can be done in addition to success spells (or as parts of them) but they are also very effective on their own. They will surround you with great fortune, luck and will promote self-confidence. Self-confidence is, after all, key when we want to be successful in life. It goes a long way in improving our negative situations. You can also use this information when creating your own success spells.

One way to attract success is with a success shrine. This can simply be a small table covered with a cloth that relates to success, such as orange or gold. You can decorate your success shrine with deities, symbols and signs of success, if you like, and place a candle of an appropriate colour in the centre. You can then perhaps sprinkle the base of your candle with marigold and sunflower petals. The candle can also be anointed with an oil that relates to success. You can also inscribe the candle with a symbol of success, such as the Wunjo rune. You can then perhaps write down on a piece of yellow paper what it is you want and place this on the shrine. You can also burn some success incense on your shrine to invite good fortune and luck. Placed in the south, a success shrine can be very effective.

To create a special success incense, mix together cedar shavings, cinnamon, sandalwood, cinquefoil and nutmeg in a small bowl. Then add three drops each of orange and lemon verbena oils. Do this on a Thursday or Sunday, the days of Jupiter and the sun, then leave the dish of herbs and oils to dry out for one week. On the following Thursday or Sunday, place the incense in a clean glass jar with a cork lid. Use two to three spoonfuls when needed. This incense blend will really empower success magic and is excellent to improve self-confidence before an important interview, review or meeting.

If confidence is a major problem for you then there are a few very effective ways that you can do to improve your self-esteem. One way is to work with confidence bath salts. Blend together three teaspoons of Epsom salts with the dried herbs of orange peel, lavender buds and lemongrass. Then add this to your bath water. Alternatively, blend together the oils of lavender, orange blossom and lemongrass with three teaspoons of Epsom salts and add this to your bath water. You can then relax in your confidence bath for as long as you will while focusing on boosting your self-esteem. You can perhaps burn some success incense in the bathroom and place crystals or stones that relate to success around you as well as candles of gold, orange and yellow to infuse your life with positive vibes. This bath is excellent for times when you are feeling low and are at your wits' end and need to build your confidence up to where it should be. If you take this bath on a Sunday or Thursday, then success will surely come.

Another way to improve your confidence is to work with confidence lotions. One of my favourites involves the oils of lemon verbena, orange blossom and lavender which are added to an unscented body lotion along with a little honey. Apply this to the skin (remember to test a little on the back of the hand first) whenever you feel that your confidence is waning. This lotion is excellent when used after a confidence-boosting bath. Without a doubt, you will feel quite different and ready to take on whatever life throws at you when you use this lotion.

Another way to build your confidence for success magic is with the use of potions or infusions. One of my favourites involves orange peel, lemongrass, lavender buds and chamomile. You can add this to a confidence-boosting bath or perhaps drink it from a yellow cup when you need to feel more confident in yourself, your abilities and your appearance. The potion is especially useful for times when your confidence has been bruised, such as after a break-up, job loss, bad results in exams or a bad review. It will help you to move on and to restore your confidence. You can then reflect on the areas where you went wrong, learn from them, so that you slowly learn not to make the same mistakes again in the future.

If you enjoy working with oils, then why not create some confidence and career oils? Confidence and career oils are excellent for enhancing success magic. They can perhaps be applied to yellow and orange candles before an important event, such as a job interview, or added to an aromatherapy lamp in your office before an important negotiation or when writing a letter to a publishing house in order to get a book published. One of my favourite oils for the above involves the oils of almond, orange, lemon verbena and lavender. Another favourite of mine involves the oils of almond, cedar, cinnamon and nutmeg. These oils will help you to bring forth good fortune and positivity into your life immensely.

One effective way to attract success is to work with the herb cinnamon. Cinnamon is a wonderful spice that is strongly associated with success and the heavenly body that strongly governs success – the sun. Cinnamon can be loaded into candles, stuffed into poppets and sachets, placed under carpets and rugs, placed around doorways, added to food, added to success baths and so on. Added to a yellow or orange sachet with a carnelian stone and carried or placed somewhere special in the home, cinnamon can be very useful to help us to attract success. If you place a four-leaf clover in your sachet or attach it to the front of it, then success will surely be yours. Alternatively, a four-leaf clover can be worn over the right breast or placed on a success shrine to invite great luck, good fortune and success.

Another way that is very useful for success magic is to work with jalap root which is also known as High John the Conqueror. Jalap root can be used to decorate the home to avert depression, improve self-confidence and attract success. It can also be added to vegetable or olive oil for the above purposes. Simply take three pieces of the root and make small cuts into them with a sharp knife, such as your bolline. Then place these roots into the bottle of the oil and place this bottle somewhere special, such as a magical pantry, to attract success. After a few weeks, the oil can be very useful to anoint candles, sachets, poppets and so on that are designed to magically attract success.

Another way to attract success is to work with ritual fires. Fire is the powerful element of success, change and transformation. Magically, it will clear away the old in order to make way for the new. It will strengthen your willpower and help you to achieve your goals. It represents your inner fire and passion to achieve your needs and goals. A blazing fire in the home can be excellent for attracting success into your life. The types of woods that are burned in ritual fires can also affect magical workings of success immensely. Rowan wood, for example, has long been associated with success. It is a wood of the sun and its element of fire that is burned in the fireplace or cauldron to empower magical workings of success and confidence. Meditating by such a fire while focusing on your needs and goals can be a very powerful thing to do. Incidently, the berries from the rowan tree make very useful charms that attract success. They can be added to poppets and sachets, for example, for this purpose.

Another thing that you may want to consider to attract success is the position in which to sleep at night. Sleep is a very receptive time when we are open to the magical powers of nature. When we dream we are highly receptive to unconscious influence. If you sleep with your head pointing towards the south, then great success shall be yours providing your will is strong and you believe in the powers of the southern quarter. South is the realm of passion, strength, confidence, motivation and, of course, success. If you place a vase of flowers and crystals or stones that relate to success in your bedroom, perhaps on your bedside table, then this will strengthen your ability to achieve success. Sleeping with your head pointing towards the south, which is strongly associated with the summer, before an important event, such as a job interview or an exam, will improve your chances of success immensely.

A Fire Success Spell

This spell utilises the element of fire to bring success. It is the spell that I have utilised to help me to get this book published and is loosely based on the spell I cast for my partner to get him his job. I cannot stress enough, however, that you also have to work hard in life, as I have with this book. You can't expect magic to do everything for you. In other words, you must be prepared to work very hard in life in addition to casting success spells. Nonetheless, this spell can be a powerful aid to help you to achieve whatever it is that you are wanting in life. Cast it before a job interview, when applying to get a book published, before an exam or whatever else your personal goal is in order for you to achieve success. The spell is most effective if it is carried out by the person who wants success but it can also be cast on behalf of someone else (with a little tweaking) as long as you explain to the person what I have stressed above. Remember also to explain to the person who you are casting the success spell for to be prepared to put their trust into the spiritual powers of nature.

Ingredients required for this spell:

- Taper orange candle.
- Matches.
- Small orange pouch.
- Two carnelian stones.
- Two yellow flowers that relate to success, such as sunflowers or marigolds.
- Small piece of clean yellow or orange paper.
- Pen with green ink.
- A fireproof bowl or small iron cauldron.
- Orange blossom oil.
- Small bowl of a mixture of success-associated herbs, such as cinnamon, nutmeg, cedar shavings, cinquefoil, ginger, lavender and so on.

Casting the spell:

On a night of a waxing or full moon, or at the noon of the sun, preferably on a Thursday or Sunday which are the traditional times of success magic, place all your spell ingredients on a flat surface, such as your altar. The candle and fireproof bowl or cauldron should be placed in the centre with a yellow flower and carnelian to either side of them. Light the candle with a match and add eight drops of the oil to the bowl of success herbs. Mix the herbs and oil together with your hands while focusing on the success of your need or goal. Then sprinkle the herbs around the base of the candle and fireproof bowl or cauldron. By the candlelight, write down exactly what the need or goal is while focusing on your success. Take your time with this process. Then allow one drop of the oil to fall on to each of the four corners of the paper. Then fold the paper three times. Then when you are ready, light the paper with the candle flame and drop it into the fireproof bowl or cauldron to allow the paper to burn to ashes. This represents the element of fire transforming your need or goal into physical reality. Then when you are ready, say these or similar words:

> *As I burn this wish in these flames of the element of fire,*
> *I ask the powers of nature to help me to bring forth my desire.*
> *O yellow petals of these success flowers,*
> *Lend this spell your wonderful and magical powers.*
> *O Mother Goddess, Father God and spirits of fire*
> *please clear my sight,*
> *And bring me the success I need that is mine by right.*
> *O beautiful elements of nature please give me the chance,*
> *To bring forth the success that I will enhance.*
> *May the success I need flow ever in my way,*
> *From this very sacred and blessed day.*
> *An' it harm none, so mote it be.*

If possible, leave the two carnelians under the light of the moon or sun for a few moments. You can then use this time to focus on your visualisation and success. Strongly visualise yourself with your need or goal. Then place the two carnelian stones and some of the herbs and petals of the yellow flowers in the pouch. You can then simply allow the candle to burn out or you can simply snuff it out. You can then carry the pouch with you wherever you go and place it under your pillow each night when you retire. Alternatively, you can hang the pouch somewhere special in your home to infuse it and your life with good fortune, luck and success. I truly do wish you all the best in your success magic. May the Goddess and God bless your life with great luck and good fortune.

Chapter Thirteen: Protection Spells

However tempted you may be to curse or hex someone who has wronged you or made your life a misery, it is important to point out that black magic is not ethical or acceptable in genuine Witchcraft or Paganism. Those who claim to be Witches and also curse people are not genuine Witches in my opinion. They are what we call corrupt magicians and are messing with forces way beyond their control and understanding. The forces of nature are very real and when we perform black magic we are messing with the dark and destructive side of it. This can be disastrous to say the least. Karma is a very real thing. Whatever we put out in life will eventually return to us – three times over. It is the natural law. So why would you want to create more misery and destruction in your life just to get gratification from seeing the person who has wronged you having misfortune or an early demise at your own hands?

The best thing you can do is try to avoid destructive people where possible. There are better ways to deal with destructive people than using black magic and this is where protection spells come in. Protecting whatever you hold dear – yourself, home, business, possessions, family, friends, pets and so on – most certainly is ethical in Witchcraft. Protection is necessary for us all. Protection magic creates an invisible force field that is a powerful, protective barrier. It prevents physical and psychic attacks of idiots, nasty people and their evil or negative vibrations (or whatever else we are wanting to protect ourselves from). Performing protective magic does not mean that you will avoid every single annoyance or misfortune in life. However, it will help you to screen out potentially harmful, negative and destructive situations.

Never allow anyone to be abusive and controlling towards you. You are a free soul, a spark of the divine, and deserve respect. If you have done nothing wrong to an abusive person, what right does he or she have to unjustly treat you bad? Abusive people, those who deliberately go out of their way to cause trouble, hardship and to hurt you or your loved ones are agents of their own destruction. Such people are weak-minded, emotionally insecure, idiotic and sadistic individuals who are on shaky ground because they will eventually have to face their karma. Such people are uneducated and have much to learn about life. They have a long road ahead of them.

The reason people may treat you bad is incredibly simple: deep down they are afraid of you in some way. They may resent your happiness and everything that you represent. Such people are wanting to take away your happiness and destroy your sound reputation. Don't let them do this. Witches are often the targets of destructive people because others may be jealous of their knowledge, powers and their relationship with the divine. As such, protection magic is something that Witches hold very dear to their hearts indeed.

Protection magic can often work in very strange and mysterious ways. Sometimes situations can get worse before they actually improve and this is something that you may have to bear in mind. If, for example, a loved one is abusing drugs or alcohol and is, in turn, abusive towards you when he or she is under the influence, the drug or alcohol problem may worsen to the point where you end up cutting him or her out of your life when your protection spell begins to take effect. Your loved one may then realise how foolish he or she has been and want to make things right in an attempt to bring you back into their life. As the person sobers up, the harsh realities of what he or she has been doing to you may hit hard and so the healing process can begin.

There are other forms of protection magic that are notable for this chapter. These are banishing and binding magic. A banishing spell basically takes away someone from your life. It basically leaves him or her free to become someone else's problem. You will have to think long and hard before you banish someone from your life. Ask yourself the questions: do I really want this person out of my life? Is this person so bad that I have to cut him/her out of my life completely? All too often, we can think irrationally when we are just at our wits' end with people. So allow yourself to calm down and to think things through properly so that you can consider your options. Once a banishing spell has taken effect it is done. There's no going back. A person who you have banished may move away and you may never see him or her again in your life. So you may just want to do a spell that protects you from their actions rather than perform a spell that banishes him or her completely.

Binding magic basically prevents people from harming themselves or others. It is a bit more complex than banishing magic. It often involves the binding of a poppet that represents someone who is abusive with a cord or ribbon to stop him or her from attacking others – whether physically, psychologically or psychically. If you wish to bind an abusive person you will have to cut him or her out of your life and break all connection for the spell to be completely effective. So a banishing spell may also be in order.

If you feel that you are under psychic attack then protection spells can be utilised for this. Many people have been known to drive themselves insane thinking that they are under the psychic attack of black magic, elementals, spirits of the dead, the wrath of ex-lovers and so on. But psychic attack from such things are actually very rare. Often, people are simply victims of their own fears, anxieties, obsessions and worries. The mind is a very powerful thing. If someone believes himself or herself to be cursed then that energy will probably manifest itself. In other words, it is his or her own creation. However, protection spells will still work regardless of whether a curse is real or it is not. If the psychic attack is not real, protection spells will, at least, protect you from your own paranoia and imagination. They will remove the negative energy around you and restore balance and harmony.

Correspondences for Protection Spells

Best Symbols: Athame, bell, broomstick, candle, cimaruta, circle, corn dolly or kirn baby, crow's foot, djed pillar, eight-spoked wheel, eye of Horus, evil eye charm, fishtail, gnome, hag stone, hand charms, horseshoe, knotted cords, labyrinth, mermaid, pentacle, protection-associated runes, phallic symbols, salamander, solar cross, spiral sun, shield, spoon, sword, sylph, triple moon, undine, wand.

Planets: Earth, Jupiter, Mars, Moon, Neptune, Saturn, Sun.

Elements: Air, earth, fire, water.

Cardinal Points: East, north, south, west.

Best Days: Monday, Saturday, Sunday, Thursday, Tuesday.

Numbers: 1, 2, 3, 4, 5, 7, 8, 9.

Colours: Black (excellent for banishing and binding), blue (for repelling negativity), brown (for stopping people from harming you without cutting them out of your life completely), gold, orange, red, silver, white.

Incense: Angelica, avens, bay, basil, calamus, cedar, cinnamon, dragon's blood, frankincense, ginseng, juniper, mugwort, myrrh, patchouli, pine, rose, rosemary, sage, sandalwood, St. John's wort, yarrow.

Plants/Trees: Acacia, agrimony, ague root, aloe, althea, alyssum, amaranth, anemone, angelica, anise, arbutus, asafoetida, ash, avens, balm of Gilead, bamboo, barley, basil, bay, bean, betony, birch, bittersweet, blackberry, bladderwrack, bloodroot, blueberry, bodhi tree, boneset, bromeliad, broom, buckthorn, buckwheat, burdock, cacti, calamus, caraway, carnation, carob, cascara sagrada, castor, cedar, celandine, chamomile, chrysanthemum, cinchona, cinnamon, cinquefoil, clove, clover, club moss, coconut, corn, cotton, cumin, curry, cyclamen, cypress, datura, dill, dogwood, dragon's blood, ebony, elder, elecampane, eucalyptus, euphorbia, fennel, fern, feverwort, figwort, flax, fleabane, foxglove, frankincense, galangal, gentian, garlic, geranium, ginseng, gorse, gourd, grass, hawthorn, hazel, heather, holly, honeysuckle, horehound, houseleek, hyacinth, hyssop, Irish moss, ivy, jalap root, jasmine, juniper, kava-kava, lady's slipper, larch, larkspur, lavender, leek, lettuce, lilac, lily, lime, linden, liquidamber, logwood, loosestrife, lotus, lucky hand, mallow, mandrake, marigold, marjoram, masterwort, meadow rue, mimosa, mint, mistletoe, molluka, motherwort, mugwort, mulberry, mullein, mustard, myrrh, nettle, oak, olive, onion, orris, papaya, papyrus, parsley, patchouli, pennyroyal, peony, pepper, pepper tree, periwinkle, pilot weed, pimpernel, pine, plantain, plum, primrose, pumpkin, purslane, quince, radish, ragwort, raspberry, rattlesnake root, rhubarb, rice, rose, rosemary, rowan, sage, sandalwood, sloe, snapdragon, southernwood, squill, St. John's wort, tamarisk, thistle, thyme, toadflax, tomato, tormentil, tulip, turnip, unicorn root, valerian, vervain, violet, wax plant, white bryony, willow, wintergreen, witchgrass, witch hazel, wolf's bane, woodruff, wormwood, yarrow, yucca. Generally spicy, stinging or thorny plants.

Crystals/Stones: Agate, amber, amethyst, aquamarine, bloodstone, carnelian, chalcedony, citrine, clear quartz, coral, diamond, diopside, emerald, fluorite, fossilised wood, fossil stone, garnet, jade, jasper, jet, lapis lazuli, lodestone, malachite, mother of pearl, onyx, peridot, pyrite, ruby, sapphire, smoky quartz, tiger's eye, topaz, tourmaline, turquoise.

Metals: Gold, silver.

Creatures: Alligator, armadillo, bear, blue jay, cat, crab, crocodile, dog, echidna, falcon, fish, goose, gorilla, hawk, horse (especially white horse), hummingbird, jackal, ladybird, leopard, lion, lynx, ostrich, mockingbird, peacock, penguin, porcupine, rhinoceros, salamander, scarab beetle, seal, shark, stag, swallow, tiger, turtle, weasel, whale, wolf, woodpecker.

Deities: Aditi, Amphitrite, Anahita, Anna Perenna, Anput, Anubis, Aries, Athena, Bes, Brigit, Cardea, Cernunnos, Cronos, Cuchulainnn, Elegua, Epona, Euryale, Frigg, Gaia, Ganesha, Hera, Horus, Hygeia, Isis, Juno, Jupiter, Kutkhu, Kwan-Yin, Mars, Medusa, Neith, Neptune, Nuada, Nut, Ochosi, Osiris, Pan, Poseidon, Ra, Rhiannon, Sarasvati, Saturn, Securitas, Stheno, Tanith, Terminus, the Dagda, the Green Man, Thor, Tlazelteotl, Varuna, Vidar, Vishnu, Zeus. Generally lunar, solar or earthy deities.

Magical Ways to Aid Protection

Here, we will look at some interesting and magical ways to aid protection. The ways in which to magically protect yourself or whatever else you hold dear are virtually endless. Over the years, magical peoples have developed many very effective ways of protection. However, in this chapter we will look at some of my own personal favourites. Many of these simple ways I have personally found very effective for protection. Give them a try if protection is something that you need at this time in your life. They will surround you and whatever else you hold dear with the protection forces of nature. You can use them on their own or in addition to protection spells (or as part of them). You can also use them when creating your own protection spells – whether for yourself or for those who come to you for help.

One very effective way to aid protection magic is to work with symbols, signs and figurines. The eye of Horus, for example, has long been used to aid protection. This beautiful symbol can be placed above a main door or near it. Alternatively, put a picture of a deity of protection above or near your door. Anubis, the jackal-headed Egyptian god of protection, would be excellent for this. As long as you trust the deity's powers, he or she will bring great protection and prevent evil or negativity from entering your home or wherever else you want to protect. If you want to specifically protect yourself then why not wear a silver pentacle? The pentacle has long been used for protection. It brings forth the protection of the sacred elements. The pentacle can also be placed above a main door to bring forth general protection to your home or wherever else you want to protect. You can also empower a piece of jewellery and wear this as an amulet of protection. In the east, names of protection deities are written on arches, doors and gates to aid protection. Even if the names are painted over, the protection will still work, according to folklore.

If you would like to create a special incense for protection, mix together bay, mugwort, yarrow, rosemary, avens, St. John's wort, angelica, basil and juniper in a small bowl. Then add three drops each of rose and sandalwood oils. Do this on a Saturday, the traditional day of protection magic, then leave the dish of herbs and oils to dry out for one week. On the following Saturday, place the incense in a clean glass jar with a cork lid. Use two to three spoonfuls when needed. This is an excellent incense blend that can be very useful for protection magic of all kinds. It will purify any area in which it is burned of evil or negativity.

Another way to aid protection is to work with herbal sachets. A herbal sachet of protection can be worn or carried or placed somewhere special. They can be filled with various herbs of protection as well as oils, amulets and crystals or stones. Herbal sachets that aid protection are something I have personally worked with for many years. I have had much success with their use and I'm sure you will if you decide to work with them.

There is another curious method of magical protection that some modern Witches carry out that is said to be very effective. This simple method is what modern Egyptians do to ward off the evil eye. This simply involves the dipping of the right hand in paint in order to make palm prints on the walls of wherever you want to protect. Blue paint is excellent for this. If you have been wondering what exactly the evil eye is then I will explain. It is the supposed glance of someone or something that wishes to cause great harm, fear, destruction and negativity or evil. The evil eye was once universally feared in all cultures and traditions.

If you enjoy working with infusions or potions then why not create a one for protection? The one I often work with is a herbal infusion of bay and rosemary as with for healing. If I ever feel threatened then this is the tea I create to avert danger or negativity and I have found it very effective. It is also very purifying and will neutralise any negativity within and around you. Another herbal infusion that is excellent for protection magic involves the herbs of mint, basil, dill and marigold. This infusion can also be sweetened with a little honey as with all herbal teas. It will bring forth great protection and ward away evil or negativity.

Another way to protect yourself is to have a familiar. The Witch's familiar, of the physical kind (Witches may also have spirit animal familiars), is an animal, a cat for example, with which the Witch has developed a special, magical, spiritual or psychic relationship. Contrary to popular belief, the Witch does not choose his or her familiar. The familiar chooses the Witch as his or her close companion. So if you want a familiar, you will have to begin establishing a very close bond with your pet. The Witch's familiar will always let his or her Witch know when danger is about. Generally, animals are sensitive to energies and can detect when these energies are good or bad. They will then let their owners know if there is negativity or evil about the house or near by. But the Witch must learn how to understand what animals are saying through their body language and the vibes that they give off. This takes time with the use of developing and awakening psychic powers.

One very effective way to protect yourself from all negativity is with an exercise known as the tower of light. To do this, you will first have to allow yourself to enter into a deep state of relaxation and meditation. Once you have done this, stand up straight with your hands by your sides. Then begin focusing on your breathing – breathe in for five seconds, hold your breath for five seconds and then breathe out for five seconds. Then visualise a blue oval shape surrounding your body. Take as long as you need to do this. Then when you are ready, visualise a globe of pure white light above your head. This represents your higher spiritual self, the part of you that is closest to the divine. Then visualise this white globe flowing down and penetrating your blue oval shape, filling it with a brilliant white light with silver sparkles. For maximum effect, repeat this three times each day. If you do this simple exercise on a regular basis it will bring ultimate protection, strengthen your aura and even your spiritual development. A blue pentagram can also be visualised on your brow during this simple method of protection. The blue pentagram can simply be visualised on your brow on any occasion when you feel under threat or in danger. It is a very old method of protection used by Witches and other magical peoples for centuries.

Dion Fortune, a respected spiritualist writer, wrote much about psychic protection. She wrote about, for example, sunlight. Sitting under the light of the sun is one of the most powerful things you can do for protection because the sun is associated with the element of fire. The element of fire is very powerful for protection. It drives away outside influences that may threaten our willpower to move forward in life. She also talked about laughter. I have always enjoyed a good laugh and enjoy making other people laugh being an Aquarius man which is ruled by the element that rules laughter – air. Laughter releases an enormous amount of magical power. Laughing at someone who is threatening you can destroy their harmful effects on you immensely. It is a simple method of protection that can create a powerful protective barrier around you.

The element of fire is very powerful for protection magic as you will know by now. You can fill your home with candles of colours that relate to protection – red, gold, blue, brown, black and so on – if this is something you feel that you need. Blue candles can be burned at night in the bedroom for protection before sleep and will also produce prophetic dreams. Brown candles can be burned to protect your pets. Kerosene lamps obviously relate to the element of fire and are a wonderful and romantic addition to your magical place of protection. If you decide to use kerosene lamps in your home or wherever else you want to protect follow the old tradition of putting a small piece of red yarn or cloth in the oil. This will prevent the lamp from exploding and will offer great protection, especially against poison or violence.

One of the most effective ways to aid protection magic is to work with the herb garlic. Garlic, which is ruled by the protective planet of Mars, is said to be extremely protective, according to folklore. Medicinally, it produces the active component allicin which is released when the garlic is crushed or chopped. This, in turn, releases other sulphides that aid great healing on the body and protect from diseases. This is why the herb, on a magical level, is considered so protective. Throughout the years, I have hung garlic near my back door to prevent evil from entering. I also did this to prevent robbers and thieves from entering and to stop envious people from entering. Biting garlic is said to drive away evil spirits. Sailors have carried it to prevent their ships from wreckage. Placed below children's pillows, garlic will protect them while they sleep. Brides, throughout history, have worn garlic for good luck at their wedding and to prevent evil from destroying their big day. If you carry garlic, it will, according to folklore, prevent all negativity or evil from coming to you.

Another herb to work with for protection is foxglove. This is one of my favourite types of wildflowers that is often present in my garden. Foxglove, which is also known as digitalis, is a poison and should not be taken internally. It is said that Pope John Paul I was assassinated with the use of this herb. It has huge effects on the heart. It has long been associated with Witches and has been used by them in their magical rites for centuries. I have always loved it, even before I fully took on the Witchcraft religion. Because it is toxic, it is considered very protective. Merely growing it in the garden will protect all those who live within the house, according to folklore. Throughout the years, housewives in Wales have used the leaves to make a black dye. This dye was then used to paint crossed lines on the stone floors of their cottages. This was believed to prevent evil from entering their homes. It is something that you may want to try.

An All-Purpose Poppet Protection Spell

This spell utilises a poppet to aid great protection. Since "opening up" to the Craft can make us very sensitive to the energies around us, it is important to renew our protection on a regular bases to shield ourselves from other people's envy, hatred and negative vibes. This protection spell will not keep you shut away from the world. Indeed, having to deal with the unpleasant situations of people is a part of life that no one can truly avoid. However, this spell will help you to filter out the very worst of the negative energies and bad emotions that dysfunctional people may direct at you. It is an all-purpose protection spell that will help to protect you from whatever you fear the most. If you do not protect yourself often you will absorb the negative energies – depression, pessimism, anger, hatred and so on – and are likely to become mentally or physically unwell. If you become unwell because of the negative energies, you cannot truly progress forward spiritually in the Craft. This protection spell will create a protective barrier around you. It is an excellent antidote to evil or negative energies.

Ingredients required for this spell:

- Taper black candle.
- Matches.
- Charcoal disc.
- Fireproof dish.
- Poppet, preferably black.
- Dried juniper berries.
- Cypress or sandalwood oil.
- Salt, preferably sea salt.
- Small bowl of a mixture of protection-associated herbs, such as basil, bay, chrysanthemum, dill, heather, lavender, rosemary and so on.

Casting the spell:

On a night of a full moon (to establish protection), preferably on a Saturday which is ruled by the protective ringed planet of Saturn, place all the spell ingredients on a flat surface, such as your altar, with the candle and poppet in the centre. Then activate your poppet. Light the candle with a match and add some salt to the bowl of protective herbs along with seven drops of the oil. Mix the herbs, salt and oil together with your hands while visualising your auric field surrounded by a protective barrier, a force field. Spend at least ten minutes doing this. Then, when you are ready, light the charcoal with the candle flame and place it on the fireproof dish. Then place some of the juniper berries on the charcoal. Put a ring of the mixture of herbs, salt and oil around the poppet and candle. This represents the protective barrier that the spell will provide for you. If your poppet can be stuffed then you can stuff it with the mixture also. Remember that you should always be visualising yourself surrounded by the protective powers of nature. Then when you are ready, say these or similar words:

> *O Mother Goddess of the silver moon above,*
> *Help me to bring forth protection with your almighty love.*
> *As I ring this poppet with these protective herbs of the field,*
> *I establish around myself an almighty, powerful, protective shield.*
> *By the powers of earth and water, of air and fire,*
> *A protective barrier around myself*
> *and my emotions is what I now desire.*
> *May no evil or negativity surround and penetrate my soul,*
> *By the powers of the three aspects of the Goddess*
> *this is my ultimate goal.*
> *May this spell bring the protection that I need,*
> *So that my mind, body and soul can be freed.*
> *O mysterious Goddess above and below the ground*
> *I do ask for your protective power,*
> *As I chant this protective song this magical hour.*
> *An' it harm none, so mote it be.*

If possible, leave the poppet under the light of the moon for a few moments. You can then use this time to focus on your visualisation and the bringing forward of protective powers. Remember that you have the power to protect yourself from evil and negative forces. Just believe in yourself. You can then simply allow the candle to burn out or you can simply snuff it out. You can then carry the poppet with you wherever you go and place it under your pillow each night when you retire. Alternatively, you can place it in a safe place in your home, perhaps in your magical pantry. Once you feel that your spell has fully taken effect you should see the poppet as nothing more than a doll and get rid of it. May you, your loved ones and anything else that you hold dear be blessed with the great protective powers of nature. Good luck.

Chapter Fourteen: Fertility Spells

Fertility is a general term that can mean many things. It can, for example, mean the birth of new ideas and theories. Witchcraft is a fertility religion that seeks to work in harmony with the earth and all its creatures and plants. The fertility of the natural world is of great importance, and also of great concern, to Witches. We understand that fertility is something that governs our lives as evinced throughout the natural world. Procreation is obviously a part of fertility and Witches celebrate it as a sacred gift of the Goddess and God. We do not see sexual activity as dirty, degrading, sinful or shameful, but rather as a sacred gift of divine energy. Healthy, safe and respectful sexuality between consenting adults is a natural part of life. Within Witchcraft, such sexuality is considered divine and what nature, or the Goddess and God, intended us to do. It is through sexual activity that procreation can be achieved. This is strongly emphasised with the Great Rite, the symbolic union of the male and female energies of the universe. Fertility spells can be a wonderful way to help a couple conceive – especially if medical science has failed.

For many people, having a child is not only a desire, it is also a complete need. This is especially so for many women. The need to conceive a baby, hold it within the womb for nine months, give birth and then nurture it as it grows older are some of the most natural instincts that a woman can ever have. They are instincts that come directly from the Goddess whose natural instinct is to create and sustain all life. Although I am not a parent, I do understand the need within women to become pregnant. This is because of my deep relationship with the Goddess and my understanding of the feminine powers of the universe. It is also because I have always enjoyed the company of women and have developed deep friendships with them over the years. Being around them and working with the Goddess throughout the years, I have come to understand somewhat of how the female psyche works. In many ways, the female psyche is very different to the male psyche. Understanding the nature of the Goddess's instincts to create and sustain life is to understand the true nature of fertility magic. Pregnancy and parenthood are sacred and should never be taken for granted. They allow us to receive a soul from the cauldron of souls of the Goddess so that we can help it to spiritually grow and develop as it aims towards spiritual perfection.

When you consider fertility spells for pregnancy, you must be patient. Souls awaiting to be reborn as children choose their parents and not the other way around and this can take time to come to fruition. Astrology plays a huge part in this. A soul that is waiting to be reborn may have already chosen you to be its parent but is waiting for the right astrological time to come to you. This is because the precise planetary positions at birth play a huge part in the soul's journey towards enlightenment. A soul must come at the right karmic time as it grows towards spiritual perfection. Any fertility spell that asks for pregnancy will allow you to appeal to the cauldron of souls that you are ready to host one of them in your womb. In other words, it will act as a catalyst. Take positive actions in your life to achieve pregnancy: speak to the full moon at night which rules the womb, sperm, menstruation and pregnancy; create a room fit for a baby; write poems, songs and stories that would be entertaining, comforting and soothing to a child; fill your life and home with loving energies and project these powers towards your future child in the knowledge that love overcomes anything; stop smoking and drinking alcohol and aim to keep as healthy as possible; and enjoy a healthy and active sex life, as a few examples. Trust yourself and keep committed to your goal of pregnancy.

Another fundamental point: if, for whatever reason, you simply can't get pregnant, be open to the idea that biology is not everything. Physically getting pregnant is not the only way that you can receive a child. You can still cast a fertility spell and then consider adopting a child. A soul that has chosen you to be its parent may be born to someone else but may only be destined for you. Adopting a child is a wonderful thing to do and is very pleasing to the Goddess. Being a true parent is not necessarily about biology. True parenting is about bringing up a child with love, care and attention. It is something that is achieved over time. Adoption can give a child a wonderful future that he or she may never have had. If you are interested in adoption, study the Egyptian story of Isis and Anubis. Anubis had been rejected as a child. Isis, who is a very mothering goddess, then adopted him and reared him as her own. Anubis then became utterly devoted to Isis. The moral of the story is that the love and bond between an adopted child and his or her parent can be just as powerful and sacred as that of a child's and his or her biological parent.

Correspondences for Fertility Spells

Best Symbols: Ankh, athame, broomstick, cauldron, chalice, corn dolly or kirn baby, cornucopia (the horn of plenty), crystal ball, cup, egg, fertility-associated runes, fishtail, gnome, Great Rite symbol, horns, key, lady riding symbol, mermaid, pentacle, phallic symbols, seashell, solar cross, spiral sun, sword, triple moon, wand, undine, yoni.

Planets: Earth, Jupiter, Moon (especially when it is full), Sun, Venus.

Elements: Air, earth, fire, water.

Cardinal Points: East, north, south (south is a potent direction for fertility in Ireland), west.

Best Days: Friday, Monday.

Numbers: 2, 3, 6, 7, 8, 9.

Colours: Brown, dark blue, gold, green, orange, pink, red, silver, white, yellow.

Incense: Basil, juniper, myrtle, patchouli, pine, violet.

Plants/Trees: Agaric, apple, banana, basil, bachelor's buttons, birch, bistort, bodhi tree, bracken, carrot, chickweed, corn, cuckoo flower, cucumber, cyclamen, daffodil, dock, fennel, fig, gentian, geranium, grape, hawthorn, hazel, horsetail, jasmine, juniper, lettuce, lotus, mandrake, mistletoe, mugwort, mustard, myrtle, oak, olive, parsley, patchouli, peach, pine, pomegranate, poppy, rice, sage, St. John's wort, sunflower, violet, walnut.

Crystals/Stones: Amethyst, aquamarine, aventurine, black coral, carnelian, emerald, fluorite, jade, jasper, lepidolite, moonstone, pearl, rhodonite, rose quartz, smoky quartz, tiger's eye, turquoise, unakite, zoisite.

Metals: Copper, gold, silver.

Creatures: Bull, cow, dove, duck, fish, frog, hare, horse, manatee, mouse, parrot, pig, pigeon, rabbit, rat, snake, stork.

Deities: Abundantia, Aditi, Adonis, Althaea, Amaterasu, Amun, Anahita, Anath, Aphrodite, Aradia, Arianrhod, Artemis, Asherah, Ashtoreth, Astarte, Atargatis, Attis, Bacchus, Bast, Belenos, Bes, Brigit, Bona Dea, Ceres, Cernunnos, Cerridwen, Cupid, Cybele, Demeter, Diana, Dionysus, Durga, Ea, El, Enki, Eostar, Epona, Eros, Father Nanna, Freya, Freyr, Frigg, Gaia, Ganga, Goda, Habondia, Haddad, Heqet, Hera, Horus, Inanna, Indra, Isis, Ix Chel, Jaguar, Juno, Jupiter, Kadesh, Khonsu, Kore, Lailah, Lakshmi, Latona, Liber, Maeve, Mardoll, Mater Matuta, Mesenet, Min, Mithras, Myrrha, Nemain, Nerthus, Oshun, Oya, Pan, Parvati, Priapus, Renenutet, Rhiannon, Rosmerta, Satyrs, Shiva, Sita, Smyrna, Sobek, Sopdet, Syria Dea, Tammuz, Tawaret, Tefnut, the Dagda, the Green Man, Venus, Zeus.

Magical Ways to Aid Fertility

In this part of this chapter we will look at some interesting and magical ways to aid fertility in Witchcraft. These are my personal favourites that can really boost any form of fertility magic that you wish to carry out. These simple ways are excellent on their own but they can also be done in addition to fertility spells (or as parts of them) to really give them a magical boost. They will surround you with the fertile powers of nature in your quest to receive a child from Mother and Father Nature. You can also use them to inspire you when creating your own fertility spells – whether for yourself or for those who come to you for help.

One very effective way to enhance fertility magic is to create a shrine dedicated to fertility and the moon. Remember that the moon governs all things, both in men and women, to do with reproduction. Its monthly cycle of waxing, full and waning particularly reflects a woman's monthly menstruation cycle. You can decorate your shrine with white and silver items and cover it with a white cloth. A white candle can be placed in the centre and some flowers of geranium and violet can be sprinckled around the base of it. The candle can also be anointed with an oil that relates to fertility, such as patchouli. You can also inscribe the candle with a symbol of fertility, such as the triple moon or the Berkano rune. You can also place a ring of moonstones around the base of your candle. You can also write down on a piece of white paper your desire for a child and place it under the candle. You can also burn some fertility incense on your shrine to infuse your life with the fertile powers of nature. Placed in the north or the west, a fertility shrine can be very effective.

To create a special incense for fertility, mix together juniper, basil, myrtle and violet in a small bowl. Then add three drops each of pine and patchouli oils. Do this on a Monday or Friday, both very potent days for fertility magic, and then leave the dish of herbs and oils to dry out for one week. On the following Monday or Friday, place the incense in a clean glass jar with a cork lid. Use two to three spoonfuls when needed. This can be a very potent incense blend that can really enhance and empower workings of fertility magic. Burning this incense while consuming an infusion of basil tea are excellent things to do to enhance magical workings of fertility (though, curiously enough, large doses of basil are not recommended for internal use if you have already become pregnant or are breastfeeding).

While I am on the subject of the herb basil, it is one of the most potent herbs for fertility. It has been used for centuries for magical workings of fertility. Merely growing it on your windowsill or growing it in your garden will aid fertility so long as you believe in its powers and you attune it with your desire for pregnancy. It is said that keeping a bunch of fresh basil hung over the bed, perhaps tied up with a ribbon of a colour of fertility, will encourage conception. Of course, you can also add basil to foods, place it in sachets or poppets and so on to aid fertility magic. It is one of my favourite herbs that is often present in my home.

When considering pregnancy you must learn to relax and enjoy a healthy sex life. Many people become frustrated when they wish to become pregnant and all this does is reduce the chances of pregnancy. It puts stresses and strains on the body and reduces harmony. In addition, some people may have problems achieving sexual arousal. In cases where sexual arousal is difficult to achieve, sexual healing may be warranted. Sexual healing basically involves a mutual understanding that you and your partner need to feel wanted and desired sexually by each other. Compliments about each other's physical appearance to enhance sexual self-esteem, providing sexual acts tailored to specific needs, indulging in erotic fantasies and erotic massages are good places to start when it comes to sexual healing. Intuition and listening fully to each other play a huge role in this. Remember that enjoying consenting, respectful and adventurous sexuality is healthy, natural and normal. It is encouraged within Witchcraft and will aid your chances of your need or goal of pregnancy and sexual healing is something that may be necessary to help you to achieve it. If you or your partner have previously been in toxic, controlling and abusive relationships, then sexual healing will most likely be necessary.

Naturally, there are many herbs that can be used to aid fertility. Merely carrying them or placing them around your home can aid your chances of becoming pregnant immensely. Carrying a bag full of hazelnuts is said to promote fertility and is traditionally given to a bride to ensure her own. A green or dark blue bag would be excellent for this. Men traditionally carry mandrake to ensure fertility and their desire for sexual activity, while women who wish for the same traditionally carry jasmine. Bistort is also a good herb for women wishing to become pregnant and a cucumber placed in the bedroom is excellent for fertility. The cucumber should be replaced every seven days. Of course, herbs can also be eaten as food to improve fertility. Some of my personal favourites include pomegranate, basil, cucumber, apple, banana, carrot, lettuce and peach. Herbs of fertility can be grown in the garden to create a magical garden that aids the fertility of a couple. Grow as many herbs of fertility to do this. A pond can be a wonderful addition to this fertility garden since water is a powerful element that rules fertility strongly.

Another way to enhance fertility is to take a fertility bath or shower. This can perhaps be done prier to sex with your partner or before a fertility spell. As you will be aware by now, water is strongly associated with fertility and having a bath or shower will help you to spiritually connect with its fertile powers. You can perhaps place crystals and stones of fertility in the bathroom, such as amethysts and moonstones, as well as symbols and signs of fertility, such as mermaids, undines and seashells. You can also burn fertility incense and candles of colours that relate to fertility, such as dark blue, white and green, to infuse the bathroom and your life with the fertile powers of nature.

If you decide to have a fertility bath, you can also work with bath salts. Blend together some Epsom salts with the dried herbs or oils of basil, juniper and patchouli and add this to your bath water. If you take your bath or shower on a Monday or Friday, then fertility magic will surely be enhanced.

Another way to enhance fertility is to work with fertility lotions. A favourite of mine involves the oils of basil, jasmine and peach which are added to an unscented body lotion. Apply this to the skin (remember to test a little on the back of the hand first) whenever you wish to enhance any magical working of fertility. The lotion will refresh you and heighten your ability to tune into the wonderful and fertile powers of Mother and Father Nature. It is excellent when used after a fertility bath or shower.

Another way to aid fertility is to work with ritual fires. Fire is a very passionate element. It represents the heat, light and power of the sun. Without the sun, this planet would be desolate of life and fertility. Making love before a ritual fire can really enhance lustful feelings as well as fertility. The types of woods that are burned in a ritual fire can give magical workings of fertility an extra jolt of power. Oak wood, for example, is excellent when burned in a ritual fire for fertility magic as is olive wood. The two types of woods will also enhance sexual potency and lustful feelings. Incidently, the acorn from the oak tree is excellent as a charm for fertility and sexual desire and olives from the olive tree are traditionally eaten by men to promote their sexual appetite. Crowns of olive leaves were traditionally worn by Athenian brides to aid fertility. Oak and olive trees are trees of the sun. They are very lustful and passionate trees of fertility.

As you will know by now, sleep is a very receptive time when our unconscious minds are most receptive to the magical powers of nature. As such, you may want to consider the position in which to sleep at night to improve your chances of getting pregnant. Sleeping with your head pointing towards the north or west are perfect for aiding fertility. They are associated with earth and water which represent the womb and the fertility of the Goddess and her power to nurture and sustain all life. You can also perhaps place herbs, crystals, stones, symbols and signs that relate to fertility on your bedside table to further improve your chances of becoming pregnant.

A Full Moon Fertility Spell

This spell, as with the love spell, utilises the power of the full moon to achieve fertility. As I explained, fertility is a general term that can mean many things, but this spell is specifically tailored for a couple who wishes to conceive a child. It assumes that a couple have a healthy sex life and that there are no major physical reasons why they cannot conceive a child. However, it can also be cast for a couple who are seeking medical science for help with achieving pregnancy. It is an appeal to nature that a couple are ready to receive a child from the pool of souls of the Goddess. It is most effective if it is carried out by the woman who wishes to become pregnant, but it can also be cast for another woman (with a little tweaking) in her quest for pregnancy as long as you feel that she is truly ready for pregnancy and the pressures of bringing up a child. Remember to remind anyone who has requested your help for a fertility spell tailored specifically for pregnancy that a trust into the spiritual powers of nature is always required.

Ingredients required for this spell:

- Tealight green or white candle.
- Matches.
- One small moonstone.
- Fireproof bowl or small iron cauldron.
- Patchouli oil.
- Small green pouch.
- White or silver cord.
- An empty walnut shell in two halves.
- Small bowl of ripe corn.

Casting the spell:

On a night of a full moon, preferably on a Monday or Friday which are very potent fertility days, light the candle with a match and place it in the fireproof bowl or cauldron. Place all your spell ingredients on a flat surface, such as your altar, with the fireproof bowl or cauldron placed in the centre. Strongly focus on fertility and your need or goal to become pregnant. Spend at least ten minutes doing this. Then, when you are ready, add nine drops of the oil to the bowl of corn and mix them with your hands. Sprinkle around the base of your fireproof bowl or cauldron some of the corn. Then, when you are ready, use the candle to add some wax to one of the sides of the walnut shell and place the candle back into the fireproof bowl or cauldron. Before the wax sets, secure the other side of the walnut shell to it. The wax within the walnut shell and the candle within the fireproof bowl or cauldron both represent the baby within the womb. Remember that you should always be utilising your visualisation. Then add to the pouch the moonstone, the walnut shell and some of the corn. Secure it shut with the cord and say these or similar words:

> *O Mother Goddess of the sea and of the earth,*
> *Mysterious woman who holds the mysteries*
> *of the seeds of new life, fertility and birth,*
> *Grant me the gift of a child so that I can fulfil my desire*
> *of self-worth.*
> *O passionate, mothering Goddess of the silver moon,*
> *I ask for a child within my womb very soon.*
> *Mother and Father Nature of the moon,*
> *sun and stars that passionately shine,*
> *Give me the gifts of fertility and parenthood and be them mine.*
> *Goddess of motherhood and water and God of fatherhood*
> *and fire,*
> *Please gently warm my goal and desire.*
> *May this fertility charm bag of green,*
> *Help me to bring forth my own fertility on which I am so keen.*
> *An' it harm none, so mote it be.*

If possible, leave the pouch under the light of the moon for a few moments. You can then use this time to focus on your visualisation and the bringing forward of the fertile powers of nature. You can then simply allow the candle to burn out or you can simply snuff it out. You can then carry the pouch with you wherever you go and place it under your pillow each night when you retire. You can repeat this until you have achieved your goal of pregnancy. Alternatively, you can hang your pouch over your bed or place it on your bedside table until you become pregnant. This will increase your chance of pregnancy each time you make love to your partner. If you are truly destined to become a parent, the Goddess and God will grant you this gift. Just believe in their powers. I truly do wish you all the best in your quest to become a parent. May the Goddess and God grant you all the strength you need. Good luck.

Part Three: Occult Aspects and Correspondences

Chapter Fifteen: Astrology

Astrology, the practice of the study of the spiritual or magical effects of the heavenly bodies and the stars upon life on our planet, is said to be the oldest known science. Since the earliest times humankind has observed the heavens with great fascination, watching the movements of the sun, moon, planets and stars with great wonder. From these observations came the great stories of the ancient gods and goddesses and a powerful heritage of myths, legends, mystery, magic and beauty. You may have heard the old saying "as above, so below". This saying is very famous in Witchcraft and other magical religions. It means that whatever happens in the heavens has a direct influence on all life on earth. Astrology is a vast subject that takes considerable study but if the basics are understood then the rest falls into place as knowledge increases. I have been studying astrology for many years now and it never ceases to amaze me that there is always something new and exciting to learn. Most Witches believe in this wonderful art. Astrology is a powerful reminder that everything within the universe is connected in some way through the great web of life. Today, astrology is just as important for the modern Witch as it was for the ancient Witch in his or her lonely cottage.

Witches understand that the positions of the sun, moon and planets at the time of birth can have a great influence on our lives and what personalities we are likely to have as people as we develop and grow older. When we are born, we breathe in the cosmic energies of the positions of the heavenly bodies against the stars of the universe. However, these positions are not the absolute determining factor. There are other influences in play as well. Things like free will, genetics, culture, environment, workplace and so on also play a role in shaping who we are. Astrology is like a form of divination. Generally, it does not tell us exactly what is going to happen to the last detail but what is likely to happen. From this information, we can try to avoid the bad things that are likely to happen and embrace the good things. The precise positions of the sun, moon and planets at birth are what the soul chooses so that it can learn and develop as it grows towards perfection in a particular incarnation. They are a map of the soul's path during its incarnation, with all its trials, tribulations, adventures, joys, misfortunes and so on.

How did astrology come about? Astrology is believed by many to have originated in ancient Egypt, but all of the surviving records suggest that the actual place of birth was probably Mesopotamia. It is believed that our ancestors observed the effects that the sun and moon had on earth so they began to believe that the other heavenly bodies had effects too. The sun was needed for the growth of plants and trees and the warmth that life depended on. The moon affected the movements of the ocean tides and the reproductive cycles of plants and animals. So, for our ancestors, the other heavenly bodies must influence the energies on earth as well. Since these ancient times, there have been many very accurate predictions made with the use of astrology.

What about astronomy? Does this play a role in modern-day astrology? The simple answer to that is yes, it most certainly does. In ancient times, astrology and astronomy were one and the same thing, but today scientists regard astronomy as a different science. Astronomy, as a modern definition, is the study of the physical nature of the heavenly bodies (weight, speed, distance, temperature and so on) and how they interact with other heavenly bodies in the universe. But, in ancient times, an astronomer was also an astrologist and vice versa. In other words, if you studied the spiritual or magical effects of the heavenly bodies then you also studied their physical nature. An understanding of the physical nature of the heavenly bodies is a fundamental part of astrology because their physical nature heavily reflects our understanding of their powers.

The Twelve Signs of the Zodiac

In most ancient systems, there are twelve signs of the zodiac that the soul can choose to be born under and this can depend on the knowledge, wisdom and experience that the soul needs in order to spiritually develop. These signs are based on the constellations of stars that appear in a wide band around the earth. The zodiac sign a soul chooses to be born under is the sign that the sun was in at the time of birth. This is known as their sun sign or star sign. The sun represents the vital life force within us. It is vitality, ego and self-expression. The positions and influences of the other heavenly bodies at birth add a little spice to our personalities and possible future events. Here, we will look at each sign of the zodiac and the characteristics associated with each to help you to further your knowledge of astrology. Bear in mind that I have only intended the following notes to be a simple introduction to each sign of the zodiac. You will have to study astrology further to get a more rounded knowledge of each.

Aries: falls approximately from March 21st to April 20th. It is a cardinal sign associated with the Golden Ram and the element of fire. Arians are considered to be the most enthusiastic of the zodiac children and typically have high energy and fast-paced lifestyles. Arians enjoy taking risks and are highly competitive. They have a straightforward outlook on life and their fiery determination often gets them far in life. However, this can encourage them to be hot-headed and rude. The Arian is able to aim high in life with great ease, grace and agility, just like the light-footed Ram that is able to climb jagged mountains with ease. Arians do things their own way with great determination regardless of outward obstacles and other people's advice. They are urgent, energetic, forthright, assertive and often selfish. Leonardo da Vinci, Elton John and Marlon Brando are some famous Arians.

Taurus: falls approximately from April 21st to May 20th. It is a fixed sign associated with the Bull and the element of earth. Taureans are incredibly famous for their romantic personalities. They are warm, sincere, affectionate, reliable, confident, loyal and persistent. They have an incredible urge to always get what they want. They are reputed to be the most beautiful of the zodiac children. Taureans have a need for financial security and they often need to have a lot of comfort, finery and luxury. However, these tendencies can encourage them to be self-indulgent, obsessive and possessive. As with the Bull that represents them, Taureans can often be slow to anger but when they are aroused they can become incredibly fearsome. Pope John Paul II, Queen Elizabeth II and Cher are some famous Taureans.

Gemini: falls approximately from May 21st to June 20th. It is a mutable sign associated with the Twins and the element of air. Geminians are communicative, versatile, lively, quick-witted, fast-thinking, intellectual, versatile people who rarely stay in the same place for long periods of time. Their communicative skills encourage them to be able to easily sway other people to their ways of thinking. Geminians hate boredom and will do anything to run away from it. Their minds have to be continuously occupied and they enjoy spreading their intellectual powers among complex tasks and people. The Twins that represents them reflects the Geminian's ability to do more than one activity at once. However, Geminians can have an inability to settle down with one thing or one person and this can create negativity and problems in relationships. People around them may find it difficult to keep up with them and so Geminians may find it difficult to form deep and lasting relationships. Judy Garland, Marilyn Monroe and John F. Kennedy are some famous Geminians.

Cancer: falls approximately from June 21st to July 21st. It is a cardinal sign associated with the Crab and the element of water. Cancerians are sensitive, imaginative, emotional, protective, loving and artistically gifted. They can, however, be moody, "crabby" and obsessed with the home and the past. Cancer is the most mothering sign of the zodiac and this strong influence can manifest even in male Cancerians. Cancerians are considered very difficult to fully understand and it may take a long time to get to know what is going on in their minds. They are complex creatures that need to be wanted and loved. As with the Crab that symbolises them, they appear to have a hard, almost impenetrable, shell that they show to the world as a form of protection. But beneath this shell lies a soft, gentle, sensitive and emotional soul with great imagination and intuition. Cancerians are famed for how far they will go to protect whatever they hold dear, especially their homes, family and friends. They often make excellent and loyal parents and friends. Princess Diana, Meryl Streep and King Henry VIII are some famous Cancerians.

Leo: falls approximately from July 22nd to August 22nd. It is a fixed sign associated with the Lion and the element of fire. Leos are the natural leaders of the zodiac children. They are generous, ambitious, outgoing, optimistic, dynamic, protective, loving, bossy, creative, impressive, enthusiastic, fiercely proud and confident. Like the Lion that represents them, they are kings of the jungle. They are party animals that believe they can do whatever they set out in life. Leos need to live life to the fullest and are wonderfully affectionate, creative and dramatic. Leos dislike narrow-minded and nit-picking people. However, they themselves can be stubborn, autocratic and dogmatic. Madonna, Napolean Bonaparte and Her Majesty Queen Elizabeth the Queen Mother are some famous Leos.

Virgo: falls approximately from August 23rd to September 22nd. It is a mutable sign associated with the Virgin and the element of earth. Virgoans are wonderfully earthy, warm, modest, hard-working, practical, creative, money-makers that represent ancient goddesses of the harvest. They often go out of their way to produce the necessities of life. Quick-thinking, meticulous, tidy, thorough and very analytical, Virgoans often have so much going on in their minds that they can be prone to stress and tension. Their quest for perfection and hard work often makes them prone to being over-critical, fussy and judgemental. They are, however, excellent at communication and persuasion. They are intellectual creatures (though they often keep this intellectual side to them hidden to appear virginal and innocent) who often win arguments. They have a great skill at winning over people. Queen Elizabeth I (also known as The Virgin Queen), Stephen King and Mary Shelly are some famous Virgoans.

Libra: falls approximately from September 23rd to October 22nd. It is a cardinal sign associated with the Scales and the element of air. Outgoing, easygoing, social, peaceful, charming, warm-hearted and diplomatic, Librans are heavily concerned with achieving balance, justice and harmony. They are often well-equipped with achieving this with their enormous reserves of charm, frankness, cleverness, persuasion, trust and communication. They are naturally laid-back people who often get an undeserved reputation for laziness. In actuality, Librans are hard-working people who are often leaders in their fields. Their laid-back nature makes them easy to work with and this is emphasised by their peaceful natures. In any situation, they often see both sides of an argument. Michael Douglas, Chalton Heston and John Lennon are some famous Librans.

Scorpio: falls approximately from October 23rd to November 21st. It is a fixed sign associated with the deadly, yet powerful, Scorpion and the element of water. Wonderfully powerful, energetic, fascinating, dramatic, passionate, exciting, intense, sexual, private, intuitive and magnetic, Scorpios are often a step away from the world and often harbour deep and dark secrets. There is often an element of "danger" around them because of their obsessive need for privacy. This is emphasised by their symbol – the Scorpion. Although this is just one aspect of their personalities. Scorpios are deep-thinkers and driven workers with an enormous ability to overcome whatever challenges are put in their way. They enormously value those who are closest to them and encourage only the best in those that they love. Prince Charles, Marie Antoinette and Richard Burton are some famous Scorpios.

Sagittarius: falls approximately from November 22nd to December 20th. It is a mutable sign associated with the Archer and the element of fire. Open, enthusiastic, likeable, wise, brave, adventurous, optimistic, tolerant, intellectual, philosophical and tactless, Sagittarians love challenges and to explore. They throw themselves into intellectual pursuits, whether physical or mental, with boundless and infectious amounts of energy. Sagittarians are optimistic, extroverts who often win the admirations and affection of anyone they come into contact with. They are exuberant and lucky people who have the potential to achieve whatever they want in life. However, they can often be foolhardy and pessimistic people who often get themselves into troublesome and worrying situations. But they often have the fiery power to get themselves out of these situations. Winston Churchill, Steven Spielberg and Walt Disney are some famous Sagittarians.

Capricorn: falls approximately from December 21st to January 20th. It is a cardinal sign associated with the Goat and the element of earth. Traditionally, the Goat was also half-fish and this dual nature is represented in the Capricornian's complex personality. One side of the Capricornian is disciplined, methodical, sensitive, sensible, ambitious, hard-working and enterprising, while the other side is lost in a world of imagined obstacles that the Capricornian is so eager to overcome. The Capricornian is a highly motivated person who is often able to set high, yet achievable, goals. Capricornians often have a prominent dark side that is hard to understand. They are often notoriously introverted, cold and boring individuals who appreciate privacy, wealth and solitude. Oliver Hardy, Joan of Arc and Elvis Presley are some famous Capricornians.

Aquarius: falls approximately from January 21st to February 19th. It is a fixed sign associated with the Water Bearer or Carrier and the element of air. Aquarians are friendly, kind, caring, warm-hearted, independent, nervous, honest and inventive individuals who are concerned with humanitarianism. They believe in equal rights for all people regardless of race, colour, religion, sex and so on. Aquarians are natural lovers of animals and will often fight for the well-being of them. Because of this, many Aquarians are vegetarians or will be at some stage of their lives. Although Aquarians often need many friends and associates, they also appreciate their own company so that they can be alone with their own thoughts. They are private individuals who are admired for their originality and creative personalities. Aquarians are often well aware of the spiritual aspects of life and so they generally make excellent priests or priestesses in whatever religion they choose to follow. They are New Agers, leaders and eco-warriors who genuinely care about the welfare of others. Robert Burns, Charles Dickens and James Dean are some famous Aquarians.

Pisces: falls approximately from February 20th to March 20th. It is a mutable sign associated with the Two Fishes and the element of water. Highly sensitive, imaginative, loving, peaceful, sensual, emotional, kind and creative, Pisceans are dreamy and vague individuals who are often natural poets. They are often easily led individuals who are concerned with other-worldly, dreamy matters. The Two Fishes that swim in opposite directions that is related to Pisceans symbolises that they are often torn between real and valuable things in the world and their private worlds of imagination and dreams. Because of this enormous and powerful pull, Pisceans are often prone to extreme nervous tension and escapism which, in turn, can often lead them to overindulging in drugs and alcohol. Pisceans often lack self-confidence but when this is overcome, they make beautiful humanitarians, poets and artists. Michelangelo, Liza Minnelli and Elizabeth Taylor are some famous Pisceans.

The Astrological Birth Chart

When beginning to study astrology one of the best places to start is your own, personal, astrological birth chart. The astrological birth chart, horoscope, natal astrology chart, natal chart, or simply birth chart, is a diagram, usually circular, that shows the precise positions of the sun, moon and planets at a person's birth. These positions will have an effect on your overall personality, health, body type, family, career and possible future events within your life cycle. To construct an astrological birth chart, an astrologer would have to know the time and date of someone's birth as well as their exact location on the earth at longitude and latitude. From this information, a unique chart can be constructed which shows the exact locations of the sun, moon and planets against the twelve signs of the zodiac.

The astrological birth chart will also show the sign that was rising over the eastern horizon at a person's birth. This is known as the rising sign or the ascendant and is also very important in determining someone's life and personality. Some astrologists believe that this sign reveals the "secret you", the sign that strongly reveals the aspects of your personality known only by yourself and those closest to you. However, other astrologers believe that your rising sign reveals the "public you", the sign that you strongly wish to show to the world. I personally believe the latter with the sign that the sun was in revealing the "secret you". The sign that was rising over the eastern horizon and the sign the sun was in at a person's birth reveals a very accurate picture of who someone is – both inside and out.

The astrological birth chart is divided into twelve segments. These are known as the houses and each rules certain aspects of life. They, therefore, add another fundamental layer to determining a person's overall personality, health, career and possible future events. The seventh house, for example, rules relationships and marriage. As well as the effects that the sun, moon and planets have against the twelve signs of the zodiac, astrologers believe that the heavenly bodies can have effects on the houses within a person's astrological birth chart. The first house always contains the rising sign. In addition to this, astrologers need to understand the relationships that the sun, moon and planets have with each other. These are known as the planetary aspects and relate to the specific number of degrees between two planets. The relationships that the planets have with each other in a person's birth chart around its circumference also influences someone's life heavily. When one planet has a specific number of degrees between another, it is said by astrologers to be in aspect with that other planet. If Mercury was trine Saturn (120 degrees apart in the birth chart circle) then this can influence you to be a very reliable and grounding person who can use your mind carefully and methodically.

Having an astrological birth chart is a wonderful thing to have. It can reveal much about yourself and what is likely to happen in your future with great accuracy. It can feel as though someone or something has secretly known you all your life, someone or something who has been peering through the windows of your soul. It can even reveal who you were in previous lives and perhaps why you may be so drawn to Witchcraft and magic in this particular lifetime. You can get a birth chart constructed by a professional astrologer but there is nothing more rewarding in astrology than constructing your own, personal, birth chart. Besides, having someone else to do your birth chart can be very costly and at least if you cast your own you will slowly develop your knowledge of astrology more efficiently. A good astrology book can help you do this. There are also many excellent sites on the internet that can do astrological birth charts.

The Heavenly Bodies

Here, we will look at each of the planets of the heavens that are about our solar system to help you to gain a deeper understanding of astrology and the planetary influences that heavily affect our everyday lives. There is much more lore and knowledge in Witchcraft and astrology about the sun, moon and inner planets (Jupiter, Mars, Mercury, Saturn and Venus) than there is for the outer planets (Neptune, Pluto and Uranus). This is because the outer planets, which are also known as the modern planets, were not known by our ancient ancestors and were only discovered in more recent times with the help of the telescope. This means that there is more magical and spiritual associations with the sun, moon and inner planets than there is for the outer planets. Still, the outer planets play a huge role in modern-day astrology and help us to expand our knowledge of this ancient art. The influence of the sun, moon and planets can have huge effects on our birth charts, our daily lives and any magical workings that we undertake. As well as using the below information to expand your knowledge of astrology, you can also use it for your spellcraft and other magical workings.

Note: You can obviously refer to chapter three for basic magical information on our own planet.

Jupiter

Jupiter is the expansive, generous, harmonising, philosophical and lucky planet associated with academic study. The Roman deity Jupiter was a god of plenty and abundance who was associated with great joy, freedom, hospitality, charity, mercy, compassion, wisdom and sexuality. He was a god associated with the father aspect of the divine who was the protector of the ancient city of Rome. He was a powerful god of self-indulgence who was king of the deities of this ancient city. His tendency towards self-indulgence and excess was to his weakness in ancient Rome. Jupiter could also be a very cruel and punishing deity who would angrily throw his thunderbolts from the sky at anyone who upset or annoyed him. On the positive side, this planet is believed to influence us to be lucky, warm, generous, popular, magnetic, benevolent, wise and sympathetic. On the negative side, Jupiter is believed to influence us to be cruel, punishing, extravagant, fanatical, hypocritical, dissipated, greedy and self-indulgent.

Apart from the sun, the planet of Jupiter is the largest and heaviest of the heavenly bodies in our solar system. It measures a massive 90 thousand miles in diameter, which represents the planet's association with plenty and abundance. Much of its mass is composed of liquid hydrogen and helium. It is so big that, apart from the sun, all the other heavenly bodies in the solar system could fit inside it (this is all down to the volume of Jupiter). It is also never less than 370 million miles from the earth and is 484 million miles away from the sun. It takes about 12 years to orbit the sun and spends approximately a year in each sign of the zodiac. Jupiter has many moons that are attracted by its powerful, magnetic field, two of which were discovered by the Italian astronomer Galileo Galilei in 1610. These are Ganymede and Callisto. Some people believe that Jupiter is dangerous to magicians in their magical workings.

Here is some magical information for this very lucky heavenly body:

Basic Energies: Expands, leads, succeeds.

Symbol: Jupiter's thunderbolt or eagle.

Elements: Air, earth, fire.

Time: Daylight hours.

Day: Thursday.

Cardinal Points: East (especially in China), north, south.

Zodiac Signs: Pisces (classical, feminine counterpart), Sagittarius (masculine counterpart).

Colours: Blue, dark blue, purple, royal blue.

Incense: Benzoin, cedar, cinnamon, fennel, ginseng, juniper, mastic, mint, myrrh, nutmeg, sage, sandalwood.

Plants/Trees: Agrimony, anise, ash, avens, balm, balsam, banyan, bay, benzoin, betony, bilberry, bloodroot, blueberry, bodhi tree, borage, cashew, calycanthus, carnation, cedar, chervil, chestnut, chicory, cinnamon, cinquefoil, clove, clover, comfrey, costmary, couch grass, dandelion, dock, echinacea, endive, fennel, fig, fir, ginseng, gospal, hart's tongue, henbane, honeysuckle, horse chestnut, houseleek, hyacinth, hyssop, jasmine, juniper, lemon, lemon balm, lilac, linden, liverwort, maple, marsh woundwort, mastic, meadowsweet, milk thistle, mint, mistletoe, mullein, myrrh, nutmeg, oak, olive, pimpernel, red rose, sage, samphire, sandalwood, sarsaparilla, scurvy grass, sassafras, sesame, star anise, unicorn root, walnut, white beet, wintergreen, witchgrass.

Crystals/Stones: Amethyst, chrysolite, lapis lazuli, sapphire, tanzanite, turquoise. Generally blue or purple stones.

Metal: Tin.

Creatures: Bee, dolphin, eagle, elephant, fish, horse, seabirds, whale.

Mythical Beast: Unicorn.

Archangel: Sachiel.

Governs: Abundance, academic study, admiration, adventures, affection, ambition, assurance, astral travel, authority, banking, benevolence, blood, bravery, business matters, cell formation, challenges, change, charity, commitment, compassion, conceit, cruelty, digestion, dissipation, divination, education, energy, energy conservation, enthusiasm, expansion, exploration, extravagance, fairness, faith, fatherhood, fertility, food assimilation, foreign countries, freedom, generosity, good fortune, greed, indulgence, joy, judgement, justice, harmony, healing, health, higher thoughts, honesty, honour, hospitality, hypocrisy, independence, insurance, intellect, knowledge, language, law, leadership, lightning, luck, magnetism, materialism, memory, mercy, money, nutrition, openness, optimism, overcoming negative situations, pessimism, philosophy, politics, popularity, power, pride, prophecy, prosperity, protection, psychic power, public acclaim, publication, punishment, rain, reading, religion, responsibility, riches, royalty, leadership, luck, searching for someone or something, sexuality, sperm, spiritual awareness, spiritual contact, success, sympathy, the immune system, the lower spiritual plane (sixth plane), things desired, thunder, tolerance, transcendence, transformation, travel, truth, uncovering mysteries, warmth, wealth, wisdom.

Mars

Mars is the war and action, red and "iron planet" that represents the intensely, dynamic, active, aggressive, masculine principle. In Roman mythology, Mars was a fiery deity of protection, defence and agriculture. He was a ferocious, bad-tempered and volatile deity but he had the intense power to bring much-needed change and transformation. He has a traditional reputation, along with Saturn, for being a malign deity who was always in conflict with the other deities. He was seen as a destroyer who was dangerous to invoke for magical workings. Always portrayed in a full battle dress, he was fortunate in battle but unfortunate in love. On the positive side, this planet is said to influence us to be enterprising, brave, independent, energetic, enthusiastic, gallant, courageous, hard-working and assertive. On the negative side, Mars is believed to influence us to be ruthless, bad-tempered, destructive, brutal, egotistic, coarse, cruel and argumentative.

Although the planet of Venus shines more brightly in the sky, Mars is seen to have a fierce, red glow and this can make it seem more striking. This is perhaps why the ancient Romans associated it with the god of war and his Greek equivalent of Aries. Mars is much smaller than our own planet and at its closest it is 35 million miles from us. It can pass as close to the sun as 129 million miles and as far away from it as 142 million miles. It also takes about 687 days to circle it and spends approximately 57.3 days in each sign of the zodiac (not including retrograde periods). It has two moons known as Phobos and Deimos. It has a 24-hour day and a pattern of seasons. It is red because it is covered in red deserts. This represents the planet's fiery associations.

Here is some magical information for this very assertive heavenly body:

Basic Energies: Acts, begins, grows, initiates, provides physical energy.

Symbol: Spear of Mars.

Element: Fire.

Time: Night.

Day: Tuesday.

Cardinal Point: South.

Zodiac Signs: Aries (masculine counterpart), Scorpio (classical, feminine counterpart).

Colour: Red.

Incense: Cypress, dragon's blood, pine, tobacco.

Plants/Trees: All-heal, allspice, aloe, anemone, asafoetida, asarabacca, barberry, basil, betony, black snakeroot, blood root, broom, butcher's broom, cacti, caper, carrot, chilli pepper, chives, coriander, cow parsnip, cubeb, cumin, curry, cypress, damiana, deerstongue, dragon's blood, galangal, garlic, gentian, geranium, ginger, gorse, grains of paradise, hawthorn, holly, holly oak, honeysuckle, hops, horseradish, hound's tongue, jalap root, leek, madder root, maguey, masterwort, mustard, nettle, onion, pennyroyal, pepper, pepper tree, pimento, pine, poke root, prickly ash, radish, reed, restharrow, rhododendron, sarsaparilla, savin, shallot, sloe, snapdragon, squill, tarragon, thistle, toadflax, tobacco, valerian, Venus' flytrap, vomic nut, woodruff, wormwood, yucca. Generally spicy, stinging or thorny plants.

Crystals/Stones: Bloodstone, carnelian, garnet, pyrite, red coral, ruby, tiger's eye.

Metals: Iron, steel.

Creatures: Fox, ram, robin, scorpion, sparrow, woodpecker. Generally stinging or volatile creatures.

Mythical Beast: Dragon.

Archangel: Samuel.

Governs: Action, aggression, agriculture, ambition, anger, argumentativeness, assertiveness, athletics, battle, birth, blood, blood formation, body heat, bravery, brutality, change, coarseness, competitiveness, conflict, contests, courage, cruelty, danger, decisiveness, defence, destruction, determination, disharmony, egotism, emotional passion, endurance, enmity, enthusiasm, exorcism, ferociousness, fevers, freedom, growth, hard work, high blood pressure, high energy, hunting, impulsiveness, independence, initiation, intensity, loyalty, lust, magnetism, motivation, moving forward in life, overcoming obstacles, physical energy, physical skills, pioneers, positivity, premature birth, passion, prison, protection, repelling negativity, rudeness, ruthlessness, selfishness, sexual drive, sexual energy, sports, strength, struggle, surgery, the lower astral plane (second plane), the masculine principle (especially the dark aspect of it), the muscular system, transformation, urgency, vitality, war, willpower, wrath.

Mercury

The planet Mercury is the fast-moving planet that represents the quicksilver messenger of the heavens. It represents the messenger that mediates between the above and the below. It governs mental processes, communication, language, adaptability, intellect, travel and movement. It has ambivalent energy that is akin to the trickster figures of legend. The planet is seen as somewhat androgynous by astrologers which represents that it contains all the opposites within. Therefore, it represents the free operator, the independent soul of a polar opposite. In Roman mythology, the god Mercury was a splendid athlete who was known as a trickster and a magician who was venerated for his enormous energy, speed and quick-witted nature. He had wings on his sandals and helmet to help him travel fast and was a messenger of the gods. His magic helmet gave him great protection as the bearer of important news. He also owned a staff with two snakes entwined around it which symbolised the planet's associations with opposites, such as good and evil, light and dark or the male and female energies of the universe. On the positive side, the planet Mercury is believed to influence us to be sensitive, quick-witted, intellectual, persuasive, brilliant, subtle, literary, good at communication, analytical and quick-thinking. On the negative side, this planet is believed to influence us to be over-critical, sarcastic, fussy, judgemental, argumentative, deceitful, unprincipled, worrying, conceited, easily bored and prone to gossip.

Mercury is a very small planet indeed. At only 3,000 miles in diameter, Mercury is so small that it could just about be dropped into the Atlantic Ocean. It is the closest heavenly body to the sun. At its closest, Mercury can be 29 million miles away from the sun. At its furthest, it can be 43 million miles away from the sun. Mercury is about 136 million miles away from our own planet. From our view on earth, it always appears very close to the sun. In fact, it is never more than 27 degrees away from it. Mercury has no moons and no air on its surface. Mercury's year only consists of about 88 days which represents the planet's association with speed and quick-thinking. It spends approximately 7.5 days in each sign of the zodiac (not including retrograde periods).

Here is some magical information for this very intellectual heavenly body:

Basic Energies: Communicates, intellectualises, mediates, moves things fast.

Symbol: Winged helmet or winged sandals.

Element: Air.

Time: Dawn.

Day: Wednesday.

Cardinal Point: East.

Zodiac Signs: Gemini (masculine counterpart), Virgo (feminine counterpart).

Colours: Mixtures of colours, orange, violet, yellow.

Incense: Anise, lavender, mint, nutmeg.

Plants/Trees: Acacia, agaric, almond, anise, ash, aspen, azalea, bean, bittersweet, bracken, butterbur, caraway, carrot, cascara sagrada, celery, cinquefoil, clover, cow parsnip, dill, elecampane, fennel, fenugreek, fern, filbert, flax, germander, goat's rue, hazel, honeysuckle, horehound, hound's tongue, lavender, lemongrass, lemon verbena, lily of the valley, maidenhair fern, male fern, mandrake, marjoram, mint, mulberry, myrtle, nutmeg, papyrus, parsley, pecan, pellitory, pimpernel, pistachio, pomegranate, senna, skullcap, southernwood, valerian, wax plant, wormwood.

Crystals/Stones: Agate, amber, carnelian, emerald, opal, peridot, smoky quartz, tiger's eye, topaz, tourmaline.

Metals: Alloys, mercury (quicksilver).

Creatures: Birds, blue jay, coyote, fly, fox, ibis, jackal, monkey, pairs of snakes, raven.

Mythical Beast: Winged horse.

Archangel: Raphael.

Governs: Acting, adaptability, ambivalence, analysing things, argumentativeness, business transactions, cleverness, cognition, commerce, communication, coordination, creativity, cynicism, debt, deceit, depression, diplomacy, divination, dyslexia, education, employment, enhancing communication skills, epilepsy, dexterity, eloquence, falsehood, fear, gymnastics, healing, health, hearing, impairment of motor functions, impairment of nerves, important news, independence, insanity, intellect, intellectual pursuits, interpretation, issues to do with the mind, language, learning, lies, love, magic of any kind, money, mediation, memory, mental agility, mental cruelty, mental perception, mental processes, messages, movement, occult wisdom of rebirth, persuasion, predictions, projects, prosperity, psychic power, reason, respiration, sarcasm, scientific theories, self-improvement, sensitivity, skills, sound judgement, speech, speech impediments, speed, teaching, the nervous system, the power of the occult, the power of opposites, the upper mental plane (fifth plane), thievery, travel, trickery, versatility, wealth, wisdom, wit, wrestling, writing.

Moon

The moon is one of the most powerful symbols of the Goddess. It is the feminine, nurturing, sensitive, reflective, emotional, mothering, changeable, creative and loving heavenly body. It influences growth, fertility, conception, imagination, instincts and our moods. The waters of the oceans, the sap in plants and all bodily fluids are influenced by the moon's waxing, full and waning phases. This is evinced by the tides of the oceans and women's menstrual cycles. Everything that grows and matures does so in accordance with the rhythms and cycles of the moon's enormous power. It is the Queen of Heaven and the Yin to the sun's Yang. It is the beautiful silver bride of the sun. It represents the cold, moist, passive, receptive and nurturing aspect of nature that receives the seed of life. It represents the Great Goddess, the mother of all nature, on whom we all depend. It has strong associations with the Elixir of Immortality and regeneration. It represents Isis, Ceres, Selene, Hecate, Diana and even the Virgin Mary of the Christian faith. The moon inspires and illuminates us and Witches draw its power in their many magical workings. She mirrors the stages of life so famously associated with women: maiden, mother and crone. It can be both cruel and kind as with all nature. Such was the importance of the moon to the ancient Pagans that the Christians tried their very best to associate it with sheer evil. On the positive side, the moon is believed to influence us to be inward-looking, sensitive, kind, sympathetic, magnetic, peace-loving, maternal, patient, psychic and imaginative. On the negative side, the moon is believed to influence us to be unreliable, lazy, confused, delusional, cruel, moody, unpredictable, negative about life, overly emotional, pessimistic and prone to evil thoughts.

The moon is a luminary, it is the earth's natural satellite, that is often called a "planet" in astrology. The word "planet" simply meant "wandering star" in ancient times (the sun, however, is the only "real" star within our solar system). In comparison to the earth, the moon is tiny. It would, in fact, take 81 moons to equal the size of the earth. Since the moon is so close to the earth, it has always had a strong influence on humankind. As with the sun, the moon was revered as a deity by our ancient ancestors in all cultures and religions, all over the world, in one form or another. At its closest, the moon can come as close to the earth as 221, 000 miles. At its furthest, the moon can be as far away from the earth as 252, 700 miles. The moon circles the earth as the earth circles the sun. It has a somewhat complex orbit around the earth. It takes 29.5 days or so to circle the earth. This means that the moon appears to grow to fullness and decrease in size. This is actually an illusion caused by how much light is reflected from the sun as the moon journeys around the earth. There is no air or weather on the moon. The moon spends approximately 2.3 to 2.5 days in each sign of the zodiac.

Here is some magical information for this very mothering heavenly body:

Basic Energies: Enchants, fertilises, intuits.

Symbol: Crescent moon.

Element: Water.

Time: Night.

Day: Monday (Moon Day).

Cardinal Point: West.

Zodiac Sign: Cancer.

Colours: Silver, white.

Incense: Coconut, ginseng, jasmine, lotus, myrrh, sandalwood, ylang-ylang.

Plants/Trees: Acanthus, adder's tongue, agave, aloe, banana, bladderwrack, buchu, burnet, cabbage, calamus, camellia, camphor, chamomile, chaste tree, chickweed, cleaver, club moss, cuckoo flower, coconut, cotton, cucumber, dog rose, dulse, eucalyptus, fluellen, fungi, gardenia, ginseng, gourd, grape, honesty, iris, Irish moss, jasmine, leafy green vegetables, lemon, lemon balm, lettuce, lily, loosestrife, lotus, Madonna lily, magnolia, mallow, melon, mesquite, moly, moonwort, myrrh, myrtle, night-blooming plants, papaya, passionflower, pea, peach, pear, periwinkle, pondweed, poppy, potato, pumpkin, purslane, sandalwood, saxifrage, sea holly, seaweed, soma, St. John's wort, stonecrop, turnip, wallflower, watercress, water lily, white rose, wild rose, willow, wintergreen, ylang-ylang, yucca.

Crystals/Stones: Aquamarine, clear quartz, jet, labradorite, moonstone, mother of pearl, opal, pearl, sea-green beryl, selenite, turquoise.

Metal: Silver.

Creatures: Cat, crab, crocodile, dog, dolphin, elephant, frog, hare, horse, ibis, moth, nightingale, nightjar, otter, owl, pig, rabbit, seabirds, seal, shellfish, snake, sparrow, spider, stag, swan, turtle, vixen, water snake, whale, white bull, wolf, wryneck. Generally aquatic creatures.

Mythical Beast: Sea serpent.

Archangel: Gabriel.

Governs: Affection, agriculture, ancestors, artistic talent, balance, banishment, beauty, benevolence, birth, celebrations, change, charity, childbirth, clairvoyance, coagulation, coldness, compassion, conception, confusion, conjunction, conjuring spirits, cooking, courage, creating a safe space, creativity, cruelty, cycles, daring, death, defence, delusions, domestic concerns, dependence, dreams, ecstasy, emotions, empathy, enchantment, enlightenment, envy, evil thoughts, family, fertility, fidelity, fluids, forgiveness, friendship, gentility, glandular secretion, growth, happiness, healing, health, illumination, illusion, imagination, infirmities caused by cold moisture, instinct, impressionability, intuition, inspiration, kindness, laziness, life, love, lunacy, magnetism, marriage, maternity, medicine, meditation, memory, menstruation, mental problems, merchandise, metamorphosis, modesty, moods, motherhood, mysteries, nervous diseases, nursing, nurture, patience, peace, personality, pessimism, pleasure, poetry, protection, psychic sensitivity, psychology, psychosis, purification, rain, reason, rebirth, recuperation, reflection, regeneration, repelling negativity, reproduction, research, rest, schizophrenia, secrets, sensitivity, sensuality, sleep, sorrow, sperm, spirituality, sympathy, the etheric plane, the feminine principle, the home, the immortality of the soul, the past, the power of the sea, the subconscious mind, the unconscious mind, the womb, thievery, tides, time, transformation, travel (especially over the sea), truth, unions of every kind, universal wisdom, unpredictability, unreliability, virginity, wishes.

Moon Esbats

Although the word "Esbat" can refer to any celebration or magical working based on any phase of the moon, it is typically associated with the full of the moon. The moon represents our Queen of Heaven and there is no better time for Witches to celebrate its power than when it is full. The full moon is a time for Witches to celebrate the mother aspect of the Goddess. The moon is cyclical, like all women, and inspires and illuminates us. Anciently, time, calendars and the seasons were all set by the moon. The word "moon" is connected to the Sanskrit word "me" meaning "to measure". However, in 46 B. C. E. the Roman general Julius Caesar proposed the Julian calendar and this took effect on January 1st 45 B. C. E. This was then gradually replaced by the Gregorian calendar which was introduced by Pope Gregory XIII in October 1582. Both of these calendars are solar-based. This means that, in modern times, there are sometimes twelve full moons in the year and sometimes thirteen. But, anciently, there were always considered to be thirteen full moons within the year that our Pagan ancestors celebrated.

Although I don't typically work with double-digit numbers in my rituals and magical workings, the number thirteen has always had a spiritual significance. As well as being connected to the traditional thirteen full moons of the year of our ancestors, it is also related to the twelve signs of the zodiac and the sun that travels through them. The traditional Witches' coven has thirteen members. This would traditionally consist of one main leader and six male Witches and six female Witches. The number thirteen even has somewhat of a connection to Christianity – Jesus chose twelve disciples to follow him. There is also a wonderful Venus figurine that is thought to be connected to the thirteen full moons of the ancient Pagan year. This is the Venus of Laussel which is believed by experts to have been created about 25, 000 years ago. It holds a horn with thirteen stripes – one for every lunar cycle of the ancient Pagan year.

One way to celebrate the full moon is with a good meal. Set the dinner table with white and silver and dress formally with the same colours for the occasion. Put lunar flowers in a vase and put this in the centre of the table and serve some lunar foods, such as creamy dishes and leafy green salads. A good white wine or special beer would be an excellent complement to this special dinner. A dinner that honours the full moon can be an excellent way to prepare for lunar rituals and spells or to replenish after them. Although the names of the full moons vary according to the traditions of specific cultures, the names below are the ones I follow for the thirteen full moon Esbats:

Ice Moon: The Ice Moon rises in January. Also known as the Wolf Moon or Cold Moon, this full moon relates to the coldness of the January air. It is a time when the waters of the earth are locked under a sheet of ice, just as Persephone was locked in the underworld with Hades as she waited to be reunited with her mother Demeter in the spring. This is a full moon associated with coldness, a time when death and winter govern the land.

Storm Moon: rises in February. Also known as the Quickening Moon, this full moon relates to the quickening of the earth when we begin to see dramatic changes within the natural world. Life begins to stir as rain falls and the oceans rage. These are the signs that the waters of the earth will ebb and flow once more as spring becomes increasingly apparent. This is a very healing moon associated with the fiery goddess Brigit.

Chaste Moon: rises in March. Also known as the Worm Moon or Awakening Moon, the Chaste Moon relates to the freshness of spring. It represents the greening of the land and the promise of the warmer days to come. It is a time when the Goddess and God dance in courtship as the animals rejoice in the increasing warmth of nature. This moon represents the virginal-fresh, clean and untouched powers of the land.

Seed Moon: rises in April. Also known as the Grass Moon or Wind Moon, the Seed Moon honours the growth of the earth as the season of spring advances. The seeds that lay on the ground over the autumn and winter show themselves as plants as the earth warms up and becomes greener. This moon represents the preparation time for the coming of the long-awaited summer.

Hare Moon: rises in May. Also known as the Flower Moon, the Hare Moon honours the sacred bond between the Goddess and God who enter into marriage at Beltane. Although the moon has its traditional colours, the Hare Moon is associated appropriately with the colour of pink because of its traditional links with love and relationships. As we welcome in the summer, our minds turn to romance and the bonds we share with our nearest and dearest at this full moon.

Dyad Moon: rises in June. Also known as the Strong Sun Moon or Strawberry Moon, the Dyad Moon honours nature and the sun at their fullest glory. "Dyad" is an old word meaning "pair" and this reflects the sacred bond between the Goddess and God at this very loving time of the year whose powers are evident all around us in the brightness of the sun and the colours of the earth.

Mead Moon: rises in July. Also known as the Blessing Moon, this moon honours the powers of nature as we prepare for the first harvest of the land. It is a joyous moon that is often celebrated with singing and dancing. Traditionally, Pagans of ancient times made mead at this full moon in preparation for the coming of the harvest celebrations. It is an Esbat associated with the rich honey mead that Witches in modern times often prepare.

Wort Moon: ises in August. Also known as the Corn Moon or Red Moon, the Wort Moon is associated with the first harvest of the land. "Wort" is an Old Saxon word which referred to the herbs and the greenery of the land and so this moon honours the plants of the earth that are to be harvested as we prepare for the cold nights of winter. It is a full moon that honours the fruits of the land as nature begins to close down and the nights become even longer.

Barley Moon: rises in September. Also known as the Harvest Moon, the Barley Moon honours the second harvest. It is a time when leaves begin to drop to the earth as nature prepares for its time of rest over the winter period.

It is a time when the God prepares to leave his physical body as the darkness governs the land and our lives.

Blood Moon: rises in October. Also known as the Tree Moon, the Blood Moon honours Samhain as we prepare for the coming of winter. It is associated with the hue of red, the colour of blood. This is because in ancient times this moon reflected the time of the slaughter of animals in order for there to be enough food in preparation for the time of barrenness over the winter period. In many places, this moon was a time when temperatures became low enough for meat to be preserved. It is a moon associated with the death of the God as the last of the leaves drop to the ground and winter approaches.

Snow Moon: rises in November. Also known as the Mourning Moon or Frost Moon, the Snow Moon honours the coming of the snow that will soon blanket the land. The earth enters into a time of slumber after the Blood Moon as it gathers strength for the coming of the spring in the following year. This is a full moon to remember that we too need to rest and retreat in order to gather our strength for the things that we want in life.

Oak Moon: rises in December. Also known as the Long Nights Moon, the Oak Moon honours winter and the dark aspect of the God as he rests in the Summerlands and is then reborn at Yule. Oak wood is traditionally burned in a ritual fire or cauldron to honour him. Oak is a wood of his symbol – the sun. This is a time of feasting and drinking with Yule foods and spicy drinks. It is a time of singing and dancing as we prepare for the coming of spring.

Blue Moon: When we do have thirteen full moons in the same year we get two full moons in the same calendar month at some point in the year. This is called the Blue Moon which is where we get the phrase "once in a Blue Moon". This is the odd moon of the year and usually falls in September or October. The Blue Moon is the second full moon in the month that it falls. Some Witches consider this moon to be extra powerful or lucky, though other Witches do not associate it with any additional power or luck. When we have a Blue Moon in September or October it is often known as the Wine Moon. This relates to the wine that Witches often make in those months from the fruits of the harvest. Witches consider wine a luxurious gift from the Goddess and God.

Neptune

The planet Neptune is the watery planet associated with the vast expanse of the oceans of the earth. In Roman mythology, Neptune was a bearded man who was the god of the sea who held a trident to symbolise his great power over the waters of the earth. He, and his Greek equivalent Poseidon, were said to rule over the ancient and mysterious city of Atlantis which some people believe had sank below the Atlantic Ocean millennia ago due to a volcanic eruption. In his stories, Neptune took the form of a horse in order to romance Ceres who he desperately loved. Ceres, the earth goddess of the harvests whose Greek equivalent is Demeter, had also took the form of a horse when Neptune decided to take his form of this beautiful creature. On the positive side, Neptune is believed to influence us to be poetic, visionary, imaginative, psychic, artistic, glamorous, spiritual and protective. On the negative side, Neptune is believed to influence us to be delusional, overly emotional, scandalous, intangible, nervous and overly indulgent (especially in drugs and alcohol).

Neptune is one of the modern planets and was only discovered in 1846. Astrologers at the time were very quick to associate it with the element of water. It is, on average, 2, 800 million miles away from the sun. Neptune is an icy, gas giant with a faint ring system. Its atmosphere consists of hydrogen, helium and methane. It has many moons – one of which is Triton that moves in a retrograde motion. Neptune's crust is icy water, methane and ammonia. The icy water is one reason why the planet is strongly linked with the element of water. Neptune is the second slowest-moving heavenly body in our solar system. It takes about 165 years to complete its cycle around the sun and spends approximately 13.8 years in each sign of the zodiac.

Here is some magical information for this very watery heavenly body:

Basic Energies: Clouds, fascinates, makes us prone to feelings of unreality.

Symbol: Neptune's trident.

Elements: Air, water.

Time: Dusk.

Cardinal Points: East, west.

Zodiac Sign: Pisces.

Colours: Mauve, sea-green.

Incense: Benzoin.

Plants/Trees: Aloe, ash, benzoin, birch, chestnut, cucumber, dandelion, lichen, lotus, melon, moss, mulberry, oak, pondweed, sage, saxifrage, seaweed, water lily, willow. Generally swampy or watery plants.

Crystals/Stones: Amethyst, aquamarine, blue topaz, celestite, coral, covellite, fluorite, jade, kyanite, lapis lazuli, sapphire, turquoise.

Creatures: Horse, marine creatures.

Mythical Beast: Sea serpent.

Governs: Affection, alchemy, altered states, artistic talent, change, clairvoyance, cloudiness of the mind, compassion, courage, creativity, delusions, dreams, ecstasy, endings, escapism, fantasy, fascination, forgiveness, friendship, glamour, guidance, hallucinations, healing, humanitarianism, illusion, imagination, indulgence, intangibility, intense emotions, issues to do with children, kindness, meditation, mysteries, nervousness, other-worldly matters, peace, pleasure, poetry, protection, psychic knowledge, psychic power, rain, relationships, safe journeys, scandal, sensitivity, sensuality, spirituality, the power of the sea, unreality, vagueness, visions.

Pluto

Pluto is the mysterious planet associated with death, darkness and the underworld. In Roman mythology, Pluto was an ancient god of agriculture who had the additional job of ruling the souls of the underworld, the land of death. The underworld was where all the souls of the dead travelled along the River Styx. He was a somewhat gloomy deity who had the power of invisibility.

He was associated with dread, inevitability and doom. He was so obsessed with the goddess Proserpina that he kidnapped her so that she could rule the underworld with him over the winter period as the earth slept. However, she returned to the land in the spring and was reunited with her mother Ceres and the result was that the earth came back to life, symbolising reincarnation and the continuation of life. On the positive side, Pluto is believed to influence us to be intuitive, psychic, powerful, energetic, fascinating, dramatic, passionate, exciting, sexually adventurous, driven, deep-thinkers and able to have the power to confront and overcome obstacles, whether physical, psychological or spiritual. On the negative side, Pluto is believed to influence us to be cruel, devious, obsessed, overly sensitive, overly critical, prone to criminality, dangerous and overly private to the point that we cut ourselves away from the outside world.

In 1930 the astronomer Clyde Tombaugh visually identified Pluto after there had been mathematical theories of its existence made by the great astronomer Percival Lowell (brother of the poet Amy Lowell) at the turn of the twentieth century. In 2006 Pluto was downgraded by astronomers from planet to "dwarf planet". This, however, has nothing to do with modern-day astrology. Pluto is no less important to modern-day astrologers than it was originally and is still regarded as a normal planet by them. Pluto is very small indeed and is close to the size of Mercury. It is about 2,700 miles wide around its equator. It is about 3,600 million miles away from the sun which means it is very dark indeed and this is one of the reasons it is associated with the darkness of the underworld. It is the slowest-moving of the heavenly bodies in our solar system. It has five moons and the largest is Charon. Pluto is actually classed as a double heavenly body with this moon. Pluto is covered with frozen methane and Charon is covered with frozen water. Pluto takes about 248 years to complete its rotation around the sun and spends approximately 20.6 years in each sign of the zodiac.

Here is some magical information for this very mysterious heavenly body:

Basic Energies: Eliminates, transforms.

Symbol: Helmet of Pluto.

Zodiac Sign: Scorpio.

Colours: Black, maroon, red.

Incense: Basil.

Plants/Trees: Anise, basil, blackthorn, bushy trees, cypress, figwort, male fern, pennyroyal, silverweed, valerian, wild thistle. Generally plants known to be beneficial for enhancing sexuality.

Crystals/Stones: Amethyst, garnet, jet, obsidian, opal, sodalite.

Metals: Plutonium, uranium.

Creatures: Scorpion, snake.

Archangel: Azrael.

Governs: Adventures, agriculture, bringing order from chaos, confrontation, criminality, criticality, cruelty, danger, darkness, death, deep thoughts, deviousness, disruption, drama, drive, elimination, encouragement, energy, excitement, fascination, group ideas, inevitability, intense thoughts, intuition, invisibility, money, mysteries, nuclear power, obsession, overcoming obstacles, passion, power, privacy, psychic power, rapid manifestation, rebirth, regeneration, reincarnation, riches, sensitivity, sexuality, the afterlife, the underworld, transformation, unification, wealth.

Saturn

Saturn is the planet of restriction, coldness, limitation, inhibition and isolation. It represents the connection between the physical world and the spiritual world. This is a representation that eternity becomes time and space. It represents the calamity we need until we master our hopes and dreams. In Roman mythology, Saturn was the god of agricultural skills and arts. He later became associated with the ancient festival of Yule which is also named after him – Saturnalia. This was a time when darkness and barrenness governed the land. So to cheer up this time our ancestors marked it with music, dancing and feasting. Although when the Christians took over this ancient festival it was moved to December 25th to coincide with other Pagan celebrations such as the birth of Dionysus, the god of the physical pleasures of life and fertility.

Saturn was often portrayed as a skeletal figure who was our Old Father Time. He mercilessly cut down the old or unworthy with his scythe. This represented the cutting away of any impurities. On the positive side, Saturn is believed to encourage us to be practical, pragmatic, honest, disciplined, sensitive, sensible, ambitious, hard-working, enterprising, able to overcome obstacles, faithful, analytical, systematic, tactful, responsible and studious. On the negative side, Saturn is believed to encourage us to be pessimistic, overly secretive, fatalistic, jealous and obstructive of positive things.

Saturn is another massive heavenly body of our solar system. It is almost 75,000 miles in diameter. It is generally considered to be the last planet that can be seen with the naked eye and this represents the planet's associations with limitations and isolations. It is famous for its extraordinary system of rings which are perhaps numbering in their thousands. These rings are made of whirling ice and rock and have been studied as far back as 1655. Saturn has many moons and the largest and most famous of which is Titan. Saturn is never less than 740 million miles from our own planet and is about 888 million miles away from the sun. It takes about 29.5 years to complete its orbit around the sun and spends approximately 2.4 years in each sign of the zodiac. Other famous moons of this planet include Rhea, Tethys and Mimas.

Here is some magical information for this very systematic heavenly body:

Basic Energies: Binds, controls, limits, obstructs, restricts, stabilises.

Symbol: Scythe or sickle of Saturn.

Elements: Earth, water.

Time: Daylight hours.

Day: Saturday (Saturn Day).

Cardinal Points: North, west.

Zodiac Signs: Aquarius (classical, masculine counterpart), Capricorn (feminine counterpart).

Colours: Black, blue, dark blue, dark brown, grey, indigo.

Incense: Aloe, copal, fenugreek, fumitory, myrrh, patchouli, spikenard.

Plants/Trees: Adder, alder, aloe, amaranth, asphodel, bachelor's buttons, barley, beech, beet, bistort, boneset, buckthorn, cannabis, comfrey, copal, cypress, daffodil, dandelion, datura, dodder, dogwood, elm, equisetum, euphorbia, fenugreek, fumitory, gladwin, heartease, hellebore, hemlock, henbane, holly, horsetail, iris, ironwood, ivy, kava-kava, knapweed, knot weed, lady's slipper, lobelia, maize, mandrake, medlar, mimosa, morning glory, moss, mullein, myrrh, pansy, patchouli, pomegranate, poplar, poppy, quince, rowan, royal fern, rupturewort, Scotch pine, shepherd's purse, skullcap, skunk cabbage, slippery elm, spikenard, spleenwort, tamarind, tamarisk, thyme, verbascum, wall fern, weeping willow, wintergreen, woad, wolf's bane, yew.

Crystals/Stones: Azurite, black coral, carnelian, coal, diamond, jet, hematite, ironstone, obsidian, onyx, pearl, ruby, sapphire.

Metal: Lead.

Creatures: Ant, beaver, crow, heron, raven, termite, tortoise, vole, worm, wren.

Mythical Beast: Dragon.

Archangel: Cassiel.

Governs: Acceptance, agriculture, ambition, analysing things, banishment, binding, blood circulation in tissues, calamity, calcination, coldness, concrete mind, control, concentration, construction, coping with death, crankiness, crying, cutting away impurities, darkness, death, dentistry, depression, destroying disease, discipline, distrust, divination, doctrines, dogmatism, endings, endurance, enterprises, evolution, exorcism, faith, fatality, funerals, hard work, history, honesty, humility, inflexibility, inheritance, inhibition, intolerance, isolation, jealousy, joints, karmic forces, knowledge, law, laziness, legal matters, lethargy, limitation, longevity, long-term memory, meanness, meditation, mercilessness, methods, mutation, obstruction, occult matters, operations concerning buildings, order, overcoming obstacles, patience, peace, perseverance, persistence, pessimism, practicality, property, protection, psychic development, rebirth, reincarnation, reliability, responsibility, rest, restriction, rheumatism, secrets, sensibility, sensitivity, sincerity, slow change, space, stability, strength, structures, studiousness, tactfulness, teeth, temperance, tenacity, tendons, termination, the afterlife, the ageing process, the connection between the spiritual and physical realities, the elderly, the lower mental plane (fourth plane), the skeletal system, the spleen, time, visions, wisdom.

Sun

The sun represents vitality, illumination, the ego, self-expression, the consciousness, passion, drive and our most basic physical and sexual needs. It represents the spirit in the flesh and the masculine principle of nature. Ancient civilisations worshipped the sun, believing its brightness and brilliance to represent the perfection of man. This is represented by the sun's metal, gold, which is believed to be a metal of perfection. There are many solar gods who the ancients worshipped. Lucifer, which is a name that has become synonymous with Satan in Christianity, was originally a positive deity of the sun. His name simply means "light-bringer" or "illuminator of the spirit". The ancient goddess Diana was known as "Diana Lucifera" which referred to her power to bring light into people's lives, though she is mostly associated with the moon. In the early Gnostic Church, Mary Magdalene was known as "Mary Lucifera" which was in honour of the Gnostic Church's power to illuminate the souls of men. Luciferians were not the evil Satanists of popular belief. They were simply people who believed that the sun represented the light of God. The sun has naturally always had a special place within religions of all cultures. It is the Yang to the moon's Yin and the handsome groom of the moon. Without the cooling, moistening powers of the moon, the sun can be harsh, burning and arid. On the positive side, the sun is believed to influence us to be enlightened, dignified, rational, inspirational, ambitious, generous, joyous, affectionate, constructive, vital, outgoing, impressive, confident, creative, optimistic and lovers of knowledge. On the negative side, the sun is believed to influence us to be pompous, despotic, overbearing, arrogant, domineering, dogmatic, stubborn and autocratic.

The sun lies in the centre of our solar system and is about 93 million miles away from us. It has a surface temperature of about 6, 000 degrees centigrade but its core can reach about 15 million degrees centigrade. Without this enormous heat, the earth would be desolate of life and fertility. You would probably have to explode 100 billion tons of dynamite to equal the enormous power of the sun. The sun is believed to be about 4.6 billion years old and astronomers believe that it is about halfway through the most stable part of its life. The sun is by far the largest heavenly body of our solar system. Its diameter is about 865, 000 miles across. About one million earths could fit inside it. The sun amazingly holds 99.8 percent of the entire mass of the solar system. The sun is basically a huge ball of incandescent gas made up mostly of hydrogen and helium. It is of average brightness compared to the other stars of the universe. It takes about 265 days for the earth to complete its rotation around the sun. The sun spends approximately 30 days in each sign of the zodiac.

Here is some magical information for this very passionate heavenly body:

Basic Energies: Achieves, creates, enlightens, governs, illuminates, inspires, promotes, provides physical energy.

Symbol: Wheel.

Element: Fire.

Time: Noon.

Day: Sunday (Sun Day).

Cardinal Point: South.

Zodiac Sign: Leo.

Colours: Gold, orange, yellow.

Incense: Angelica, benzoin, bergamot, cinnamon, clove, copal, frankincense, myrrh, olibanum, sandalwood.

Plants/Trees: Acacia, angelica, ash, bay, benzoin, bergamot, birch, bistort, bromeliad, broom, burnet, butterbur, carnation, cashew, cedar, celandine, centaury, chamomile, chicory, chrysanthemum, cinnamon, citron, clove, copal, everlasting, eyebright, frankincense, ginseng, goldenseal, hazel, Helen's flower, heliotrope, hibiscus, hollyhock, juniper, lime, liquidamber, lotus, lovage, marigold, mastic, mistletoe, myrrh, oak, olive, orange, palm, peony, pineapple, rice, rosemary, rowan, rue, saffron, sandalwood, sesame, St. John's wort, sundew, sunflower, tangerine, tormentil, viper's bugloss, walnut, witch hazel.

Crystals/Stones: Amber, blood-red carbuncle, chrysolite, diamond, ruby, tiger's eye, sunstone, topaz.

Metal: Gold.

Creatures: Beetle (especially scarab beetle), blackbird, cat, eagle, falcon, lion, orange butterfly, ram, rooster, white horse, yellow butterfly.

Mythical Beast: Sphinx.

Archangel: Michael.

Governs: Achievement, action, activity, affection, ambition, anger, arrogance, authority, awakened understanding, banishment, body heat, bone marrow, brightness, brilliance, business matters, buying things, career goals, challenges, change, clarity, coagulation, combustions, comfort, competitions, concentration, confidence, conflicts, conjunction, construction, contests, courage, courtrooms, creativity, cycles, desires, destruction, digestion, dignity, discharges from the eyes, dogmatism, drama, drive, electricity, employment, encouragement, energy, energy distribution, enlightenment, enthusiasm, eruptions, excitement, exorcism, fatherhood, fertility, financial issues, freedom, friendship, fulfilment, generosity, good fortune, greed, happiness, hard work, harshness, healing, health, heat, heritage, honesty, hope, illumination, inheritance, inspiration, intellect, issues to do with children, joy, justice, kingship, knowledge, law, leadership, legal matters, lightning, longevity, luck, lust, money, motivation, optimism, organisation, passion, perceptions, perfection, personal power, philosophy, physical energy, physicality, pompousness, positivity, pride, promotion, protection, purification, purpose, rapid growth, rational thought, reactions, rebirth, recognition, responsibilities, self-esteem, self-expression, selling things, sexual needs, sexual potency, sight, speeding up matters, spiritual attainment, sports, stimulation, strength, stubbornness, success, survival, the brain, the conscious mind, the ego, the heart, the life force, the masculine principle, the power of urge, the upper spiritual plane (seventh plane), thunder, transformation, trust, truth, vitality, war, wealth, willpower, wisdom, youth.

Uranus

Uranus is the eccentric and ecstatic planet of shock, change, abrupt upheaval and disruption. This is all symbolised by the Tower in the tarot deck. In Greek mythology, Uranus was the god of the sky and was the son of the Earth Mother. He entered into an incestuous relationship with her and from this came all living things on earth. Uranus was caught by Cronos and his army and was vengefully dethroned and castrated as punishment. His castrated testicles then produced Aphrodite, the Greek goddess of love and erotic sexuality. The significance of the deity Uranus is that his associations with sudden and ruthless change is a reminder of the impermanence of life and that the greatest achievements of life can be taken away from us abruptly and in an instant. This is often karma at work and the deity represents its forces at work in their most dramatic. The planet of Uranus has become somewhat of a "cult" ruler of futuristic fantasy, science fiction and space exploration. On the positive side, Uranus is believed to influence us to be original, versatile, sexually adventurous, independent, innovative, exciting, social, friendly, intuitive and illuminating. On the negative side, Uranus is believed to influence us to be overly eccentric, rebellious, prone to criminality, sexually deviant, crude and rude.

Uranus was discovered in 1781 by the English astronomer William Herschel. It has a diameter of about 29, 300 miles and is about four times the size of our own planet. It is about 1, 600 million miles away from the earth. It is a gas giant and is covered in methane clouds that absorb red light. Uranus has many moons. Oberon and Titania are the largest which were discovered in 1787 by the astronomer who discovered the planet itself William Herschel. Uranus takes about 84 years to obit the sun and spends approximately 7 years in each sign of the zodiac.

Here is some magical information for this very eccentric heavenly body:
Basic Energies: Changes, disrupts, excites, overthrows, replaces, shocks.
Symbol: Zodiac wheel.

Zodiac Sign: Aquarius.

Colours: Electric blue, rainbow.

Incense: Cedar, cinnamon, clove, nutmeg.

Plants/Trees: Allspice, apple, cedar, cinnamon, clove, elder, fruit trees, goldenrod, lady's slipper, mandrake, nutmeg, orchid, pomegranate, skullcap, spikenard, tonka bean, tree of heaven, valerian, wild carrot.

Crystals/Stones: Amethyst, aquamarine, aventurine, blue topaz, clear quartz, diamond.

Archangel: Uriel.

Governs: Adventure, animal magic, animal welfare, astrological knowledge, bizarre occurrences, brilliance, change (especially unexpected change), creativity, criminality, crudeness, destruction, disruption, drama, ecstasy, eccentric actions, eccentric ideas, ecology, electricity, excitement, extremity, fantasy, friendship, healing, health, higher thoughts, honesty, humanitarianism, humour, illumination, impermanence, independence, innovation, intellect, intuition, inventiveness, karmic forces, kindness, laughter, leadership, mental health, nervousness, novelty, originality, overthrow, privacy, rebellion, reform, restlessness, rudeness, science fiction, sexuality, shocks, social awareness, space exploration, spirituality, strangeness, sudden and abrupt upheaval, technology, the urge for freedom, versatility, transformation, truths, wisdom.

Venus

Venus is the planet of love, erotic sexuality, art, friendship, music, family, beauty, fertility and emotion. It helps to mediate between opposites and diverse elements. It basically brings the elements of life into a harmonious balance. In Roman mythology, Venus was the beautiful goddess of love who had a close connection with finery, cosmetics, luxury, clothes and harmony. She was linked to venereal diseases which were once thought to be caused by Venusian influence. The closest to the goddess Venus that the Christians could get was Mary Magdalene who has become associated with prostitution. Although the Christians had never venerated female sexuality, Mary Magdalene was a reminder of the importance of the female role within life. In the ancient temples of Venus, there were hidden corners where the early worshippers could make love. The planet itself is said to have strong associations with the Elixir of Immortality. Although there is no immortality of the physical body, the planet is a reminder of the immortality of the soul. On the positive side, Venus is believed to influence us to be loving, cheerful, popular, friendly, idealistic, gentle, tactic, romantic, diplomatic, kind, poetic, artistic and harmonious. On the negative side, Venus is believed to influence us to be sentimental, obsessive, overly lustful, vulgar and vain.

The planet of Venus is brighter than anything else in the night sky, except for the moon, which is why it has always fascinated humankind. Its orbit lies between the earth and the sun. Apart from the moon, it is our closest neighbour. It comes within 24 million miles of us. This may seem quite far away but it is, in fact, at least 10 million miles than Mars can ever come to us. From our view on earth, Venus appears very close to the sun indeed. Venus is very similar to the size of our own planet. It is covered in clouds of sulphuric acid and its atmospheric pressure is 90 times that of earth. Much of its surface is covered by undulating plains. Venus takes about 225 days to circle the sun and spends approximately 18.7 days in each sign of the zodiac (not including retrograde periods).

Here is some magical information for this very loving heavenly body:

Basic Energies: Harmonises, leads on, pleasures, seduces, sexualises.

Symbol: Scallop shell.

Elements: Earth, water.

Time: Midnight.

Day: Friday.

Cardinal Points: North, west.

Zodiac Signs: Libra (masculine counterpart), Taurus (feminine counterpart).

Colours: Green, indigo, pink, red, rose, royal blue, scarlet.

Incense: Benzoin, jasmine, rose, sandalwood, storax, valerian, violet.

Plants/Trees: Acacia, Adam and Eve, alkanet, alder, alfalfa, aloe, ambrosia, apple, apricot, artichoke, aster, avocado, bachelor's buttons, balm of Gilead, banana, barley, bean, benzoin, birch, bishop's weed, blackberry, bleeding heart, blue flag, buckwheat, bugle, burdock, caper, cardamom, catsfoot, catnip, cherry, chestnut, coltsfoot, columbine, corn, cowslip, crocus, cuckoo flower, cyclamen, daffodil, daisy, damask rose, dropwort, elder, eryngo, feverfew, fig, figwort, foxglove, geranium, goldenrod, gooseberry, groundsel, heather, hibiscus, huckleberry, hyacinth, iris, jasmine, kidneywort, lady's mantle, larkspur, lesser celandine, lilac, linden, lucky hand, magnolia, meadowsweet, mint, moneywort, motherwort, mugwort, myrtle, olive, orchid, peach, pear, pennyroyal, periwinkle, plantain, plum, primrose, quince, ragwort, raspberry, rose, sandalwood, sanicle, sea holly, silverweed, soapwort, sorrel, strawberry, storax, sycamore, tansy, thyme, valerian, Venus' flytrap, verbena, vervain, violet, willow, yarrow.

Crystals/Stones: Amber, aventurine, coral, emerald, jade, lapis lazuli, malachite, opal, pearl, rose quartz, sodalite, turquoise.

Metal: Copper.

Creatures: Bull, butterfly, deer, dove, hare, lynx, rabbit, scallop, swallow, swan.

Mythical Beast: Sea serpent.

Archangel: Anael.

Governs: Acceptance, adaptability, affection, artistic talent, attraction, averting depression, balance, beauty, breasts of women, cell and nerve formation, charm, cheerfulness, cleverness, clothing, cold and moist diseases, communication, complexion, confidence, cosmetics, desires, devotion, diplomacy, diuretic and emetic processes, emotion, enhancing female power, environmental issues, erotic sexuality, family, fashion, fellowship, female genitalia, fertility, fidelity, finery, frankness, friendship, garden or herb magic, gentility, good will, growth, happiness, harmony, idealism, immodesty, impracticability, indecisiveness, indulgence, instinct, joy, justice, kindness, law, leadership, leisure, love, loyalty, lust, luxury, marriage, material matters, music, obsession, partnership, passion, peace, persistence, persuasion, pilgrimage, pleasure, poetry, popularity, positivity, possessions, proportion, prostitution, receptivity, reconciliation, relationships, reliability, romance, seduction, sentimentality, sex magic, sexual needs, sincerity, social awareness, society, strangers, the ability to see both sides of an argument, the immortality of the soul, the kidneys, the power of love, the power of the sea, the sense of smell, the upper astral plane (third plane), the womb, trust, vanity, venereal diseases, vulgarity, youth.

Chapter Sixteen: Herbal Lore

One area of the occult that draws many people to the Craft is the herbal lore or herbalism. Witches and other Pagans are famed for their love and knowledge of herbs on both magical and medicinal levels. Ever since I was a young boy I have always been deeply fascinated by plants and trees. According to my mother, however, I was terrified of them as a toddler and would cry if I came into close contact with one. Perhaps even then I knew that herbs were alive and had mystical powers associated with them. As you will be aware by now, herbs are wonderful manifestations of divine power. They have been used in magical workings and healing since humans became intelligent enough to understand more about the world around them. Almost all plants and trees have the most wonderful and fascinating folklore associated with them which helps us to expand our knowledge of their uses. Herbal lore is a vast subject but it is very interesting and as your knowledge increases you will undoubtedly be hooked.

The word "herbs" comes from an Old Sanskrit word *bharb* meaning "to eat" and this word later became *herba* which is the Latin word meaning "grass" or "fodder". The Old Saxon word for herb was *wort* and this is why using herbs on both magical and medicinal levels was originally known as *wortcunning* by the country folk of olden times. The word wort is actually still preserved in many names of herbs. St. John's wort, figwort, moonwort, spiderwort and masterwort are just some examples. The magical and medicinal uses of herbs truly is ancient and it is only in recent times that scientists and those in the medical professions have turned their backs away from the natural medicinal side of herbs that nature provides for us in favour for very debatable, man-made drugs. We must not forget, however, that much of our knowledge of drugs comes from thousands of years of the medicinal and healing properties of herbs.

Although in Witchcraft today the medicinal and magical uses of herbs are classed as separate, originally these two aspects of herbal lore were one and the same thing. For our Pagan ancestors, medically healing someone with a herbal infusion, for example, was just as magical as using herbs in ritual and magic. Separating the medicinal and magical uses of herbs would have been strange and somewhat bizarre for our ancestors. They simply saw the medicinal and magical uses of herbs as one and the same thing – the science of herbal lore. For them, the science of herbs was a gentle way of helping them to achieve their needs and goals. It was a healthy and natural way of achieving the balance of the mind, body and soul. Interestingly, the word "pharmacy" is derived from the Greek word *pharmakeia* which referred to not only the construction of herbs for physical or mental ailments, but also the construction of potions for ritual and magic. In modern times, however, the medicinal and magical sides of herbs are treated as separate due to the fact that some herbs can be dangerous when used for a specific ailment of the body.

Plants and trees truly are nature's precious gifts and without them we would not be here. We depend on them for food and the air we breathe. Plants and trees absorb carbon dioxide that we breathe out and exchange it for oxygen which we need to survive. Everything in nature works in total balance and harmony and since we get so many uses from plants and trees, they should be greatly respected. They are the lungs of the Earth Mother and beautiful manifestations of the Goddess and God. Always treat any herbs that you use with great respect for without them you would not be here. When you take herb materials from herbs, always ask their permission first and trust your instinct as to whether it feels right to take from them. You can then perhaps leave them a gift as a token of respect. In addition, never take more from the herbs than what you need and generally do not take all of a particular herb so that it has enough materials to survive and grow.

In modern times, many peoples have lost almost all of their spiritual closeness with the natural world. Modern civilisations have cut themselves away from the true occult lores and powers of nature. This is not so for the modern Witch and the use of herbal lore is one excellent way for us to remember our true connection to the powers of the natural world. Plants and trees contain the life force of the universe within them. Each has unique powers that can be utilised in our magical workings. They absorb the mighty powers of the God's symbol (the sun) and the loving powers of the Goddess's symbol (the moon). They stretch their roots deep into the dark and nourishing earth to absorb nutrients. All of these powers mix together within the plants and trees to create the plant kingdom that Witches know and love today. Witches understand that plants have emotional feelings. They respond to both good and evil. Many gardeners will say that plants respond to kindness (my grandfather always used to say this). This is true and Witches have always known it. It is not unusual to see Witches walking barefoot through woodlands and hugging plants and trees. It is one excellent way for us to ensure that we do not lose our connection to the great powers of Gaia.

Witches and Trees

Witches have always had an affinity with trees and tree lore. There is some wonderful and remarkable beliefs and traditions regarding these beautiful additions to the plant kingdom. It is known by those who deal with occult matters that our Pagan ancestors respected and honoured the spirits of trees and that they understood the spiritual and magical energies that were locked inside them. The tree lore of our ancestors still somewhat exists today in some forms. The old belief among many modern folk that you should "touch wood" or "knock on wood" for luck or to ensure that something bad will not happen again comes from the ancient, divine associations regarding trees as magical beings of luck believed by our Pagan ancestors. The fact that many people in modern times still decorate a Yule tree, decorate their homes with holly and burn Yule logs or eat a Yule log chocolate cake around the time of the winter solstice are powerful reminders of our ancient, spiritual connection to trees.

Trees are an amazing addition to the plant kingdom. They can live for hundreds or thousands of years and record in their growth historical, meteorological and geological upheavals. They provide homes, food, shelter and shade for animals and other plant forms. The wood can provide us with the necessities of life and can make our own habitat remarkably beautiful. People have become so used to the uses of trees that these beautiful life forms are underestimated and not given the respect that they truly deserve.

Trees teach us spiritual lessens. They are rooted in the deep, dark and strong foundations of the Earth Mother and grow towards the heavens, reminding us all of our connections between earthly matters and the powers of the heavens. They respond to the seasons of nature. They awaken in the spring with new growth, become full in the summer, shed their leaves in the autumn and finally rest in the winter in order to gather strength for the following spring. This is the wisdom of the natural cycles of life. It is birth, death, rest and reincarnation – the life lessons that nature is so eager to express to us, if only we would take the time to look deeper. It is not at all surprising that our ancestors honoured the Tree of Life as a universal symbol of creation and existence. Trees have long played a part in ancient creation myths and legends and have played special, magical roles in religions and cultures since time immemorial.

If you ever feel completely drained and just at your wits' end with the stresses and strains of life, then you can appeal to the power of a tree for help. This is something that I have often done throughout my life. Find a tree that really appeals to you, a good solid and strong one, perhaps a one in your garden or local woodland. An oak tree would be excellent. Then sit on the ground with your back against the trunk. Close your eyes, relax and allow yourself to enter into a deep state of meditation for at least ten minutes. After some time, you should start to feel better. Your anger, frustration, tiredness or any other negativity will gradually fade away. This will then be gradually replaced by a glowing warmth and feelings of contentment, love and comfort. You may begin to feel a pleasant tingling sensation rising up from your feet to your head. You may feel the strength once again to get through whatever life throws at you. These wonderful feelings are aided by the tree. Accept them with peace and be glad. When you feel completely whole again, give the tree a big hug and thank it. Then walk home in the knowledge that you have become just that little bit closer to the great powers of the natural world.

Herbs and the Moon

You will understand by now that herbs are linked to astrology and the heavenly bodies of our solar system. The moon, however, is the most important heavenly body when it comes to the powers of herbs. As you will be aware by now, everything that grows and matures does so in accordance with the natural powers of the moon. The moon influences both the magical and medicinal properties of herbs as she waxes, becomes full and wanes into darkness. As a rule of thumb, you should be planting your herbs when the moon waxes and then collecting their materials when the moon becomes full. Research has shown that the medicinal properties of herbs are far greater when the moon is full. So, for Witches, their magical powers are at their most potent as well when the moon reaches the peak of her cycle. Magical peoples have been collecting herbs for their workings at the full moon since time immemorial. Of course, herbs will still have powers no matter what phase the moon is at but it is always good to remember that they will be at their most potent if you collect them at the full moon. Herbs picked at the full moon will really help to strengthen and empower your magical workings. They will truly give your magical workings an enormous boost.

A Witch's Herbal

Here, we will look at an alphabetical list of some popular herbs that Witches may use in their magical and medicinal practices. It is a Witch's herbal but it is far from complete. Even a book dedicated to herbal lore would only scratch the surface of this wonderful subject. This guide, however, will be enough to get you started in your quest to expand your knowledge of herbalism as you perform and devise rituals and spells. I have also explained some of their medicinal properties since I believe that this part of herbalism should be a priority for any Witch's development. I cannot stress enough, however, that caution should always be taken when working with herbs. It can be fatal to ingest some herbs. If you are not sure about a specific herb and the effects it may have on the body, then leave it alone and find an alternative. In addition, some herbs should not be used for the body unless you know how to properly prepare them. It is also wise not to use too much of some herbs for the body in one go. Regardless, I'm sure you will find the below information very useful. The information I have given on each herb will serve as an introduction. A more rounded look at each herb, however, will require more research.

Acacia: Acacia is a masculine herb that is strongly linked to the sun and the element of air. It is sacred to the deities Diana, Osiris, Ishtar, Astarte and Ra. The wood is used to burn sacred fires in India. When the wood is burned with sandalwood, psychic powers are said to be stimulated. A spring of the wood placed in the bedroom is said to ward away evil or negative influences. The wood of acacia is traditionally carried for protection. Use acacia for magical workings involving protection and psychic powers. The flowers can also be used in magical workings of love. Medicinally, acacia can be utilised to relieve pain and irritation. It also helps to ease coughs and sore throats. It can also be used to heal wounds and it restricts blood loss. It is a good source of fibre that is believed to reduce body fat. A study on rats has shown some evidence that acacia could potentially treat diabetes.

Agaric: is a masculine type of fungus that has strong connections to the planet of Mercury and the element of air. It is the famous toadstool with a red cap with white spots and is sacred to Dionysus and Bacchus. Scientists nowadays don't necessarily see fungi as plants. They see them as having their own, unique kingdom. But I always see them as plants for simplicity. Interestingly, there is a whole system of fungi beneath the ground that some people call "nature's internet". This is because plants and trees communicate with each other through this system. There is a belief that mystery religions of ancient times centred their secret magical workings with the use of agaric. Agaric is used in magical workings that increase fertility. It is, however, poisonous and so some people consider it not very wise to use it. It can cause terrifying hallucinations.

Agrimony: is a masculine herb that is strongly linked to the planet of Jupiter and the element of air. It is often placed into sachets to banish negative energies and evil spirits. It has long been used by Witches and magicians to break curses. Throughout history, agrimony was believed to detect Witches. Agrimony is excellent for magical workings of protection. It can help to powerfully banish the evil and negative intentions of others. Medicinally, the anti-inflammatory properties of agrimony make it useful for treating skin rashes, stomach upsets, sore throats, mouth ulcers and rheumatism. The cooled infusion of this herb can be applied to a cloth and then used to treat irritated skin and improve blood circulation. Drinking the infusion will improve digestion because it will stimulate the stomach and gallbladder. It will also treat irritable bowels. It can also be used to treat wounds since it helps blood to clot.

Alfalfa: is a feminine herb that is strongly linked to the planet of Venus and the element of earth. It can be kept in the home or about your person to protect against poverty and hunger. It can be placed in small jars for these purposes and then these jars can be placed wherever you want. The herb can also be burned to ashes and then sprinckled for these purposes of protection against poverty and hunger. It is excellent for all magical workings of prosperity, anti-hunger and money. Medicinally, alfalfa is excellent for high cholesterol, asthma, osteoarthritis, diabetes and stomach upsets. It is also useful for kidney, bladder and prostate problems. It is used to increase healthy urine flow. It is also an excellent source of dietary nutrients for the body. It is high in calcium, protein and vitamins.

Aloe: is a succulent, feminine herb that is strongly linked to the moon and the element of water. It is a popular plant that people enjoy keeping in their homes. It is a protective herb that protects against evil or negative influences as well as household accidents. In Africa, it is hung over houses and doorways to stop evil from entering and to bring forth luck. It is used in all forms of magical workings of protection, success and luck. Medicinally, aloe stimulates the immune system and has powerful anti-inflammatory, antibiotic and antiseptic effects. It is used to treat skin problems, such eczema and psoriasis. It is excellent when used as a moisturiser for the skin. It can help to heal burns, wounds, acne, anal fissures and haemorrhoids. Since aloe is also quite a strong laxative, it is best to use the herb primarily as an external remedy.

Anemone: is a masculine herb that is strongly linked to the planet of Mars and the element of fire. It is sacred to the deities Adonis and Venus. The blossoms are traditionally wrapped in a red cloth and then worn to prevent disease. Red anemones are particularly excellent when grown in the garden to protect both it and the home. Anemone is traditionally carried for healing. It is excellent for all magical workings of protection, health and healing. Medicinally, anemone treats tension headache, hyperactivity, insomnia, boils, asthma, lung diseases, earache, neuralgia, restlessness and problems with the urinary tract. Anemone is excellent for those who suffer from nervous tension and panic attacks (also known as anxiety attacks).

Angelica: is a masculine herb that is strongly linked to the sun and the element of fire. It is sacred to the goddess Venus. The herb is grown to aid protection and made into incense that aids both protection and exorcism. When the herb is sprinckled in all four corners of the home, it helps to ward away evil or negative influences. Added to ritual baths, angelica can help to remove curses or any other spells cast against you. American Indian tribes carried the root in the pocket as a form of a gambling talisman. The incense is used in healing rituals and smoking the leaves of this herb is said to aid visions. It can be used in all magical workings of exorcism, protection, healing and causing visions. Medicinally, angelica is used for the treatment of heartburn, flatulence, loss of appetite (good for anorexia), circulation problems, insomnia, nervous tension and respiratory catarrh. Some women use angelica to start their menstrual periods.

Anise: is a masculine herb that is strongly linked to the planet of Jupiter and the element of air. The seeds of the anise are placed inside a small pillowcase to keep away nightmares. The seeds are also placed in purification baths. These baths would be especially useful for purification if there are also bay leaves in the water. The fresh leaves of the anise placed in a room drive away evil or negativity. They are also placed around the magic circle to protect the Witch or magician from evil entities or spirits. They also protect against the evil eye. Anise can be useful for calling forth spirits in magical workings. A spring of the herb placed above the bedpost will help to restore youth and vitality. Anise is excellent for all magical workings of protection and purification. Medicinally, anise has many health benefits. It is a powerful plant that is rich in nutrients. It is used to treat stomach ulcers, blood sugar levels, depression, menopause, indigestion, flatulence, menstrual period pains and bronchitis. It is also believed to help libido in both sexes.

Apple: is a feminine herb that is strongly linked to the planet of Venus and the element of water. It is sacred to the deities Venus, Aphrodite, Olwen,

Dionysus, Apollo, Athena, Zeus, Iduna, Hera and Diana. There is so much folklore attached to the apple tree. It is one of the most potent representations of immortality. It is said that the apple tree marks a boundary between the worlds. The tree was incredibly sacred to the Celts and the Norse peoples. The fruit of the apple tree is peeled and then the peel is thrown over the left shoulder to discover the initial of a future partner. The apple is excellent for all magical workings of love, health, healing, garden magic and fertility. Medicinally, the benefits of the fruits of the apple tree are thought to be many and varied. The fruits are also highly nutritious and a good source of vitamins and minerals. They are thought to be good for weight loss, reducing cholesterol, reducing the risk of heart disease, reducing the risk of diabetes, preventing cancer, bone health and improving brain health. Apples contain compounds that can help fight asthma. They regulate the digestive system and neutralise the effects of high fatty foods. They purify the blood, prevent gallstones and clear gout and rheumatism. They also help to keep the teeth clean. The tea made from the bark of the apple tree is an old remedy that is used as a potent tonic for diarrhoea, boils, insect stings, rabid dog bites and toothache.

Ash: is a masculine herb that is strongly linked to the sun and the element of fire. It is sacred to the deities Uranus, Poseidon, Neptune, Thor, Odin, Mars and Gwydion. Sacred to the Celts and the Norse peoples, the ash tree symbolised the Yggdrasil to these peoples, the Tree of the World and was, therefore, highly revered. The branches of the tree are made into solar crosses (equal-armed crosses) as protective devices against drowning while at sea. The ash tree is said to prevent the power that resides within water and is thus used in sea rituals. The leaves are said to induce prophetic dreams when placed beneath the pillow. The leaves are used in protective sachets and rituals and are also placed in all four directions of an area to aid great protection. The leaves are also carried to attract the opposite sex. The ash tree is used in all types of magical workings involving protection and sea magic. Medicinally, ash can be used to treat rheumatism, kidney stones, gout, water retention and obesity. It has anti-inflammatory, analgesic and antipyretic effects. It may also stimulate the immune system.

Basil: is a masculine herb that is strongly linked to the planet of Mars and the element of fire. It is sacred to the deities Vishnu and Erzulie. The scent of fresh basil is thought to cause sympathy between two people and can thus calm tempers between them. The fresh leaves can also be rubbed on the body as a natural love perfume. Basil is excellent when added to purification baths. It is also strewn on the floor or burned as incense for protection, exorcism and purification. Small amounts are often placed in each room for these purposes. Basil is used in all forms of rituals involving love, fertility, purification, protection, exorcism, prosperity and money. Given to someone as a gift, basil is said to bring luck to a new home. Medicinally, basil is used to treat spasms, loss of appetite, flatulence, bloating, indigestion and sore throats. It can also be used to heal wounds and cuts. The oil also combats worms and infections. Its antibacterial properties are good for people who suffer from acne. Basil is one of my favourite herbs.

Bay: is a masculine herb that is strongly linked to the sun and the element of fire. It is sacred to the deities Apollo, Ceres, Aesculapius, Faunus and Eros. The bay tree is an evergreen and so the leaves are used to decorate the home at Yule to remind us that the earth will be green once again. Ancient priestesses chewed or burned bay leaves to induce the prophetic powers of Apollo. Bay leaves can be brewed to make a potion that aids clairvoyance and visions. They are also placed below pillows to aid prophetic dreams. They are also used as amulets to ward away evil or negativity. They are also traditionally burned or scattered during exorcism rites and hung up to prevent poltergeists from being mischievous. Placed on the windowsill, bay leaves protect the home from the ill effects of thunderstorms and lightning. Grown in the garden, bay protects those in the home against illness. Use bay for all forms of magical workings involving strength, love, money, healing, protection, purification and psychic powers. Burning bay with sandalwood can be utilised to remove evil spells. Holding a bay leaf in the mouth is said to ward away bad luck. You can also write your wishes on the leaves and then burn them to help you to make them come true. Medicinally, bay is excellent for treating aches, pains, rheumatism, bruises, sprains, fungal infections, mouth ulcers, inflammation and digestive disorders.

Blackberry: is a feminine herb that is strongly linked to the planet of Venus and the element of water. It is sacred to the goddess Brigit. Traditionally, blackberries are baked into a pie to honour the ancient festival of Lughnasadh. There is a tradition that if you walk between the arch of the blackberry bush backwards and forwards three times rheumatism, boils, coughs and blackheads will magically disappear. The herb is used in all magical workings of money, healing, protection and prosperity. Medicinally, blackberry is used to treat diarrhoea, sore throats, mouth ulcers, gingivitis, inflammation of the mouth, skin ulcers and wounds. Both the leaves and the berries are used medicinally.

Borage: is a masculine herb that is strongly linked to the planet of Jupiter and the element of air. The blossoms of the herb are traditionally carried to strengthen courage. The blossoms are also traditionally placed in buttonholes to aid protection. Borage is excellent for all forms of magical workings involving psychic powers, money, prosperity and courage. Medicinally, borage is thought to be useful for treating stress on the cardiovascular system, sore throats, skin ailments (such as dryness and loss of elasticity due to ageing), rheumatoid arthritis and lung problems. Borage may be harmful to some people.

Chamomile: is a masculine herb that is strongly linked to the sun and the element of water. It is a member of the daisy family. An infusion of the herb is traditionally used to wash the hands before gambling. An incense of the herb is traditionally made to calm the mind and induce sleep. Because the herb is related to the sun, it is traditionally used to combat evil spells. It is also used to prepare the mind, body and soul for magical workings since it helps to open psychic doors. Chamomile is excellent for all rituals involving psychic powers, sleep, meditation, money, prosperity, healing, success, love, purification and protection. Medicinally, chamomile has been used throughout the ages to treat digestive disorders. It is also a mild sedative and is calming on the nervous system. It is, therefore, used to treat insomnia. Chamomile is also excellent for menstrual period pains, eye irritation and oral hygiene.

Cinnamon: is a masculine herb that is strongly linked to the sun and the element of fire. It is sacred to the deities Venus and Aphrodite. The ancient Hebrew folk used the oil of this spice as a holy anointing oil. The leaves were also utilised by the Romans to make wreaths that decorated their sacred temples. Ancient Egyptians used the oil for their mummification process. When burned as incense, cinnamon is said to have various magical uses. The incense raises high spiritual vibrations, aids healing rituals, aids love rituals, aids success rituals, aids lustful thoughts, induces psychic powers, draws money, draws prosperity and produces protective energies. The herb is also traditionally made into a tea or placed into sachets, poppets and Witch-bottles for these purposes. It is a very uplifting herb. Medicinally, cinnamon is used to treat a variety of digestive problems including indigestion, poor appetite, nausea, belching, flatulence, intestinal spasms, trapped wind and diarrhoea. The oil is also excellent for cramps, joint pains, rheumatism and neuralgia. Cinnamon is excellent for treating minor cases of tiredness and fatigue.

Coriander: is a masculine herb that is strongly linked to the planet of Mars and the element of fire. It has long been used in lustful and love sachets and spells. The seeds are traditionally made into a powder and then added to a warm wine to make an effective lustful drink. It is said that if pregnant women eat coriander their children will be ingenious. Coriander is excellent for all forms of magical workings involving love and lust. Medicinally, coriander is used to treat digestive problems, diarrhoea, influenza, high cholesterol and bacterial or fungal infections. Coriander seed oil can ease the pain of haemorrhoids and joints affected by rheumatism.

Cypress: is a feminine herb that is strongly linked to the planet of Saturn and the element of earth. It is sacred to the deities Mithras, Aphrodite, Pluto, Artemis, Cupid, Apollo, Jupiter and Ashtoreth. The ancient Minoans honoured and worshipped this herb as a divine symbol and the cult spread from Cyprus to Crete. The Egyptians used the wood to make coffins. Throwing cypress into the grave of a loved one is said to give the deceased luck and love on the other side. The herb is also a symbol of eternity and immortality and so it is carried to lengthen life. Cypress is traditionally carried during times of grief or crisis, such as during funerals. Cypress is also traditionally grown in the garden to aid protection. Cypress is excellent for all forms of magical workings involving longevity, healing, comfort and protection. Medicinally, cypress has antiseptic, sedative and diuretic properties. It also has antispasmodic actions and is used to treat coughs. It is famed for its ability to treat all kinds of vein problems, including varicose veins and haemorrhoids.

Daffodil: is a feminine herb that is strongly linked to the planet of Venus and the element of water. The flowers are traditionally placed in the bedroom to increase fertility and are also placed on love shrines or are carried for the purpose of attracting love. Wearing a daffodil next to the heart is said to bring good luck. Use the daffodil for all magical workings involving success, luck, love, fertility and healing. Daffodil is a poison and should not be taken internally.

Dandelion: is a masculine herb that is strongly linked to the planet of Saturn and the element of air. It is sacred to the goddess Hecate. The root of this wonderful herb is traditionally dried and ground (like coffee) to make a very useful tea that induces psychic powers. The tea will also help to call spirits when placed by the bed. It is also said that blowing the seeds from the head in the direction of a loved one will send forward what you want to say to him or her. Dandelion is excellent for all magical workings involving divination, psychic powers and wishes. The root is traditionally used in healing rituals. Medicinally, dandelion is well-known for its diuretic properties. In fact, the Old English for the herb was piss-a-bed. This may seem crude and humorous but it is the truth. It is, therefore, used to stimulate urination in cases of water retention, cellulite, kidney problems and obesity. It also contains potassium to replace the potassium that is lost during increased urination. Dandelion is also a mild laxative.

Dill: is a masculine herb that is strongly linked to the planet of Mercury and the element of fire. Dill is traditionally hung around doorways and placed into sachets to aid protection. It is also placed in cradles to protect children. It is said that if dill is placed over the door, no one who wishes you harm can enter. Because dill produces many seeds, it is used in almost countless magical workings of money and prosperity. Added to ritual baths, dill is said to make us irresistible and if it is smelled or eaten lust will surely be stimulated. It is said that dill will cure hiccups if smelled. Use dill in all magical workings of protection, money, prosperity, love and lust. Medicinally, dill is used to treat swelling, pain, flatulence, digestive problems, nausea, bruises and gum infections. It is also used by breastfeeding women with blocked and overloaded breasts.

Elder: is a feminine herb that is strongly linked to the planet of Venus and the element of water. It is sacred to the deities Holda and Venus. Witches and spirits were believed to live within the elder tree. This was why it "bled" red sap when cut, according to folklore. The tree has long been used in Britain for burial rites. Hanging the tree over doorways and windows is said to keep away evil or negativity. The elderberries are also carried for the purpose of protection. Grown in the garden, the elder tree will offer great protection, especially against evil magicians and lightning strikes. Rubbing a fresh green elder twig on a wart and then burying it in the ground to rot is said to cure the wart. The sticks of the elder placed about the home will offer great protection, according to folklore, especially against robbers and snakes. Pregnant women traditionally kiss the elder to bring good fortune for their future children. Elderberries placed under the pillow are said to help us sleep peacefully. Elder can be utilised in all magical workings involving exorcism, healing, protection, sleep, money and prosperity. The elderberries are also useful in magical workings of love. Medicinally, the flowers of the elder tree can be used to treat sunburn. The flowers are on the tree around the time of Litha – when sunburn is more likely. The infusion of the flowers is a good blood purifier. The root of the elder tree is thought to kill lice. Badgers rub their bodies against them to kill infestations within their fur. The elder tree is also highly useful for treating influenza, colds, catarrh, sore throats and gingivitis. The raw berries can cause vomiting and nausea and should not be ingested.

Foxglove: is a feminine herb that is strongly linked to the planet of Venus and the element of water. It is quite a famous herb associated with Witches. Dr. William Withering (1741-1799) became very famous when he published information about the medicinal uses of this herb. Much of this information, however, was taken from a Witch. The foxglove is traditionally grown in the garden to protect both it and the home. Throughout history, housewives in Wales have made a black dye from the plant in order to make crossed lines on the stone floors of their cottages. Foxglove is excellent in all magical workings of protection. Although foxglove is known to have some medicinal properties, it is actually a poison and should not be ingested.

Fumitory: is a feminine herb that is strongly linked to the planet of Saturn and the element of earth. Rubbing the infusion of this herb on the shoes or sprinkling it around the home are said to draw money and prosperity. Burning the herb is said to exorcise evil spirits and bad energies. This is a practice that has been done for centuries. Fumitory is excellent for all rituals involving money, prosperity and exorcism. Medicinally, fumitory is traditionally used to treat skin problems. It is excellent for acne, eczema and psoriasis. Fumitory is also excellent for digestive problems, high blood pressure, asthma, gallbladder problems and irregular heartbeat.

Garlic: is a masculine herb that is strongly linked to the planet of Mars and the element of fire. It is sacred to the goddess Hecate. It was traditionally eaten to honour this goddess. It was also left at crossroads as a sacrifice in her name. It is used in rituals to absorb diseases by rubbing an affected area of the body. The garlic is then traditionally thrown into running water. When garlic is worn, it is traditionally said to protect against bad weather. The ancient Romans ate it for courage. It is also traditionally hung near doorways to protect the home. I have done this for years. It is said to be especially protective if it is hung around doorways of a new home. Garlic is excellent for those who wish to induce lustful thoughts. Use it in all magical workings involving healing, exorcism, protection and lust. Medicinally, garlic reduces the formation of clots and so it helps to prevent heart attacks. In fact, it is excellent for the overall health of the heart and cardiovascular system. It is also used to treat intestinal worms, digestive infections, respiratory infections, circulation problems and bronchitis. It is very healing on the body and protects from diseases. It is also good for repelling insects.

Geranium: is a feminine herb that is strongly linked to the planet of Venus and the element of water. The geranium is traditionally grown in the garden to aid protection. It is said that where geranium grows snakes will not come. The herb is excellent in all types of magical workings involving fertility, love, protection and healing. Medicinally, the oil of this herb is used to treat anxiety, depression, pain and infections. Geranium is said to have powerful anti-inflammatory properties.

Ginger: is a masculine herb that is strongly linked to the planet of Mars and the element of fire. Eating this spice before magical workings is said to give them power. This is especially so with love rituals. The root of the herb is planted to attract money and prosperity. The root is also ground into a powder for this purpose and placed into magical items, such as sachets. Ginger is also traditionally chewed and spit out to cure illness. This practice is also done at sea to halt an oncoming storm. Ginger is excellent for all magical workings involving money, success, prosperity and love. Medicinally, ginger is used to treat nausea, vomiting, poor digestion, menstrual period pains, diarrhoea, flatulence, painful muscles, painful joints, viruses, circularity problems, rheumatism, coughs and fevers. Ginger is thought to have powerful anti-inflammatory properties. An overdose of ginger can cause stomach upsets and drowsiness.

Hawthorn: is a masculine herb that is strongly linked to the planet of Mars and the element of fire. It is sacred to the deities Cardea, Flora and Hymen. It was once used to decorate Maypoles. Superstitious people once believed that hawthorn trees were Witches who had transformed themselves into these trees. Traditionally, Witches dance and perform their magical workings beneath these wonderful trees. Traditionally, the hawthorn has long been used in wedding rites because of its association with fertility. This is especially so for those that were performed in the spring. Carrying the herb is said to aid happiness and to avoid depression. Placing hawthorn in the home protects it, especially from lightning strikes and spirits. The ancient Romans placed hawthorn in cradles to protect babies. It is also said that a Witch's garden should contain at least one hawthorn tree. Hawthorn is said to be sacred to the faery folk. It is said that if the trees grow together a person will be able to see these spirits. Hawthorn is excellent for all magical workings involving fertility, happiness, protection, faery magic, love and success. Medicinally, hawthorn is used to treat heart problems, high blood pressure and minor sleeping issues. It is said to strengthen the cardiovascular system. It also has calming effects on the nervous system. Both the berries and the flowers are traditionally used in medicine.

Heather: is a feminine herb that is strongly linked to the planet of Venus and the element of water. It is sacred to the goddess Isis. It is traditionally carried to protect against rape or other violent crimes. Carrying the herb is also said to bring luck and success. Burning the herb with fern is said to attract rain. Heather can be utilised in magical workings to attract spirits. It is excellent in all magical workings involving success, protection, luck and attracting rain. Medicinally, heather is used to treat bladder and kidney problems. As an external wash, heather is excellent for treating eczema and psoriasis.

Hibiscus: is a feminine herb that is strongly linked to the planet of Venus and the element of water. The blossoms of the herb are traditionally placed into sachets and poppets to attract love. Red hibiscus flowers are traditionally made into an infusion as a love and lust-inducing potion. This love potion was thought to be so powerful that women were forbidden to drink it in Egypt. In the tropics, the blossoms of the hibiscus are used in wreaths in marriage ceremonies. Hibiscus is excellent in all magical workings of love, lust and divination. Medicinally, hibiscus is used to treat heart problems, nerve problems, constipation, liver problems and colds. Hibiscus is also a diuretic and increases urine production. Hibiscus may also lower body temperature and blood fat levels. It may also promote weight loss.

Jasmine: is a feminine herb that is strongly linked to the moon and the element of earth. It is sacred to the god Vishnu. The dried flowers of the herb are used in various love sachets and mixtures to attract a deeply spiritual love. The flowers are said to induce sleep when smelled before retiring. Burned in the bedroom, jasmine is said to cause prophetic dreams. Jasmine is excellent for all magical workings involving love, money, prosperity, protection, purification and fertility. Medicinally, jasmine is used to treat hepatitis, cirrhosis of the liver, stomach pain, dysentery and insomnia. Jasmine is also said to heighten sexual desire. It may also treat cancer.

Juniper: is a masculine herb that is strongly linked to the sun and the element of fire. It is a protective herb that is used to stop theft. The herb is said to be one of the earliest that was used by Mediterranean Witches as incense. It is burned during exorcism rites and hung around doorways to protect against sicknesses and evil or negativity. Wearing the herb is said to protect against wild animals and accidents. The berries are traditionally carried by men to induce sexual desire. When burned, the herb will help to induce psychic powers. Juniper is excellent in all magical workings involving protection, exorcism, love, lust in men, psychic powers and fertility. Medicinally, juniper is used to treat muscle pains, rheumatism, tendinitis, digestive problems, flatulence and urinary problems. It also stimulates the appetite. There is also evidence that juniper may also treat diabetes and viruses.

Lavender: is a masculine herb that is strongly linked to the planet of Mercury and the element of air. The fragrant flowers of this herb are traditionally placed in drawers with clothes to attract love. Rubbing the herb on paper is an excellent and traditional way to make love notes. When worn, lavender is also said to protect someone against the cruel treatment of a spouse. The scent of lavender is said to particularly attract men and for this reason it was worn by prostitutes to attract business. If someone is depressed, then he or she should simply gaze at the plant and all negative thoughts shall depart, according to folklore. The depression will then be replaced by a joyful feeling. Scattered around the home, lavender flowers aid a peaceful atmosphere and help to maintain it. Burned or smouldered, lavender flowers are said to induce sleep and rest. Lavender is also used in healing mixtures and sachets and is traditionally worn or carried to see spirits and to protect against the evil eye. Added to bath water, lavender is excellent for purification. Lavender is excellent in all magical workings involving protection, money, prosperity, health, healing, success, love, sleep, longevity, happiness, peace and purification. Medicinally, lavender is used to treat nervous disorders, minor sleep problems, digestive problems, menstrual period pains, depression, anxiety, tension headache, flatulence, asthma, minor skin complaints, insect bites, burns, blood circulation and rheumatism. It is also used to improve the passage of bile.

Mandrake: is a masculine herb that is strongly linked to the planet of Mercury and the element of fire. It is sacred to the deities Hecate and Hathor. It is quite a famous herb associated with Witches. There is a legend associated with the mandrake that came about in the seventeenth century. Supposedly, when a man was hanged he would get an erection and ejaculate. The sperm falling to the ground would then produce the mandrake. Placing the mandrake root about the house is said to bring forth money, prosperity, fertility and protection. Hung above the bed, mandrake is said to offer protection during sleep. Carrying the root will attract love and will also stop illness from coming to the holder. The root of the mandrake often takes on a humanoid shape and so it is often used in image magic. It can make an excellent poppet. The scent of mandrake is said to induce sleep and it is said that if mandrake is placed next to money, especially silver coins, it will double. Mandrake is excellent in all magical workings involving fertility, money, prosperity, love, health, healing and protection. Mandrake is a poison and should not be ingested.

Marigold: is a masculine herb that is strongly linked to the sun and the element of fire. Scattering marigolds under the bed are said to induce prophetic dreams and will also protect during sleep. Strung on doorsteps, marigolds prevent evil or negativity from entering. Placed in bath water, marigolds are said to help us to win the respect and admirations of everyone we meet. Carried in the pocket, marigolds help with justice when attending courtrooms. Gazing at the flowers is said to strengthen sight. It is also said that if a girl touches the petals of marigolds with her bare feet then she will soon be able to understand the language of birds. Marigold is excellent in all magical workings of psychic powers, protection, legal matters and success. Medicinally, marigold is used to treat cracked skin, insect bites, cuts, sunburn, mouth infection, fluid retention, bleeding and muscular spasms. Marigold is also used cosmetically for the skin. A cream made from marigold and applied to the skin is very anti-ageing.

Marjoram: is a masculine herb that is strongly linked to the planet of Mercury and the element of air. It is sacred to the goddesses Aphrodite and Venus. Carrying the herb or placing a bit of it in each room of the home (renew every month) is said to offer protection and the herb is added to food to strengthen love. Merely growing the herb in the garden is said to shield against evil or negative forces. Mixed with violets, marjoram is excellent for repelling colds during the winter months. Marjoram is also traditionally used in money mixtures and sachets and when it is given to a depressed person happiness is said to come to him or her. Marjoram is excellent in all magical workings involving happiness, love, protection, money and prosperity. Medicinally, marjoram makes a good nerve tonic. The herb is used to improve blood circulation. It also treats stomach pains, digestive disorders, dizziness, paralysis, tension headaches, colds, coughs and depression.

Mint: is a masculine herb that is strongly linked to the planet of Mercury and the element of air. It is sacred to the deities Pluto and Hecate. Mint is traditionally used to make healing sachets and infusions. Rubbing the fresh leaves against the head is said to cure headaches, while wearing the herb on the wrist is said to guard against sicknesses. Placing a few fresh leaves in the pocket, wallet or purse will attract money. In fact, placing the fresh leaves in any place in which money is usually kept will attract it. Fresh mint on the altar will attract favourable spirits and will aid magical workings of all kinds. Grown in the home or garden, mint will offer protective powers. Mint is excellent in all magical workings of protection, lust, love, money, prosperity, health, healing, travel and exorcism. Medicinally, mint is used to treat bad breath, digestive disorders, asthma, colds, headaches, obesity, acne, nausea, morning sickness, stress, insomnia and depression. Mint is excellent for oral hygiene. Studies have shown that mint may improve cognitive functions and memory (brain power). The juice from mint is excellent for the skin. It cleanses, clears and gives the skin a youthful glow. Mint is one of my favourite herbs.

Mugwort: is a feminine herb that is strongly linked to the planet of Venus and the element of earth. It is sacred to the deities Artemis and Diana. Stuffing the herb into a pillow used to sleep on will induce prophetic dreams. Placing the herb in the shoes before long walks and runs will give strength. The tea of mugwort is drank to awaken psychic powers. The tea is also rubbed on scrying mirrors and crystal balls for the same purpose. Ancient tradition tells us that carrying the herb ensures that we cannot be harmed by poison, wild beasts and sunstroke. The herb is also placed in buildings to prevent evil or negativity from entering. It is also traditionally placed by the bed to aid astral travel. The herb is also traditionally carried to cure diseases and insanity. Carrying the herb is also said to aid lust and fertility. Mugwort is excellent in all magical workings involving psychic powers, lust, fertility, divination, strength, protection, healing and astral travel. Medicinally, mugwort is used to treat menstrual period pains, intestinal worms, digestive problems, loss of appetite, intestinal cramps, bacterial infections, fungal infections, fevers, skin inflammation and rheumatism.

Myrrh: is a feminine herb that is strongly linked to the moon and the element of water. It is sacred to the deities Isis, Marian, Adonis and Ra. The healing associations of myrrh were widely known throughout the ancient world. In ancient Egypt, myrrh was burned to honour the deities Isis and Ra. Myrrh is said to increase the powers of any other incense that it is burned with. When burned, it is said to create a peaceful atmosphere, lift vibrations, aid healing and purify the area. Myrrh may also be added to healing sachets and poppets. The smoke of this herb is used to consecrate ritual tools. The smoke also aids meditation. Myrrh is excellent for all magical workings involving protection, exorcism, healing, peace, purification, consecration, meditation and success. Medicinally, myrrh is used to treat minor wounds and oral problems, such as inflammation in the mouth and gum infections.

Nettle: is a masculine herb that is strongly linked to the planet of Mars and the element of fire. It is sacred to the deity Thor. It is traditionally placed in protective sachets and poppets. It is said that sprinkling nettle around the house will keep out all negative or evil vibrations. Placed in a pot, freshly cut nettles can be placed beneath an ill person's sickbed to speed up recovery. Nettle is also traditionally thrown into a fire to stop danger, held to ward off spirits and worn to keep negativity far away. Mexican spiritualists advocate the use of nettle in purification baths. Nettle is excellent in all magical workings involving healing, purification, protection, exorcism and lust. Medicinally, nettle is used to treat rheumatism, gout, bleeding, eczema and urinary problems. It may also treat hay fever and high blood pressure. Nettle contains a variety of nutrients that are beneficial to good health. It is said to be excellent for the overall health of the liver.

Oak: is a masculine herb that is strongly linked to the sun and the element of fire. It is sacred to many deities including Jupiter, Zeus, Thor, Hecate, Pan and the Dagda. It is a powerful symbol of strength and wisdom. The oak was one of the most famous trees associated with the Druids and they would not traditionally meet unless an oak tree was present. Some people believe that the words "oak" and "Druid" are related. Witches are said to traditionally dance below the oak tree (I have personally cast spells under oak trees with amazing results) and religious idols were traditionally fashioned from oak wood. The oak tree often lives for over five thousand years and for this reason it is a symbol of endurance and the continuity of traditions. Carrying the wood is said to protect against all harm. Burning the wood is said to draw off illness. Carrying the acorn can be an excellent way to aid longevity, protection against illness and preservation of youth. Carrying the acorn will also aid fertility and strengthen lust. Carrying any part of the oak will draw luck. Oak is excellent in all magical workings involving protection, success, strength, wisdom, fertility, health, healing, luck and lust. Oak leaves are traditionally used in magical workings involving money and prosperity. Medicinally, oak is used to treat mouth diseases, skin problems, toothache, rheumatism, eye infections, ear infections, stomach problems, dysentery, abscesses and swollen spleens.

Parsley: is a masculine herb that is strongly linked to the planet of Mercury and the element of air. It is sacred to Persephone. Eating the herb is said to aid fertility and to strengthen lust. The ancient Romans traditionally tucked a sprig of parsley in their togas every morning to aid protection. Parsley is also added to food to stop contamination. Parsley is utilised in purification baths. When placed in the bath, parsley will also prevent all misfortune or bad luck. A wreath of parsley placed on the head is said to prevent (or at least delay) drunkenness. Parsley is excellent in all magical workings involving purification, protection, fertility and lust. Medicinally, parsley is a diuretic and is used to treat urinary problems. It is also used to treat obesity since it helps to remove excess fluid from tissue. Chewing parsley can help cure bad breath. Parsley is also excellent for menstrual problems, digestive disorders and the leaf infusion is a good eye, hair and skin tonic.

Passionflower: is a feminine herb that is strongly linked to the moon and the element of water. Despite the name of this plant, it is placed about the house to bring forth peace and tranquillity. It is used to calm down any troubles that life throws at us. Traditionally, it is also carried to increase popularity and attract friends. Sleep is also said to come with ease when passionflower is placed below the pillow. Passionflower is excellent for all magical workings involving peace, friendship, sleep and healing. Medicinally, passionflower is used to treat anxiety, nervous agitation, muscle spasms, palpitations, insomnia and digestive problems of a nervous origin.

Plantain: (not to be confused with the banana plant plantain) is a feminine herb that is strongly linked to the planet of Venus and the element of earth. Plantain is traditionally hung in cars to ward off the intrusion of evil spirits and a piece of the root protects against snakebites. Plantain is traditionally bound together with red wool to cure headaches. This can also be placed beneath the feet to remove weariness. Plantain is excellent in all magical workings involving healing, protection and strength. Medicinally, plantain is used to treat toothache, bed-wetting, middle-ear infections, coughs, colds, bronchial inflammation and catarrh.

Rose: is a feminine herb that is strongly linked to the planet of Venus and the element of water. It is sacred to many deities including Hathor, Aphrodite, Venus, Hulda, Isis, Eros and Cupid. Whenever I think of the rose I think of the song "The Rose" which was recorded by Bette Midler for the 1979 film of the same title. It is one of my favourite songs. The herb has strong associations with emotions and love. It is, therefore, traditionally used in love mixtures and potions. The thorns are removed from the branches. The branches are then used to make love chaplets while performing love rituals. A single rose on a love shrine is a powerful addition to workings of love. The hips, or fruit, of the rose are strung together to make love beads. An infusion of rosebuds that is drank before sleep aids prophetic dreams. Rose petals and hips are traditionally used in healing mixtures. The petals of the rose are sprinkled around the home to calm the atmosphere and to calm stress and tension. Rose is excellent in all magical workings involving love, calming atmospheres, prophetic dreams, enhancing psychic powers, healing, luck, protection and success. Medicinally, rose is used to treat headaches, digestive problems, inflammation, coughs, colds, influenza, diarrhoea, stomach weakness, depression, grief, insomnia, scurvy and anxiety. The hips of the rose are an excellent source of vitamin C.

Rosemary: is a masculine herb that is strongly linked to the sun and the element of fire. It is quite a famous herb associated with Witches. Grown near the doorway, rosemary is said to aid protection. Burning rosemary is said to emit powerful vibrations. It is burned to cleanse and purify an area of negative energy or evil spirits. The smoke is said to offer great protective powers. Placed under the bed, rosemary is said to protect the sleeper from harm of any kind. Placed below the pillow, rosemary is said to ensure a good sleep and to keep away nightmares. Carrying the herb is said to keep us healthy. The herb is also hung around doorways to stop robbers from coming to the home. Rosemary is also placed in purification baths. The wood smelled often is said to preserve youth but the infusion can be added to bath water for the same purpose. Rosemary is also traditionally stuffed into healing poppets or sachets. The infusion is also used to wash the hands to aid healing work. Rosemary is traditionally used to preserve the memory and so it is placed on remembrance shrines or used in death rites to ensure that we will always remember those who have passed on to the Summerlands. Rosemary is excellent for all magical workings involving protection, death rites, exorcism, purification, love, lust, healing, sleep, preserving youth and strengthening mental powers. Medicinally, rosemary is used to treat stomach cramps, exhaustion, gout, headaches, constipation, bloating, muscular pain, poor circulation, memory loss, rheumatism and bacterial or fungal infections. The infusion used as a wash is said to strengthen hair and improve its growth. Rosemary is also said to be very good for detoxifying the liver.

Rowan: is a masculine herb that is strongly linked to the sun and the element of fire. It is sacred to the deity Thor. The wood is traditionally used to construct wands and dowsing rods. The leaves and berries can be used to make incense for psychic work and divination. Carrying the berries or the bark aids recuperation. They are also added to sachets that bring forth healing, health, success and luck. The twigs can also be tied together to make equal-armed crosses that aid protection. Kept in the home, rowan guards against lightning strikes. When the rowan is planted on a grave, it is said to prevent the deceased from haunting. Planted in the garden or nearby, rowan is said to offer protection to the home. Rowans growing near stone circles are said to be the most potent.

The berries of the rowan are used to seal bargains. Rowan is excellent in all magical workings involving protection, growth, healing, health, psychic powers, success and luck. Medicinally, rowan is used to treat stomach problems, bleeding, sore eyes, rheumatism, asthma, colds, oral thrush, sore throats and poor appetite. The berries are a rich source of vitamin C and are traditionally made into a jam.

Sage: is a masculine herb that is strongly linked to the planet of Jupiter and the element of air. This herb is said to be loved by toads. Carrying sage is said to promote wisdom and a horn filled with the herb is said to protect against the much-feared evil eye. Sage is also traditionally added to healing and prosperity sachets, charms and poppets. Curiously enough, it is said to be bad luck to plant sage in your own garden – a stranger should do the work. Sage is excellent for all magical workings involving longevity, wisdom, protection, purification, money, prosperity, health, healing and fertility. Medicinally, sage is used to treat night sweats, digestive problems, loss of appetite, diarrhoea, flatulence, depression, memory loss, overproduction of saliva, fatigue, sore gums and sore throats. The tea makes an effective mouthwash and is drank as an antiseptic nerve and blood tonic.

Sunflower: is a masculine herb that is strongly linked to the sun and element of fire. Cutting a sunflower at dusk while making a wish is said to make it come true by another sunset as long as you do not ask for something too grand. The seeds of the sunflower are traditionally eaten by women who wish to become pregnant. A sunflower placed under the bed is said to help you to become aware of the truth of any matter. Grown in the garden, sunflowers are beautiful additions that grant the gardener excellent luck. Sunflower is excellent for all magical workings involving fertility, getting the truth of a matter, success and luck. The seeds are also traditionally used in magical workings of money and prosperity. Medicinally, sunflower is used to treat high fevers, sores, swellings, snakebites, spider bites, malaria, tuberculosis, inflammation of the windpipe, coughs, cardiovascular problems and infections. The seeds have diuretic properties and the root is a laxative.

Thistle: is a masculine herb that is strongly linked to the planet of Mars and the element of fire. It is sacred to the deities Minerva and Thor. Carrying thistle is said to renew strength and bring forth energy. Placing thistle in a bowl is said to bring forth vitality. Thistle growing in the garden is said to stop robbers from coming to your home. Growing thistle in a pot near the door is said to stop evil or negativity from entering the home. Throwing thistle on a fire will stop the ill effects of thunderstorms and lightning. Placing a thistle flower in the pocket is said to protect the holder. Thistle is also strewn about the house to exorcise evil or negativity. Thistle is excellent in all magical workings of protection, exorcism, vitality, gaining strength and hex-breaking. Milk thistle is particularly excellent for magical workings of healing. Medicinally, thistle is used to treat rheumatism, toothache, indigestion and bleeding piles. It is also used to treat worms in children. Milk thistle is particularly excellent for treating chronic hepatitis and cirrhosis of the liver.

Thyme: is a feminine herb that is strongly linked to the planet of Venus and the element of water. Keeping thyme about your person is said to promote good health and healing. Placing the herb below the pillow will stop frightening nightmares and will also promote a good sleep. If thyme is worn, it is said to induce psychic powers. Women who wear thyme are said to become irresistible. Smelling thyme is said to offer courage and energy and wearing it is said to make the holder see faeries. Thyme is excellent in all magical workings involving health, healing, enhancing psychic powers, protection, faery magic, purification, courage, love and sleep. Medicinally, thyme is used to treat belching, bloating, flatulence, inadequate bile flow, coughs, sluggish digestion, nasal congestion, insect bites, insect stings, gum disease, tonsillitis, wounds, aching muscles, acute bronchitis and intestinal problems.

Turnip: is a feminine herb that is strongly linked to the moon and the element of earth. At Samhain, turnips are traditionally hollowed out and then eerie faces or sacred symbols are then carved into them and candles are then placed inside them. These are then placed about the home to repel negative energy or evil spirits. Placing a dish of turnips in front of a person who is obsessed with you will repel them and stop them from pestering you. Turnips placed about the home are excellent charms of protection. They are said to repel all evil or negativity. Turnip is excellent in all magical workings of protection and ending relationships with people. Medicinally, the nutrients in turnips are thought to have a wide range of health benefits. Turnips are thought to relieve intestinal problems, reduce the risk of getting cancer, lower blood pressure, aid digestion and aid weight loss. They are a rich source of vitamin C.

Valerian: is a feminine herb that is strongly linked to the planet of Venus and the element of water. The root of this herb has a foul smell. It is ground into a powder and added to sachets and poppets designed to protect. Women who wear valerian are said to become irresistible to men. Placing valerian in the pillow is said to induce sleep. Hung around the home it will guard against the ill effects of thunderstorms and lightning. An argumentative couple are said to be calmed when the herb is introduced into the room. The ancient Greeks hung valerian around windows to ward off all evil. Throughout history, the root of valerian was powdered and used as "grave dust". Valerian is excellent in all magical workings involving purification, protection, money, prosperity, sleep and love. Medicinally, valerian is used to treat high blood pressure, intestinal problems, headaches, eczema, anxiety, insomnia and nervous disorders. Valerian is a natural herbal tranquilliser. It is a herb that I have used over the years because I am quite a nervous person who has suffered from insomnia.

Violet: is a feminine herb that is strongly linked to the planet of Venus and the element of water. The ancient Greeks wore this herb to calm anger and to promote peace and sleep. It is said that if you pick the first violet of spring your most dearest wish will be granted. The leaves of the violet are used in green sachets to heal wounds and to prevent evil spirits from making the wounds worse. A chaplet of violets is traditionally worn to cure dizziness and headaches. Violet is excellent in all magical workings involving healing, success, fertility, protection, love, lust, wishes and peace. Medicinally, violet is used to treat sore throats, colds, respiratory problems, insect bites, eczema, varicose veins and haemorrhoids.

Walnut: s a masculine herb that is strongly linked to the sun and the element of fire. It is said that in Italy Witches danced under the walnut tree in their secret rites. Since the nut of this tree is shaped like a human brain, it was traditionally thought that by eating the nuts memory and concentration would be improved and strengthened. It is also said that walnuts should not be carried during an electrical storm as they attract lightning. When carried, walnuts are said to strengthen the heart and ward away the pains of rheumatism. If a bag of walnuts is given to someone their wishes are said to be granted. It is also said that sunstroke and headaches can be prevented by placing the leaves of the tree in a hat or around the head. Walnut is excellent in all magical workings involving fertility, strengthening mental powers, health, healing and wishes. Medicinally, walnut is used to treat acne, eczema, skin infections, ulcers, diarrhoea and intestinal infections. Leaf preparations are said to improve circulation and immune health.

Willow: is a feminine herb that is strongly linked to the moon and the element of water. It is sacred to many deities including Persephone, Ceres, Hecate, Mercury and Hera. The wood of this tree is used to make magical wands that honour the moon. The leaves of this wonderful tree are also carried to attract love and used in love mixtures. Any part of the tree can be placed in the home or carried to aid protection magic and knocking on the tree is said to ward off evil. The Witch's broomstick is traditionally bound together with a willow branch. Willow is excellent in all magical workings of protection, psychic power, healing and love. Willow is also traditionally used in love divination. Medicinally, willow is used to treat ulcers, fever, headaches, inflammation, diarrhoea, intestinal infections, influenza, rheumatism, pains and wounds.

Wolf's Bane: is a feminine herb that is strongly linked to the planet of Saturn and the element of water. It is sacred to Hecate. Its name relates to the fact that the Germans used it to poison wolves. Wolf's bane is traditionally used in sachets and poppets that aid protection magic. Wolf's bane is excellent in all magical workings of protection and banishment. Wolf's bane is a poison and should not be ingested. Contact with the skin can cause severe irritation and dermatitis. Some say it is best to leave this plant alone.

Yarrow: is a feminine herb that is strongly linked to the planet of Venus and the element of water. It is one of my favourite herbs. Holding yarrow in the hand is said to stop fear and grant courage. Wearing the herb will offer great protection. Dried yarrow is used in marriage decorations and hung over the bed to ensure love that will last at least seven years. Carrying yarrow is said to bring love and attract friends and distant relatives. In other words, it attracts the attention of the people who you wish to see. The flowers of yarrow are traditionally made into a potion to aid psychic powers. Washing the head with the potion of yarrow is said to prevent hair loss. Yarrow has also been used for centuries to exorcise evil or negativity from people, places or anything else. Yarrow is excellent in all magical workings involving courage, exorcism, love, psychic powers and protection. Medicinally, yarrow is used to treat trapped wind, flatulence, intestinal worms, respiratory problems, bacterial infections, digestive disorders, rheumatism, haemorrhoids, eczema, mouth infections, fever, uterine cramps and high blood pressure. When taken regularly, yarrow can help to regulate menstruation. Yarrow is also excellent for treating greasy skin and so it is often found in cosmetic products.

Chapter Seventeen: Crystals, Stones and Metals

Crystals, stones and metals are surely some of the earth's most beautiful treasures. They are magical gifts from the Earth Mother that make wonderful compliments to our magical workings. Throughout my time as a practising Witch, astrology and the herbal law have been two of my main interests but in recent years I have really taken an interest in the wonderful jewels and precious metals that nature provides. For many Witches, there is nothing more down-to-earth than the rocks of the earth upon which we walk. Crystals, stones and metals have always been a great fascination for magical peoples. As far back as archaeology can tell us, our ancestors have always considered them to have magical, spiritual and healing properties. They are the very bones of the Earth Mother with each having unique powers that can strongly give our magical workings an enormous boost.

Some magical peoples believe that crystals, stones and metals are not chosen by their owners, but rather that these precious items choose their owners. In my experience with them, this would seem to be completely true. Once these treasures of the earth have served their purpose they can "disappear" or their owners may feel completely compelled to give them to someone else who may be in need of their help. Some of these nature's treasures, however, can stay with their owners for years and years and sometimes even until death and this can depend on the energies that are needed in their owners' lives. Some crystals, stones and metals simply stay with their owners because of the spiritual attachment and sentimental value that has developed.

Stones with holes in them are particularly regarded as extraordinary and have always been regarded as having potent magical properties. These strange stones were known as "hag stones". This is because it was said that they protected against the evil intentions and spells of old hags. The country folk of olden times believed them to be the harbingers of life. This was because the holes represented feminine fertility and so the hag stones became strongly associated with the moon goddess Diana. It is traditional to collect twelve crystals or stones along with a heart-shaped one. The crystals or stones can then be arranged into a circular shape to make a personal sacred stone circle. It is said that any object or spell within will be particularly empowered.

The idea that the treasures of the earth have magical, spiritual and healing properties has been largely, if not entirely, dismissed by the scientific community. In our modern times, we live in a very scientific world in which everything must seem "plausible", "rational" and "sensible". But for the Witch not everything can be measured by modern-day science. There are some things in life that boil down to personal experience and this is where crystals, stones and metals come in. The more you work with these precious gifts of the earth the more you will come to understand their spiritual, healing and magical benefits. Just because something is not "accepted" or can't be measured by modern-day science does not mean that it does not exist. Witchcraft truly opens our eyes to the world around us and working with crystals, stones and metals is one excellent way to help us to understand the occult powers of the earth and of the universe. In modern times, crystals, stones and metals are used in various forms of technology (watches, computers, laser technology and so on) and this can be considered very magical if only we would take the time to think about it and look deeper.

Crystals, stones and metals are often considered very important to modern Witches. They are used in various forms of magical workings. In healing work, for example, they are used to pass energy (typically from the universal source) from the Witch to the person, animal, plant, tree or whatever else is requiring the healing. These treasures of the earth can also be used to clear and clarify the human aura of negativity so that we can live full and productive lives. They can be used to release suppressed fears, depression, anxieties and any other destructive or negative emotion. Crystals, stones and metals can also be used to balance the chakras. These are energy points or balls of energy that run along your spine. Each has a different colour and a different function. The chakras range from your most basic, earthly needs at the bottom of your spine to your higher spiritual needs at the top of your head. If one chakra spins too fast or too slow there will be too much or too little activity in that area which can cause negativity and imbalance in your life. If your heart chakra (which is located in your chest area) was spinning too slow, for example, your ability to love properly or feel empathy may be stunted. A rose quartz crystal, for example, can help you to balance this out.

Witches and Alchemy

Alchemy is an incredibly ancient art. Originally, alchemy was concerned with the transmutation (changing or transforming) of base metals into more valuable and precious ones, particularly gold. That is to say that our ancestors believed that metals could be changed or transformed into other metals. This may sound far-fetched and silly today but for our ancestors metals were alive and they grew in the soil very slowly. These metals grew, just like plants, and progressed through stages. The base metals were very young metals and would eventually transform or transmute into other metal forms. The longer they were left in the earth the more "pure" and valuable they would become, just as a fine cheese or wine matures over time. Gold, which was considered the metal of perfection, would be the eventual outcome of any metal. Though this may take millennia to achieve. This is why we have the phrase "the golden years" to describe a person's later life when he or she has gained wisdom, knowledge and maturity. Alchemy was concerned with finding the correct procedures to speed up this process. This is very symbolic and metaphorical to modern Witches. It represents that spiritual enlightenment can be achieved over time. The darkness of ignorance is overcome through the progression of time. It represents that the base human soul is made divine through the experiences and karmic forces of life.

The English word *"alchemy"* is believed to be Arabic and translates as "the science of the black earth" or "the Egyptian science". The fascinating word *"alchemy"* is from the Arabic words "al" (meaning "the") and "Khemeia" or "Kimia" (meaning "Egyptian"). Ancient Egyptians referred to their country as *"Kemet"* which means "the black land". Therefore, the word "alchemy" is literally referred to as "the black art". This term today is often used to describe evil or negativity. But, in ancient Egypt, the colour black represented fertility, abundance, growth, eternal life and reincarnation or resurrection. In short, it was a divine, positive colour. For the Egyptians, red was the colour of malevolent magic because it was associated with danger. Throughout history, alchemy reflected the human connection to the unknown and the blackness and darkness of the universe. It represented the soul's yearning for perfection and humankind's unification with the divine. It symbolised the method of perfecting whatever nature has left unfinished or imperfect. It represented the transformation of the raw human soul into the cooked and perfected human soul. Witches today use alchemy primarily to understand the spiritual and magical properties of metals for their magical workings and the ancient symbolism of alchemy and metals help us to speed up our own spiritual development and closeness with the divine.

Caring for Crystals, Stones and Metals

To really get the most out of your crystals, stones and metals it is always best to cleanse and charge them on a regular basis. Your precious treasures of the earth are very sensitive to the energies around them and can pick up negative energies which can make them less effective. Generally, new treasures and those that have become dirty (except for those that are water-soluble, corrosive or too fragile) can benefit from simply washing them with soap and water. This will remove any dust and grime and restore freshness. On a more spiritual level, however, your treasures should be energetically cleansed on a regular basis. Over time, your treasures will absorb energy from their surrounding areas in their very structures and this can create imbalance. Not cleansing treasures regularly will cause them to become overloaded and tired which can reduce their effectiveness in your magical workings. You will know when a treasure is cleansed because it will look different. It will look brighter, feel lighter and feel more pleasant in your hands. Following are some of the ways that you can cleanse and charge your treasures:

- Running water. Water is the great cleanser and healer. Holding your treasures under running water can really bring them back to life and restore their vitality and make their energies more effective. You can use tap water for this but it is best to take them to a natural stream. This method, however, is not suitable for treasures that are water-soluble, corrosive or too fragile.

- Moonlight or sunlight. You will be aware by now of just how important the sun and moon are for the magical workings of Witches. They both have enormous power. You can place your crystals, stones and metals under the light of the sun or moon to restore vitality. The full moon and the noon of the sun are the best times to cleanse and charge your treasures.

- Sound. Another way to cleanse and charge your treasure is with the use of sound. You can do this by striking or ringing a bell near your treasure. This can be a very effective method of charging and cleansing.

- Incense. An ancient method of cleansing your treasures is with the use of incense. Use a good incense that is known for its cleansing and purifying properties, such as sage or rosemary. You can simply pass your treasures through the smoke until you feel that they are fully charged and cleansed.

- Salt. You can place your treasures in a bowl of sea salt and then leave them overnight. Alternatively, you can place them on a bed of rock salt overnight. Salt has always been used to cleanse and charge magical materials.

- Breath. You can breathe on your treasure several times for effective cleansing and charging and imagine the negativity being blown away. Your breath represents the sacred breath of life.

- Crystal clutters. You can restore natural energy levels of your treasures by placing them on large crystal clutters.

- Essence sprays. You can spray your treasures with sprays that are made from herbs that are known for their cleansing and purifying qualities for very effective energetic cleansing.

A Guide to Specific Crystals, Stones and Metals

Here, we will look at an alphabetical guide to specific crystals, stones and metals to help you to expand your knowledge of these wonderful treasures of the earth. The earth produces many different kinds of crystals, stones and metals so this guide is far from complete. As with the subject of herbal lore, a book dedicated to the subject of crystals, stones and metals would only scratch the surface. This guide, however, will be enough to get you started on this wonderful subject as you devise your own rituals and spellcraft. If you own crystals and stones but are not sure exactly what they are you can always use their colours. Green ones for fertility and growth, brown ones for grounding and balance, red ones for success and passion, blue ones for sleep and meditation and so on. The following notes will serve as a simple introduction to each treasure. A more rounded look at each, however, will require further study.

Agate: is a variety of quartz. It is crystallised silica with bands or clouds of colours that can look similar to petrified wood. It is strongly related to the planet of Mercury and the element of earth. The agate has long been used to treat alcohol dependence and skin eruptions. Tradition has it that the agate can staunch blood from wounds. An agate with two snakes entwined on it is said to heal snakebites or scorpion stings. Agates make excellent amulets against poison, venom, thunder and fiendish possession. They were once used to make drinking vessels because they were believed to be hostile to poison. The agate is excellent in all magical workings involving grounding, travel, protection, prudence, garden magic, balance, eloquence and improving the personality. Agate can come in many different forms and colours with each having its own specific uses. Green agate, for example, is excellent for magical workings of love.

Alloys: are combinations of metals or metals combined with other minerals. An example of an alloy is a combination of gold and copper which produces red gold. Alloys are strongly related to the planet of Mercury and the zodiac sign of Pisces. In ancient Egypt, alloys were believed to possess magical powers.

Aluminium: is a soft and ductile metal of the element of air. It is excellent in all magical workings involving invisibility, mental powers, travel, image magic and magic that requires a high strength-to-weight ratio.

Amazonite: is usually a greenish blue colour and is a variety of feldspar. It is strongly related to the element of earth. The amazonite is traditionally used in meditation and divination to access distant memories and past lives. It is also used in these practices to tap into the energies of our ancestors. The amazonite is excellent in all magical workings involving divination, balance, love (especially sending it), money, prosperity, dispelling fear and worry, improving self-confidence, calming the nerves, creativity, personal expression, communication, releasing blocked emotions, enhancing psychic powers and easing problems with the nose, throat, ears and nervous system. Amazonite is excellent for balancing the heart chakra. It is excellent for the Virgo person. The gem essence of the amazonite has long been believed to embody universal love.

Amber: is the fossilised resin or sap of coniferous trees. It is a hard, translucent yellow substance that is strongly related to the sun and the element of fire. It is not a crystal or stone but I always see it as such for simplicity. It has been used for thousands of years as a precious gem for jewellery. The ancient Greeks referred to this substance as electron. Amber has long been used to symbolise the sun, divinity and the life force. It is sacred to Apollo, Electra, Amberella, Benjamin, Oshun and Electrides. It has long been used to harness or concentrate solar power. Washing amber is said to cause urination in women who are not virgins. Amber necklaces are excellent protective devices against sore throats and for the protection of children. Amber run along the spinal column – head-to-feet – is said to release nervous tension. Amber is excellent in all magical workings involving improving memory, courage, success, luck, protection, historical issues, healing, health, love, balance, strength, beauty, solar power, fire magic, invigoration, improving nervous problems, generating enthusiasm, boosting energy, sharpening thinking processes and enhancing spiritual awareness.

Amethyst: is a crystallised form of quartz with a beautiful and stunning purple or violet colour. It is strongly related to the planet of Jupiter and the element of fire. Once referred to as the Violet Ray of Alchemy, amethyst has long been the favoured gem of royalty. Its name is Greek and means "not drunken" since it was used to cure drunkenness, unruly behaviour and encourage clarity of the mind. It was once thought that it would be impossible to become drunk if alcohol was drank from a vessel of amethyst. Sacred to Alahah, Manasseh and Issachar, the amethyst is an excellent all-round healer. Healing can be promoted by lying on the ground and taking eight amethysts and placing one above the head and one below the feet and placing the rest spread evenly around the body. All the amethysts should be pointing inwardly for this. This simple healing method can be amplified by lying on a violet or yellow cloth. Amethyst is excellent in all magical workings involving protection, balance, peace, sleep, calming the mind and harsh emotions, inspiration, transformation, meditation, health, healing (good for psychological healing), hunting, enhancing psychic powers, fertility, chastity, self-esteem, sobriety, purity, love (good for divine love), vision quests, understanding emotions, victory over enemies, happiness, temperance, courage, psychic dreams, enhancing spiritual awareness, stilling the mind, vigilance, encouraging self-control, stability and overcoming compulsive behaviours. I often keep an amethyst by my bed to help calm my mind and encourage sleep.

Aquamarine: is a popular greenish blue form of beryl. The impurities of iron determine its colouring. It is strongly related to the moon and the element of water. It is sacred to sea goddesses. Aquamarine is traditionally worn as a pendent midway between the throat and heart chakras when energy is low and infections are frequent. This is said to boost the immune system and balance energy levels. Aquamarine is also combined in a layout with rose quartz crystals to calm and soothe on all levels. Aquamarine is excellent in all magical workings involving protection, psychic work, peace, tranquillity, sea magic, compassion, scrying, health, soothing the heart, boosting the immune system, balancing the heart and throat chakras, clearing negative emotions, encouraging unique skills, finding imagination and inspiration, encouraging optimism, encouraging creativity, fertility and healing. Aquamarine eases grief, pain and difficult situations.

Aventurine: is a variety of green and sometimes bluish quartz. It is strongly related to the planet of Venus and the element of earth. It has a very long history for its use in healing and carving. In Tibet, it was used to increase perception and sharpen eyesight. Aventurine is traditionally placed in the centre of the chest. Four clear quartz crystals are then placed around it with the points facing outward. This is done to stabilise the emotions and open the heart. If emotions are disturbed, another aventurine can be placed on the throat chakra and another grounding stone can be placed below the feet. Aventurine is excellent in all magical workings involving healing, luck, money, energising the nervous system, developing mental powers, good fortune, meditation, grounding, tranquillity, clarity, balance, enhancing creativity, joy, encouraging positivity, calming and stabilising emotions, encouraging spiritual growth, gratitude, prosperity, success and fertility.

Azurite: is a blue colour and forms when copper ores oxidise. It has a similar chemical structure to green mineral malachite. It is strongly related to the planet of Saturn and the element of earth. Four pieces of azurite are traditionally placed on and around the body to encourage expression of consciousness and understanding – one above the crown, one to either side of the head and one on the solar plexus. Azurite is excellent in all magical workings involving intuition, increasing psychic awareness, understanding things, accessing deep levels of body-consciousness, communication, encouraging creative flow and drawing out old memories and stress so that they can be released later during healing work.

Beryl: is a mineral composed of beryllium aluminium cyclosilicate that comes in a variety of different colours. The Christians hold beryl sacred to St. Thomas. A crow with a crab below its feet engraved on beryls were once thought to bring joy, union, exultation, lasciviousness, acquisition and conjugal love. The beryl has long been used to treat liver dysfunctions and jaundice. Beryl is excellent in all magical workings involving healing, rain magic, scrying and eternal friendship. It is excellent for sending forth energy. Beryl actually comes in a variety of different forms with each having their own, specific uses. Emerald and aquamarine are two example forms of beryl.

Bloodstone: is essentially a green variety of jasper. It is a variety of quartz streaked with red, brown or yellow markings created by iron oxides. It is strongly related to the planet of Mars and the element of fire. It is known as a warrior's stone. The ancient Egyptian amulet of protection, called the Isis Knot, was composed of bloodstone. Warriors throughout history have carried bloodstones to stop or restrict blood from flowing from wounds. Holding a heart-shaped bloodstone in the right hand that has been wetted with cold water is said to stop bleeding. Bloodstone is excellent in all magical workings involving money, prosperity, health, healing (especially physical healing), longevity, mental balance, overcoming enemies, breaking free of restrictions, increasing business, aligning energy along the spinal column, increasing a good reputation, encouraging a fiery disposition, opening spiritual doors, meditation, protection, increasing worldly influences, stimulating the physical systems of the body (especially blood circulation), motivation, encouragement, clairvoyance, strength, courage and energising the heart and root chakras. Bloodstone is said to remove toxins from blood and a bloodstone ring was once a treatment for haemorrhoids.

Brass: is an alloy of copper and zinc and is strongly related to the element of fire and the zodiac sign of Taurus. It is excellent for all magical workings involving auditory magic, music, communication, building resilience and opening spiritual doors.

Bronze: is an alloy mainly consisting of copper and is strongly related to the zodiac sign of Taurus. It is excellent in all magical workings of matriarchal power and all those associated with brass.

Carnelian: is a variety of chalcedony that is red or reddish orange and semitransparent. It is strongly related to the planet of Mars and the element of fire. The red carnelian is sacred to St. Bartholomew in Christianity. According to the Egyptians, heart-shaped carnelians brought the protection of Osiris and Ra. It is traditionally worn for confidence, courage and protection from harm. Carnelian is excellent in all magical workings involving sexual energy, confidence, courage, protection, money, prosperity, health, longevity, healing, inner work, good fortune, success, fertility, sexuality, accessing information from past lives, preventing or destroying fascination, destroying depression, treating anger, ridding skin problems, enhancing creativity, repairing subtle bodies and reducing stress, anxiety and trauma. Despite its relation to Mars and fire, carnelian can also be used to create peace and harmony. Carnelian enhances wisdom.

Chrysolite: is a yellow, olive or brownish variety of olivine. It is strongly related to the planet of Jupiter and the element of fire. Christianity holds it sacred to St. Matthias. The yellow chrysolite is said to be the golden cup of Hercules and is sacred to the Hebrews who say that it corresponds to the Month of Repose. Placed with gold, yellow chrysolite is said to protect against night terrors. Chrysolite is excellent in all magical workings involving treating delirium and preventing fevers and foolishness. Yellow chrysolite is particularly excellent for preventing madness and other issues to do with the mind.

Clear Quartz: is a clear or white substance composed of silicon and oxygen atoms. It is easy to identify with its distorted, hexagonal, cross-section and six-faced termination. It contributes to over a tenth of the earth's crust. It is strongly related to the moon and the element of water. The ancient Greeks referred to this crystal as *crystalos* meaning "permanent ice". This was because they believed that it was ice frozen so much that it could not melt. Ancient Shamans and healers prized this crystal and used it to help them to access the spirit world. Placed with other stones, clear quartz is said to amplify their energies. Placed in an area with negative energies, clear quartz crystals are said to absorb them. Placing a clear quartz crystal on the third eye chakra will aid purification and open up psychic and spiritual awareness, allowing you to "see" the spiritual or magical realms. Clear quartz made into crystal balls are excellent for scrying rituals and can be used in lunar rituals. They can also be used in solar rituals to kindle sacred fire. Clear quartz is excellent in all magical workings involving vitality, clarity, psychic work, mental stimulation, revealing the truth of a matter, divination, bringing about calmness, releasing blocked emotions, clearing away negativity, purification, shifting energies, inspiration, confidence, amplifying the aura, strengthening the aura, sharpening perception, meditation, contemplation, finding organisation, blessings and protection.

Copper: was one of the seven key noble metals of the ancient peoples. It is strongly related to the planet of Venus and the element of water. It is sacred to Oya, Venus, Aphrodite and Copper Woman. Ancient people referred to this metal as Venus because of its easy union with other metals. Copper is said to ward off bacterial infections and to build up and strengthen the generative function in people. A copper disc placed on the abdomen is said to ward off cholera. Wearing this metal, perhaps in the form of a bracelet, is said to reduce the aches and pains of rheumatism and arthritis. Copper is excellent in all magical workings involving love, beauty, fertility, money, prosperity, easing conflicts, positive outcomes of negative situations, emotional harmony, enhancing brain function and releasing tension and frustration. Copper is said to reduce the problems caused by cosmic and astrological influences.

Coral: is the skeletal remains of marine invertebrates. It is a stony substance that can come in a variety of different colours. It is strongly related to the planet of Venus and the element of water. It is sacred to sea goddesses. Red coral is the most valuable and is honoured in India, Tibet and by Native Americans as a promoter of the energy of life and fertility. Bells attached to pieces of coral were once given to children as amulets that frighten away evil spirits. The Romans give children pieces of coral as charms of protection and healing. The weapons and helmets of Gauls were adorned with coral for extra protection. Shaped like horns or hands, coral is said to protect against the evil eye. It is said that if a man wears coral it will deepen in colour and if a woman wears coral the colour will become paler. Coral is also believed to grow very pale if its wearer is burdened with illness. Coral was also once believed to be a good brain tonic and was used by women to regulate menstruation. Powdered coral mixed with seeds protects crops from blight, locusts and caterpillars as well as the ill effects of thunderstorms and lightning. Placed at the root, sacral and brow chakras, red or pink coral is said to gently stimulate the circulatory system. Coral is excellent in all magical workings involving healing, personal transformation, banishing foolishness, counteracting poison, protection, love and heightening the awareness of the needs of others. Black coral is particularly excellent for fertility. Coral is said to help us understand how all life is connected.

Diamond: is a very hard form of crystallised carbon. It is strongly related to the sun and the element of fire. Diamonds were once thought to keep the limbs whole, tame wild beasts and to be good antidotes to poison when worn in rings. It is said that diamonds are most powerful when they are received as gifts rather than when purchased. Diamonds are traditionally worn to drive away evil and bring strength and courage. Worn on the left arm, diamonds are said to aid victory and to help us overcome madness and adversaries. It is said that the power of a diamond is multiplied when placed with a lodestone. It was also once thought that only goats' blood can break diamonds. Diamonds are excellent in all magical workings involving courage, strength, clarity, invisibility, joy, peace, happiness, purity, protection, virility, healing, health, spiritual ecstasy, withstanding adversity, honour, detoxification, repelling emotional blocks, meditation, spiritual ventures, exorcism, love and transforming sluggish and mundane thought processes into a broader and universal view. Diamonds can also be used to treat mental problems, indigestion and possession by evil spirits. They avert panic, ghosts, nightmares, strife, pestilence, sleepwalking, riots, sorrow, calamities and invasion of fantasies or illusions caused by wicked or evil spirits.

Emerald: is a very precious variety of mineral beryl that is bright green in colour. It is strongly related to the planet of Venus and the element of earth. It is sacred to the deities Mercury, Venus, Vishnu and Sudurjaya. The Christians hold the emerald sacred to St. John. Its colours can look like the deep woods in the springtime which is why it has always had an association with the growth of plants as well as fertility and abundance. It is said in some myths that demons and evil spirits guard the mines of emeralds. Wearing emeralds on a Friday is said to bring good fortune and luck. An emerald is said to change its appearance when a lover is unfaithful or there is false witness to the truth. It is also said to be a bad omen when an emerald drops from its setting. Wearing emeralds on a necklace is said to shield against epilepsy and fear. An emerald ring is said to improve the memory and stop giddiness. Placing an emerald on the heart chakra restores balance and brings calming and peaceful feelings. The emerald is excellent in all magical workings involving love, protection, harmony, abundance, garden or herb magic, balance, money, prosperity, purification, success, fertility, health, healing, improving the memory, increasing understanding, emotional recovery, prophecy, finding the truth of a matter, honesty, friendship, meditation and banishing hidden fears and anxieties. Emeralds are said to speed up the cleansing and purifying processes of the body. They are also reputed to be excellent amulets against nightmares, eye problems, nocturnal emissions and other disturbances.

Fluorite: is crystallised calcium fluoride that can be clear, purple, green, yellow or blue. It most commonly, however, comes in a rich purple colour. It is strongly related to the planet of Neptune and the element of air. Placing a fluorite in a study or workplace is said to bring orderliness. Placing a fluorite by the bed will help you to find new ideas and solutions to problems while you slumber. Carrying a fluorite on the upper body is said to improve coordination skills. Fluorite is excellent in all magical workings involving innovation, coordinating resources, mastering physical skills, improving dexterity and balance, encouraging self-worth, protection, fertility, assimilation of new ideas, understanding fine levels of awareness and grounding energy. The purple variety of fluorite is said to be excellent for manifesting changes within life. Green fluorites are thought to be excellent for balancing the hormones, recovery after childbirth, puberty and menopause.

Gold: was one of the seven key noble metals of the ancient peoples. It is strongly related to the sun and the element of fire. It is particularly sacred to male solar and fiery deities. It has long been associated with power and wealth – at least ten thousand years. The ancients perceived it to be one of the most spiritual and precious of substances. The ancients used gold to make a Tincture of the Sun. It was once thought that gold was the congealed breath of white dragons. The Saxons believed gold to be a metal of honesty and integrity. It is said that the energies within gems are increased by this wonderful substance. Carrying gold balls in the palms of the hands promotes vitality. Placing gold on blocked or painful areas of the body is said to stimulate healing. Gold is excellent in all magical workings involving protection, fertility, success, authority, longevity, solar work, youth, vitality, increasing wisdom, purity, strength, comfort, legal matters, happiness, finding the truth of a matter, health, healing, averting depression, financial issues, prosperity, fulfilment, stimulating the life force, bringing spiritual attainment and influencing cosmic forces and the astral planes.

Iron: was one of the seven key noble metals of the ancient peoples. It is strongly related to the planet of Mars and the element of earth. It is sacred to the deities Mars, Aries, Jarn Saxa (Iron Dirk) and Ogun. It is known as the warriors' metal. This is because the ancients discovered the secret of melting the metal down in order to make weapons that were way more powerful than those made of bronze. The ancients also used iron to make farming tools which is perhaps another reason why it is linked to the god Mars who was also a god of agriculture. It is said that iron is a charm against spirits who are said to find it obnoxious. Cemeteries surrounded by iron fences were once thought to contain the souls of the dead. Iron is excellent in all magical workings involving strength, grounding, astral travel and courage. Iron is said to heavily reflect the saying "as above, so below" because it is abundant in the earth itself and the celestial bodies of the universe.

Jade: is a compact variety of hornblende that may be green, white, grey or bluish. It is strongly related to the planet of Venus and the element of water. It is sacred to the Aztec goddess Chalchiuhtlicue whose skirt is of jade. It is known as a stone of perfection and is held sacred in China as the Jewel of Heaven. The Chinese folk believed it to be a masculine symbol that represented nine virtues: righteousness, purity, virtuous action, knowledge, benevolence, moral conduct, music, endurance and ingenuousness. Jade is considered to have relevance to the spirits of our ancestors and to the protection of the dead. Strangely, it is known to change colour when it is buried with the dead, normally to shades of brown. Jade is considered a jewel of good luck and is thought to be a happy omen. It is known as a diviner of judgements. If you wish to restore energy when you feel disconnected from your past or the place in which you live, place jade at the base of the spine, sacral chakra or throat. Wearing a jade necklace is said to rid urinary gravel and break up bladder and kidney stones. Jade is excellent in all magical workings involving longevity, protecting the spirits of the dead, contact with ancestors, luck, success, good fortune, balancing the heart chakra, improving relationships with others, increasing a sense of belonging, enhancing the ability to act appropriately and efficiently, healing, health, money, prosperity, protection, fertility, relaxation, charity, love, garden or herb magic, weather magic and balancing the Yin and Yang.

Jasper: is a type of quartz that is coloured by a variety of impurities. It can be red, brown, yellow or green in colour. The green jaspers that have red flecks are the most valuable. Jasper is strongly related to the element of earth. The Christians hold it sacred to St. Peter who is traditionally regarded as the first Pope by the Roman Catholic Church. It symbolised the rock on which Christ built his Church. Jasper has a very long history. It has been used to make talismans, amulets and ornaments for centuries. Wearing a jasper necklace is said to strengthen the stomach. Engraving a scorpion on a jasper while the sun is in Scorpio is said to be an excellent charm against kidney stones. Jasper is excellent in all magical workings involving healing, health, visions, success, protection, fertility, good fortune, luck, eloquence, finding solutions to practical problems, relieving pain, strengthening brain power, gently grounding the mind and body, focusing on the practicalities of life, encouraging enthusiasm and drive, aiding recovery and repairing and nurturing damaged areas of the body to aid a fast recovery. Green jasper is particularly good for encouraging empathy.

Jet: is an intensely black or dark brown colour that is made of carbon. It is actually the fossilised wood of waterlogged monkey puzzle trees. It is strongly related to the moon and the element of earth. It is sacred to the earthy god Pan and can be worn when invoking Cybele. It became popular when Queen Victoria wore jet as a symbol of mourning for her husband Prince Albert. Jet is said to have very calming, cooling and balancing properties. It is said to help us to "return to oneself". Working with jet can make us feel as though we are under the branches of ancient, protective trees. Placing jet below the waist, such as in a pocket, is said to be helpful when we are overburdened with worry or are too analytical about certain situations of life. Jet was once boiled with wine for toothache. Burning jet is said to repel serpents, diagnose epilepsy, confirm virginity and bring women out of trances. Wearing jet is said to stop nightmares. Jet is excellent in all magical workings involving health, healing, divination (especially good for scrying), confronting your dark side, perceiving hidden things, activating spinal energy, avoiding depression, calming the mind, safety, comfort and protection.

Lapis Lazuli: is a metamorphic rock that is deep blue with white and gold flecks. It is strongly related to the planet of Venus and the element of water. It is sacred to Isis, Levi and the Babylonian moon god Sin. It has a history of over five thousand years. It was considered very powerful by the pharaohs of ancient Egypt. Their craftsmen would make charms of scarabs, hearts and eyes of lapis lazuli. Placing lapis lazuli on the forehead is said to bring deep insight, courage, clarity and memory recall. Necklaces of lapis lazuli are said to drive away fright from children. Worn over the heart, lapis lazuli helps us to make a strong connection between the heart and the mind. Lapis lazuli is excellent in all magical workings involving psychic work, love, visions, joy, fidelity, understanding things, bringing higher wisdom and thoughts, cosmic connection, gentleness, seeking possible future events, truth, seeking balance, justice, steadfastness, courage, memory issues, clarity, deep insight, making a strong connection between the heart and mind, bringing out anxieties, communication and meditation. Lapis lazuli has been used over the ages to strengthen the heart and the eyesight. It is also believed to stop fainting and miscarriage. It is also believed to treat the spleen, sores, recurrent fever, epilepsy, boils, depression and other mental problems.

Lead: is the most base of metals, was one of the seven key noble metals of the ancient peoples. It is strongly related to the planet of Saturn and the element of earth. It is sacred to the gods Saturn and Cronos. In medieval alchemy, lead and silver were often extracted from the same mixed ore. The ancient Greeks used lead plates for binding magic as well as dark and destructive magic. They would engrave the lead plates with people's names and then bury them. Lead is excellent in all magical workings involving meditation, stability, grounding, overcoming additions, focusing on your deep spiritual self and breaking negative thoughts and patterns. Lead is said to quicken lust and aid communication with the underworld.

Lodestone: is a magnetic iron ore that is used in compasses. Unlike other iron oxides, lodestone is pure. It is strongly related to the element of earth. When the earth was formed billions of years ago, heavy metals such as iron were pulled to the core and this is where the earth's magnetic field is generated. Lodestone is, therefore, useful to help us to remain in harmony with the energies of the earth. Lodestones have been used in African-American folk magic (called Hoodoo) in magical workings known to draw things such as luck, power, blessings, gifts, success and so forth. In Hoodoo, they are traditionally placed in sachets, anointed with oil, "fed" with iron fillings known as magnetic sand and used in magical workings of love and sex. They are also traditionally left in oil with other magical items to make attraction oils. In healing work, lodestones are utilised to help us avoid loss of direction. Lodestones are also traditionally used in magical workings that neutralise the pollutions of the environment caused by modern urban living. Rotating a lodestone pendulum through someone's auric field is said to remove electromagnetic pollution. This simple method is very useful for those who feel drained of energy after using electrical equipment. Talismans of sapphires, diamonds and lodestones are said to give someone near-invisibility. Lodestone is excellent in all magical workings involving love, protection, healing, health, success, luck, sleep, reconciliation (especially in marriage), finding the right path, turning adverse situations around, aligning the chakras and subtle bodies, grounding, releasing stress, revitalising things, attuning with the earth, neutralising things and seeking forgiveness from a husband for infidelity. Lodestone is known as the leading star.

Malachite: is a beautiful bright green colour with black markings. It is a secondary mineral of copper deposits. It is strongly related to the planet of Venus and the element of water. It is also strongly associated with the solar plexus and the heart chakra. Malachite has long been used for protection against the evil eye. It has also been used to guard against cholera and colic. A piece of malachite held in each hand counteracts long-term exposure to electromagnetic radiation. Holding malachite over painful areas of the body will reduce pain, according to folklore. Several pieces, however, may have to be used to thoroughly absorb any imbalances. Malachite is excellent in all magical workings involving success, luck, protection, love, emotional balance, reducing stress and tension, relieving pain, aiding recovery after exhaustion, developing new ideas and theories, encouragement, money, prosperity, overcoming difficult situations, growth, abundance and strengthening the mind, body and inner eye.

Mercury: Also known as quicksilver, mercury represents the female principle of nature and was one of the seven key noble metals of the ancient peoples. It is strongly related to the planet of Mercury and the element of water. It has strong connections with the zodiac signs of Gemini and Virgo. Although mercury has been used in alchemy and other magical traditions since ancient times, it is poisonous and should not be ingested. Contact with the skin for long periods of time should be avoided. Those who wish to work with this substance should always take caution. Mercury is excellent in all magical workings involving transformation and dramatic change. Mercury is said to be excellent for shape-shifting and the power to become fluid.

Moonstone: is a soft, pearly, opalescent variety of mineral feldspar that is usually bluish or silvery. It is strongly related to the moon and the element of water. It is sacred to Aphrodite and all moon goddesses. In India, the moonstone is regarded as a perfect charm for women to wear given the fact that it is so related to the moon, the Goddess's symbol, and all things that are feminine. A moonstone placed above the head, one on each shoulder above the armpits and one on each hipbone will soothe and calm the body, harsh emotions and the mind. This is said to be amplified if you lie on a dark, blue cloth. Moonstones are traditionally given to brides by their grooms as good luck charms. The moonstone is excellent in all magical workings involving psychic work, love, success, luck, good fortune, serenity, healing, female health, emotional balance, increasing awareness of natural cycles, enhancing feminine qualities, lunar work, conveying the energy of the Goddess, fertility, growth, balancing blood and lymph systems, encouraging empathy, stabilising emotions and relieving stress, anxiety, tension, stress-related indigestion, menstrual cramps and other female issues. Moonstones are said to treat obesity and balance hormones.

Obsidian: is a dark, usually black, volcanic glass-like substance that is formed from cooling lava. It is mostly found in volcanic regions. It is strongly related to the planet of Saturn and the element of water. Obsidian is famous for its use in scrying rituals. Crystal balls of obsidian and obsidian discs have been used for centuries in scrying rites. My own crystal ball is obsidian and I have used it for scrying for years with amazing results. Dr. John Dee, the astrologer of Queen Elizabeth I, reportedly used obsidian with Edward Kelley to receive angelic messages. Obsidian can be added to sachets and given to those who are struggling to make important changes within life. Obsidian is excellent in all magical workings involving psychic work, divination, binding, transformation, money, prosperity, dramatic change, grounding, insight and revealing hidden issues, emotions and traumas. Obsidian is said to be excellent for rebalancing the digestive system.

Onyx: is a variety of agate that usually has black and white bands, though it can sometimes just be black. It is strongly related to the planet of Saturn and the element of earth. Onyx means "fingernail" in Greek and this is because the thin white bands of many onyx stones resemble the edge of a fingernail. In Roman mythology, Cupid used his arrow to cut the nails of Venus as she slept. The clippings then fell into the Indus River where they were transformed into onyxes. Gazing at a banded onyx is said to help us to explore hidden aspects of a situation. It is also said that wearing onyx can make the wearer less noticeable to others. Onyx is excellent in all magical workings involving self-control, defence, emotional balance, introspection, calming harsh emotions, withdrawal from everyday activities, cleansing, purification, quietening the mind, protection, stillness and revealing underlying causes of situations. Onyx is said to be good for treating epileptic seizures when worn around the neck. Unfortunately, onyx has a somewhat bad reputation for causing depression and strange dreams. However, wearing a sard is said to neutralise these effects.

Opal: is a quartz gemstone that can come in a variety of different colours. It is usually milky and iridescent. It is strongly related to the planet of Mercury and the element of air. It is sacred to Hercules. Carrying an opal wrapped in a bay leaf is said to confer invisibility and blind those nearby. Opal is excellent in all magical workings involving improving confidence, linking the physical to the higher planes, inner beauty, seeking past lives, victory, astral travel, emotional balance, gaining access to cosmic consciousness, invisibility, unblocking negativities, inspiration, hope, love, success and good fortune. Unfortunately, opal has a traditional, though undeserved, reputation for being unlucky. It is believed by some to be the embodiment of the evil eye. In reality, however, the many types of opal have a wide range of positive magical benefits. Fire opal, for example, is excellent for working with the element of fire and is very useful for promoting recovery after emotional stress, while tree opal strengthens the ability to bring organisation.

Pearl: is a hard, usually white or bluish grey, lustrous mass that is formed within the shell of a pearl oyster or other bivalve mollusc where there is irritation from sand or parasites. It is strongly related to the planet of Venus and the element of water. It is sacred to Marian, Muttalamman (the Pearl Mother) and Yemaya (Holy Queen Sea). Pearls are hard to find. They are, therefore, highly prized. In mythology, pearls were said to fall to the earth when celestial dragons went into battle. Pearls represent tears, emotions and femininity. Wearing a pearl is said to bring the blessings of Isis. Pearls are excellent in all magical workings involving sea magic, love, healing, purity, luck, success, good fortune, fertility, money, prosperity, restoring the spirit, chastity, encouraging emotional clarity, calming extreme situations, encouraging a good flow of things, regulating glandular function, balancing emotions, increasing tolerance, energising the sacral chakra, focusing on the core of the self and reducing worry, anxiety and frustration. Pearls have also been used to treat infections and indigestion.

Peridot: is a deep olive form of chrysolite that symbolises the thunderbolt. It is strongly related to the planet of Mercury and the element of earth. It symbolises the vibrant energies of the natural world. The ancients highly valued peridot because they believed that it had the power to dispel terror and evil spirits, especially if it was set in gold. Peridot used as a pendulum is said to release stress and encourage increased levels of perception. Peridot is excellent in all magical workings involving healing, love, money, prosperity, banishing negative thoughts and emotions, letting go of the past, strengthening personal identity, health, attraction, sleep, purification, protection, dispelling terror and evil spirits, releasing stress, encouraging increased levels of perception, stimulating the mind, emotional balance, opening the heart, unblocking things and balancing the mind and body. Peridot is said to be excellent for reducing toxins in the body.

Platinum: a precious silvery white metal, has feminine energy. Its name comes from the Spanish term *platino* meaning "little silver". It has a history in Egypt of over three thousand years. It is strongly related to the zodiac signs of Virgo and Pisces. Jewellery made of platinum is said to help ease constipation. Platinum is excellent in all magical workings involving clairvoyance, divination and enhancing psychic powers. It is also said to be good for boosting nutrients in the body and treating spasmodic disorders and headaches.

Plutonium: Plutonium is strongly related to the planet of Pluto and the zodiac sign of Scorpio. This metal should never be used because it has far too much radioactivity.

Pyrite: is iron disulphide that is a light brass yellow colour with a dark tarnish. It is sometimes known as iron pyrites or fool's gold and is found in all kinds of rock. It is strongly related to the planet of Mars and the element of fire. The name of pyrite derives from the Greek word *pyr*, meaning fire and this is because when struck pyrite sparks with ease. It has been associated with fire-making since ancient times. Placing pyrite in a room will brighten it and lift depression. Placing pyrite on areas of the body prevents sluggishness. Pyrites are also carried or worn to support diets and detoxification. Pyrite is excellent in all magical workings involving revealing the truth of a matter, encouraging vitality, strengthening willpower, health, healing, cleansing, increasing enthusiasm, protection (especially from pollutants and negativity), success, luck, good fortune, strengthening logical thinking, creating a grounded sense of reality and reducing anxiety, depression and frustration. In healing work, pyrite is utilised to improve the circulation of the body.

Rose Quartz: is made up of silicon and oxygen atoms and its colour is usually considered as due to small amounts of titanium, iron or manganese. It is strongly related to the planet of Venus and the element of water. It is often placed on the heart chakra to balance out any negativities to do with it. Twelve rose quartz crystals placed evenly around the body while lying down can increase self-worth and feelings of nurture. This would be especially potent if you lie on a pink cloth. Wearing a rose quartz, perhaps on a necklace, can be an excellent way to rapidly release emotional stress and bring forth success. Rose quartz is excellent in all magical workings involving success, love, harmonising relationships, friendship, emotional balance, ending loneliness, beauty, releasing emotional stress, easing a broken heart, fertility and uncovering the underlying cause of negative problems (such as a negative outlook of body image).

Ruby: is a form of red mineral corundum that is coloured by chromium oxides. It is strongly related to the sun and the element of fire. Ruby is valued as an occult stone that has a somewhat psychic, magnetic influence on the people who wear it. It is believed that a ruby will become dark red and cloudy when evil is about to come to the wearer. The ruby is utilised to strengthen the heart chakra. The ruby is excellent in all magical workings of longevity, health, healing, vitality, success, luck, good fortune, balancing the heart, confidence, security, enthusiasm, self-esteem, leadership, compassion, protection, high energy, joy, love, opening the heart and healing an unhealthy relationship with a father. Rubies are said to avert danger, nightmares, wicked spirits, sadness and foolish or evil thoughts. Rubies are said to warm and steady us and soothe our relationships with others. As a solar treasure, the ruby acts as a reliable source of life-energy and brings us those qualities associated with the sun. It is excellent in solar rituals that honour the God and bring us closer to him.

Salt: and water have long been used in ritual and magic. Salt is strongly related to the element of earth. Salt has antiseptic and cleansing properties and so it is known as a magical substance of purification. It has long been used to preserve foods such as meat. It is used magically for purification, cleansing, consecration and removing negative energies. Sea salt is sacred to sea deities and is excellent for sea rituals and working with undines and merfolk. Rock salt lamps are a wonderful and romantic addition to the home and magical workings. They are an excellent way to bring forth the purifying energies of salt.

Sapphire: is a variety of mineral corundum that is usually blue. Red mineral corundum is ruby. Sapphire, however, is strongly related to the planet of Jupiter and the element of air. It is sacred to Apollo and Prometheus. Christianity holds it sacred to St. Andrew. It is said that star sapphires are the most potent. Buddhists believe that sapphires have sacred magical powers that reconcile humans with the divine. Applied to the forehead, sapphires are said to open and sharpen the third eye chakra and to stop nosebleeds and the inflammations that cause them. Sapphire is excellent in all magical workings involving psychic work, peace, meditation, devotion, encouraging safety, healing, sharpening intellect, opening and sharpening the third eye chakra, health, clarity, finding the truth of a matter, increasing personal expression, prosperity, money, luck, success, good fortune, love, protection, defence, pacifying enemies, spiritual awakening, making animal spirits flow, spiritual strength, attracting blessings, attracting favourable spirits, prophecy, encouraging wisdom and stimulating the higher mind. Sapphires are said to avert depression, fear, enemies, captivity and negative thoughts. They are said to be excellent for calming, regulating and reducing tension in the solar plexus that is created by fear and anxiety. They are also said to balance the endocrine system.

Selenite: is a transparent, common form of crystallised mineral gypsum. It is strongly related to the moon and the element of water. With its luminous, moon-like glow, selenite is named after the lunar, Greek goddess Selene. Selenite was formed from ancient seas and the salty waters of ancient lakes. Placing a selenite crystal on the sacral chakra is said to remove stress, tension, trauma and stubborn imbalances within the body. Merely holding a wand of selenite can help to purge the stresses and strains of the day as well as painful memories that may be difficult to remove from the mind. This will be enhanced if you imagine breathing in through the top of your head and then breathing out along the wand. You can then visualise all your problems flowing out of the stone, harmless and neutralised. Selenite is excellent in all magical workings involving lunar power, inspiring the mind, clearing away the darknesses of life, avoiding difficulties, unblocking stagnant energy, releasing negative emotions, bringing clarity of the mind and expanding the consciousness.

Silver: has been a valued metal for thousands of years. Alchemists and astrologists refer to this substance as luna. Just as gold strongly represents the sun, silver epitomises the moon and its element of water. It has strong connections with the zodiac sign of Cancer. It is sacred to female deities – especially moon goddesses. It symbolises the feminine, moist and loving nature of the moon in the night sky as its light reflects on the waters of the earth with a romantic, silvery glow. Placing a silver sample in a glass of drinking water for an hour and then removing it is said to make an excellent drink to protect against infections or to soothe when feeling unwell. Carrying silver balls in the palms of the hands clears the head. Silver is excellent in all magical workings involving fertility, lunar work, psychic development, health, success, divination, healing, protection, money, stability, banishing negativity, working with the Goddess, female sexuality, menstrual issues, motherhood issues, good luck, wishes, love, peace, sleep, relationships, intuition and attuning with the rhythms and cycles of nature. Silver is said to ease the flow of energy in the body and to clear out any impurities. It was one of the seven key noble metals of the ancient peoples.

Smoky Quartz: is made up of silicon and oxygen atoms and can be a smoky brown to brownish black colour. It is strongly related to the planet of Mercury and the element of earth. The smoky colour is thought to occur when clear quartz is affected by radioactive decay within minerals that are nearby. It is a very earthy and mysterious crystal that can help us to feel peacefully radiant. Holding a smoky quartz in one hand and a clear quartz in the other can help to balance "receiving" and "broadcasting" energies. Smoky quartz is excellent in all magical workings involving money, prosperity, protection, fertility, calming the mind, peace, grounding, concentrating energy, meditation, creativity, strength, physical stamina, sex magic, stimulating primal energy, attuning with the earth and transforming negativity into positivity.

Sodalite: is generally a royal blue colour with white veining that is found in lava rock. It can, however, be green, white, yellow, pink, grey or a normal blue colour. It is strongly related to the planet of Venus and the element of water. Placing a piece of sodalite on the brow, throat and sacral chakras releases subconscious blockage, according to folklore. Sodalite is excellent in all magical workings involving physical healing, health, transformation, dramatic change, opening up the throat chakra, communication with others, contact with others, transmission of messages over vast distances, enhancing the immune system, stabilising emotions, clarifying perception, meditation, expanding awareness of things and encouraging calmness, peace and contentment. Sodalite is said to be excellent for cleansing the lymphatic system.

Steel: is an alloy of iron with typically a small percentage of carbon. It is strongly related to the planet of Mars and the element of fire. It has strong connections with the zodiac signs of Aries and Scorpio. It can be a good substance for athames and swords. It has strong connections with weapons and armour. Steel is excellent in all magical workings involving strength, courage, grounding and astral travel.

Sunstone: belongs to the same family as the moonstone (feldspar) but has sparkling inclusions similar to the warm, golden light of the sun. It is excellent for working with solar power and the male aspect of the divine. Placing a sunstone on the solar plexus and surrounding it with four clear quartz crystals with the points out will lift sadness and depression, according to traditional healing. Merely looking at a sunstone and meditating with it will lift your mood which is especially good for those who become depressed or sad during the cold, dark, winter nights. Sunstone is excellent in all magical workings involving solar power, lifting depression, lifting sadness, bringing optimism, promoting self-worth, promoting a positive self-image, bringing warmth, bringing comfort, supporting a willingness to stand up for who we are, brightening life, health, healing, vitality, strength, male issues, success, good fortune and luck.

Tiger's Eye: is a member of the quartz family and consists of the fibres of the common rock-forming mineral amphibole. These are embedded in the quartz in highly packed bands. Tiger's eye is usually brown or gold in colour. It is strongly related to the planet of Mars and the element of earth. It is sacred to the deities Bast and Sekhmet. The ancient Romans wore engraved tiger's eyes as protection amulets. Placing a tiger's eye under the tongue was once believed to aid wise judgement and prophecy. Placing tiger's eyes on the root, sacral and solar plexus chakras activates practical energy according to folklore. Tiger's eye is excellent in all magical workings involving money, justice, prosperity, luck, protection, courage, gambling, beauty, bringing comfort, bringing contentment, divination, psychic power, treating depression, diverting unwanted energy, releasing stuck or congested states, confidence, contact with others, success, good fortune and fertility. Tiger's eye is said to be excellent for protection against the evil eye and wicked or evil spirits. It is a treasure that brings pleasure and helps us to distinguish between need and desire.

Tin: is a rather soft metal that was one of the seven key noble metals of the ancient peoples. It is strongly related to the planet of Jupiter and the element of air. It has strong associations with the zodiac signs of Sagittarius and Pisces.

It was considered a magical gift from the deity Jupiter who was king of the ancient city of Rome. Tin actually has strong connections with British Witchcraft and this is because tin was abundant in Britain. This was so much so that the Greeks and Romans referred to Britain as "the Tin Isles". The Romans called it *plumbum album* meaning "white lead" and they used it to make mirrors and even coins. Tin is excellent in all magical workings involving sexuality, rejuvenation and the sacral chakra. Tin is also said to be a good bactericide. Because Jupiter is associated with thunder and lightning, tin is said to be most potent if it is magically charged during thunderstorms and lightning.

Topaz: is mineral corundum that can come in a variety of colours. It can be yellow, orange, pink, white, blue, clear, grey, green or brown. Some varieties of topaz can lose their colour in sunlight, while in other varieties the colour becomes more intense in sunlight. It is strongly related to the planet of Mercury and the element of air. It is sacred to the god Ra. Christianity holds it sacred to James the Less. The rarity of this stone means that it has long been associated with success, luck and good fortune. A long crystal of topaz is said to make an excellent wand that can help its owner to channel large amounts of energy. Placing a topaz on the diaphragm is said to relax the body very quickly and to balance the upper and lower regions of the body. Set in gold and worn on the left arm as a bracelet or worn as a necklace, topaz is said to brighten wit and make you express your desires with ease. It is also said that applying topaz to the nose will stop nosebleeds. Topaz is excellent in all magical workings involving protection, money, prosperity, health, healing, success, luck, good fortune, fostering self-assurance, leadership, expressing desires, releasing physical tension, stabilising emotions, confidence, increasing motivation and harmonising layers of subtle energy.

Turquoise: is a bluish green or light blue stone that forms when water acts on aluminium and copper which gives the stone its beautiful colouration. The shades of colour form from iron impurities. It is strongly related to the moon and the element of water. During the European Renaissance, gentlemen wore a ring with a turquoise to ward away riding or dwelling accidents. The Native American nations held the turquoise sacred and used it in their medicine or charm bags. In Germany, turquoises were given as tokens of love. The Germans believed that love would last as long as the colour of the turquoises did. Turquoises are said to alter their colour according to the health and well-being of their owners. They are believed to grow pale with sadness or ill health and completely lose colour once death occurs. However, the colour is believed to be restored slowly with new and healthy owners. Turquoise is excellent in all magical workings involving love, friendship, success, spiritual contact, strengthening the health of the organs, balancing the subtle systems (especially the heart, thymus and throat chakras), neutralising environmental negativity, luck, good fortune, calming emotions, calming overactive thoughts, enhancing intuition, psychic power, health, healing, cheering the soul, manifestation of spiritual qualities on the physical plane, happiness, fertility, protection, courage and strengthening or enhancing the auric field.

Uranium: is a metal of the planet of Pluto and is strongly related to the zodiac sign of Aquarius. It is too radioactive to be used in magical workings.

Zircon: can come in various colours and is crystalline mineral that occurs as small pyramidal or prismatic crystals in igneous rocks. It is hard and very resistant to erosion. It can, therefore, be found in rivers and sandstones. The clear variety of zircon is often used to imitate diamonds, though it is often used simply as a gemstone in its own right. It is strongly related to the element of water. Zircon is excellent in all magical workings involving enhancing wisdom, honour, driving away evil spirits, transformation, dramatic change, revealing hidden realities, sleep, correcting emotional over-sensitivity, encouraging a flexible attitude and avoiding delusions or fantasies. Zircon is said to cleanse and regulate the digestive and endocrine systems and allow us to experience a valid, practical, psychic awareness. Jacinth is an orange or reddish variety of zircon and is excellent for magical workings of money and prosperity.

Chapter Eighteen: Animal Kingdom

Such is my love of animals and their unique associations and powers that this chapter seemed inevitable from the very start of me writing this book. Ever since I was a little boy I have always loved animals and have always felt a spiritual and loving bond with them. Witches call upon animal powers to strengthen and enhance their many magical workings. Witches have a great love for animals and the animal kingdom in general. We understand that each has unique energies that can bring forth the powers that we may be lacking in our lives, helping us to further our development as we progress spiritually within the Craft. Witches never bring harm to animals within our rituals and spells because, as you will be aware by now, the ritual sacrifice of any living creature would be the ultimate way to violate our law of harm none.

Many of the spells of olden times required strange ingredients that referred to animal body parts. But in actuality these were just different names for specific types of herbs. This is known as "The Magician's Herbal Code" and is simply various folk names that were given to herbs. You may have heard of the famous "eye of newt", for example, and this name simply referred to lavender, a favourite herb among many Witches. The knowledge of magic was once so closely guarded from ordinary people that Witches and magicians used secret codes. The whole idea that Witches killed to enhance their magical workings is a result of the teachings of Christianity. Unfortunately, the Christians did their very best to degrade the Craft and make Witches look evil.

In the Craft, it is only lawful and acceptable for Witches to use animal parts when they are no longer of use. A dead starfish, for example, can be dried out and used to work with the element of water and sea deities. Cat claws, as another example, can be used to protect from slander and arguments, while a snail's shell can be used to give stability in money and business and aid patience and meditation. Witches may simply visualise animal parts instead of using actual animal parts to aid image magic or call upon deities that relate to specific animals.

If you seek to know more about animals and the animal kingdom, there is much you can do besides read about them from books. Make an effort to meditate with their energies. Surround yourself with figurines of animals and think about their behaviour. Meditate on the ancient, animal cave paintings of Europe and other places around the world and how animals have played a role in religions. Focus on how animals have always had a special, spiritual link to humans and our understanding of the world. Make an effort to watch nature programs and to go for walks to see animals in action. While you do so, think of the male and female roles in the world around you. Watch how many male animals fight to protect their clan and think of the God's role in the world. Watch how many female animals suckle their offspring and protect their young at all costs and think of the Goddess's role in the world. Animals often come to Witches and other magical people to reveal secrets, enhance wisdom, aid meditation, aid our connection to the spiritual energies of nature and support our rituals and spells.

Another term that you may come across within the Craft is animal totem. An animal totem is an animal that symbolises a single person, a family or a group of magical people (such as a coven of Witches). In ancient times, the Shamanic tribes often each had a specific animal that symbolised their group. It comes as no surprise that even in modern times groups who are not magical will often have animals to symbolise their groups. This is evident in various sports teams or clubs. It all comes from ancient Shamanism when people understood what animals can symbolise for their group. The fact that children often receive animal toys, such as teddy bears and bunny rabbits, is another reminder of the symbolism of animal spirit totems and our ancient connection to the spirit world. Finding your own animal totem can be a wonderful part of your inner work and a powerful way to find your spiritual path to enlightenment.

The spirit world, which is actually made up of many levels or dimensions, is populated by countless, non-physical beings. These invisible beings are actually all around us all the time and are not distant, in "heaven", as it were.

It is within the spirit world that what we call elementals, angels, deceased loved ones, spirit animals and so on exist. All are extensions of the Ultimate Deity, or the Goddess and God, that can aid our lives and magical workings if only we would take the time to show a willingness, that is a conscious effort, to understand them, to work with them and to acknowledge their spiritual powers. As with the Goddess and God, they can't help us if we don't acknowledge them and call upon their powers. Calling upon the spiritual powers of animals is one of the most powerful things that a Witch can do to aid his or her work. They can truly strengthen and empower our work.

The Witch's Familiar

Witches may have familiars of two types. One type may be a non-physical animal, a spirit being, known as a power animal. The other may be a physical or material creature, such as a cat, a toad, a rabbit or a tortoise. Whether the animal is a spirit, a non-physical being, or a material being it is an animal with which the Witch has developed a special, magical, spiritual or psychic bond. The familiar is one with which the Witch has gained an empathetic relationship and will offer deep companionship, spiritual and magical support, protection and typically unconditional love. The bond that Witches share with their familiars can be very intense and unshakeable. It can be a love that can never truly die and this is speaking from personal experience.

The belief in non-physical animal familiars, also known as spirit animals or animal spirit guides, has its origins in ancient Shamanism. These are highly specialised spirits that come to help and guide Witches. They may come to Witches in dreams as well as during meditation, visualisation or other techniques that allow us to gain access to the spirit world. If a specific animal continuously shows itself during these altered states, it may well be your power animal trying to communicate with you. An animal spirit guide is a wonderful thing to have. It is a highly specialised and personal relationship that only a Witch has with his or her animal spirit familiar. The animal spirit familiar may reflect your own personality and characteristics, helping you to enhance them or it may bring forth those energies that are needed in your life to enhance your spiritual development. The spirit animal familiar may well be an animal known to us on earth or a mythical beast, such as a fire-breathing dragon or phoenix.

The familiar of the physical kind is just as powerful as the non-physical kind. This is a deep and loving bond that is different to that of a bond with another animal pet. A Witch may not love a different pet any less, but the bond shared with their pet that is a familiar is more intense because it is deeply spiritual and psychic. Acquiring a familiar takes time and effort. It requires patience and an understanding with your pet. If a deep, spiritual trust is gained then your pet may well choose to work with you magically and become your familiar. You cannot force this as the pet will choose you as his or her magical partner rather than the other way around. Gaining a familiar in this way can be very rewarding to say the least. Your familiar will not only be a very close companion and a magical helper in your workings, he or she will offer great protection and will let you know if there is evil about so that you can take action.

Unfortunately, the word familiar meant something quite different to the Christians of the persecution times of Witches. The Christians were convinced that Witches always had a familiar with whom they worked with. The familiar was believed to be the Witch's demon-helper sent by Satan to aid the Witch in his or her evil workings. Cats, dogs, rats and toads were believed to be the animals that were most likely to be evil Witches' familiars. Witches' familiars were believed to be demons that had took the form of animals in order to disguise themselves. These demon-helpers were believed to be fed blood or psychic energy by Witches using a secret nipple or teat. This may seem amusing to modern-day folk but, believe me, it was no joke at the time. So if the suspected Witch bore an unusual mole or wart then she was instantly doomed and put to death. Most often, the suspected familiars were burned with the Witch and especially cats which were believed to be able to easily change their shape in order to wreak havoc that was invoked by the Satanic Witch.

As you will be aware by now, Witches do work very closely with the energies of the four sacred elements of nature and the elemental spirits that represent them. This is because we understand that there is much more to nature than what meets the eye. They are not sheer evil beings of Satan, but simply the powers and forces of nature that Witches harness to empower their work. Trees, plants, crystals, stones, mountains, rivers, ponds, metals and so on all contain the life force and are guarded by the deva or djinn powers or spirits of the elements. They are the neutral spirits that create the wonderful magic of the earth and our universe – not the evil entities imagined by the Christians. Some Witches may well refer to these elemental spirits as familiars.

A Guide to Specific Animals and Mythical Beasts

Here, we will look at an alphabetical guide to specific animals and mythical beasts to expand your knowledge of these wonderful creatures. There are obviously many animals and mythical creatures to explore so this guide is far from complete. This guide, however, will be enough to get you started on your road to expanding your magical knowledge of animals and mythical beasts as you devise your rituals and spellcraft. To call upon animals in your magical workings you can perhaps write invocations for them in much the same way as for deities, decorate your sacred space or home with them or call upon specific deities associated with them, as a few examples. The information I have given below will also tell you what each animal means spiritually. If an animal, symbol or sound of that animal, shows up at least three times in a short period, perhaps in dreams or during meditation, it is most likely trying to give you a spiritual message. If it shows up often over a prolonged period of time it may well be your power animal or animal totem. Although I have given the traditional meanings of animals below, it is important to understand that your perception of a specific animal is key to what it may mean for you specifically. A rat, for example, can symbolise something quite friendly if you have kept rats as pets but if you are afraid of rats, perhaps because you have been bitten by one, a rat can symbolise something to be cautious of in your life. Intuition plays a large role in this. The following information will serve as a simple introduction to each creature. A more rounded look at each, however, will require more research.

Alligator: a reptile that symbolises survival, aggression, protection, assertiveness and adaptability. It is sacred to Cipactli who is the Aztec symbol of the Earth Mother. If an alligator shows up it means that perhaps you need to think about what you are currently learning rather than rushing ahead. An alligator showing up to you can also symbolise that you need to be protective. It is advising you to be assertive about what is yours and setting your boundaries. The alligator showing up to you can also mean that you are emerging from a dark period of your life and into a period of renewal and new beginnings. The alligator showing up to you could also be urging you to gather all the facts of a situation before passing judgement or making any harsh decisions. The alligator may also be urging you to show respect and honour to your ancestors at this moment in your life. If the alligator is your power animal or animal totem you may well be someone who keeps to yourself most of the time but when others get to know you they will feel a strong and powerful presence. Call on the alligator for magical workings involving protection, assertiveness, keeping things hidden or secret, moving on in life, making amends, enhancing wisdom, enhancing patience and gaining knowledge.

Ant: are insects that are strongly related to the planet of Saturn and the element of fire. They symbolise teamwork, self-discipline and friendship or family. They are sacred to Ahriman who is the Persian god of darkness. If ants show up to you it means a cherished project or goal that you have been considering doing needs to be started and needs to be seen through to the end. Ants can also symbolise that friends and/or family are very important to you right now and it is time to seek their support rather than isolating yourself. Ants showing up to you may well be urging you to trust yourself in accomplishing your hopes and dreams. Ants showing themselves to you may also be advising you to take your time and have patience in any goals or projects that you are involved in. If the ant is your power animal or animal totem you may well be a person who works best in group effort rather than in isolation. You may be a person who understands that what you put into group work is for the benefit of everyone rather than just what is in it for you. Call on the ant for magical workings involving success, luck, good fortune, teamwork, bonding with others, projects, friendship, family issues, completion, enhancing patience, motivation, coordinating efforts between people, adapting to situations and avoiding frustration.

Antelope: The antelope is a mammal that is sacred to the deities Vayu, Saraddevi and Dedoun. If the antelope shows up it means that you should be cautious with people around you who have harsh or aggressive energy. In such situations where these types of people are around you, the antelope may be encouraging you to surround yourself with golden light to physically protect yourself. If you have a cherished wish or desire, the antelope may be encouraging you to make a clear and firm decision to begin working towards it with high energy. The antelope showing up may be also urging you to pay attention to new opportunities and to take good advantage of them. You may well regret it if you don't. The antelope may also be encouraging you to finish your goals that you have already started as quickly as you can. The antelope may also be warning you that you have been spending too much time on your own and it is now time to seek out the company of friends and family. If the antelope is your power animal or animal totem you may well be an innately psychic person who is highly intuitive and quick-witted and able to effectively deal with any situation you become involved with. Call on the antelope for magical workings involving boosting your energy levels, unblocking things, getting things moving within life, wishes, making decisions, taking advantage of new opportunities, seeking the company of friends and family, psychic power and dealing with situations effectively.

Badger: is a mammal and it was once believed that by putting its powdered eye or feet into someone's food it would make him or her fall in love with you. This to me sounds absolutely disgusting. The feet and eyes of badgers were once believed to confer invisibility. If a badger shows up it may be urging you to stick with a project no matter what happens. You may well regret it if you don't. The badger may also be a warning to stop depending too much on others and to understand that you can do things on your own. The badger may also be urging you to always defend your beliefs or principles and to face your challenges head-on without thinking you cannot. If the badger turns up it can also indicate that now is the time to transform your anger, frustration and aggression into constructive action without cutting others to pieces. If the badger is your power animal or animal totem you may be a very determined person who can stick to your goals until you achieve them. However, you do not like confrontation but if necessary you will defend yourself. Call on the badger for magical workings involving self-reliance, healing, success, luck, good fortune, the completion of projects, determination and defending your beliefs and principles.

Bat: is a mammal that I adore. A wonderfully complex creature with amazing hearing, the bat is a guardian of the night associated with the winter festival of Samhain. The Chinese people associate the bat with great luck and happiness. Bats are strongly associated with the element of air. They are sacred to the deities Shang Kuo-Lao, Alcithoe, Arsippe, Fu-hsing and Camazotz. If the bat shows up it means that it is time to embrace necessary changes that are long overdue and to let go of habits, attachments and unnecessary baggage that are no longer needed. The bat may also be advising you that an ordeal that you may be facing is necessary for your spiritual development. The bat may also be urging you that time with others is necessary and so now may be the time to go out and socialise, perhaps by joining classes or group activities that you may personally enjoy. The bat may also be urging you to confront your fears and in doing so be trusting that beneficial changes are on the way. If the bat is your power animal or animal totem you may be a very social person who thrives in group activities. You may also be a person who can easily see in others what they try to keep hidden and perhaps even hear what they are thinking. Call on the bat for magical workings involving embracing changes, letting go of things that no longer serve you well, confronting ordeals, social awareness, dramatic and beneficial changes, group work and seeing things that the people around you try to keep hidden.

Bear: is a mammal and a well-known Celtic and American power animal or animal totem. It is strongly related to the element of fire. It is sacred to many deities including Mercury, Artogenus, Ursula (Little Bear) and Callisto (Queen of Bears). It has been strongly revered in Britain and throughout Europe for its ferocity and strength since time immemorial. In Zuni tradition, the bear is associated with the west. The bear has always been associated with the ability to marry our inner strength with our intuition. In other words, the bear can symbolise an ability to show sensitivity without appearing weak. It symbolises kingship, healing, power, mother-cunning and gentle strength. The teeth of the bear were once thought to be very potent magical charms. If the bear shows up to you now is the time to clear your boundaries and do not compromise despite any pressure from others. The bear may also be urging you to get on with a creative project that has been on your mind and to stop putting it off. The bear may also be advising you to spend some time alone to gather your thoughts and to take some time away from your usual routines. The bear may also be telling you that physical or emotional healing is needed. The bear may also be urging you to be gentle and affectionate to those closest to you. If the bear is your power animal or animal totem you may well be a very good healer with enormous emotional strength who is assertive and confident with a very strong presence. Call on the bear for magical workings involving strength (especially inner or gentle strength), intuition, healing, clearing boundaries, assertiveness, getting on with creative projects, solitude, confidence, success, luck, good fortune, dealing with adversities, courage, strengthening integrity and protection.

Beaver: is a mammal that is a Native American power animal or animal totem. It symbolises building, the ethic, construction, purpose and effort. It is strongly related to the planet of Saturn and the zodiac sign of Taurus. It is sacred to the deities Castor, Great Beaver and Wishpoosh. The beaver appearing to you can represent that now is the time for avoiding contemplation or procrastination. It can be an indication to direct your energy head-on towards purposeful activities. The beaver can also be an indication that now is the time to change your surroundings or environment so that you can feel more comfortable and secure. The beaver may also be advising you to balance your activities by allowing time for rest and social time with family and friends. The beaver may also be urging you to be aware of wasting time and energy on unnecessary matters. If the beaver is your power animal or animal totem you are probably a person who likes to get a job done and to keep busy. You may also be very loyal to your friends and are able to make long and lasting friendships with others. Call on the beaver for magical workings involving construction of things, getting things done, friendship, comfort, security, social awareness, balancing work and play, keeping busy, loyalty, keeping focused, organisation, ideas, visions, getting out of relationships that make you feel trapped, resolving conflicts in relationships and overcoming things that are daunting.

Bee: is an insect that is strongly related to the planet of Jupiter and the element of fire. It is sacred to Ah Muzencab, Callisto (Queen Bee), Cybele (the Queen Bee), Usins, Mellonia and Neith. The honey bee is sacred to Melissa. The bee showing itself to you symbolises a time to approach your projects with commitment and dedication. If you do this, you will achieve your goals beyond your wildest expectations. The bee may also symbolise that now is the time to get more organised within your life and to get on with a creative idea that you have been meaning to do. The bee can also symbolise that now is the time to involve others in a life-affirming venture, one that will benefit everyone. The relation the bee has to honey means that now is the time to enjoy the sweetness of life. If the bee is your power animal or animal totem you may well be a person who is very committed to your goals and you have what it takes to be successful in anything that you attempt. You may also be a person who is a little slow to anger but when you are aroused you can sting people with your words. Call on the bee for magical workings involving commitment, creative ideas, projects that involve persistence and perseverance, group work, enjoying the sweetness of life, social skills, finishing things, organisation, responsibility, cooperation of everyone involved in shared tasks, luck, good fortune and success.

Blackbird: s a bird of the sun and the element of air. It was once believed that if the feathers of the right wing of the blackbird were tied up with red thread and then hung from the middle of a house that had never been occupied it would be impossible for anyone to sleep until they were removed. If the blackbird turns up to you now is the time to focus on your singing. Let go of any inhibitions and just sing without any concern for how you sound or what other people think. The blackbird is advising you to appreciate the gift of song. The blackbird showing itself to you may also be an indication that the archangel Uriel is trying to communicate with you. The archangel may well be watching over you and helping you to connect with nature and its spiritual powers. The blackbird may also be urging you to enhance your awareness of the non-physical realities and your own true spiritual path. The blackbird may also be advising you to take note of any signs or omens that are shown to you in this time of your life so that you can act accordingly. If the blackbird is your power animal or animal totem you may well be a person who is gifted with the ability to sing well, someone who can use your gift of song to soothe others during difficult times. You may well be a very cheerful and gentle person, but if someone violates your boundaries you may well become aggressive. Call on the blackbird for magical workings involving singing, chanting, letting go of inhibitions, working with the archangel Uriel, connecting with the spiritual powers of nature, finding your true spiritual path, setting boundaries and bringing periods of cheerfulness and gentleness.

Blue Jay: is a trickster bird that is strongly related to the planet of Mercury and the element of air. If the blue jay shows up now is the time to pay close attention to non-verbal clues that indicate someone is being deceitful towards you. Take note of any body language and facial expressions. The blue jay may also be urging you to attack something, both boldly and courageously, that has caused you great fear rather than shying away from it. The blue jay may also be encouraging you to take a note of your gifts and talents and to begin planning on how to best use them in order to take purposeful action. If the blue jay is your power animal or animal totem you may well be a fearless person who will not back down from any threat or challenge. You may well be able to mimic other people's voices or impersonate them. Call on the blue jay for magical workings involving protection (especially from people who may be stronger or more capable than you are), defence, overcoming threats, overcoming challenges, seeing deceitful people for who they are, commitment, success, difficult choices and exploring things.

Buffalo: is a mammal that is a Native American power animal or animal totem. It is known as the builder of life and the provider of sustenance. It is very symbolic of plenty, abundance, prayer, sacredness, determination and harmony with the earth. It is sacred to the deities Oya, Yama and Mahish. If a buffalo shows up it can symbolise that you must trust that you will always have your basic needs. The buffalo may also be urging you to always appreciate the things that you have in life now. The buffalo showing up may also be telling you to stop feeling sorry for yourself and just be aware of the resources that you do have. The buffalo is telling you to use them well. Stay positive and have faith in the natural abundance of life. The buffalo appearing to you could well be an indication that now is the time to expand your awareness of your interests, perhaps by starting a new hobby or recreational activity. A white buffalo appearing to you could well be an indication that peace and calmness are coming your way and that you should expect a miracle of some sort. If the buffalo is your power animal or animal totem you may well be a very confident and determined person who understands that you will always have what you need. You may well have a very harmonious relationship with the earth and trust in the abundance of life and nature. Call on the buffalo for magical workings involving money, prosperity, abundance, determination, harmonising with the earth, appreciation, expanding awareness of interests, projects, overcoming challenges, confidence, getting through times of intense struggle and restoring faith in the abundance of life.

Bull: a mammal that is a Native American power animal or animal totem. It symbolises creativity, fertility and virility. It is strongly related to the planet of Venus and the element of earth. The white bull is strongly related to the moon. The bull strongly represents the zodiac sign of Taurus and is sacred to many deities including Adad, An (the Bull of Heaven), Dionysus, Vishnu, Ra and Jupiter. Bulls are actually calm animals and they can be slow to anger but when they are aroused they can become incredibly fearsome. When a bull shows up to you it could be an indication that you are experiencing an incredibly fertile and dynamic period and so perhaps it is time to indulge in those creative projects that you have been considering. If there is one particular goal that means more to you than others, get committed to it and move forward to it with a steady and persistent attitude. However, don't rush this as you may make mistakes. The bull may also be asking you to work with the God, the masculine energy of the universe, whether you are male or female. If the bull is your power animal or animal totem you may well be a very determined and committed individual, though you may have a somewhat stubborn side. Call on the bull for magical workings involving fertility, creative projects, determination, commitment, virility, working with the God, success, good luck, strength, boosting endurance and overcoming difficult or challenging tasks.

Butterfly: The butterfly is an insect that symbolised perfection to the Aztecs. It is strongly related to the planet of Venus and the element of air. Yellow and orange butterflies strongly correspond to the sun. The butterfly is sacred to the deities Great Butterfly and Itzpapalotl (Obsidian Butterfly). The significance of the butterfly is change, metamorphosis and transformation. The change of caterpillar to pupa and then to butterfly symbolises the natural cycles of life and the changes that come with them. If the butterfly turns up to you now is the time to stop taking life so seriously and to lighten up a bit. The butterfly may also be an indication that a big change is on the way. If you have been thinking about changing an old habit, a way of thinking or a way of lifestyle, the butterfly may well be encouraging you to do so. The butterfly may also be saying to you that despite any challenges, you will get through these transitions. If the butterfly is your power animal or animal totem you may well be a person who understands and appreciates the natural cycles of life. You may well be a very flighty and attractive person who is drawn to exotic and colourful things. Call on the butterfly for magical workings involving transformation, dramatic change, cheerfulness, overcoming challenges, encouragement, romance, encouraging relaxation and love.

Camel: is a mammal that is sacred to the Arabian deities Azizos and Arsu. It symbolises strength, faith, replenishment, nourishment, stability and continuity. If the camel shows up to you it may be that more then ever you need to listen to your intuition for guidance. You may well have a lot more energy and durability to deal with a specific task than what you think. The camel may also be warning you that the road ahead may well be difficult but you must see it through to the end and trust that you will get through it. The camel may also be advising you to store some money and supplies for future use. If the camel is your power animal or animal totem you may well be a very adaptable person who has the ability to endure any condition within life. You may be a person with considerable inner strength who is very kind and patient. Call on the camel for magical workings involving inner strength, keeping the faith, replenishing energy, nourishment, stability, keeping continuity, new adventures, money and prosperity.

Cat: is a mammal that has a long history with Witchcraft. Witches often have cats as their familiars. I have always adored them. The cat strongly corresponds to the moon, owing to its nocturnal habits, and the element of fire, owing to its volatile nature. It is sacred to many deities including Artemis, Cat Annis, Bast, Cerridwen, Diana, Demeter, Sekhmet (the Great Cat) and Tefnut. Cats have long be revered as mysterious creatures and have played a role in myths, legends, rituals, spells and magic. It is said that cats can see spirits with ease. The ancient Egyptians adored these creatures and always held them to be incredibly sacred. If the cat shows up to you perhaps now is a period of independence and self-sufficiency. Perhaps you need to trust your instincts and capabilities where necessary. The cat may also be an indication that an ancestor is trying to communicate with you and so you should listen very carefully to your own intuitive guidance. The cat can also be telling you that you need to open up to your sensuality, perhaps by dancing slowly and enjoying the power of touch and intimacy. As a very magical creature, the cat showing itself to you can be an indication that you should be aware of any signs and omens that may help to guide and direct your life positively. If you have recently released something that is not good for you, such as a bad habit or toxic relationship, the cat may be telling you that the negativity will be replaced with something more suitable to you personally. If the cat is your power animal or animal totem you may well be a very independent person who is a creature of the night. You may well be a very intuitive person who is naturally drawn to all things that are magical. Call on the cat for magical workings involving independence, self-sufficiency, communication (especially with ancestors), enhancing instincts, enhancing capabilities, enhancing sensuality, transforming negative situations into positive ones, exploring new things, relieving boredom, intuition, psychic power, healing and protection.

Cow: is a mammal that is sacred in Hindu cultures and traditions. It is strongly related to the element of earth. It is sacred to a whole host of deities including Damona (Divine Cow), Indra (Lord of Cows), Ushas (Mother of Cows), Io, Brigit, Juno, Diana, Hathor, Inanna, Lakshmi, Astarte and Aditi. If the cow shows itself to you it may be an indication that you are entering a period of great nourishment and so you should involve yourself in anything positive that is offered to you. As a symbol of healing and motherhood, the cow showing to you may well indicate that you need to heal your relationship with your mother, whether she is here physically or she has passed into the spirit world. The cow could also be advising you that you have been worrying unnecessarily and that you should trust that you will always have your needs despite any fears or doubts. If you have recently made a solid decision, the cow may be telling you to stand by it and not let anyone sway you away. The cow can also be an indication that some sort of sacrifice is needed in order to make life better for you. If the cow is your power animal or animal totem you may well be a very generous, compassionate and caring person who is always willing to put the needs of others before your own. You may well be a person who needs stillness and calmness so that you can think and do things at your own leisure. Call on the cow for magical workings involving nourishment, seeking opportunities, healing (especially with a mother), avoiding worry, making decisions, generosity, bringing compassion, bringing calmness and stillness, issues to do with children, keeping the faith, abundance, money, prosperity and fertility.

Coyote: is a mammal and is a trickster creature. It symbolises honour, insight, playfulness, humour, laughter, duality, sarcasm and the power to see both sides of an argument. It is strongly related to the planet of Mercury and the element of fire. The coyote is sacred to the deities Hermes and Mercury and all other trickster gods. If the coyote shows up perhaps now is the time to not take life so seriously and get a better sense of humour, perhaps by going to see your favourite comedian. The coyote can also indicate that something rather unexpected may happen and this may not be welcome. If you have been feeling guilty about something you have done, the coyote may be telling you to forgive yourself and look for any lessons learned. The coyote showing itself may also be an indication that you should try to adjust to something rather than fighting or running away. If the coyote is your power animal or animal totem you may well be a very humorous individual, a practical joker, who always sees the fun side to things. You may well be a survivor who can adapt to almost anything that life throws at you. Call on the coyote for magical workings involving insight, adaptability, forgiveness, learning from past regrets, regaining a sense of humour, solving problems and finding creative solutions.

Crab: is a marine crustacean creature that symbolises the world of dreams. It is strongly related to the moon and the element of water. It is a symbol of the zodiac sign of Cancer. It is sacred to the deities Toko'yoto and Nzambi. I have always loved crabs. The crab showing itself to you can be an indication that you are becoming increasingly intuitive, psychic and clairvoyant. You may find that you can see things that others cannot. If so, now is the time to take note of any dreams or visions that may help to guide your life and your soul's path. The crab can also be an indication that there will be some sort of unexpected shift or change in your personal life or feelings that will benefit the path of your soul. If life has become stressful, the crab may also be advising you to take your mind off things by listening to some music that you enjoy and then dancing to it. If the crab is your power animal or animal totem you may well be a very intuitive and psychic person who is very sensitive to your surroundings. You may well be an individual who is very protective of your feelings, your home and your personal space. Call on the crab for magical workings involving protection, psychic power, dream work, clairvoyance, transformation, dramatic change, adaptability, cleansing and purification.

Crocodile: is a reptile that is strongly related to the moon and the element of water. It is sacred to the deities Itzam Na, Nuga, Osiris, Set, Khentekhai, Sobek (the Rager), Nyakaya and Hao. It was once believed that the left eyetooth of a crocodile was a potent charm against fever. As a close relative of the alligator, the crocodile basically has all the same spiritual associations and so you can refer to the alligator above for information about the crocodile.

Crow: is an often feared bird and is a Celtic power animal or animal totem. It is strongly related to the planet of Saturn and the element of air. It is sacred to many deities including Apollo, Athena, Cronos, Saturn, Yangwu (Sun Crow), Badb (Crow of Battle), Maeve and Rhiannon. In Italy and Greece, the crow symbolises long life. If the crow shows up to you there may be something that you have been working towards for some time that is about to finally manifest. The crow can be an indication that a very big change is on the way to you. The crow showing itself to you can also be a warning that you are about to notice an imbalance or injustice that hasn't been addressed and this must be spoke up about. The crow can also be an indication that you will soon see a glimpse into a possible future event that may affect you directly. The crow showing itself to you can also be an indication that you should take good notice of any signs or omens around you over the next couple of days as these can be indications that help to guide your life and its direction. If the crow is your power animal or animal totem you may well be a very social person but you much prefer to spend time with your most closest friends and family. You may well be a person who is very much guided by the voice of spirit and your own personal integrity. Call on the crow for magical workings involving longevity, manifesting goals, dramatic change, transformation, social awareness, friendships, family, seeking the guidance of spirit, enhancing personal integrity, creativity, inspiration, intuition, psychic awareness and healing.

Deer: is a mammal that symbolises sensitivity, gentleness, kindness, wisdom, spirituality, purity of purpose, gracefulness and walking in the light. It is strongly related to the planet of Venus and is sacred to the deities Artemis and Nemesis. Unlike many other animals, the deer does not hibernate in the winter. It does, however, rest a lot more in the winter than at other periods of the year. It eats as much as it can in the autumn to store as much energy as possible for the winter when food is not as available. It then rests in the winter to conserve energy as it prepares for the coming of spring. If a deer shows itself to you it could be an indication that you are about to enter a period of discovering your sensitive side. You may begin to understand the feelings of others even before they do. The deer showing itself to you can also indicate that you are about to embark on an exciting adventure that will lead to many possibilities. The deer could also be warning you that you need to seek safety from aggression or negativity. If the deer is your power animal or animal totem you may well be a very sensitive and intuitive person who is aware of masculine and feminine qualities. You may, however, relate to those that are most closely associated with your own gender. Call on the deer for magical workings involving gentleness, kindness, spirituality, finding purity of purpose, enhancing wisdom, gracefulness, sensitivity, enhancing intuition, psychic awareness, understanding the feelings of others, seeking safety, understanding masculine and feminine qualities, enhancing creativity, love, inspiration, projects, avoiding harm and seeking strength and endurance through difficult times.

Dog: is a mammal that symbolises healing, loyalty, devotion, love (especially unconditional love), protection, faith, service, determination, appreciation and the future. It is said to be the oldest domesticated creature and is strongly related to the moon and the element of earth. It is sacred to many deities including Mars, Anubis (Guardian of the Dogs), Sarama (Heavenly Bitch), Aries, Garm (Hell-Hound), Dharma, Sucellos and Ishat (Bitch of the Gods). The dog was believed to howl when a death was about to occur because it could see the Angel of Death at work. Bitches and white dogs are said to represent corn spirits. If a dog shows up to you it may be an indication that you must always keep the faith in any situation. Perhaps the dog is encouraging you to do some form of volunteering service, such as charity work, simply to help those less fortunate than yourself. If you have recently faced some form of negativity or disappointment, the dog showing itself to you may be telling you to remain determined. The dog may also be reminding you that love and loyalty are important right now and that you should be showing these qualities to your nearest and dearest. If the dog is your power animal or animal totem you may well be a very loving and loyal person who shows commitment to people and any situation of importance. You may well be a gifted speaker or singer who is eager to work towards helping humanity in any way you can. Call on the dog for magical workings involving loyalty, devotion, healing, love (especially unconditional love), protection, defence, keeping the faith, determination, appreciation, commitment, humanitarianism, clairvoyance, psychic awareness, guardianship, metaphysical knowledge, companionship, social awareness, group work and overcoming very difficult challenges.

Dolphin: is a sea mammal that the Native Americans see as a creature that brings us the teachings of the element of water. They regard the beautiful creature as a bridge between humans and the ocean. It is strongly related to the moon and the element of water. It is sacred to the deities Aphrodite, Neptune, Venus, Delphinus, Apollo, Poseidon, Atargatis and Hat-Mehit. It is often said that the Child of Promise often came on a dolphin. Dolphins symbolise kindness, joy, playfulness, communication, breath control, spiritual awakening, sexuality and the sacred breath of life. The dolphin has wonderful myths and folklore that date back to ancient Greece. If a dolphin shows itself to you perhaps now, more than ever, is the time to do some meditation while listening to your favourite music. If you have been experiencing difficulty with a specific person, the dolphin may be advising you to behave more positively towards him or her. The dolphin may also be advising you that you need to listen more to others and the natural world rather than talking too much. If the dolphin is your power animal or animal totem you may well be a very sensitive person who is a master at communication. You may well be very aware of other people's feelings, even the ones that others would rather keep hidden. Call on the dolphin for magical workings involving communication, kindness, joy, spiritual awareness, sexuality, meditation, enhancing positivity, understanding the feelings of others, intuition, psychic awareness, sea or water magic, compassion, empathy, counselling others, telepathy, playfulness, breathing freshness into your life, releasing tension, unblocking harsh emotional issues and enhancing creativity.

Dove: is a wonderful bird that symbolises love, long life, clear vision, prophecy, spiritual renewal and domestic issues. The Hebrew folk regard the dove as a symbol of deliverance. A pair of doves is a powerful symbol of love and represents wedding bliss. The dove is strongly related to the planet of Venus. It is sacred to Aphrodite, Venus, Lupa, Maia, Rachel, Turan and generally love goddesses. If a dove shows itself to you perhaps now is the time to show your love to as many people as possible. You can do this by saying the right words and doing the right deeds. The dove may also be telling you that you are about to go through a time of prophecy and clear vision so you may get insight into possible future events. A dove showing itself to you can also be an indication that you are about to experience a sense of spiritual renewal and this is after an intense period of self-examination and difficult challenges. The dove may also be advising you that now, more then ever, is the time to enjoy your home and your domestic side. You may need to also nurture yourself with loving care. If the dove is your power animal or animal totem you may well be a very calm person and have the ability to calm others. You may have a strong, loving side to you and you are aware very much of the spiritual side of life, yet you may be very grounded and down-to-earth. Call on the dove for magical workings involving love, longevity, prophecy, spiritual renewal, domestic issues, clear vision, marriage, nurture, keeping grounded, peace, calmness, security in relationships, deepening spiritual faith, comfort, seeking loved ones who have recently passed and fertility.

Dragon: is a mythical creature, a fantastic beast. The dragon is strongly related to the planet of Mars and the element of fire. There are, however, many different kinds of dragons. Cave-dwelling dragons, for example, can symbolise the element of earth. The dragon is sacred to Medea (Dragon Queen), Illuyankas (the Dragon), Ryujin (Dragon King), Godi and Goru. It can be positive or negative. In the eastern traditions, the dragon was seen as a beast who enlightened darkness. In Celtic traditions, however, the dragon was thought to bring chaos, infertility and ruin. In Tao, the dragon symbolises the Yang, the male principle of nature. The auspicious Chinese dragon dates back thousands of years. In folklore, the Emperor Shi Huangdi was said to have been immortalised as a dragon in order to be able to ascend into heaven. The dragon then became a very powerful symbol of imperial power and so it flew on the Chinese flag. If a dragon shows itself to you perhaps you are about to enter a new phase of life. This new phase will be a period of risk-taking, but from this you will make many positive changes. The dragon may also be advising you that now is the time to do meditation and from this you will gain much insight and inspiration. If the dragon is your power animal or animal totem you may well have had many past lives in the east and are drawn to that type of spirituality. You may well be a very open-minded person who is accepting of other people's beliefs, ideas and theories. Call on the dragon for magical workings involving enlightenment, working with the Yang aspect, imperial power, dramatic change, transformation, embracing a new phase of life, taking risks to make way for positive change, meditation, insight, inspiration, spirituality, keeping open-minded, expression, finding the truth of a matter and embracing mystical arts.

Dragonfly: is an insect of carefree life, swiftness, whirlwinds, change, transformation, insight, joy, luck, clairvoyance, magic and mystery. It symbolises the messenger. It is strongly related to the element of air. It is sacred to Kangalogba and Toro. If the dragonfly appears to you then you can probably count on a message of importance coming to you and this will most likely be good news. The dragonfly may also be warning you to be aware of any falsehood, illusions or deceit that may be clouding a situation or relationship. The dragonfly may also symbolise that meditation is needed right now so that you can recharge your psychic energy or powers. The dragonfly showing itself to you can also be an indication that a major change is on the way and that you should enjoy a time of big transformation, perhaps a much-needed one. The dragonfly can also symbolise that you are about to embark on a path of reawakening, one where you will appreciate the magic and mystery of life. If the dragonfly is your power animal or animal totem you may well be a very intense and passionate person who has a love of nature and gardening. However, you may be a very nervous individual and so you will have to learn how to balance this energy, perhaps by doing grounding exercises. Call on the dragonfly for magical workings involving swiftness, dramatic change, finding the truth of a matter, transformation, insight, joy, luck, clairvoyance, sending messages, meditation, psychic power, reawakening energy and expressiveness, passion, working with nature spirits and avoiding falsehood, illusions and deceit.

Eagle: is a bird of opportunity, new beginnings, fearlessness, great spiritual awakenings, divine energy, creativity, inspiration, success, power in battle, clear vision, prosperity and the soaring spirit. It is strongly related to the sun and the element of air. It is sacred to many deities including Jupiter, Zeus, Sumul (Mother of the Eagles), Hirgab (the Father of the Eagles), Tonatiuh (Soaring Eagle) and Agni. The Native Americans considered the eagle a divine spirit and a primary servant of the sun. If an eagle shows up to you perhaps now is the time to take advantage of an opportunity that is being offered. There may also be a new beginning of some sort that will put you in the right direction in life after a period of struggle. The eagle showing itself to you may also be an indication that you are about to experience a closeness with the divine. In other words, there may be a great spiritual awakening. The eagle may also be making you aware that karmic forces are at work in your life right now so now is the time to learn from them. If the eagle is your power animal or animal totem you may well be a very spiritual person who has a very close relationship with the divine. You may well be a born leader who is able to embrace challenges head-on because you know you can get through them. Call on the eagle for magical workings involving opportunities, embracing new beginnings, avoiding fear, great spiritual awakenings, success, good luck, good fortune, power in battle, inspiration, working with divine energy, solar power, enhancing creativity, leadership, challenges, spiritual insights, revelations and avoiding routine and the mundane.

Eel: is a fascinating, snake-like, aquatic creature. The Hebrew folk once found the eel to be a taboo. It is strongly related to the moon and the element of water. It is sacred to Riiki, Te Tuna (Phallus) and Suijin. If the eel shows up to you there may be a period of enhanced sexuality. There may be people around you, both male and female, who are attracted to you, especially sexually. If there has been a question or puzzle that has been bothering you, the eel appearing to you can be an indication that you will soon get to the bottom of it. An eel appearing to you can also be a sign that you are about to go on a spiritual pilgrimage, one that will profoundly open your eyes and senses to who you truly are to the point that it will change you dramatically. This change may be so profound that others will not recognise you. If the eel is your power animal or animal totem you may well be very drawn to the sea and generally the energies of water. You may well be a very sexual person who has considerable depth to your personality that is not readily apparent to others unless they get to know you properly. Call on the eel for magical workings involving solving problems, sexuality, sea magic, spiritual journeys of any kind, attracting people, discovering the secrets of dreams and avoiding difficult and draining situations.

Elephant: is a mammal that symbolises wisdom, ancient power, greatness, loyalty, family, royalty, devotion, strength, heightened sexuality, joy, memory and life span. It is strongly related to the moon. It is sacred to the deities Devata Bandara, Gajana, Ganesha, Ganapati, Lakshmi, Mahaganapati, Parvati, Airavata, Dadimunda and Tarri-Pennu. The elephant is abundant in mythology and folklore and the creature is held sacred to Buddhists. If the elephant shows itself to you perhaps now is the time to help others who are less fortunate than yourself, such as the elderly or the young. The elephant may also be reminding you that you should never let anyone or anything get in the way of any goals that are of great importance to your life and spiritual development. The elephant may also be a sign that you should always remain loyal to those closest to you. Whatever challenges are put in your way, the elephant may be telling you that you have the determination and persistence to overcome them. If the elephant is your power animal or animal totem you may well be a person who has an insatiable hunger for knowledge, someone who always seeks to understand things on a much deeper level. You may well be a very determined individual who is quite able to achieve your goals. Call on the elephant for magical workings involving money, prosperity, success, good luck, good fortune, abundance, loyalty, enhancing wisdom, family, devotion, strength, enhancing sexuality, joy, memory issues, helping those who are less fortunate than yourself, determination, persistence, avoiding loneliness, overcoming obstacles, vitality, confidence, leadership and understanding the cycle of life and death.

Falcon: is a bird that is strongly related to the sun and the element of air. Calling upon falcons is said to be good for omens. The falcon is sacred to many deities including Circe (She-Falcon), Freya, Khonsu, Mentu, Sopedu and Yah. If the falcon shows itself to you there may be a decision that you have to make. But before you do so you must step back from it and look at it very closely from a broader perspective. The falcon coming to you can also symbolise that an opportunity is heading your way but you must show patience and trust your instinct as to when the time is right to act on it. The falcon showing itself to you can also be a sign that now is the time to really listen to the natural rhythms and cycles of your body and its surroundings. They may be able to teach you a lot. If the falcon is your power animal or animal totem you may well be a very independent person who needs much time alone. You may well be a very intense individual who is able to focus on complex tasks without becoming distracted. Call on the falcon for magical workings involving healing, health, seeking omens, protection, making wise decisions, opportunities, patience, independence, solitude, enhancing concentration, guidance, precision and speeding up matters.

Fox: is a very interesting mammal that I have always adored. It symbolises prophecy, cunning, twilight, intuition, intelligence, freedom of expression and female magic. It is strongly related to the planet of Mercury and the element of fire. The fox is sacred to corn spirits and the deity Demeter. If the fox shows itself to you perhaps now is the time to be very careful around someone who is trying to trick you in some way. You must trust your intuition around this person. The fox may also be telling you that you are much better off in your life right now to blend into the background rather than take an active role in leadership. From that position, you can exert your influence in a positive way. The fox may also be advising you to trust your senses right now. They may be able to tell you much about your life and surroundings. If the fox is your power animal or animal totem you may well be a creature of the night. You may well be an individual who gets the most work done at night or twilight while others sleep. Call on the fox for magical workings involving prophecy, enhancing intuition, female magic, intelligence, freedom of expression, blending into the background, enhancing wisdom and diplomacy.

Frog: is an amphibian that I have always adored. The significance of the frog is change, transformation, metamorphosis, rebirth, teeming life and emotions. It is strongly related to the moon and the element of water. It is sacred to the deities Heqet (Egyptian frog-headed goddess), Ah Hayaob (Great Frog), Herst and Nun. The ancient Egyptians associated the frog with resurrection as did the Christians. The heart of a dove and the head of a frog, dried, powdered and then sprinkled on the breast of a sleeping woman was once believed to make her confess any wrongdoings. However, the powder had to be removed before she woke to stop delirium. To silence dogs, frogs fed to them in their meat were said to be effective charms. If a frog is seen during the day, rain will surely come soon. If a frog shows up to you perhaps now is the time to release any emotions that may be burdening you. You can do this by crying as much as you need to or by having a purification bath or shower. Singing (frogs sing as well) is another effective way to release any emotional baggage. The frog showing itself to you can also indicate that you are about to enter a phase of plenty and abundance, a time where you will have your needs. The frog can also be telling you that a slow and steady phase of change and transformation is on the cards, a time of positive movement from an old way of life and into a new one. If the frog is your power animal or animal totem you may well be a very sensitive soul who is able to express your emotions with ease. Your singing voice and how you word things may well arouse deep emotions in people but in a very soothing way. Call on the frog for magical workings involving money, prosperity, abundance, fertility, transformation, dramatic change, emotional issues, purification, cleansing, moving on in life, adaptability and rain magic.

Goat: is a mammal that has long been associated with sex magic and virility. It is strongly related to the element of earth. It is also associated with the zodiac sign of Capricorn. The goat is sacred to many deities including Artemis, Athena, Dionysus, Holda, Bacchus, Olwen, Pan and Silvanus. The Orphic cup contained honey and goat's milk and was drank at dawn. Feta cheese can be utilised in magic that calls upon the goat's powers. If the goat shows up to you perhaps now is the time to keep moving forward with a goal you have been working on no matter what. Symbolically, you will always land on your feet if you slip and you will be able to overcome any obstacles. If you are feeling vulnerable in your life right now, the goat may be telling you to seek the support and guidance that you need. The goat showing to you can also be an indication that now is the time to spend time outdoors amongst the beauty and powers of nature. Symbolically, the goat showing itself can also be a sign that you should stop butting your head against a wall with people – if they are not listening or not accessible don't waste your time and energy. If the goat is your power animal or animal totem you could well be a very determined person who is able to achieve your goals. You may well be a very sexual person who is very creative in your sex life. Call on the goat for magical workings involving success, good fortune, good luck, projects, sex magic, virility, earth power, moving forward in life, determination, overcoming obstacles and seeking support and guidance.

Griffin: or gryphon, is a mythical creature, a fantastic beast. It is the legendary creature that has the body, tail and back legs of a lion and the head and wings of an eagle. It is sacred to Nemesis and sometimes has an eagle's talons as its front feet. Since the lion was traditionally known as the king of the jungle and the eagle was considered king of the birds, the griffin has been considered an especially magical, mystical, powerful and majestic creature. If the griffin makes an appearance to you there may be some sort of dramatic and positive change coming your way. However, you should be very careful not to disregard the advice of other people with regards to this change. The griffin can also indicate that you will have the strength, power and fortitude to get through whatever challenges that come your way. The griffin showing itself to you can also indicate that a promotion may come your way and this will make your popularity grow. If the griffin is your power animal or animal totem you may well be a very mystical and powerful individual who is admired by your social peers. You may well be a very majestic person who has the strength to overcome whatever challenges are put in your way. Call on the griffin for magical workings involving wisdom, alertness to danger, kingship, enhancing power, dramatic change, transformation, strength, courage, fortitude, promotion, popularity, admiration and overcoming challenges.

Hare: is a mammal that has long been associated with Witchcraft in the Celtic traditions. It was believed in the persecution times of Witches that hares were demon-helpers of Witches or Witches in disguise that should be shot with a silver bullet. The hare is strongly associated with the moon. Hares are sacred to many goddesses of fertility. One of the most famous is Eostar or Ostara. The animal is the origin of the Easter Bunny that many have known and loved throughout the ages. The hare was thought to be a taboo in ancient Britain and hunting hares was suspended on May Eve. If you have been working on a project, the hare showing itself to you may be urging you to move faster with it yet remain flexible. The hare showing itself to you can also be a warning to be careful of anyone who may be trying to trick you or decieve you. The hare appearing to you can also indicate that you should pay close attention to lunar energies and try to work your life around their cycles more efficiently. The hare can also be a sign that there will be some unexpected and rapid changes coming your way in the next few days or weeks. If the hare is your power animal or animal totem you may well be quite a sensitive and fertile person who has quite a talent for artistic ventures. You may well become very nervous around others and so you much prefer your own company. Call on the hare for magical workings involving fertility, lunar power, dramatic change, transformation, getting things to move ahead quickly, intellect, opportunities, projects and female mysteries.

Hedgehog: is a mammal that I have always adored. It was once believed that pixies took the form of these wonderful creatures. If the hedgehog shows itself to you perhaps now is the time to really enjoy life no matter what is going on. The hedgehog appearing to you can also be an indication that you are entering a very creative period of life, one in which you can perhaps express your artistic side. The hedgehog can also be a sign that you should retreat from the mundane activities of life for at least a day or two so that you can refresh and rejuvenate your mind, body and soul. The hedgehog appearing to you can also indicate that you should honour your natural curiosity. If the hedgehog is your power animal or animal totem you may well be a very gentle, wise and nurturing person who people often come to for advice or help. You may well be a very unique person who does not yet understand how special you are, someone who can often feel like an outcast, but once you accept your individuality you can become a very powerful presence. Call on the hedgehog for magical workings involving enhancing creativity, artistic talent, breaking routine, exploration, enhancing wisdom, nurture, weather magic, garden magic, enhancing your sensitive side and enhancing your gentle side.

Horse: is a mammal that symbolises power, strength, stamina, devotion, loyalty, sexuality, endurance, spirituality, love and sacred kingship. The creature is strongly related to the moon and the element of fire. One of the reasons the horse is related to the element of fire is because the hooves of the horse often strike sparks. The horseshoe is a very powerful symbol of good luck and healing. The horse is sacred to many deities including Poseidon, Neptune, Demeter, Ceres, Rhiannon, Epona, Belenos, Minerva and Pegasus. If the horse shows itself to you there may be a very unexpected adventure coming your way, one in which you will have to move with speed. If you have been feeling constricted in some way the horse appearing to you may be urging you to free yourself, both emotionally and physically. The horse may be telling you that you are much stronger and more powerful than what you think. The horse showing itself to you can also be a sign that you need to work very closely with family members, friends or the community right now in order for things to be bountiful. If the horse is your power animal or animal totem you may well be a very spiritual person who appreciates personal freedom, someone who will not let anyone get in the way of that. You may well be a natural leader who brings forth confidence in anyone you meet. Call on the horse for magical workings involving love, protection (the white horse is especially good for protection), fertility, strength, devotion, loyalty, sexuality, leadership, stamina, enhancing spirituality, adventures, romance, family, friendship, kingship, enhancing creativity, moving things ahead quickly, freedom, confidence, travel and new territories.

Jackal: is a mammal that is strongly related to the planet of Mercury. It is sacred to the deities Wepwawet, Duamutef, Anubis (Egyptian jackal-headed god) and Shmashana-Kali. If the jackal shows itself to you then you may have been considering some sort of travel – whether physically, mentally or spiritually – and in any case you should be aware that you will be well protected and guided. The jackal showing itself to you may also be an indication that you have had past lives in Egypt and may well be drawn to Egyptology. The jackal appearing to you can also be a sign that you should be willing to embrace any opportunities that come your way in the next few days. The jackal can also indicate that you will be aware of any danger that comes your way and you will have the power to avoid it. If the jackal is your power animal or animal totem you may well be a very cleaver and intelligent person who is involved with death and the dying, someone who can help souls pass into the spirit world with ease. You may well be a very loyal person who commits to those you have bonded with. Call on the jackal for magical workings involving protection, Egyptian magic, travel of any kind, adventures, guidance, opportunities, enhancing intelligence, coping with death and cooperation with family or friends.

Kingfisher: is a bird that is strongly related to the element of air. It is sacred to the deities Ceyx and Alcyone. It is said that the bird has the magical ability to subdue or quieten storms. The dried body of a kingfisher was once an amulet against the ill effects of lightning. If the kingfisher shows itself to you perhaps now is the time to really express yourself but you must do this as clearly and concisely as possible. The kingfisher showing itself to you can also be a sign that you are about to enter a period of abundance and prosperity and so you should welcome and receive it with gratitude. If the kingfisher is your power animal or animal totem you may well be a very verbal person who is excellent at communication. You may well be a person who is willing to make sacrifices for the people who you greatly value. Call on the kingfisher for magical workings involving communication, expressing yourself, abundance, money, prosperity, new projects, peace, meditation, stillness, joy, success, good luck, good fortune and opportunities.

Ladybird: is an insect that is strongly related to the element of fire. If the ladybird shows itself to you perhaps there is something in your life that you thought was lost that will soon return to you. The ladybird appearing to you can also represent that you may need to spend a certain amount of time each day to reflect, relax and meditate in order to gather your thoughts. The ladybird appearing to you can also indicate that you are about to enter a period where you will be shielded and protected from irritations, bad thoughts and ill behaviour of others. If a ladybird falls on you make it your mission to make a cherished wish and it is said that the wish will be granted. If the ladybird is your power animal or animal totem you may well be a very delicate, passionate and family-orientated person who has traditional values and morals. Call on the ladybird for magical workings involving money, prosperity, protection, recovery of things lost, reflection, relaxation, meditation, cherished wishes, passion, family, integrity, values, morals, increasing spiritual development, faith, joy, happiness and releasing fears or anxieties. You can also call on the ladybird when you want to keep pests to a minimum in your garden.

Lion: is a mammal that symbolises courage, royalty, protection, strength, personal power and dignity. It is strongly related to the sun and the element of fire. It is sacred to many deities including Artemis (A Lion Unto Women), Hathor, Cybele, Helios, Hercules, Inanna, Ishtar, Khnemu (Governor of Lions), Sekhmet, Tefnut and Vishnu. The eyes of the lion were once believed to confer invisibility. In ancient Egypt, beds were decorated with lions to guard against hostility while people slept. They are known as the king of the jungle and are associated with the zodiac sign of Leo. If the lion shows itself to you perhaps now is the time to hold your head up high and keep your dignity in the face of any problems. The lion may also be an indication that you are much stronger than what you think and you will need to call upon your own inner emotional strength to get through uncomfortable situations that life may soon throw at you. If you have been facing a very tough decision lately, the lion showing itself to you may be telling you to follow your heart rather than what you think should be done. If the lion is your power animal or animal totem you may well be a very powerful person with enormous reserves of dignity and emotional strength. You may well be a natural leader with enormous compassion for other people. Call on the lion for magical workings involving money, prosperity, success, good luck, good fortune, protection, courage, strength, dignity, kingship, increasing personal power, leadership, self-confidence, dealing with difficult situations, integrity, authority and group activities.

Lizard: is a reptile that symbolises agility, dreams, sensitivity, intuition and stillness. It is strongly related to the element of fire. It is sacred to Abas, Atum and Saurus. There is a night goddess called Evaki who stole the sleep away from the eyes of lizards and gave it to all living creatures. If the lizard shows itself to you perhaps now is the time to take a particularly close attention to your dreams. You can do this by meditating on their meanings and keeping a dream journal. They will reveal deep secrets about your life and spiritual direction. The lizard showing itself to you can also be a sign that you need to prepare for a situation that will require stillness and calm before you can make a move. When this move comes, you will do it quickly and efficiently. The lizard showing itself to you can also be an indication that you are very sensitive to your surroundings right now and so you should be very careful who you place yourself with and the places in which you dwell. The lizard showing itself to you can also be telling you to listen to your own intuition instead of what other people say. If the lizard is your power animal or animal totem you may well be a very relaxed person with an acute awareness of your surroundings. You may well be a very dreamy and visionary person with a gift for clairvoyance. Call on the lizard for magical workings involving dream work, agility, enhancing intuition, clairvoyance, stillness, calmness, bringing relaxation, visions, overcoming emotional or physical hardships, releasing the past, vitality and overcoming sadness and depression. There are many different types of lizards and each has their own uses in magical workings. The iguana, for example, can be called upon for healing (especially good for healing skin problems) and the chameleon, which is sacred to the African god Leza, can be called upon when you want to express your emotions.

Lobster: is a large marine crustacean creature that is strongly related to the planet of Neptune and the element of water. I have always been fascinated by these aquatic creatures. If the lobster appears to you this may be a time in your life where you are experiencing a powerful time of change and transformation. Each phase of this process may well prove that you are trying out different expressions of who you are. The lobster showing itself to you can also be an indication that patience is key right now in your life for the things that you want. It may be that you have to wait for your desires rather than actively pursue them. The lobster appearing to you may also be an indication that you may well find yourself looking through things that you have had stored away for some time and you will most likely find some very useful things. If the lobster is your power animal or animal totem you may well find that you prefer to work on an evening after sundown and that this is the time when you get most of your work done. You may well be a person with an amazing ability to concentrate and as you get older you will probably acquire great wisdom. Call on the lobster for magical workings involving enhancing wisdom, dramatic change, transformation, expressing your inner self, patience, enhancing concentration, letting go of the past and encouraging privacy and solitude.

Mole: is a mammal that is strongly related to the element of earth. My late cat Molie, a beautiful creature with only one eye, was named after the mole because she reminded me and my partner of this creature. We loved her so dearly and she still often visits me in spirit. The mole has strong connections with our own planet and earth power. It was said that of all animals the mole is the most admired creature among magicians. If the mole appears to you then you may be entering a period in which you will have to trust in what you feel rather than what you see or hear. The mole may also be advising you that your sense of touch is important right now. You may need to seek to physically touch those closest to you. This may involve hugging your partner or close friend or giving appropriate physical gestures. The mole appearing to you can also be an indication that you are entering a period of self-examination. This may involve you digging up deep secrets about yourself and inner emotions. From this, you will come to understand your deep spiritual self. The mole can also be an indication that you will find that you get psychic impressions whenever you physically touch others and you should always trust them. The mole appearing to you can also be an indication that you must learn how to properly ground yourself in order to keep up with your vitality and good health. If the mole is your power animal or animal totem you may well be a very grounded and earthy person who prefers solitude. You may well be a very intuitive person who has a very healing touch. Call on the mole for magical workings involving health, healing, vitality, earth power, nurture, enhancing the power of the sense of touch, self-examination, discovering inner secrets, enhancing your deep spiritual self, psychic power, grounding, seeking solitude and enhancing intuition.

Monkey: is a mammal and is a symbol of curiosity, cleverness, creativity, communication and innovation. It is strongly related to the planet of Mercury. It is sacred to Sugriva, Hanuman, Sun Hou-Shi and Sun Wu Kong. If the monkey shows itself to you perhaps acceptance is in order. In other words, you should accept the things in your life exactly how they are. Once you have done this, you will be able to find creative ideas and solutions for any problems that you have and utilise them. The monkey may also be advising you that communication is very important in your life right now and you should express yourself with the right words, actions and body language. The monkey showing itself to you can also be an indication that nature spirits are in close communication with you and so you should seek their help for any problems that you may have. If the monkey is your power animal or animal totem you may well be a very intellectual person who is excellent at communication. You may well be a clever and adaptable person who is excellent at solving problems. Call on the monkey for magical workings involving success, good fortune, good luck, enhancing creativity, communication, intellect, solving problems, innovation, expression, nature spirits, acceptance, finding solutions, adaptability, ancient wisdom and lifting depression or sadness.

Mouse: The mouse is a mammal and is sometimes associated with the faery folk and corn spirits. It is strongly related to the element of earth. In the ancient temples of Apollo, white mice were kept as charms against the plague and rats. If a mouse shows itself to you it may be an indication that you need to pay very close attention to everything that is going on in your life. You can then get rid of anything that no longer serves you well. However, be careful not to get rid of things that are important. You need to be vigilant so as to avoid anything that will cause significant loss. The mouse showing itself to you can also indicate that you may be missing something or looking for something and the answer or solution is obvious or right in front of you. The mouse appearing to you can also mean that you need to stop only focusing on one or two activities as you may miss great opportunities. If the mouse is your power animal or animal totem you may well be a very organised person who pays very close attention to detail. However, you may need to be careful with this as you may often lose track of the bigger picture. Call on the mouse for magical workings involving fertility, faery magic, vigilance, purification, organisation and keeping focused in life.

Octopus: is a fascinating, eight-limbed mollusc marine animal that many of us find frightening. It symbolises camouflage, original thinking, eccentric behaviour, sexual peak and mental agility. Since it is an aquatic creature, it is strongly related to the planet of Neptune and the element of water. If the octopus shows itself to you perhaps soon you will find that your clairvoyant skills will increase. You may well become very sensitive to the energies around you. If you have been thinking about making your body more flexible, the octopus making an appearance to you may well be a sign that you should think about doing yoga. The octopus may also indicate that you may want to think about exploring the possibility of helping those who are about to make their journey into the spirit world. The octopus may also be a sign that mental agility is needed right now to help you get through whatever goals or desires you are seeking. If the octopus is your power animal or animal totem you may well be a very flexible person who is agile in mind, body and soul. You may well be a person who works with death and the dying. Call on the octopus for magical workings involving health, healing, camouflage, enhancing originality, sexuality, mental agility, clairvoyance, enhancing sensitivity, helping the dying, death rites, enhancing flexibility, regeneration and recovery of things.

Owl: is a bird that has long been associated with Witchcraft and magic. It symbolises dreams, messages, wisdom, prophecy and the collective unconscious. It is strongly related to the moon and the element of air. It is sacred to the deities Hecate, Artemis, Athena, Persephone, Tlazelteotl, Minerva, Medusa and Lilith. The owl was once seen as the dreaded messenger of death. The ancient Romans called the owl a funeral bird and believed that it was an omen of death. The Christians once associated owls with demonic possession. Witches and owls were once both known as hags by the Anglo-Saxons. If an owl appears to you perhaps there is a need in your life for meditation in darkness to see what will be revealed to you. The owl may also be an indication that you need to pay very close attention to your environment so that you can look for any signs and omens that may reveal answers to any question that you may have in your life. The owl showing itself to you can also indicate that you are about to enter a period of wisdom and prophecy and during this period you may well become aware of things before they happen. The owl appearing to you can also be an indication that you are about to embark on a very creative cycle, one in which your best work will be done in the evenings. If the owl is your power animal or animal totem you may well be a highly intuitive and wise person who can see the truth behind any falsehood. You may well be someone who has a very close connection with the spirit world. Call on the owl for magical workings involving success, good fortune, good luck, dream work, messages, prophecy, enhancing wisdom, meditation, seeking the truth of a matter, creativity, enhancing spirituality, confidence, overcoming challenges, dealing with death, death rites, clairvoyance and loyalty. The owl is my power animal.

Peacock: is a bird of love and inner wisdom. It is strongly related to the element of air. It is sacred to Hera, Juno, Isis and Mahamayuri (Great Daughter of the Peacock). The tail of the peacock spread out can symbolise the stars of the heavens. The feathers of peacocks are excellent in love spells. If the peacock makes an appearance to you there may well be a great vision coming to you that will affect your life and its direction immensely. If you have been worried or are fearing something, the peacock may also be an indication that you are worrying unnecessarily because you are well protected. The peacock showing itself to you can also be a sign that some sort of risk is necessary to make way for positive change and new opportunities. The peacock may be telling you to speak your truths instead of holding yourself back. If the peacock is your power animal or animal totem you may well be a person with enormous reserves of dignity and personal integrity. You may well be a showy or flashy person who is very loving and has much inner wisdom. Call on the peacock for magical workings involving love, success, good luck, good fortune, protection, star magic, visions, taking risks, making decisions, self-esteem, self-confidence, seeking the truth of a matter, enhancing inner wisdom and enhancing personal integrity or dignity.

Phoenix: is a mythical creature, a fantastic beast, the bird that was reborn or regenerated from its own ashes. The red phoenix has strong associations with longevity. It is sacred to the Chinese goddess of longevity Hsi Wang Mu. The Chinese believe it to be a masculine symbol. In rituals, the Egyptians painted the wings of an eagle to represent the phoenix. If the phoenix shows itself to you perhaps now is the time to let go of the past so that you can make positive plans for the future. The phoenix can indicate that you are about to experience a dramatic "rebirth" of a new you. This may be so much so that you will hardly recognise the person you once were. The phoenix can be a very positive sign if it shows itself to you. It can indicate that any past negativity will be gone and you can soon embrace a bright and positive future, one in which you will have so much more clarity. The phoenix appearing to you can also indicate that you will soon find better and more positive ways of communicating with others. If the phoenix is your power animal or animal totem you may well be a very positive person who is able to easily communicate with other people. You may well be a very optimistic person who understands the natural cycles of life. Call on the phoenix for magical workings involving transformation, dramatic change, communication, enhancing positivity, understanding the natural cycles of life, longevity, letting go of the past and clarity.

Praying Mantis: is an insect that is strongly related to the element of fire. It is sacred to I Kaggen. If the praying mantis shows itself to you it may be a sign that now is the time to listen to your instincts or intuition as to whether it feels right to move forward with something or to retreat from it. The praying mantis can also indicate that prayer and meditation are needed right now and this would be most beneficial outside amongst the beauty and powers of the natural world. As a good fighter, the praying mantis showing itself to you can also indicate that you may well benefit from the discipline of some sort of martial-art, such as Kung Fu. The praying mantis appearing to you can also be an indication that you should focus more on the things that are working in your life rather than wasting time and energy on those that are not working. If the praying mantis is your power animal or animal totem you may well be a very balanced and centred person who is very tuned into your instincts. You may well be a very focused individual who enjoys the power of prayer and meditation. Call on the praying mantis for magical workings involving meditation, enhancing intuition or instincts, prayers, discipline and balancing and centring the mind.

Rabbit: is a mammal that symbolises alertness, nervousness, fertility, vigilance and creativity. It is strongly related to the moon. It is sacred to Inaba, Kaltesh, Mexith, Wenet and Master Rabbit. It is said that rabbits are very sensitive to the evil eye. They are also often associated with faeries. The movements of rabbits were believed to be excellent for divination. If a rabbit shows itself you may well be about to embark on a very creative period of your life so you should embrace and take advantage of any opportunities that come your way. These opportunities may come to you very unexpectedly so be prepared. The rabbit showing itself to you can also be a warning that vigilance is important right now. If, over the next few days, you find yourself in threatening situations, leave and seek safety. The rabbit showing itself to you can also be a sign that a period of stillness and peace is coming your way but this will be followed by a sudden surge of intense activity and movement. The rabbit showing itself can also be an indication that there is a need to show your love freely and readily right now to your nearest and dearest. If the rabbit is your power animal or animal totem you may well be a very loving and intellectual person who can use your common sense very well. You may well be a very sensitive person who can get yourself out of uncomfortable and unpleasant situations with great ease. Call on the rabbit for magical workings involving love, fertility, creativity, vigilance, faery magic, seeking opportunities, enhancing intellect, enhancing common sense, seeking stillness and peace, avoiding threatening or unpleasant situations, making progress with projects and vitality.

Ram: is a mammal that is known as the bighorn sheep. It is a Celtic totem creature with strong associations with the zodiac sign of Aries. It is strongly related to the planet of Mars. It is sacred to many deities including Zeus, Jupiter, Angi, Osiris and Poseidon. If the ram makes an appearance to you perhaps now is the time to move forward with a creative project that you have been considering. This may involve intellectual, educational or career interests and it is a good idea to make a plan so that you can put it into action and move forward in life. The ram showing itself to you can also indicate that there is an imbalance in your life and you may need to work out exactly what this is so that you can put it right. The ram showing itself to you can also be a sign that the timing is right for new challenges and you will experience a willingness to charge ahead with them with ease, grace and agility. The ram showing itself to you can also mean that you are about to embark on some sort of spiritual initiation that will awaken a different sense of who you truly are. If the ram is your power animal or animal totem you may well be a very confident person who does not question your ability to climb high in life and achieve your goals. You may well be a detached and somewhat unemotional person who keeps things to yourself. Call on the ram for magical workings involving success, good fortune, good luck, taking risks, determination, assertiveness, overcoming obstacles, seeking new challenges, initiation, career, strength, virility and vitality.

Rat: is a mammal that symbolises caution, impending wealth, plenty and abundance. If the rat appears to you it could be that a project or investment is about to pay off in a way that you could never have imagined despite any fears or insecurities. The rat showing itself to you can also be a sign that you will always have what you need so do not worry unnecessarily. The rat making an appearance to you can also indicate that you may need to be cautious so that you can anticipate the things that lie ahead of you. If you have been meaning to clean out something, the rat may be encouraging you to do so and you can make good use of the things you find and throw out or recycle the things that no longer serve you. If the rat is your power animal or animal totem you may well be a very adaptable person who can live on whatever is available to you. You may well be a very clever and cunning person who enjoys the feeling of success from whatever you have achieved. Call on the rat for magical workings involving money, prosperity, abundance, success, good luck, good fortune, friendship, fertility, projects and adaptability.

Raven: is a bird of prophecy. It is strongly related to the planet of Saturn and the element of air. It is sacred to many deities including Apollo, Athena, Freya, Odin, Saturn, Cronos and Rhiannon. It symbolises shape-shifting, changes in consciousness and Shamanic power. It is considered to be a teacher and a trickster to the Native Americans. If the raven shows itself to you it could be an indication that magic is in the air and something very special is about to happen to you. The raven may also be telling you that close attention to dreams or visions is of great importance to you right now as they are very prophetic. The raven can also be a sign that you are slowly emerging into a more confident, powerful and spiritually-based person and you will continuously grow, especially if you let go of past events and the old you. The raven showing itself to you can also be an indication that you should be very clear in any aspect of your life what exactly your intentions are so that they can manifest in the way that you want. If the raven is your power animal or animal totem you may well be a very spiritual person who prefers your own company. You may well be a great teacher and a spiritual healer with a strong presence who is able to communicate with animals with great ease. Call on the raven for magical workings involving healing (especially spiritual healing), health, coping with death, death rites, success, good fortune, good luck, Shamanic power, dream work, visions, prophecy, confidence, seeking mystical power, enhancing spirituality, manifestation, teaching, animal magic, solitude and reclaiming innocence and joy after a painful childhood. The raven is my animal totem.

Robin: is a bird that symbolises aggression, joy, new growth, challenges and laughter. It is strongly related to the planet of Mars and the element of air. It is sacred to the Celtic god Belin. If a robin shows itself to you perhaps now is the time to let go of the past and to make positive plans for the future. In other words, sow the seeds for future success. The robin appearing to you can also indicate that you need to let go of any drama so that you can allow laughter and joy into your life instead. The robin showing itself to you can be a sign that you should allow new growth in many areas of your life. The robin can also indicate that your spiritual path will have challenges, but you will make slow and steady progress and eventually achieve what it is you are looking for. A robin appearing to you is also a good time to make a wish and if you believe in yourself and the spiritual powers of nature it may well manifest. If the robin is your power animal or animal totem you may well be a very positive and happy person who enjoys singing or whistling. You may well be a very spiritual person who continues to grow and evolve as time goes by. Call on the robin for magical workings involving success, good fortune, good luck, assertiveness, letting go of the past, new growth, happiness, spiritual awakening, confidence, challenges, projects, bringing joy, wishes and lifting sadness and depression.

Salmon: is a type of fish that was very sacred to the ancient druids and other Pagan folk. Since it is an aquatic creature, it is strongly related to the moon and the element of water. It is sacred to Anaulikutsaix, Tsa'qamae and Fintan. The salmon is famous for the way it returns to its place of birth to spawn and then die. It faces many challenges along the way as it jumps and battles upstream with great determination. This is all symbolic to the cycles of life. If the salmon shows up to you perhaps now is the time to keep on keeping on with any goal that you have in mind despite any challenges or discouragement. The salmon showing itself to you can also indicate that there may be some sort of loss in your life. Although this may cause sadness, remember that this will give you a chance to start a new beginning. The salmon can also be a sign that it is important to trust your intuition at this time in your life, especially around people who may have hidden agendas. The salmon can also be a warning that some sort of sacrifice is necessary in your life right now. This will allow you to renew and refresh yourself as you experience a "rebirth" of yourself. If the salmon is your power animal or animal totem you may well be a very wise person who others turn to for help or counselling. You may well be a very determined person who always knows how to get things done. Call on the salmon for magical workings involving money, prosperity, abundance, success, good fortune, good luck, wisdom, challenges, determination, enhancing knowledge, new beginnings, enhancing intuition, renewal, finding a sense of purpose in life, understanding life lessons, courage, family ties, goals, projects and spiritual journeys.

Scorpion: is a predatory arachnid that has strong associations with the zodiac sign of Scorpio. It is a powerful creature of folklore that is strongly related to the planet of Pluto and the element of fire. It is sacred to Ishara, Scorpion Man, Seth, Selket and Ahriman. If the scorpion shows itself to you perhaps a close friend or family member will soon ask you to keep a secret. The scorpion showing itself to you can also indicate that your sex life will improve with great intensity and passion. The scorpion can also be a sign that you will have to learn how to contain and control your temper in order for any changes to fully come to fruition and run smoothly. The scorpion appearing to you can also be an indication that you are about to go through an intense period of transformation, one in which you will release a lot of negative habits and toxic people. If the scorpion is your power animal or animal totem you may well be a very powerful and influential person who has considerable strength of character. You may well be a very intense and solitary person who will "sting" others with your words if they cross you. Call on the scorpion for magical workings involving secrets, enhancing sexuality, dramatic change, transformation, releasing negative habits, dealing with death, death rites, releasing toxic people, enhancing power, enhancing strength of character, solitude and containing and controlling temper.

Sea Horse: is a very fascinating marine creature that symbolises healing and confidence. The male sea horse is equipped with a pouch into which the female sea horse deposits as many as a thousand and a half eggs. The male then carries the eggs for some time and then releases the young. So effectively the male is the one who becomes pregnant. Since it is a marine creature, the sea horse is strongly related to the planet of Neptune and the element of water. If a sea horse shows itself to you it could be an indication that you may have to sacrifice your needs so that you can help others or some sort of cause. The sea horse showing itself to you can also be a sign that you should try swapping gender roles by doing things that you associate with the opposite sex. If the sea horse is your power animal or animal totem you may well be a very gracious and polite person who can easily blend into the background should you feel the need. You may well be a person who harbours gentle strength, serenity and balance. Call on the sea horse for magical workings involving health, healing, confidence, invisibility, seeking balance, gentle strength, serenity, stability, self-esteem and understanding the male and female balance. Calling upon the sea horse during pregnancy can help the man to become more intimately involved.

Sea Serpent: is a fantastical, mythical, marine creature that resembles an enormous snake. It is the legendary sea monster that is strongly related to the moon and the element of water. It is sacred to various sea deities. Throughout the years there have been many people who have claimed to see sightings of sea monsters and it has been suggested by cryptozoologists that the sea serpents are relict plesiosaurs or other Mesozoic marine reptiles. Such an idea is often associated with lake monsters such as the Loch Ness Monster. The sea serpent making an appearance to you can indicate emotional and spiritual transformation. It can represent your need to discover your deep spiritual and emotional self. It can be an indication that meditation and other spiritual practices are needed for you to discover this deep spiritual side to yourself. If the sea serpent is captured or otherwise in captivity perhaps you are keeping your emotions contained and this may be harmful to your spiritual well-being over time. It may represent that you need to open up about your feelings and emotions to avoid them building up too much inside you. If you keep your emotions contained for too long you may erupt into a burst of anger. If a sea serpent with a head at each end of its body makes an appearance to you then it can indicate that you might soon become emotionally torn between two things that are very important to you. If the sea serpent is your power animal or animal totem you may well be a very spiritual and emotional person who is highly gifted psychically. You may well be a person who enjoys meditating by the sea, especially on a full moon night. Call on the sea serpent for magical workings involving sea magic, lunar power, emotional or spiritual transformation, meditation, enhancing spirituality or emotions, dramatic change and psychic power.

Shark: is another fascinating sea creature that I have always loved to study. Since it is generally a volatile creature it is strongly related to the element of fire. It symbolises adaptability, survival, sensitivity, dignity and self-respect. If a shark shows itself to you perhaps you are very sensitive to your environments and situations right now and so you should be very careful about the places in which you surround yourself. The shark showing itself to you can also indicate that you are very protected and you will have the ability to ward off any negativity that comes your way. The shark making an appearance to you can also indicate that you should be careful what you eat so as to maintain your physical and emotional balance. The shark can also be a sign that self-respect and dignity are very important right now, something you may need to remember no matter who or what comes your way. If the shark is your power animal or animal totem you may well be a very active person who has difficulty resting or staying still. You may well be a very authoritative person with enormous reserves of self-respect and discipline who needs long periods of time to rest in order to avoid anxiety and irritation. Call on the shark for magical workings involving success, good fortune, good luck, protection, adaptability, physical and emotional balance, self-respect, self-esteem, confidence, enhancing dignity, authority, discipline, motivation, clarity and getting things to run smoothly.

Snake: is a reptile that represents the beast of the fire from within the earth. There are many different types of snakes but generally speaking they are strongly related to the moon and the element of fire. They symbolise fertility, sexuality, renewal, change, transformation, lunar mysteries, temptation, intuition, power, healing and spirituality. Two snakes, especially when they are entwined, relate to the planet of Mercury and symbolise the power of opposites, such as good and evil or light and dark. The snake is sacred to many deities including Mercury, Hermes, Brigit, Athena, Demeter, Hades, Pluto, Hercules, Persephone, Proserpina, Tlazelteotl, Medusa, Hathor, Isis and Tefnut. The Christians associate the serpent with the Devil. If the snake shows itself you may well be about to experience a time of intense and dramatic change and transformation in your life. This may feel so strong that you may feel as though you don't recognise your old self as your new self emerges. The snake appearing to you can also be a sign that some sort of intense and unexpected healing is coming your way and this could come from something you did not expect. The snake making an appearance to you can also indicate that you are about to experience a sudden surge of renewed energy, an energy that will dramatically open you up to new channels of awareness. The snake appearing to you can also indicate that a long-standing issue will finally be resolved and from this you will see things in a new light. If the snake is your power animal or animal totem you may well be a very sensitive person who is a natural healer. You may well be a very sexual and wise person who appreciates ancient, magical practices. Call on the snake for magical workings involving healing, health, fertility, sexuality, renewal, transformation, dramatic change, enhancing spirituality, lunar power, enhancing intuition, opening up to new channels of awareness, resolving long-standing issues, enhancing sensitivity, enhancing wisdom, shedding old attachments, moving on in life, vitality and enhancing power. The rattlesnake is especially good when called upon for healing.

Sphinx: is a composite, fantastical, mythical beast with the head of a human, a cat, a falcon or sheep and the body of a lion with the wings of an eagle. In Greek mythology, the sphinx had the head of woman, the haunches of a lion and the wings of an eagle. The sphinx is strongly related to the sun and is sacred to Ashtaroth, Athena, Osiris, Horus and Astarte. If the sphinx makes an appearance to you then your spiritual wisdom may well be about to increase dramatically. This can involve the people or spirits who support and watch over you. The sphinx showing itself to you can also indicate that the rebellious side to you will become very strong – the part of you that wishes to resist or rise up against authority, tradition, the government or anyone else you feel is controlling you in some way. The sphinx can be a warning not to rebel too much against authority where you have no input or control. The sphinx making an appearance to you can also be a warning to be careful around toxic and controlling people. If the sphinx is your power animal or animal totem you may well be a very spiritual and wise person, though there may be a strong rebellious side to you. You may well be a person who does not appreciate controlling people or those that you consider to be a threat to your personal beliefs. Call on the sphinx for magical workings involving wisdom, enhancing spirituality, sexual desire, standing up for yourself or beliefs and avoiding toxic or controlling people.

Spider: is a predatory arachnid and its web symbolises the web of life. It symbolises the pattern of life, creativity, determination, intelligence, completion, meditation, deep wisdom and other dimensions. The spider is strongly related to the moon and the element of air. It is sacred to Arachne, Anansi, Spider Grandmother, Great Spider, Nareau (the Old Spider) and Thinking Woman. Spiders have caused considerable fear among many people over the years. But generally they are harmless and will only bite if provoked. I am one of the few people in this world who loves spiders. If you come across a spider in your home never kill it, if possible simply put it in a jar and put it outside. If it were not for spiders we would be overrun with pests that carry disease. Some Witches use the webs of spiders to scry. If a spider shows itself to you perhaps now is the time to access your deep thoughts and inner wisdom and apply them to your everyday life. The spider can also indicate that you should be very careful about becoming involved in any traps that you are tempted by. The spider can also indicate that you should allow yourself to be willing to explore other dimensions and realities rather than becoming limited to the everyday mundane world. The spider can also be a sign that you should allow yourself some time to write creatively. So perhaps now is the time to think about writing your Book of Shadows or journal. If the spider is your power animal or animal totem you may well be a very creative writer who can weave words together with great ease. You may well be very slow to anger but once you are aroused your bite can hurt a lot. Call on the spider for magical workings involving determination, enhancing creativity, enhancing intelligence, meditation, completion, enhancing wisdom, exploration, scrying, divination, accessing inner wisdom, writing, transformation, dramatic change and seeking balance.

Tiger: is a mammal that represents the ability to remain focused and patient. The tiger is strongly related to the element of fire. It is sacred to the Hindu goddess Durga. If the tiger makes an appearance to you perhaps now is the time to remain focused and patient with regards to a goal that you have been working on. If you do this, you will achieve it more quickly than you would have expected. If you have been ill recently, whether physically or mentally, the tiger showing itself to you can be an indication that you will heal very quickly and this will be followed by a sudden increase of vitality. The tiger showing itself to you can also indicate that there will be a sudden increase in passion and power after a time of waning self-confidence. The tiger making an appearance to you can also be a sign that an adventure is coming your way, one that will introduce many challenges. But from these, you will see some dramatic changes in your life that will benefit you positively. If the tiger is your power animal or animal totem you may well be a very clairvoyant person who has the ability to heal people with great ease. You may well be a very confident person who needs to take many adventures. Call on the tiger for magical workings involving healing, health, success, good fortune, good luck, protection, patience, accomplishment, vitality, enhancing power, steadfastness, enhancing passion, self-confidence, self-esteem, adventures, challenges, transformation, dramatic change, clairvoyance, psychic power and the ability to remain focused.

Toad: is an amphibian that has been revered as a magical creature since time immemorial. Toads were once more popular pets than cats and dogs. It is said that burnt toad worn around the neck in a sachet will cure bed-wetting. The toad symbolises psychic power and intelligence. Toads are said to be very sensitive to spirits. If the toad shows itself to you perhaps now is the time to spend some time alone so that you can gather your thoughts on more emotional, psychic or spiritual matters. The toad showing itself to you can also indicate that you'll soon have time to review and clear a past issue that has been upsetting or uncomfortable to think about. The toad making an appearance can also be a sign that you will achieve personal and spiritual growth. This growth will allow you to identify with a new "you". If the toad is your power animal or animal totem you may well be a very shy and secretive person who prefers solitude. You may well be a person with a high strength of character who can depend on inner strength to solve your problems. Call on the toad for magical workings involving success, good fortune, good luck, solitude, enhancing intelligence, psychic power, enhancing spirituality, emotional matters, overcoming negativity, personal or spiritual growth, renewal, enhancing strength of character, secrets, solving problems, dramatic change, transformation, accomplishment and enhancing sensitivity.

Tortoise: is a reptile whose season is winter. It is strongly related to the planet of Saturn and the element of earth. It is sacred to the deities Lugh and Kurma. The tortoise is said to carry the world on its back. If the tortoise makes an appearance to you perhaps now is the time to consider that you are taking on far too many of the worries and troubles of other people. Therefore, allow yourself some time on your own so that you can focus on you only. The tortoise can also symbolise that you need to slow down in life and just enjoy it. The tortoise making an appearance can also indicate that you need to be patient with a goal or project you have been working on. With your determination, you'll get what you're after before you even know it. The tortoise showing itself to you can also be a sign that a vegetarian diet is necessary right now, even if only for a little while. If the tortoise is your power animal or animal totem you may well be a great listener who can help to solve the problems of others. You may well be a person who needs to be careful not to take on too much of the problems of others. Call on the tortoise for magical workings involving patience, projects, goals, determination, solving problems, slowing things down, the ability to keep on keeping on and accomplishment.

Unicorn: is a fantastical, mythical beast that is strongly related to the planet of Jupiter and the element of earth. It does, however, have strong connections also to the element of spirit. It is said that only a virgin can capture a unicorn. The horn of the unicorn symbolises the spiral of immortality. If the unicorn shows itself to you perhaps now is the time to work on any creative or artistic projects that have become suppressed. The unicorn showing itself to you can also symbolise that you will soon discover your connection to the spiritual powers of nature and the spirits that it holds. If you are burdened with worry, the unicorn showing itself to you can also indicate that you should let go of it for a while so that you can just play and have fun. The unicorn making an appearance to you can also be a sign that you will encounter some very creative children who have talents that you have never seen. From these children, you will learn much. The unicorn showing itself to you can also indicate that you are about to experience a sudden surge of power that will benefit you greatly. If the unicorn is your power animal or animal totem you may well be a very artistic and creative person with strong connections to the spirits of nature. You may well be a very psychic person who enjoys working with children. Call on the unicorn for magical workings involving enhancing spirituality, understanding the cycles of life, children, enhancing creativity, artistic talent, enhancing your connection with nature spirits, letting go of negativity, enhancing power and psychic power.

Whale: is a sea mammal and is said to be a record keeper. It is strongly related to the planet of Jupiter and the element of water. The killer whale is sacred to Masset San and Sga'na. The whale is a symbol of royalty. If the whale shows itself to you perhaps now is the time to express your emotions by singing or chanting. The whale making an appearance to you can also indicate that you are about to embark on a very creative period of your life, one in which you can express your artistic side from the depths of your imagination. The whale can also symbolise that you are about to become aware of your ability to expand your spiritual awareness and the more you learn how to clear your mind, perhaps with regular meditation, the more you will be able to do this. The whale making an appearance to you can also indicate that you need to psychically insulate yourself and you can do this by meditating and imagining yourself surrounded by a blue or white light. If the whale is your power animal or animal totem you may well be a self-contained and contemplative person who is very psychic and highly intuitive. You may be a very caring and expansive person with a great appreciation for the Earth Mother. Call on the whale for magical workings involving money, prosperity, protection, royalty, enhancing creativity, enhancing imagination, spiritual awareness, meditation, clearing the mind, psychic power, enhancing intuition, expansion, caring for others, abundance, peace, enhancing calmness and emotional issues. Calling upon the whale is said to be good for all activities that involve music.

Winged Horse: flying horse, or sky horse, is a fantastical, mythical beast. It is strongly related to the planet of Mercury and the element of air. It is sacred to Pegasus, Eros, Helios and Apollo among others. If the winged horse makes an appearance to you it can indicate your divine ability to aim high in life. It represents that the sky is limitless and you should never allow anyone to get in the way of your goals. The winged horse can also be an indication that you need to release the inner child within you to discover the big wide world. It can indicate the need to open up to your inner child qualities that may have been dormant for some time. From this, you can explore the things that you have always wanted to. The winged horse showing itself to you can also be a sign of your communication skills with those closest to you. So perhaps there is a need to work on them in some way. It may be that you need to make sure your lines of communication are open and strong with the people that are important to you. The winged horse making an appearance to you can also be an indication that you are about to embark on a very creative and artistic period of your life. If the winged horse is your power animal or animal totem you may well be a very artistic and creative person who has the strong need to aim high in life. You may well be a very communicative person who enjoys the company of children. Call on the winged horse for magical workings involving challenges, aiming high in life, inner child qualities, exploring things in life, communication, psychic awareness, working with children, enhancing creativity, artistic talent, freshness, new beginnings, enhancing intelligence and clarity.

Wolf: is a mammal that has strong connections to the ancient Celtic and Native American peoples. It is strongly connected to the moon and the element of earth. It also has strong connections with the beautiful star of Sirius. It is sacred to many deities including Apollo and Artemis. The prints of wolves symbolise keeping track of things and movement. If the wolf makes an appearance to you perhaps now is the time to let go of any characteristics and behaviours that no longer serve you. As you let go of these, you can then embrace new insights, ideas and teachings that will serve you well so pay very close attention to them. The wolf appearing to you can also indicate that you need to maintain your self-esteem, self-confidence and integrity, despite any misunderstandings. The wolf showing itself to you can also be a sign that you are strongly protected at all times on both psychic and spiritual levels. If the wolf is your power animal or animal totem you may well be a very intuitive person who values your friends and family. You may well be a very expressive person who will fiercely defend those who are closest to you. Call on the wolf for magical workings involving love, friendship, courage, health, healing, success, good fortune, good luck, protection, stability, moving on in life, loyalty, perseverance, letting go of the past, insight, ideas, teaching, self-esteem, self-confidence, integrity, family, expression, defence, projects, career, finding your path or purpose, communication and finding the truth of a matter.

Chapter Nineteen: Dreams and Dream Work

The universe has many ways of communicating with us about our lives and one way is through dreams. Every single human being has dreams, but some of us are more advanced at remembering them. Since everybody dreams, they must be a fundamental part of human existence. Witches believe that dreams open the door to many different levels of consciousness and dimensions of reality. The symbolism in dreams can reveal hidden fears and anxieties and how these may be overcome as well as unresolved issues, possible future events, how to achieve our goals and even who we may have been in past lives. Some dreams can be so pleasant, often sexual, to the point that we are disappointed when we wake up, while others, known as nightmares (*"mare"* in this word is from the Old English meaning a mythological demon or goblin who torments people with terrifying dreams), can be so frightening that when we wake up, often with the heart pounding and our skin covered in sweat, we are relieved that it was all just a nightmare. Whether our dreams are good or bad, however, they can give us huge insight into what is really going on in our lives. All we really need to do is pay very close attention to our dreams.

In the field of psychology, the sequences of images, thoughts, sensations and other dream experiences are all believed to come directly from the unconscious mind. The conscious mind is believed to play a role in provoking dreams with thoughts about the events of life that we have experienced, but everything we experience in dreams is the work of the unconscious mind. Most dreams occur during a process of sleep known as rapid eye movement. Scientists have been wondering for centuries why we dream and what purpose dreams play in humans and animals. Some scientists have proposed that dreams are a cleaning process, helping to refresh the brain, while other scientists have proposed that dreams help us to store memories. While both of these are probably true, Witches know that there is much more to dreams than that. Dreams can be utilised to empower our personal lives and our connection with divine energy in ways that we could never have imagined. Dreams spring forward valuable information from the unconscious mind to the rational, conscious mind.

The unconscious mind is the magical or psychic part of the brain. It holds ancient wisdom and sees things through images, symbols and signs. It is much more than a depository of information, only holding things like memories and instincts, and it is able to use the experiences of life and then draw conclusions as to where a person is heading in life and how to best act to overcome any problems. As I have explained, the mind is an amazing thing. It knows things that are happening within life even if we are not consciously aware of them. Dreams are like a portal to the unconscious mind and are a way for us to access spiritual wisdom about our lives that may not be otherwise available to us. This is why Witches believe that dreams are very important and that we should take notice of them. Although we dream every night, the dreams that are most memorable and vivid are the most important so please take effort to interpret them. This will open you up to other dimensions of your life, helping to guide you in ways you never knew you could.

Most important to Witches is that dreams help us to connect with the divine more deeply. When we dream, the filters of the conscious mind are switched off and so we are able to connect with deity more efficiently. When we are awake, we can often become so cluttered with information that we don't listen to what is really there in the energies around us. When we dream, things are different. The filters of the conscious mind are no longer there and so the Goddess and God and other spiritual beings or energies are able to directly communicate with us more effectively than within the everyday mundane world. This can open us up to a whole world of possibilities. A clairvoyant dream, for example, can help you to gain information that is out of sight or in a different location. From this, you may be able to find out how someone truly feels about you and how you can act around him or her accordingly. You can even go as far as to have telepathic dreams in which you will be able to communicate with someone who you don't have physical access to.

The best and most simplest way to keep track of your dreams is to keep a record of them in a dream journal. This is known as dream work. You can do this by keeping a notebook and pen on your bedside table and then writing your dreams down as soon as you awaken. You can write down every dream you recall or just the ones that you feel are more meaningful. Writing your dreams down as soon as you wake may be important to you personally because many people unfortunately forget about their dreams within minutes of waking up. At regular intervals, carefully study your dreams from your dream journal and consider how they relate to important things that may be going on in your life or the lives of those around you. Then use books and your intuition to interpret their symbolic meanings in your life and the lives of others who are important to you. Reviewing your dreams regularly can reveal important patterns and issues and how to best overcome any negativity. It can be an incredible way to validate any predictions and premonitions.

Dreams and the Moon

As you will be aware by now dreams are linked to the moon. The moon governs the magical part of the brain, the unconscious mind, and the dreams that spring from it. As such, you may want to keep a close eye on how different your dreams are at different phases of the moon. You can do this by writing down the phase of the moon by each dream in your dream journal. As Witches develop and deepen their relationship with the energies of the moon, they may become profoundly aware of how its cycles affect their dreams. You may find, for example, that your dreams at the dark or new moon may reveal things that need to be banished so that you can move on and sow the seeds for future success. You may find, as another example, that your dreams at the waning of the moon may give you deep insight on how to best balance your mind, body and soul perhaps after a period of stress and tension. It is said by many people who deal with the occult that dreams at the full moon can seem to be wild, bizarre, vivid and the most prominent. So it is a very good idea to particularly take notice of your dreams at the full moon. They may reveal secrets to the most potent spiritual and psychic aspects of your life. Working with the phases of the moon in dream work can be an excellent and wonderful way to connect with the feminine energies of the divine – the Goddess. Recently, some scientists have come to believe that the moon does, after all, affect the sleeping cycles of humans and the dreams that we have. Studies have shown that the sleep hormone melatonin is altered during a full moon. This leads to a much higher disturbance of the dreams of humans. Why does this happen? It's all down to the energies of the full moon. It has enormous power. This is something that Witches and other Pagan practitioners have always known.

Astral Travel

Astral travel, or astral projection as it is otherwise known, is an advanced form of a dream state. It may occur during deep relaxation states, such as meditation or concentration, or during sleep. It occurs when the soul or consciousness actually leaves the physical body completely and travels to other realities or dimensions. During this process the soul is not bound by time, space or gravity. This can be a frightening experience to those who are not used to it but it is actually perfectly normal, natural and safe. You cannot get stuck in the other astral realities, nor will you not be able to find your way back to your physical body. You are attached to your physical body by something called the silver cord. This cord is the part of you that keeps your soul attached to your physical body – the cord will only be broken when you physically die. It is this cord that will allow you to snap back into your body during astral travel should anything negative happen at your home or wherever else your physical body is. It is during the process of astral travel that you may meet spirit guides, such as power animals or deities, who may come to help you through your life's problems.

Throughout my life, I have been able to achieve astral travel quite easily, though I must admit that most times it happens without me even thinking about it. This may relate to my zodiac sign of Aquarius which is ruled by the element of air. Those of the zodiac signs of earth may well find it difficult to achieve astral travel since they tend to be more bound to more "earthly" and physical matters. My earliest experience of astral travel occurred when I was around 5 or 6 years old. I remember going to bed one night and then soon after I began seeing my physical body on the bed from the ceiling. My physical body was kicking and moving about like crazy. I remember wondering what on earth was going on. Since I was so young, the experience terrified me but, even from that very young age, it helped me to open up to the fact that there is more to life than what meets the eye and that there is a such thing as the human soul. Since then, whenever I am able to achieve astral travel I just enjoy the experience and go with the flow, learning what I can from the experiences I have during the process. Astral travel can teach you much about yourself. It can reveal secrets about your life and your magical path to enlightenment.

If you would like to learn how to consciously achieve astral travel you will have to be very patient. If you try to rush the process you will probably achieve nothing. Regularly meditate and surround yourself with meditation devices – recordings of nature sounds, incense, crystals, herbs, stones and so on. If the devices relate specifically to astral travel as well then all the better. Then, when you are ready, lie on your bed and on your belly. Then visualise yourself looking down from the ceiling. After some time, you may find yourself actually doing it. When you are able to achieve this you will soon find that your soul or consciousness travels to different levels of reality. It can be very exciting to say the least. You may find that colours are different and that things are much brighter and clearer. After some time of achieving astral travel, you may have a particular objective as to why you want to travel on the astral levels. You may want to tell yourself before your travel, for example, that you wish to travel to the astral realms to meet your power animal or a much-loved family member who is deceased physically. Once you learn how to master astral travel you may find yourself doing it most nights when you go to bed without even thinking about it. Many Witches will often say that they can't wait to get to bed at night just so they can travel on the astral realms. You may well feel like this each night too. Good luck and just enjoy the experience.

Universal Dream Symbolism

Following are some very common forms of dream symbolism. This guide will be enough to get you started on the traditional meanings of dreams. Many forms of dreams are very common. Many people dream of being attacked and of being chased by something terrifying for example. Most dream researchers, however, haven't truly settled on an interpretation for these dreams that can apply to every single one of us. There is a simple reason for this. The images that appear in dreams can have different meanings for everyone. Age, workplace, culture, geography, genetics, environment, astrology and personal circumstances all play a role in shaping what dreams can mean. Therefore, intuition plays a vital role in understanding what each dream can mean for a particular person. Dreaming of flying can be terrifying to some people and can indicate something negative, while dreaming of the same thing for other people can be a pleasant experience and can indicate something positive. It really all depends on the person. Nonetheless these are the traditional meanings of some of the most common, and most famous, dreams that you can use to enhance your knowledge of the world of dreams. Although many dreams are unfavourable, ultimately you generally have control over your own life and its future. Let any dreams that you have help you to make the right decisions for a bright and more bountiful future. I have only intended the following notes to be a simple introduction to each form of dream symbolism. You will have to study dreams further to get a more rounded knowledge of each.

Note: You can obviously refer to chapter eighteen for the meanings of specific types of animals for dreams. You can also obviously refer to previous chapters for other things that I haven't covered here and simply use your intuition to what they can mean. Dreaming of the goddess Aphrodite, for example, can indicate a need for love, finery and luxury, while dreaming of the colour red can indicate a need for strength and courage around a difficult situation.

Abandonment: A dream of abandonment can denote that you will have much difficulty making plans for your future success. If it is a house that you abandon it can be a warning that you may well experience some sort of grief, especially when it comes to fortune. If it is your romantic partner that you abandon it can be a warning that you may well fail to recover things and people that are extremely valuable to you. If you abandon a mistress, you may well enjoy an unexpected inheritance of great value. If you abandon children, it may well be an indication that you will lose something valuable due to lack of calmness and judgement.

Abbey: Dreaming of an abbey can be an indication that peace and tranquillity are needed. If you have been experiencing distress, the abbey can be a sign that you will soon have these qualities as well as safety. However, the abbey is an indication that this safety is only temporary. You will soon have to just get on with life's challenges. The abbey, however, is a symbol that you should have enough time to recuperate and heal from your distress. If you dream of suddenly being inside of an abbey you may well receive a much-needed helping hand. It is very favourable in a dream during distress.

Abroad: Dreaming of being abroad can indicate a much-needed trip away from people. These can be people who may cause you distress and worry. The dream of being abroad can be a signal that you need necessary change from your surroundings. If you do not make these changes, your life will not properly move forward. A dream of being abroad can also indicate that you will experience some dramatic changes and transformation. Dreaming of being abroad can also indicate that you have been working too hard in life and it is now time to just stop and take a break.

Abscess: Dreaming of an abscess is an indication that something in your life that is harmful is growing and you may not even be aware of it. This can be dangerous and it may need addressing. This can represent an emotional issue that is deep within you or a very toxic relationship. Dreaming of an abscess can represent a physical illness or an emotional one that you may not be aware of. Therefore, it is always best to get a medical examination.

Absence: A dream of experiencing absence of someone you adore can represent that some sort of repentance is needed in order for you to truly progress forward in life and secure your friendships and relationships with people. If, however, you rejoice over the absence of a friend it can denote that you will soon finally get rid of a horrible adversary. Dreaming of someone or something that is absent can also indicate a sense of loss of something very valuable to you and you may want to somehow fill the void.

Abundance: Dreaming of something that comes in abundance can represent a desire for independence. It can also represent that you are very comfortable in life and that you are confident in a current situation. Therefore, dreaming of abundance can indicate that you should just move forward with it. Trust in your abilities. Dreaming of abundance can also indicate that your needs are cared for and you will not fear any sort of loss in the near future. It represents your ability to achieve the things you need in life. It can be very favourable.

Accident: A dream of an accident can foretell that something will happen that you may not have planned for. It can represent possible danger. Therefore, you may need to be very careful around a troublesome situation. Dreaming of an accident can also indicate the coming forward of hidden aggression and this may erupt due to people who have been negative in your life. A dream of an accident can also indicate that you should avoid travel for some time.

Actor/Actress: A dream of a favourite actor or actress can indicate a desire for recognition. It can mean that a cherished wish will soon come to fruition. If you have been working on a project, then you may well reap the benefits. Dreaming of a favourite actor or actress can also indicate that you may have to play an uneasy role in life to suit other people. This may be uncomfortable but in the long run it will make your life easier. Dreaming of a favourite actor or actress can also indicate your feelings about how other people perceive you.

Adultery: A dream of adultery can represent some form of hidden guilt. Something that you may have done in the past may well be coming back to haunt you. This may be karma at work. However, you will soon learn from your mistakes and move on in life and you will remember not to repeat them. Dreaming of adultery can also indicate some sort of betrayal or insecurity in a relationship. This can result in you never trusting a particular person properly ever again.

Aeroplane: Dreaming of an aeroplane can indicate some sort of spiritual achievement. It can indicate that you will soon overcome any sort of obstacles that come your way. You may also rise to some sort of high status and prominence that will deeply benefit you. If you are in control of flying the aeroplane you may well soon become very much in control of your destination in life. You may well have a sense of confidence and self-assurance in your decisions and achievements.

Angel: To dream of an angel is very positive. It can indicate that you have complete protection in any sort of venture that you undertake. It can indicate that you are a very positive soul and that you will soon experience great comfort, guidance and tranquillity. The angel in your dream can also represent someone who you dearly love who has gone out of their way to help you overcome your problems. Dreaming of a specific angel can represent a need for something positive in your life. If you dream of the archangel Raphael, for example, there may well be a need for communication and healing of some sort in your life.

Arrow: To dream of an arrow is very positive. It can represent pleasure and festivity and that suffering will soon become a distant memory. It can represent your positive energy directed towards a specific goal or desire. To dream of shooting an arrow can represent a need to take action regarding a specific goal or desire in order to achieve the outcome. Old or broken arrows in dreams can foretell some sort of disappointment in business or love.

Ashes: Dreaming of ashes can represent some sort of disappointment or regret. The ashes can represent failed relationships, friendships or business endeavours. It can represent that you may be feeling that the best part of your life is over and there isn't much left to look forward to. Always remember, however, that these feelings are only temporary and you can make positive changes for a brighter future. Just have faith and believe in yourself. Ashes in a dream can also represent the ending of things and a need for positive and constructive change.

Author: Dreaming of an author can foretell that you may have difficulty expressing your creative potential. If you dream of being an author who has been rejected you may well experience doubt about an important issue but this will soon be overcome and you will achieve whatever you are looking for. To see an author looking at his or her work with great anxiety can denote some sort of worry, but if you put the hard work in you will soon get over your worries and be confident in any endeavours that you undertake.

Baby: To dream of a baby can represent the birth of new ideas and theories. It can also represent your innocence and warmth, but you may need to be careful not to be so innocent that you miss the underlying negative potentials in people around you. Dreaming of a baby can also represent that you may soon have a sudden overwhelming feeling of emotions and so you may need to have a good cry. Something that you want out of life may also need patience in order for it to fully come to fruition. There may also be a need for laughter and pleasure. You may also experience some sort of frustration when it comes to things you have planned for. A dream of a baby can also obviously indicate that an actual baby is coming to you.

Bachelor: Dreaming of being a bachelor for a man can be an indication that you have an urge for freedom in life. If you are a female, dreaming of a bachelor can be an indication that something negative in your life is holding you back from your true potential. For men who dream of being a bachelor it can be a warning to be aware of any negativity surrounding women.

Baptism: in dreams is a positive indication. It can represent the birth or emergence of new love and happiness. The water involved in the baptism is a symbol of renewal and rebirth. The baptism can represent that something planned for will be very beneficial and you will soon reap the rewards. Baptism in dreams can also represent a renewed strength of character.

Basement: To dream of being in a basement can represent very earthy energies in your life. It can represent that you will soon be very thoughtful about your darkest emotions and memories. This, however, may only be temporary and it will help you overcome negativity. It is actually a healing process. Dreaming of a basement can also indicate that a problem or situation may worsen if you don't take appropriate action. Alternatively, dreaming of a basement can indicate that you will soon see prosperous opportunities but you will have to be careful around pleasure that turns into frustration and trouble.

Battle: in a dream can represent internal conflict. It can also represent that you will soon overcome troublesome situations if you are triumphant in your dream. You may well overcome very difficult problems. Dreaming of battle can also indicate that you should be very careful around people who don't like you. They may well have a well-prepared attack for you. If you are defeated in a battle you may well have to be aware of people who give you bad deals and prospects.

Beauty: in a dream is favourable. It can denote the beauty in your own life and you should be grateful for what you have. To dream of a beautiful woman or child can be a sign that a much-needed pleasure or profit of some sort is coming to you. If you are a man who dreams of beauty, you may well need to accept some sort of responsibility but in the long run this will benefit you and highlight your good character and sound reputation. Beauty in a dream can also indicate a fruitful and happy union.

Bell: a traditional symbol of protection. Dreaming of a bell can be an indication that this is needed in your life around difficult people and situations. It can mean that you may need to banish people who are toxic in your life. Dreaming of a bell can also indicate that you are about to enter a very spiritual period of your life, one in which you will gain much wisdom and experience. As a very feminine symbol, the bell in a dream can indicate a need to learn much from the Goddess and the women around you. Dreaming of a bell can also foretell much fulfilment and joy around very important issues that you are passionate about. A bell in a dream can also indicate joyous victory over someone or something.

Bicycle: To dream of being on a bicycle can be a very intriguing and interesting experience. It can represent a need for balance and harmony in certain situations of your life. It can also represent that you will have to put the hard work in around projects that are of great importance to you. If you are a woman who is riding the bicycle down a hill, you may well need to take good care of your good character and health. Riding a bicycle can indicate for anyone that you are on the right road in life and you will learn much about the cycles of life.

Bird's Nest: in a dream can represent your feelings about the place in which you live. It can represent your contentment and you should not worry that this will be taken away from you. To see a bird's nest full of eggs can be a happy omen. It can indicate the onset of peace, prosperity and good results in all engagements. If there are young birds in the nest, you may well experience very successful journeys and dealings. If, however, you see a bird's nest without anything in it and you feel negative about it, you may well experience a dull and gloomy outlook regarding business and projects.

Bottle: Dreaming of a bottle can be a positive indication if the bottle is full of transparent liquid. It can be an indication that you will overcome any obstacles that may be burdening you. This can include passionate matters of the heart and prosperous engagements. On the other hand, a bottle in a dream can signify aggression and aggressive behaviour. This can be aggression that you have held within for some time that will soon erupt. Dreaming of drinking from a bottle can indicate that some important changes are needed in your life in order to progress forward positively.

Bridge: Dreaming of a bridge can represent the overcoming of very problematic situations within your life. It can represent that better times are on the way and that you will soon have a sense of connection, progress and stability. The bridge in a dream can also represent that you will soon enter a fresh start, one in which you will have a good sense of renewal. Dreaming of a bridge can also indicate that you will soon go on some sort of travel or transition and you will learn much. If a bridge gives way in a dream you should be careful around false friends or admirers who have ulterior motives.

Burial: in a dream can mean that you have finally got rid of bad habits and negative patterns in your life and that you can now enjoy the freedom from them. It can represent the end of a negative phase of life and you can now take a new direction. You can now learn from the past negatives. On the negative side, however, to dream that you are being buried can signify that you have taken on too much and are burdened with stress and tension. Only you can save and free yourself of this negativity. The dream may be urging you to take positive action to rid yourself of any negativity. Dreaming of a burial can represent hidden fears and anxieties.

Castle: To dream of a castle can mean many things. The castle can represent wealth, ambition, travel, family, the home, extravagance, luxury and loyalty. Generally, dreaming of a castle can represent significant wealth that you will always have so there may be unnecessary worry and stress regarding your financial situation. Dreaming of a castle can also mean that you will enjoy much travel and you will meet a lot of different kinds of people along the way. To dream of leaving a castle can denote that you will lose valued possessions or someone very dear to you.

Cave: Dreaming of a cave can be a very earthy experience. It represents your need to retreat or take refuge perhaps after a time of stress and tension. It can represent a need to take time away from something that is causing problems in your life so that you can just think and perhaps meditate. It represents emotional retreat, sanctuary and a good psychological safe haven. The dream of a cave can represent the means by which you can escape your problems, pain and anything else that can be harmful to your ego. The cave can appear in your dreams when you are going through a very traumatic transition or situation. For a woman to dream that she is walking into a cave with her lover can be a warning that she will fall in love with a villain and lose trusted friends in the process.

Cemetery: The dream of a cemetery can be a symbol that you are thinking too much about death and what will happen to you after your own death. It can also mean that you are too concerned about what will happen in your future and this may be causing fear and anxiety. In other words, the dream is advising you to just live in the present and take life as it comes. Learn to embrace the good things in life and learn how to overcome the bad things. You will gain much wisdom if you do this. For a mother to take beautiful, fresh flowers to a cemetery can denote that she can expect excellent health of her family.

Children: The dream of children can be a very positive one. It can indicate happiness, playfulness, blessings, cheerfulness, love, curiosity, contentment, prosperity, self-discovery, celebrations, temptation and an overwhelming urge to discover the big wide world. To dream of seeing children studying or otherwise working can denote that very peaceful times are ahead. However, to dream of seeing disappointed children can foretell trouble from enemies and fake friends.

Circle: in a dream can be a very positive indication. It can represent your certainty around areas of your life that are of great importance. It can represent the completion of projects that you have been working on. If you dream of seeing a complete circle it can represent that everything in your life is about to fall into place very nicely. Dreaming of the circle can also represent your collective unconscious and a need to protect yourself from outside influences. Circles in dreams can appear in the form of everyday mundane objects.

Climbing: To dream that you are climbing up something can be a positive sign. It can mean a self-mastery process and the raising up of your own consciousness. It can reflect a much higher level of thinking. It can also mean your ability to overcome your issues and the rising above a challenge. It can reflect your ability to improve your methods of doing things to achieve your desires. The climbing of something in a dream can denote your struggles in life and also your determination and ambition to get what you want.

Clock: in a dream represents the passage of time and its importance to you and the issues around you. It can also represent the need to take appropriate actions in life. The clock can also symbolise the ticking of the human heart and so it can represent the emotional issues in your life. Sometimes clocks in dreams can represent some sort of danger from a foe. Traditionally, if a clock stops or strikes in a dream then the death of someone may well be imminent. This may come after a long illness.

Comedy: To dream of seeing comedy can represent your need to stop taking life so seriously. It can represent that part of you that needs to step back from stressful and worrying situations in order to have a more carefree attitude to life. Perhaps you have taken on too much in life and it is now time to just enjoy yourself and let go of things that are bothering you, if only for a short time. You can then return to things that need sorting, with a feeling that you are a little less stressed and more able to cope. Alternatively, dreaming of seeing comedy can represent that someone is making a mockery out of a situation that you are involved in. It can also represent foolish and short-lived pleasures.

Crying: Dreaming of seeing yourself crying in a dream is usually a representation of your inner emotions. It could be that you long to express your fears and anxieties to someone very dear to you but you may find this difficult as your dear loved one may not be very approachable. It could be that there are many people you long to express your deep emotions to but you simply can't as it may be inappropriate to do so. Crying in a dream can represent your inner anger, frustration, joy, agony or ecstasy. It can represent those suppressed emotions that are intense or perhaps overwhelming. If someone close has hurt you or is otherwise treating you bad you may often find yourself crying in dreams. It has often happened to me throughout my life.

Cupboard: To dream of a cupboard can signify that you are perhaps exploring those things within your life that you are doing to see that your needs, desires and goals are met or accomplished. It can represent the sorting of your mind so that you can achieve them. If the cupboard is clean and full of shiny and interesting things then pleasure and comfort may well soon be yours. An empty and dusty cupboard can represent your distress or frustration around areas of your life that are holding you back or stopping you from achieving what you want out of life. Dreaming of a cupboard can also denote your emotions, feelings and parts of your personality that you wish to hide from others who perhaps wouldn't understand you.

Dance: can be very favourable in a dream. It can represent your renewed sense of happiness, freedom, joy and liberation. This can be very welcoming after a period of your life of stress and tension. When you see yourself dancing in a dream it can mean that you are expressing yourself in your life to your fullest potential and perhaps that some unexpected good fortune will soon come your way. Dreaming of seeing the elderly dancing can represent a much brighter outlook when it comes to business.

Darkness: in a dream represents your subconscious fears and anxieties that may soon surface in your life. However, with inner strength and perhaps help from others you will soon overcome them. This is especially so if the sun breaks the darkness in your dream. Darkness in a dream can represent unfamiliarity and obscurity in certain areas in your life and so you should be careful around certain people and situations that may cause you problems. Try to remain especially in control in matters of business and love as darkness in dreams can foretell problems with them. Dreaming of darkness can also represent your failure to connect with your inner self or a spiritual endeavour. Only you can truly learn how to overcome this negativity.

Death: in a dream can represent the end of one cycle and the beginning of the next. It can represent the death of an unpleasant situation and from this you can finally move on in life. It can represent the long-awaited opportunity for change, transformation and new beginnings, just like the ice-cold winters that melt into spring. Often people become fearful that seeing death in a dream can represent the actual death of the dreamer or a dear loved one. But dreams of this nature are rare. Death in a dream is usually only a symbol of much-needed change and transformation.

Divorce: in a dream is another indication of change and transformation. It can mean that you need to recognise and perhaps reset any priorities in your life. This can involve the parting or separation from things that no longer serve you or are holding you back in some way. Divorce in a dream can also represent that you fear seclusion and the anxieties you experience when you are alone with your own thoughts. Divorce in a dream can also denote that you are unsatisfied with your partner and some much-needed changes are needed for the relationship to be a happy one.

Doctor: As a figure of authority, a doctor in a dream can represent your need to appreciate your roles and position within your life and perhaps career. It can also represent the inner healer within you and your ability to heal yourself and others with whatever means you have. This can often be in the form of spiritual healing with traditional methods and skills within you that are unique. The doctor in your dream can be an indication that you need to learn how to relax your mind or you may become overburdened with stress and tension. A dream of a doctor can be a prediction of disagreement with family members or some sort of illness, but it can also indicate wealth, prosperity and good health.

Earthquake: in a dream can be very unfavourable. It can symbolise destruction, disaster, business failure, distress, obscurity and uncertainty about the future. So you will have to look at those areas of your life that may cause these things in order to avoid any negativity. Remember that you have the power to be able to do this. Dreaming about an earthquake can indicate an uncertainty about going through the necessary changes in life. It can indicate that there needs to be a change to your routine in order to move forward in life.

Ecstasy: Dreaming of experiencing ecstasy, an intense feeling of pleasure, can sometimes indicate some sort of delusion. It can represent a fear of facing the realities of your life and the hardships that come with them. It can represent unbalanced fantasies and unhealthy feelings you have towards achieving things that you know deep down are probably unattainable. This is especially so if you experience a disturbing dream involving feelings of ecstasy. On the other hand, a dream about ecstasy can mean that you will soon be reunited with a long-absent friend.

Education: Dreaming of education can mean that some sort of promotion in life is coming your way. It can indicate your need to move forward in life to achieve your hopes and desires. Dreaming of education can indicate that you will have to learn new skills and abilities to be able to have the positivity that you are after. The dream of education can indicate that you have a very strong desire for knowledge and as you attain it in life you may well be very successful in any project that you undertake.

Eye: The dream of eyes can represent some sort of self-examination. It can represent the depths of your soul and how you truly feel about who you really are. It can represent that you are being called to understand the basic principles of life and your own personal integrity. If you see your own eyes it can indicate that you will soon understand and experience love, family values and the blessings that you have in life. Dreaming of eyes can also indicate that you will have to be very watchful around people who may not be all that they seem to be. They may cause trouble and hardship for you.

Falling: If you experience falling in a dream then it can indicate that you feel that you are not living up to the expectations of others around you. It can represent insecurities, anxieties, fears and instabilities in life. You may be experiencing some sort of overwhelming feeling in your life that you are out of control of a situation. So you will have to address this negativity and seek the appropriate actions in order to move forward properly in life. If you experience much fear as you fall in a dream it traditionally means that you will experience great struggle but you will soon rise above it and achieve your goals. If you become injured in your dream of falling you may well lose friendships.

Family: The dream of the family can indicate that you may feel that you need to protect yourself and those closest to you. If you dream of being a child being looked after by your family it can indicate that there are perhaps situations in your life that are out of your control. A dream of the family can also denote that you will soon experience an argument with a family member. If you dream of being surrounded by a happy and harmonious family you may well enjoy a future of good health and easy circumstances.

Farm: The dream of a farm can indicate that there may be significant hard work coming your way that will require you to have a strong and productive mind-set. You may well experience that you will have to try very hard in life to make a success of a cherished wish or goal. The dream of the farm often foretells that you will be fortunate as long as you do work hard. If you dream of buying a farm you may well experience a profitable deal of some kind or perhaps a safe voyage. To dream of visiting a farm is an indication of pleasant associations.

Flying: is very common in dreams. For those who are scared of heights it can be an unpleasant experience and can indicate something negative in your life. It can represent the fear and anxiety you have in life about loss of control and your longing for stability. For those who love heights it can indicate something positive such as a sense of freedom and the ability to aim high in life. Generally, flying can indicate your ability to look down in order to understand the wider picture. It can indicate that you can soon achieve a wider and more broader perspective of things. It can indicate a sense of personal power and that you are on top of a situation.

Garden: Dreaming of being in a garden can be very earthy and favourable. It can represent that something very positive is developing within your life. This can be a cherished wish or it can be your own personality and wisdom. You may well see new areas of your life developing if you dream of being in a garden. The dream of a garden can also indicate that some sort of project, new skill or other experience will take time to develop but it may well go according to plan. If the garden is filled with vibrant green plants and colourful flowers you may well enjoy a great sense of comfort and peace of mind.

Giant: The dream of a giant can mean that you are feeling very powerless and unable to control something. This can involve the influence of a person close to you or perhaps a negative situation. You may have a sense that you are enslaved in life and you don't know how to stop whatever it is that is making you feel this way. The dream may be urging you to seek the appropriate actions to overcome this negativity. Never let anyone or anything make you feel this way in life. You should be in control of your own life. If the giant runs away from you in your dream you may well soon experience good health and prosperity.

Gift: Dreaming of receiving a gift can mean that you are experiencing feelings of positivity and abundance within your life. You may well feel very happy, fortunate and that you have everything that you need. It can mean that you will never become behind with any important payments and that you may well be unusually fortunate in matters surrounding love and friendship. Giving a gift can be a sign that you need to show more gratitude for those who have helped you in your life or it may indicate a loss of something valuable.

Graduation: is often a very favourable indication in a dream. It can mean that you have completed a very difficult phase of life and are now entering a new and easier one. It can represent that all your hard work is about to pay off and you will soon experience the benefits and a sense of great honour. Any anxieties or uncertainty that you experienced during the difficult phase of life will soon be banished and you will enjoy a good sense of achievement, inner strength and power.

Hair: in dreams, can be a symbol of your thoughts, creativity, inner strength, inner beauty and your sense of empowerment. It can represent that prosperity and your knowledge will increase over the coming weeks or months. If the hair is long in your dreams then your spiritual and physical strength may well increase to levels beyond what you expected. It can also indicate that you will soon rediscover the enjoyments of sexual pleasures. Dreaming of grey or silver hair can indicate your sound ability to think wisely in life.

Hammer: Dreaming of a hammer can represent your power to move forward in life. It can represent your inner strength to straighten out a difficult situation or to resolve and overcome it. If you are frantically looking for a hammer or have misplaced it in your dream it can represent that you may be feeling powerless around a difficult situation. If the hammer is deformed you may need to take a broader perspective around a difficult situation as you may not be seeing it for what it really is.

Harp: in a dream can represent your inner peace, serenity and your connection with the divine. It represents the divine creativity and clarity that falls upon your soul like the beautiful droplets of rain. If you see yourself playing a harp you may well be about to experience a period of peace, tranquillity and rejuvenation. However, playing the harp can be a warning not to be too trusting and confident around others who may not be all that they seem to be.

Heart: is one of the most potent symbols of love. The pairing of two hearts symbolises the joining of two people in love, romance and even marriage. Dreaming of the heart can symbolise that you will soon have a beautiful sense of trust, romance, courage and love. However, sometimes dreaming of the heart can represent an internal struggle with emotional matters and the heart is encouraging you to find a way to deal with your emotions.

Horseshoe: is a traditional symbol of great luck. It can symbolise matters of your life involving good fortune, luck, success, money, prosperity, protection and healing. Dreaming of a horseshoe can be a sign that you will soon develop a deep bond with someone who will mean a lot to you. A woman dreaming of a horseshoe is a traditional sign that she will be lucky in any engagements. If you see a horseshoe attached to a gate you may well achieve success in anything you have been working on beyond your wildest dreams. If you find a horseshoe on a road when out on a walk in your dream you may well profit from some source that you knew nothing about. A broken horseshoe in a dream, however, can indicate some disappointment, misfortune or illness.

House: Dreaming of a house represents your whole self and your conscious interest in spiritual matters. The rooms within it can represent different aspects of your consciousness. The bathroom, for example, is the cleansing aspect of you and can represent the things within your life that you no longer desire, while the living room is a social place and can represent your social life with family, friends and associates. If you dream of building a house you may well make very wise choices within your affairs. If you dream that you own a big and elegant house, you may well soon move away from the house in which you live in your waking life to a better and more convenient one. Old and deteriorating houses in dreams can represent a fear of ageing and declining health. It can also indicate failure in business matters.

Ice: in a dream can indicate a coldness of character and that someone may need to learn how to warm to other people. Dreaming of ice can also represent those situations of life that are frozen or in a state of limbo in some way. It can be a sign that there are issues within your life that you feel you cannot resolve. It can represent that there are obstacles that may be blocking you from moving forward in life. It may also represent your resistance of necessary change. If you do not make the necessary changes in life, you can't really expect to properly move forward for a brighter future. Remember that there is always a way around your problems.

Illness: Dreaming of illness can represent your boredom or disappointment with life or certain aspects of it. It can also represent some sort of delay in certain situations of life and this may be causing your distress and anxiety. It may mean that you have to wait for some time before things can truly move forward. Although this may be discouraging, you will learn much about the value of patience. If you are experiencing illness in your dream you may well be looking for an easy way out of a current, difficult situation. Unfortunately, illness in a dream can represent some sort of emotional breakdown and unpleasant changes, but out of any despair there will always be something good that comes from it – from darkness comes light. This is evident throughout the natural world.

Insanity: A dream of being insane can represent your fears and anxieties about not being in control of your thoughts and emotions. If you dream of doing things that you would simply never do in your waking life because of the insanity, you may feel that you have lost total control of yourself and the situations around you. You may feel that your thoughts are somewhat dark and disturbing in your waking life when you have dreams of insanity. Therefore, your dream of insanity may be urging you to take control now rather than letting your dark thoughts and emotions to continue to build up. This may involve some sort of counselling or letting loved ones know how you truly feel. If you don't take control now you may well lose total control in the future. It is said that the utmost care regarding health should be taken when we have dreams of insanity.

Jail: Dreaming of being in jail can represent that you are feeling trapped in some way in your waking life. It can represent your feelings of confinement, frustration, disappointment and your inability to act appropriately. There may be many complications in your emotional, spiritual or material situations that need addressing in order for you to move forward in life. If you dream of being sent to jail you may well meet someone who will initially make you happy, but you may well soon feel trapped in the relationship. Dreaming of being in jail can also indicate that you are feeling guilty about something you have done in the past and you now fear punishment. This may be karma at work.

Jewellery: Dreaming of jewellery can represent how you feel about yourself. It can represent your self-image, self-confidence and self-value. It can also represent the people and things around you that are very important and valuable. Dreaming of jewellery can also indicate that you will make the right choices in life that will ensure the success of your goals and desires. The dream of jewellery can also indicate that you will go through some form of transformation and change that will be beneficial. However, broken jewellery can denote some form of disappointment or disagreement.

Journey: Dreaming of taking a journey can represent how you feel about your life so far. It can represent that things have been difficult and a slow and steady process but you got there in the end. It can reflect perhaps your thoughts and feelings about how difficult and complicated your life has been right up until this point. You may feel that you have learnt so much and you can use your experience and new skills for a much brighter and more positive future. It can represent your growing or maturing personality and your spiritual advancement. If you begin a journey in your dream you may well be starting a project that will take a long time to achieve but the rewards will be worth it. If you take a journey that is expected to take a long time but it does not, you may achieve things in life much quicker than you expected.

Key: in a dream can symbolise that you will soon discover the answer or solution to a problem or puzzle. It can be an indication that you will soon have a sense of control, independence and freedom. This can be after a period of feeling that you have no control over certain situations or perhaps people in life. On the other hand, the key in a dream can represent repressed feelings and that you are in denial. It could be that you do not want to share your emotions and feelings for fear of judgement and that others will not understand you. Keys in dreams also symbolise unexpected changes and fertility in all its forms.

Kiss: Dreaming of kissing indicates affection, satisfaction and completion. If you are romantically involved with someone, kissing him or her in your dream can indicate that you are very content in the relationship and that you feel a sense of wholeness and completeness. It can indicate that future happiness and harmony will be abundant in your relationship with him or her. If you dream of kissing your mother you may well enjoy a future in which you are greatly honoured and loved by your family and friends. Kissing your mother in your dreams can represent much success in your future. It can also obviously represent your strong relationship with her in your waking life.

Ladder: in a dream can represent your ability to climb high in life. It can represent you searching for new heights. This represents a wish for where you want to be as you go through life. This can involve career, relationships, friendships, self-esteem, self-confidence, self-development and your spiritual life. This can be a very potent dream that represents your ability to rise above anything despite people who pull you down.

Lightness: If you dream of seeing lightness it can indicate that you have overcome the negatives of life. You may well have a sense of clarity about where you need to be in life. You may well feel that you have overcome the darkest shadows of your life and that you can reap the benefits. Dreaming of lightness can also indicate that someone who is close to you may be about to pass over to the spirit world and so you should prepare for it. Dreaming of lightness can also indicate that you have a renewed sense of hope within your life and there may be some sort of success coming to you after a period of worry and stress.

Marriage: Dreaming of being married represents contentment and fulfilment. Something that you have been working on is about to pay off and you will soon reap the benefits. Dreaming of being married can represent your commitment to something that you cherish. To dream of marriage can denote high enjoyment in the future. If the guests are wearing black in the marriage there could be some sort of disappointment in your life.

Mask: Wearing a mask in your dream can represent your desire to hide something that has been on your mind. It can represent your need to hide your thoughts and emotions. You may well be feeling a sense of shame, discount and hypocrisy. If you see others wearing masks you should be careful with those around you as they may have ulterior motives. There could be a lot of falsehood around you. If you dream of dressing with a mask perhaps you should analyse your relationships so that you can discover any difficulties at the moment. Wearing a mask in a dream can represent your need to hide your true feelings and that there are spiritual hidings to discover.

Mirror: Dreaming of a mirror can represent how you feel about yourself. It can represent your true, inner emotions. It can also represent your need to reconsider a certain situation of your life that has been bothering you. If you look into the mirror and see someone else staring back at you perhaps you are giving this person too much of your personal identity and perhaps you should learn to back off from him or her. To see other people in the mirror can indicate that they will act unfairly towards you to promote themselves in life. Dreaming of a mirror can also indicate matters of your unconscious mind and your connection to the spirit world.

Mother: If you dream of a mother figure it can indicate your need to nurture and look after yourself. You may have been going through a difficult time and now is the time to care for yourself rather than other people. Those around you may well be taking advantage of you and you should be careful as they may well hurt you in unexpected ways. You may well be seeking comfort after a time of hardship and this may be something you need in order to progress forward in life. Dreaming of your own mother can also obviously reflect your relationship with her. There may be unresolved issues that need to be addressed. Dreaming of your own mother can also represent pleasing results in the future in anything you undertake.

Nudity: Dreaming of being in the nude can represent your urge for freedom. It can represent a need to rediscover those child-like qualities that are locked inside you. It can represent your need to express yourself around a current situation without any falsehood. However, dreaming of being in the nude can represent that you are too exposed and you may need to back off from people who may have ulterior motives. It can represent scandal and unwise engagements. If you dream of suddenly becoming naked you may well rediscover who you truly are after a time of not knowing. If you are trying to conceal your nudity you may well be trying to hide your true feelings.

Nun: To dream of a nun represents that you are giving up something for the greater good of your life. This can involve materialistic desires, goals and sexual interests. Traditionally, if a woman dreams of a nun it can indicate separation from her lover and a need to take care of herself. Dreaming of a dead nun can represent a need for more worldly pleasures rather than matters of a spiritual nature. I often dream of a specific nun: Sister Margaret Veronica. She was a dear friend of mine from childhood. She helped to open me up to many spiritual matters and I believe my dreams of her are her way of communicating with me in spirit. It is very comforting.

Ocean: Dreaming of the ocean is all to do with your inner emotions. You may feel that you are overwhelmed by them and are not properly grounded.

The dream of the ocean may be warning you that you need to find ways to ground yourself appropriately. You can do this by practising meditation or visualisation. To dream of the ocean can also indicate that many opportunities are coming your way so you should choose wisely. To sail on a calm ocean in your dream can represent that prosperity is on the way. Dreaming of the ocean can also represent that the desires you have are unrealistic in your waking life.

Old Man/Woman: To see an old man or woman in a dream can indicate your increasing knowledge and wisdom. To see an old woman in your dream can represent that you need to pay close attention to your feelings and emotions. The old woman can represent your repressed feelings and your desire to understand your inner voice. She can represent what it is that your unconscious mind is trying to tell you so that you can take appropriate actions in your waking life. To see an old man in your dream can be an indication that you need to pay close attention to things in the mundane world. It can represent the necessities that are needed for your environment, workplace and physical health. To dream that you are an old man can indicate that there is much to learn in life before you reach your desires or goals.

Party: To dream of a party denotes your feelings towards other people who are in your life. It can indicate your feelings towards your social life. If you dream that you are happy and content around the people you love, then this can indicate that you are happy in your current surroundings. However, if you feel uncomfortable with the people in your dream then this can indicate your social anxiety. It can indicate that you are insecure with those closest to you and this can erupt in your social life. Dreaming of a party in which you experience much pleasure can indicate that there is going to be much enjoyment coming your way, especially with people who you adore.

Picnic: Dreaming of going to a picnic can indicate that you want to get away from the everyday mundane world. It can indicate that you want to be more carefree. It could be that you have a holiday planned and you are anticipating it. Perhaps you should stop worrying about it and just go with the flow. Dreaming of a picnic can also indicate that you crave some time in places where you can just be yourself. It can indicate that you just want to be carefree and not worry about the things that are important. If you dream of people assaulting you at a picnic it could be that there are people around you who want to take things from you.

Police: To dream of the police can indicate your feelings towards the people who you consider authoritative. Perhaps you have been let down by those who were supposed to protect you from the people you fear the most. It may be that dreaming of the police can indicate your need for assistance and direction in your life. If the police arrest you in your dream you will be successful in life but there will be delays.

Pond: Dreaming of a pond can indicate your deep emotions. It could be that you are uncertain about things that you were previously confident with. You may feel an uncertainty to try new things. Your confidence to try a new challenge without embarrassing yourself may be on your mind but if you don't try new things you will never get forward with the things that you want to achieve. Remember that you only have yourself to answer to regardless of how you feel about trying something that may upset and annoy those around you. A muddy pond in a dream can indicate that there will be quarrels with those closest to you.

Pope: is a symbol of great authority. If you see him in your dream it could be that you want to retain your moral authority. Perhaps there are people in your waking life who are going against your beliefs and you need to keep them in line in some way. You perhaps believe that everything you say should be believed and the people around you should welcome you with open arms. If you speak to the Pope it can indicate that you will receive great honours in everything you do. If you meet the Pope and he seems sad or displeased with you, it could indicate that you will feel sorrow of some kind with the things that are most important to you.

Priest: in a dream is another symbol of authority. It may be that you are struggling with internal emotions and you need advice from those closest to you. You may be experiencing anxiety, stress and tension. These feelings may be making you feel that you don't know where to turn in life. The priest in your dream can indicate that you need to pay close attention to yourself.

There may be a need for a break from the everyday cares and frustrations in your life. If you dream that you are in love with a priest it can indicate that you are delusional about some sort of aspect in your life.

Pyramid: in a dream can represent your struggles to achieve the things that you so desire. It can indicate the worries and frustrations that you are facing to achieve them. Perhaps this negativity is so great that you feel that you can't achieve what you want but if you keep on keeping on the rewards will be great. Dreaming of studying the ancient mysteries of the pyramids can denote that you will fall in love with the mysteries of nature and you will soon become very knowledgable and perfected in some way.

Quarantine: Dreaming of being in quarantine can represent your need for solitude and peace. You may feel that you just want to get away from the world. Perhaps there has been people around you that you want to escape from. It may be that you need to protect your deepest emotions in some way. You may feel a need to protect whatever you hold dear. Dreaming of being in quarantine can also represent that you will be placed in positions that you do not agree with. This can involve very malicious enemies.

Rain: in a dream can represent your deepest emotions. There may be something very sad happening in your life and there may be a need to recuperate from it. It may be that you have lost something and are now experiencing sadness and depression. Remember that this is only temporary and you will soon overcome it. You will emerge stronger and more able to cope with the negatives of life. Dreaming of the rain can also indicate that you need to express your emotions with those who are closest to you. The rain in dreams can also indicate your passionate love and your desire to show it to those closest to you.

Resurrection: To dream of resurrection can indicate that you have overcome the darkness of life. It can mean that you are now emerging into a new sense of who you truly are. You may have overcome the darknesses of your life and are now stronger as a person. Dreaming of resurrection can also indicate that something that you thought was lost has now been restored and you may be amazed by this revolution. It could be that this will make you feel a renewed sense of your dignity, respect and power. A dream of resurrection can also indicate that a restoration of love is coming to you with someone you thought you had lost.

Ring: in a dream is one of the best symbols of love. It can represent your commitment to your partner. If you have been in a long-term relationship the ring in your dreams can indicate that your partner is about to propose marriage to you. It could be that your partner has already brought up the prospect of marriage but is afraid to ask you officially. Alternatively, it can represent your commitment to your goals and desires in life. It can represent your loyalty to your responsibilities, beliefs and those who are important to you. A broken ring can represent some sort of loss or separation.

River: Dreams of rivers can indicate your journey towards peace, happiness, joy, contentment and relaxation. Perhaps you have worked hard in life and now is the time to take care of your own needs. This is especially so if the river is crystal clear. Dreaming of rivers can also indicate that there are new opportunities coming to you and you should seize them wisely. Dreams of rivers can also indicate that some sort of healing is needed. This is especially so with emotional matters.

Sacrifice: in a dream can represent your need to give up something in order to achieve the greater good. It could be that you need to sacrifice the needs of things important to you in order to give yourself time to heal. Perhaps you need to overcome some sort of pride in order to move forward in life. Dreaming of sacrifice can also indicate that there needs to be some sort of forgiveness in your life – whether from yourself or from others who you have perhaps hurt.

School: To dream of being at school can represent your need to regress back to your childhood. Perhaps you are longing for the feelings you had as a child. It can also indicate fears, anxieties and inadequacy that stem from your childhood that are unresolved. Dreaming of a school can also indicate your quest for knowledge and distinction. Perhaps you are striving for literary attainment and you want to teach others. It may be that your dream of a school is telling you that you are learning the greatest lessons from life and from this you will achieve great wisdom.

Scissors: in dreams can represent your need to cut away the things that are no longer important to you. This can represent situations and people. Perhaps you can no longer cope with the situations and people of your life and you long to get rid of them. This can be after a period of discontentment, stress, tension and worry. Alternatively, scissors in your dreams can represent someone who is making you feel hurt by their cutting remarks and spiteful tongue. If scissors are broken in your dreams there may be quarrels and some sort of separation coming your way.

Sex: To dream of having sex can indicate a lack of pleasure in your life. Perhaps you have been working too hard and you want to just enjoy the benefits. Dreaming of sex can indicate in a relationship that something you desire from your partner is lacking. This can actually be sex. Perhaps you don't know how to explain your feelings about your desires to your partner. Dreaming of sex in which you have a proper orgasm can represent satisfaction and completeness in your life. It can represent a culmination of this that you have been working for, much like the symbolism of the full moon or the sun at the Sabbat of Litha. You may now have a sense of stability and security.

Ship: To dream of a ship can be a very positive omen. It can indicate your optimism about things that you have desired for some time. It can indicate very positive outcomes for things you have worked hard for. This can mean that you will soon have a sense of happiness and contentment. From this you may experience very positive and unexpected surprises. To dream of a shipwreck, however, can indicate that female friends and family may be about to betray you. You may well have an upsetting turn of affairs to do with them.

Skeleton: To dream of a skeleton traditionally means your fear of death, the unknown and becoming unwell. It may be a warning that you should be very careful around people who may cause you trouble. Dreaming of a skeleton can also indicate unnecessary worry and that you should seek a milder sense of yourself. To see many skeletons in a dream can indicate that some sort of shock or failure is coming your way. But from this you will learn a lot and perhaps remember not to repeat any mistakes. Dreaming of a skeleton can also indicate the final ending of something. This may be something that has been burdening you.

Soldier: Dreaming of a soldier can indicate a need for self-discipline. Perhaps you feel that there are things in your life that you can't control. The dream of a soldier can indicate a need to take action for things you want in life. Only you can do this. Dreaming of a soldier can also indicate that something is missing from your life and you long for it to be there. There may be inner battles to do with this. This can involve your battle between your heart and your mind. The dream of a soldier can also indicate that your quest for perfection and discipline may create an unexciting and boring future. There may be a need to seek things that give pleasure and excitement.

Table: Dreaming of a table can represent your need to connect with those closest to you. It can represent a need for stability with them. Perhaps you need to sit down with someone who is close to you and discover what he or she is truly thinking. Perhaps there are unresolved issues to do with this person. If you see an old and broken table it can indicate some sort of stress and tension with regards to people and situations around you. You may be experiencing a sense of insecurity and only you can mend the things within your life that are unbalanced. If you dream of setting a table it can indicate very happy unions with those closest to you and perhaps prosperity in projects.

Telescope: Dreaming of a telescope can indicate a bright outlook on life and your sense of feeling content. If you look at distant planets or stars through a telescope there may be very pleasurable journeys coming your way, but be careful that you will not have too much financial loss. However, it can also indicate unfavourable energies to do with projects, family and friends. It can represent your frustration to do with these matters. Perhaps the things that you care about the most are too far away from you and you feel that you can't truly handle them properly. The dream of the telescope may be urging you to be strong-hearted around situations that are out of your control.

Thief: If you dream of a thief you may experience some sort of loss or fear of it. There may also be a lot of insecurity within your life right now. There may also be something in your life in which you highly value that someone wants to take away from you. This may be without your knowledge and it could be something literal, as in physical, or symbolic. There may be a period coming to you in which you experience a loss of time and energy, a relationship, a friendship or business if you do not cherish and care for the things that are of great importance to you. If you overcome a thief in your dream you may well overcome your enemies in your waking life.

Thunder: Dreaming of thunder can represent your anger and hurt in your waking life. Perhaps you are angry with the way someone is treating you and you have a very stormy relationship or friendship with him or her. Alternatively, the dream of thunder can foretell that you will experience guilt for something you have done in the past. Thunder in dreams can be a warning that there are hard times on the way. It can symbolise very turbulent feelings of anger, disappointment, grief, loss, bitterness, hurt and revenge. But after this period you should emerge stronger as a person and be able to move forward in your life. After a thunderstorm the air is cleared.

Travelling: Dreaming of travelling can often be a very positive omen. It can symbolise your path and movement towards your goals and desires. It can be an indication that you are progressing forward towards what you want out of life after much work and effort. It can represent some sort of advancement and this may well be of a spiritual nature. You may be about to experience both profit and pleasure. However, if you dream of travelling through rough and unknown places, you may have to be careful around people and situations that could be harmful or may not be all they seem to be. Dreams of this can also foretell some sort of sickness.

Twins: Dreaming about twins can indicate your ego and your alter ego. Perhaps you work in a profession that requires you to have an alter ego. Traditionally, the dream of twins indicates security and balance in business and a content home life in which there is much harmony. Alternatively, the dream of twins can indicate that you are torn between two situations of your life. This may be causing you conflict or disharmony so you may have to weigh up your options. If the twins are ill in your dream there may be some sort of grief or disappointment in your life.

Umbrella: The dream of an umbrella can represent your need for security or shelter from trouble, worry, stress or any other difficult situations in your life. Seeing an open umbrella in your dream can indicate that you should always seek help when you need it. If you see others carrying umbrellas in your dreams you may well be asked for help. If you carry a new umbrella during sunshine, you may well be about to experience intense pleasure in your waking life.

Uniform: Dreaming of being in a uniform can be a desire in your waking life for some sort of recognition. Perhaps you have been working hard on projects and you want to reap the benefits. Perhaps you have been working hard to please someone and you want appreciation for what you have been doing for him or her. Dreaming of a uniform can also indicate that you will soon meet some very interesting and influential friends who will help you to get far in life and achieve your goals or desires. A dream of a uniform can also indicate that some sort of order is needed in your life. There may also be some identification with some authority in your waking life with dreams of this sort.

Vampire: is a mysterious creature originating from Slavic folklore and often represents something negative in dreams. This is especially so if you fear the vampire in your dreams. If you dream of being a vampire or becoming one you may be feeling very empty, emotionless and dead on the inside in your waking life. The dream of the vampire can indicate that you may well be experiencing much fear and insecurity. Perhaps you have done things in your life that you are not proud of and these may be coming back to haunt you in some way. These negative feelings may be draining you of vital energy and stopping you from moving forward in life. Dreaming of the vampire can be a warning that you need to face up to your own inner demons in order to move forward in life. Alternatively, the dream of the vampire can indicate that there are negative people around you who drain you of your energies. It can indicate people who have no good intentions towards you. Spot the signs in people who are idiots and move on is my advice. Such people are often known as psychic vampires.

Virgin: Dreaming of a virgin can represent your feelings about innocence. You may be wishing that you could turn back the hands of time in order to return to the innocence of your childhood. Perhaps you long to have that carefree attitude that you once had as a child. There may be a need for you to return to childhood feelings where you can feel content and happy. This may be after a period in your life where you have experienced much stress and tension. Alternatively, the dream of a virgin can indicate a renewed understanding of something very important to you. The virgin in a dream also has the traditional meaning that you will have comparative luck with regards to your speculations.

Volcano: The dream of the volcano can represent your intense emotions and sexual needs. Perhaps you have been experiencing much frustration, anxiety, stress or anger and you need a sexual release. This is especially so if the volcano erupts in your dream. Volcanoes in dreams can represent that there are blockages in your waking life that need to be purged. Therefore, you may have to find ways to release your tension or resolve your problems. Dreaming of a volcano can represent violent disputes and so the dreamer should be careful. There could be potential for reputation to be destroyed with dreams of this sort.

Wall: Dreaming of a wall can represent frustration and an inability to move forward in life. There may be things in your life that are getting in the way of your success. This is especially so if you can find no way to get over the wall in your dream. However, if you find that you can get over the wall with ease in your dream you may find that you can overcome any obstacles in your life. If you build a wall in your dream you may well be building the solid foundations in your waking life for a very bright and successful future. If you demolish a wall you may well overcome your enemies with ease. Dreams of walls can also indicate that you need to shield yourself from outside influences.

Wind: Dreaming of the wind often has very positive meanings in your waking life. It can indicate inner strength and your connections with the divine and the spirit world. Perhaps you have been asking for help with current situations in your life and you want to have a sense of direction. The dream of the wind can indicate that there are important changes coming your way that should be embraced. It can indicate that spirit is guiding you towards these necessary changes. A strong wind can indicate a huge and unexpected change. If the wind blows you in a desired direction you may well go to places in your waking life in which you want to go. It can also indicate that you will meet people who will help you to achieve what you want.

Witch: The dream of a Witch can often represent your need to seek spiritual or healing help and advice. Perhaps you have been going through much difficulty in your waking life and you don't know who or what to turn to. The dream of the Witch can also indicate your increasing knowledge and wisdom about the fundamentals of life. Perhaps you have learned much and now have a sense of who you truly are. Dreaming of a Witch can also indicate that your magical abilities are increasing to levels beyond your expectations. You may be experiencing psychic or magical powers that you never knew existed. You may find that your eyes have been opened to things that you never knew were there. Dreaming of a Witch can also imply that you will soon seek hilarious and joyous adventures.

Wreath: The dream of a wreath made of fresh flowers can indicate some great opportunities, celebrations and honours coming your way. Perhaps you have been working very hard in life and you can now reap the benefits. These benefits will soon give you feelings of enrichment and encouragement. If you see a bridal wreath you may well experience a very happy ending to engagements that you have been uncertain about. On the other hand, however, a withered wreath can represent self-pity and can indicate some sort of sickness or wounded love.

Zombie: is a frightening figure from folklore. It is a dead, soulless body that walks the earth and often seeks to eat the flesh of human beings. It often, therefore, represents something negative in your life if you dream of it. You may well be experiencing an overwhelming situation in which there is a lot of stress and tension. There may be things in your life that you feel you have no control over, things that are eating you away so to speak. There may be a negative habit or addiction that you are finding very difficult to overcome. You may well be feeling like you are losing your power and control over things or perhaps that someone is trying to take these qualities away from you. You may well be feeling empty, emotionless and dead inside in your waking life. Perhaps your fear of loss of power and control is making you feel like this. Remember that only you can truly make the necessary changes in life to move forward in it.

Chapter Twenty: Divination

Divination, a common practice of Witches and other Pagans, is the magical art of using tools to discover unknown information. This can include the tarot cards, scrying, clouds, flames, smoke, I Ching, playing cards, runes, among other forms. In this chapter, we will look at two example forms of divination that I have worked with the most over the years. These are scrying and the tarot cards. Most Witches are drawn to divination because of our natural thirst to understand more about the world around us and our need to help and to heal those who seek our help. Divination works by using tools to seek patterns or symbols which can reveal things about our lives and possible future events. It is a way for the conscious mind to make contact with the psychic mind (unconscious mind) through various tools. It is a way for us to develop our psychic abilities and for the male and female energies of the universe to speak to and through us. For those with a strong psychic ability, divination isn't always necessary. But for those who have a weak psychic ability, divination can help to develop psychic powers immensely.

Witches believe that everyone is born psychic and that everyone has a psychic ability to a degree throughout life. This is called gut instinct or intuition. However, you can't really say that you are psychic, or are a psychic, if you haven't developed your psychic powers to a certain level. Regular meditation, visualisation and divination methods, for example, can help to awaken your psychic powers if you feel that you are not especially psychic. Most people are able to awaken their super psychic senses. All it takes is a willingness to at least try. You can use whatever methods of divination that really appeal to you and investigate them. Many bookstores have books and kits on many different divination forms. It can be a fun and entertaining thing to do to find the forms that you are most drawn to and then study them. You will find that many things are revealed to you about yourself and the world around you as you do this.

Many people experience fear and become uncomfortable around the subject of divination. This is because of the misunderstanding that divination reveals someone's unchangeable destiny. But this is not really what divination is actually about at all. Divination is about being grounded in the current situations of life and growing and evolving into the future. It gives us a chance to seek knowledge and wisdom from deep within the unconscious mind in order to understand the present and possible future events. It can give you an idea or insight of what is likely to happen in the future based on how energies are flowing in the present in the universal scheme of things. Generally speaking, however, you have the power to change the events of your future. Divination can help you to avoid any negativity and embrace positivity in order to live a full and productive life. In other words, it can help you to make the right choices in life.

Divination is not necessarily about telling the future or predicting it in the way most people in the general public think. Time is not linear. In other words, it does not move in a straight line. The universe is in a constant state of flux and variability. Things in the future can change according to choices, astrology, environment, culture, workplace and behaviour, despite what is said in a reading. A divination reading can really only tell you how energy is flowing in a situation and the eventual outcome if the energy continues to flow in the same direction. In other words, it can tell you the future conclusion of a given situation in the present if no significant changes are made. It can give someone the chance to understand the current situation so that he or she can decide what to do for a brighter and more positive future. It should never be thought of as sealing someone's fate.

Divination is made possible because everything that exists is interconnected. That is to say that all energy is linked through the great web of life. The web of life is the Goddess and God. People are a part of this linked energy or great web of life. When we perform divination we receive information through the power of the mind directly from the Goddess and God and from all planes of existence. Divination is a powerful way for the rational, conscious mind to draw information from this ocean of energy. It is a way for Witches and other magical peoples to heighten their awareness of the energies all around us. It is an effective way for us to expand our consciousness so that we can perceive and understand these energies.

Divination is a way for Witches to help and to heal others. It is a form of counselling – psychic counselling. There is a good bit of advice when it comes to giving a divination reading: the first thought is divine and the second thought is self-doubt. That is to say that the first thoughts you have during a reading are usually correct so you must learn to trust yourself more. If you start to doubt your instincts you will begin to squash your intuition and the reading will probably be not as powerful or potent. Just have faith and believe in yourself and your abilities. Always bear in mind when you read others that your wording is very important. Your words can shape the lives of others so you must learn to get them right. If you misjudge a reading or say the wrong things you can bring much discomfort, unhappiness, distress or trouble to people's lives who you were actually trying to help. It can be a heavy burden to read others so never perform a reading until you feel totally comfortable and confident to do so. Read much about divination and first practise much on yourself. Nobody wants to go to someone for a psychic reading who isn't any good.

Mediumship

Another thing that is noteworthy for this chapter is mediumship. It is something that I have decided to talk a little about here because I am a spiritual medium and I am very passionate about it. I have been helping people to commune with their deceased loved ones for many years now and it is very rewarding. Mediumship is basically the ability to commune with the spirits of the dead through psychic means. As you develop your super psychic senses with your divination tools, you may feel drawn to this aspect of the occult. Mediumship requires us to develop our psychic powers even further. A spiritual medium acts like an intermediary between the living and the spirits of the dead. Mediumship has become very popular over the last few hundred years, but it is actually ancient. Witches and other Pagans have been famous for their ability to commune with the spirits of the dead since time immemorial. It can be very comforting to be able to do it.

Mediumship usually involves something called clairvoyance. This term is often used to describe a wide range of psychic skills and abilities. It has, however, a very specific meaning. It literally means "clear seeing". If a psychic can see a spirit, whether vividly in the mind's eye or perhaps as though the spirit is alive in a physical body right in front of the psychic, that psychic is said to be clairvoyant. When a spiritual medium wants to commune with the spirits of the dead he or she may use a psychic skill called clairaudience. Clairaudience in mediumship is the ability to hear and understand the voices, noises and other sounds that spirits may create to let the psychic know that they are about. Another way in which a medium may communicate with spirits is with clairsentience. This is where the medium is able to psychically understand the sensations and emotions that belong to the spirits and perhaps the people who are wishing to commune with them. The clairaudience and clairsentience are the two forms I personally use the most for mediumship, though I do literally see spirits as well.

There is a fundamental point when it comes to mediumship: you must be very careful when embarking on this aspect of the occult. Not all spirits have good intentions. I would suggest that you find a reputable spiritual medium or other spiritual expert who is at hand and is able to give you advice when needed. He or she can help you until you master your psychic skills. You can also ask your power animal or other spirit guide for help and protection. Never dabble in dangerous spiritual exercises, such as Ouija boards, unless you know what you are doing and how to protect yourself. Although many people enter things of a spiritual nature light-heartedly and see it all as just a bit of fun, it is a serious matter. You do not want to open psychic doors that will let negative entities in that you can't control. Spirits are easy to summon but often very difficult to get rid of. Generally speaking though, as long as you are reasonable, sensible, respectful to all beings and walk in the power of love and light you should be fine.

The Art of Scrying

Scrying (meaning "to discern" or "to descry"), also known as seeing or peeping, is an ancient art and form of divination that I have always enjoyed from being a young boy. It can be very relaxing, meditative and revealing to say the least. It can be used for spiritual guidance, prophecy, inspiration, receiving messages from spirits and revelation. Scrying basically involves gazing into a "facilitator" to calm and still the conscious mind so that we can make contact with the psychic (unconscious) mind. The images that appear on the "facilitator" can reveal events in the past, present and possible future as well as events that are happening far away. Crystal balls, candle flames, polished copper sheets, bowls or pools of black water and obsidian black mirrors are all excellent as tools used for scrying rituals. If you can learn how to do this wonderful form of divination it can be very spiritually uplifting to say the least. There is much symbolism in this book to help you to interpret any symbols and signs you see during a scrying ritual, but your own intuition is the most important when scrying as always with anything else of this nature.

Whenever I think of scrying Michel de Nostradamus, a gifted French physician who lived in the sixteenth century, always comes to mind. It is said that he was able to predict many future events with the use of scrying and astrology, including the French Revolution, the Great Fire of London, the rise of Napoleon Bonaparte, the rise of Adolf Hitler, the execution of King Charles I, the first moon landings, the September 11 attacks, to name just a few. It is also said that the astrologer of Queen Elizabeth I, Dr. John Dee, used this form of divination to contact angelic forces, particularly the archangels Uriel and Michael, with a man named Edward Kelley who was said to be very gifted at scrying. Aleister Crowley, a controversial ceremonial magician, was said to be the reincarnation of Edward Kelley. Scrying has ancient links to China, the Middle East, Egypt and Greece and remains popular among many modern-day magical peoples.

A Simple Scrying Ritual

Here, we will look at a simple scrying ritual that you can use should you wish to explore scrying for yourself. This ritual is only a basic guide – you can tweak it how you like to suit yourself. To perform scrying you need to learn how to enter into a deep state of relaxation and meditation. This can put you in a dream-like state and this is what you should be aiming for to get the most out of scrying. You can perform all the steps in chapter eight that are required for a spell in high magic if you like – casting of the magic circle, invocation of the elements, invocation of the Goddess and God or specific deities and so on. You can simply tweak them to suit the scrying ritual. The circle will help you to screen out any distracting psychic energy that may be present in the everyday mundane world. Try not to feel upset or frustrated if nothing happens when you perform this simple scrying ritual. Such feelings will block you from any future success anyhow. With patience, relaxation and meditation you will eventually learn how to perform effective scrying.

Ingredients required for this ritual:

- Taper blue or black candle.
- Matches.
- A teapot filled with a herbal infusion that will aid psychic powers (marigold, mugwort, rose, bay and yarrow are good for example).
- Small iron cauldron or black bowl.
- Black ink.
- Pen with blue or black ink.
- Notebook.
- Sandalwood incense.
- Two obsidian crystals.

Performing the ritual:

On a night of a full or waning moon, place all your ritual ingredients on a flat surface, such as your altar. The cauldron or bowl and candle should be in the centre with an obsidian crystal to either side of them. Then, with a match, light the incense and then the candle and focus on its colour and that colour's link to psychic development. You can also focus on the crystals and their link to psychic work. Then, when you are ready, allow yourself to enter into a deep state of meditation. Take as long as you need to do this. Then pour the infusion from the teapot into the cauldron or bowl and add three drops of the black ink into the infusion in the cauldron or bowl. Make sure the flame of the candle is reflecting on the surface. Then, when you are ready, bring forward in your mind's eye any questions you want answers to. You can say them aloud if you wish. Then gaze at the surface of the infusion in the cauldron or bowl. Allow yourself to really focus on the surface while still focusing on any questions. After some time, you may begin to see a cloudy apparition on the surface and then symbols. If you are really lucky, you may even see events or even deceased loved ones who may come to let you know they are around you. Try not to force yourself to see any images. Simply allow them to come naturally. You can blink normally during this process as this does not affect scrying rituals. When you do not see anything else after some time, write down any symbols and experiences in your notebook while your memory is still fresh for later interpretation. Remember to always believe in yourself and I wish you every success in your scrying work. Good luck.

The Art of the Tarot

Tarot cards are perhaps the most common form of divination that Witches and other Pagans use to seek information. The symbolism on the cards strongly reflects the events of life and appeals to the unconscious (psychic) mind. Most Witches own a set of tarot cards. The tarot cards are one of the easiest ways to open up your psychic powers. The tarot cards can truly open up your inner wisdom. Each card has specific meanings that represent the trials and tribulations of life. The stories of the ancient gods and goddesses that the cards symbolise reflect this. No matter which cards are picked they are always right, even if you do not think so. The accuracy of the reading with the tarot cards always depends on the reader's psychic powers. The tarot cards consist of seventy-eight cards. These are divided into two parts. These are the Major Arcana (Arcana means "secret" and "changes") and the Minor Arcana. The Minor Arcana consists of fifty-six cards and is further divided into four parts. Each part consists of fourteen cards each – an Ace up to ten and then four court cards: Page, Knight, Queen and King. We will look at the Major Arcana and the four parts of the Minor Arcana later in this chapter.

Nobody truly knows where the tarot cards originate from and there has been much debate on the subject. The tarot cards have been linked to many places including Spain, Greece, India and Egypt. The debate on where the cards originate from is partly because the Christians taught that the tarot cards were the work of the Devil and his demons. Their true origin has been lost due to this fact. The Christians wanted to hide anything that would sway the people away from their ways of thinking. If anyone was found to own a pack of tarot cards during the infamous Pagan persecutions and the Witch hunts he or she was instantly doomed. Such cards were seen as a temptation away from the "true God" of Christianity and for this reason many of the tarot decks were hidden or disguised to avoid persecution. The tarot cards are thought to have come about in Europe during the twelfth century, though nobody truly knows where they originate from. Since ancient times, however, the tarot cards have hardly changed at all.

If you would like to work with tarot cards choose a deck that really appeals to you. There are many different designs to choose from. My personal tarot cards resemble strongly the ancient mythology of the gods and goddesses, specifically from Greek mythology. If you are beginning on this form of divination, choose a deck that really displays the stories of the gods and goddesses to help you understand the stories of life. As you study the cards, it will be easier for you to perform divination readings. This means that you will not have to keep referring to books to understand their symbolism. Remember that you should treat your cards with respect because each time you handle them they will absorb your energies and thus the more powerful your readings will be with them. Keep them in a safe place when they are not in use, such as a magical pantry. To discover the cards in more detail I would suggest that you start from the beginning. You can leave each card out in a given day and study its specific meanings. You can then use books and your intuition. Do this over seventy-eight days to cover all the cards and repeat this whenever you think that your knowledge is waning.

When you perform any reading for others in divination you are the reader and the person who you are reading becomes the querent (meaning client). Readings for ourselves makes us become both the reader and the querent. In tarot readings, the cards are shuffled while the querent thinks about their life and any questions that he or she may have. When the cards are shuffled energies are absorbed from deep within the unconscious mind and so the reading can proceed. Chosen cards are then drawn for interpretation. In addition, the reader must understand the relationship between each card that is drawn for a specific reading.

There are many different spreads to explore for tarot readings – from a single-card reading, to a three-card reading to a more complex reading involving the Celtic Cross. The best advice is to start small and gradually build up higher when your confidence grows. The single-card reading is excellent for discovering how a day or week is going to be and the emotions that are likely. The three-card reading, which is the type I mostly use, is excellent for discovering the secrets of the past, present and possible future events. For example, if the querent receives the cards the Devil for the past, the Death card for the present and the Sun card for the future, this reading can indicate some sort of addiction in the past (the Devil card influence), the need to put an end and overcome this influence of the querent (the Death card influence), in order for there to be a brighter, happier and more positive future (the Sun card influence). Each reader has to decide how to best interpret a reading based on intuition and their developing psychic understanding. The more a tarot reader does tarot readings the stronger he or she will become.

Always treat tarot readings, as with all divination readings, as special occasions. Make it your mission to make yourself and the querent as comfortable as possible. You are, after all, doing a form of healing and psychic counselling. I would suggest that any reading is performed in a quiet room where you will not be disturbed. You can fill this room with divination devices as well as tools to aid your psychic powers. If you are reading another person it is best to record the reading, perhaps on a tape recorder. If you are reading yourself, you can perhaps write down everything about the reading in a notebook or your Book of Shadows. As with any divination reading, remember to always believe in yourself and your abilities. Performing a divination reading with the tarot can really enhance your wisdom and psychic powers in ways I can't even explain. Good luck with any divination readings that you give and learn to relax and know that each time you give a reading you are gaining wisdom.

The Major Arcana

The Major Arcana consists of twenty-two cards and relates to the element of spirit and the centre of the magic circle. The Major Arcana represents the most significant changes of life. It represents big influences of the unconscious mind. It symbolises the big passages of life that we often face. In other words, it represents esoteric journeys, huge events or major turning points within life. Always bear in mind that the unconscious mind only communicates with pictures and symbols to convey human emotions, behaviours and experiences, not necessarily language. This, as with any divination readings, should be understood when performing a tarot reading. Some tarot readers may only use the Major Arcana for readings. You can obviously decide for yourself. Here are the twenty-two tarot cards of the Major Arcana and some brief discussions on them:

The Fool: also known as the Joker, relates to the deity Dionysus. It represents beginnings, innocence, risks, the unexpected, foolishness and intelligence. Often, when this card appears in a spread it can indicate that risks may have to be taken in order for a brighter and more positive future. There may be a new opportunity coming when this card appears in a tarot reading. There may also be an unexpected turn of events coming. The fool can also indicate that a lot needs to be learned from a current situation. This card has strong relations to the element of air and its astrological influence is Uranus.

The Magician: also known as the Magus, relates to the deity Hermes. It represents action, initiative, confidence, change, creativity, talents, untruth and hidden knowledge. When the Magician appears in a spread it can indicate that the querent has all the ingredients for positive and constructive change. If the querent thinks that he or she does not have what it takes to make dreams or desires happen, the Magician can represent that things are possible. It can represent the hidden knowledge needed to make things happen. When the Magician appears in a spread there could be a burst of creativity and a need to take important journeys. The astrological influence of this card is Mercury.

The High Priestess: also known as the Female Pope, relates to the deity Persephone. It represents inner wisdom, decisions, inner thoughts, rites of passage, authority, dreams, occult knowledge, leadership, guidance and creative potential. When this card appears in a spread, there may be a need for some sort of guidance and knowledge. Perhaps the querent needs to seek these qualities from an important female figure. The querent may be about to seek the advice from this female figure in order to make a big decision within life. When the High Priestess appears in a spread it is an indication that the querent seeks advice rather than letting internal conflicts to carry on. The astrological influence of this card is the moon.

The Empress: relates to the deity Demeter. It represents harmony, abundance, domestic comfort, fertility, motherhood, productivity, security, love and all emotions associated with femininity. When this card appears in a spread, there may be some sort of birth. This can involve a baby or the birth of new ideas and theories. If the querent has been experiencing financial difficulties, this card can indicate that the problems will alleviate and that there may be a promise for more financial security. The Empress can also indicate a strong relationship with the mother. The astrological influence of this card is Venus.

The Emperor: relates to the deity Zeus. It represents rulership, responsibility, logic, fatherhood, visions, authority, willpower, expansion, strength, counselling, traditions, aggression and creativity. If this card appears in a spread there may be an authoritative male figure with strong traditions within the querent's life. This may be a father or a father figure. This male may be very dynamic and creative who the querent respects very much. It may be that the querent is trying very hard to build a good relationship with this male figure but is finding it very hard. The male figure may have a very strong personality with a good sense of judgement. The astrological influence of this card is Jupiter and Aries.

The Hierophant: relates to the deity Chiron the Centaur. It represents spiritual authority, inspiration, approval, unlocking truths, enlightenment and support from universal power. When this card appears in a spread there may be some very inspiring words that come from a very respected figure. This may be a priest of some sort, a family member or a friend. Whoever the words come from, the person may be very spiritual and religious. The querent may be about to embark on a period of much learning and discovering, especially of a spiritual nature. There may also be an unlocking of truths and a new sense of freedom. When the Hierophant appears in a spread there may be a need for the querent to seek comfort during very difficult times. The astrological influence of this card is Taurus.

The Lovers: relates to the deity Aphrodite. It represents growth, love, maturity, choices, harmony, desire, infatuation, opportunities, decisions, friendship, relationship issues, passion and obsessions. When this card appears in a spread there may be a relationship coming for the querent in the future. The querent may have to make a crucial decision in the future as well. This can involve some sort of commitment. There may also be many conflicts within the querent's life that will soon be resolved. The Lovers in a reading can also indicate that the querent needs to follow the heart rather than the head. The astrological influence of this card is Gemini.

The Chariot: relates to the deity Aries. It represents travel, progress, determination, change, discipline, overcoming problems, rewards, limitations, seeking balance, struggle and triumph. When this card appears in a spread there may be a sense that the querent has been working very hard in life and will soon experience the benefits. This will be entirely deserved. Perhaps the querent has been struggling very hard to maintain his or her position with career. The querent may feel the need to protect whatever he or she holds dear. There may also be a sense that the querent should just enjoy the benefits of the hard work that has been put into any important projects without worrying too much. The astrological influence of this card is Cancer.

Justice: also know as Adjustment, relates to the deity Athena. It represents balance, resolution, fairness, clarity, finding solutions, morality, decisions, summing up and equality. When this card shows itself in a spread there may be some sort of settlement that will be initiated. This usually involves things to do with the law. On a more personal nature, Justice appearing in a spread can indicate the summing up of a long-standing issue. There may be agreements that will benefit the querent immensely. This, however, may only come if the querent has acted morally and fairly. The astrological influence of this card is Libra.

The Hermit: also known as the Trailer, relates to the deity Cronos. It represents solitude, separation, individualism, withdrawn emotions, inner knowledge, isolation, deep thoughts, lack of support, inner wisdom and meditation. When the Hermit appears in a spread perhaps the querent may need to withdraw from people or situations in order to gather his or her thoughts. Perhaps the querent is tired of people or situations and just needs some time to recuperate. The Hermit appearing in a spread can also indicate that the querent may have to do things of importance on his or her own without the support and guidance of other people. There may also be a need for the querent to look very deeply to understand what he or she has learned so far within life. This is a card I often get being a Solitary Witch. The astrological influence of this card is Virgo.

The Wheel of Fortune: relates to the three goddesses of fate known as the Moirai. It represents change, endings, beginnings, chances, choices, ideas and the flow of events. When this card appears in a spread there may be a sudden major change in events in life and overall circumstances. This major change in life can transform the whole way in which the querent thinks and lives. This can be good or bad. Regardless, this card indicates a chance for new growth and a new phase of life. Whatever has happened within the querent's life, new things can be learned for a brighter future. The astrological influence of this card is Jupiter.

Strength: also known as Fortitude, relates to the deity Hercules. It represents struggle, inner strength, possible danger, courage, self-discipline, talents, collisions and the need for balance around a situation that requires much strength. If Strength appears in a spread perhaps there is a situation around the querent's life that needs gentle strength and an intuitive response if a resolution to a troublesome situation can be reached. Symbolically, the querent must not slay the lion but rather use errant negotiations and peaceful control in order to ensure a steady progress. Often, this card will appear when the querent has some sort of inner battle around a situation or decision in which he or she must balance the male and female qualities in order for success. The astrological influence of this card is Leo.

The Hanged Man: relates to the deity Prometheus and the element of water. It represents the unconscious mind, hope, waiting for things, letting go, sacrifice, loss of faith and a change in attitudes. When the Hanged Man appears in a spread there may be a need for the querent to look at a situation differently. The card can indicate that there is unconscious wisdom at play within the querent's life and so intuition may well be very important. On a more mundane level, the Hanged Man can indicate that there may be a period of waiting around for the outcome of something very important. This can involve employment or perhaps a pending contract of some sort. There may also be some sort of sacrifice needed within the querent's life in order to attain something else of greater value. The astrological influence of this card is Neptune.

Death: also known as the Close, relates to the deity Hades. It represents endings, new beginnings, change, opportunities, new ventures, growth and the chance to move on from a toxic relationship. When the Death card appears in a spread the end of a cycle may well be coming. This will allow the querent to experience new opportunities and new growth. Perhaps there has been a very negative situation that needs to be put to an end in order for a brighter and more positive future. The letting go of past pain, negative habits and associations can allow the querent to finally move on and embrace a new phase of life. Although the card can seem a little gloomy at first glance, it does usually indicate great opportunities ahead for the querent. The astrological influence of this card is Scorpio.

Temperance: relates to the deity Iris. It represents reconciliation, finance, compromise, growth, self-control, balance, renewal, group work, adjustment and the connection between the conscious mind and the unconscious mind. When this card appears in a spread, it may well be time for the querent to pay very close attention to detail in order to get the right balance around an important situation. If not, the potential rewards or benefits will soon evaporate and disappear. There may also be a possibility for balance and harmony if the querent learns how to reconcile past behaviours with who he or she is right now. Temperance appearing in a spread can also indicate a happy and harmonious relationship or marriage. The astrological influence of this card is Sagittarius.

The Devil: also known as Temptation, relates to the deity Pan. It represents struggle, manipulation, decisions, temptation, misconceptions, addiction, shame, personality disorders, unethical issues, instincts, enslavement, constriction, confrontation and being tied to a negative person or situation. When the Devil appears in a spread the querent may well be tied to a negative situation or person and this may be causing displeasure. The querent may well have entered into a relationship, contract, career commitment or financial agreement with high hopes, but things may not have turned out the way that was hoped. Whatever situation the querent has entered into, it has become more like enslavement rather than liberation. Therefore, it may be time for the querent to follow his or her instincts and to remember that in one jump freedom can be on the horizon. The astrological influence of this card is Capricorn.

The Tower: also known as the Fire From Heaven, relates to the Famous Labyrinth of King Minos which was struck down by the angry god Poseidon. It represents breakdowns (whether emotional or physical), change, upheaval, breakthroughs, shocks, insight, speed, recovering the ego, disaster and an inability to control events. When the Tower appears in a spread the querent may well feel that there are situations and events that are undoing hard work or whatever the querent holds dear. There may be a feeling that a creative idea is collapsing or becoming undone. Although this card can seem very unfavourable, perhaps there is a need for change in order for life to move on. The querent should understand that the ego can still be recovered and new growth and ideas will come again for a positive future. There is always something positive that comes from any disaster if we take the time to think about things. The astrological influence of this card is Uranus and Mars.

The Star: relates to the deity Pandora. It represents happiness, imagination, new life, vigour, dreams, hope, clarity, wisdom, thoughts, promise, faith, opportunities, meeting others and an interest in astrology. When the Star appears in a spread there may be a fresh start on the horizon and a wonderful sense of renewed hope and faith. The card is very favourable if the querent has started a new project or relationship. It can indicate much creativity and imagination with these. The querent may also have a sense of renewed energy and be able to put his or her hopes and dreams into reality. The Star, however, can indicate that the querent should be careful of blind hope. If the necessary actions are not put into things that are important, then they will not happen. The astrological influence of this card is Aquarius.

The Moon: relates to the deity Hecate. It represents indecision, solitude, perspective crisis of faith, instincts, gossip, risks, confusion, uncertainty, mental health problems, feminine issues and intuition. When the Moon appears in a spread the querent may have much doubt about his or her positions in life. The querent may have to look to intuition in order to gain insight into possible solutions. Things can appear to look different under the light of the moon (blood can appear black for instance) and this represents the need to look to the inner self rather than just accept things at surface values. There may be a risk involved within the querent's life that will take him or her away from familiar surroundings. The querent may need to understand that only he or she alone can make any decisions at this time. The astrological influence of this card is Pisces.

The Sun: relates to the deity Apollo. It represents innocence, joy, health, protection, creativity, trust, success, positive attitudes, pleasure, comfort, youth and moving forward in life. When the Sun appears in a spread there may well be a sense of achievement within the querent's life or this may be about to come. This achievement may be the result of much hard work and determination. The card can indicate a period of great happiness, success and love. There may also be the birth of a child on the way. Whatever the querent is working on, the card appearing can indicate much good fortune and success. If the querent has been working hard in life to achieve their goals, the Sun can indicate a need to relax and enjoy the benefits. The querent may want to rediscover those child-like qualities within himself or herself after this period of intense hard work. The astrological influence of this card is, unsurprisingly, the sun.

Judgement: relates to the deity Hermes the Psychopomp. It represents rewards, second chances, conclusions, taking responsibility for actions, spiritual awakening, forgiveness, learning from experience, reaping what has been sown and things that come back to haunt. When Judgement appears in a spread there may be a sense that the querent has a second chance to put right the things that he or she has done wrong in the past. Perhaps the querent has been experiencing some sort of guilt and has an incredible urge to make amends. The querent should use this opportunity very wisely as there is an excellent chance to spiritually reinvent himself or herself. Judgement appearing in a spread can also indicate financial rewards and progress in a new project for past efforts. If the querent has failed in a past project, he or she may well have success the second time around due to experience and hindsight. The astrological influence of this card is Pluto.

The World: relates to the deity Hermaphroditus, the child of Hermes and Aphrodite. It represents completion, endings, successful outcomes, beginnings, birth, fulfilment, spiritual understanding, completion, movement and travel. When the World appears in a spread there may be a very successful outcome of something very important. The card can indicate triumph and a final conclusion of a matter after a period of very hard work. The outcome of a cycle may well be reached and the querent will soon experience the need to start the next phase of life after much accomplishment. This is symbolised by the dancing Hermaphroditus who becomes the foetus, ready to start the next phase of life, just as the Fool emerges from the cave at the start of the Major Arcana. In other words, one chapter of life is now closing and a new one is beginning. The success achieved by the querent may make him or her want to do some travelling around the globe which is another meaning of the World in the tarot deck. The astrological influence of this card is Saturn.

The Minor Arcana: Pentacles

Pentacles, or Coins, of the Minor Arcana correspond to the element of earth and the direction of the north. Their season is winter and their zodiac signs are Capricorn, Taurus and Virgo. They relate to all day-to-day events that correspond to the element of earth, such as wealth, the physical body, physical possessions, employment, stability, growth, prosperity, money and dedication. They are associated with worldly matters basically and all things of a very earthy nature. Here are the fourteen tarot cards of the Pentacles and some brief discussions on them:

Ace of Pentacles: When the Ace of Pentacles appears in a spread perhaps the querent has a sense of the appreciation for what money can bring. He or she may have those feelings that come with complete material accomplishment. There may have been very wise investments made by the querent that have paid off and the querent may now feel secure on the financial scene. On the other hand, when the Ace of Pentacles appears in a spread, a win of some sort may well be coming if the querent has been entering competitions or has been entertaining other gambles. With this card, there is usually a very happy period of prosperity in which the querent can enjoy comfort, material abundance and satisfaction.

Two of Pentacles: When the Two of Pentacles appears in a spread it can reveal some sort of harmony regarding a business partnership. The card in a spread can mean that the querent may well have to be a master at juggling the demands of time and money. Money and energy are likely to be readily available with the appearance of this card for important projects which may well develop into something rewarding in the future. However, the querent must be willing to put in the hard work and embrace opportunities that arise. This card is considered very favourable for those who know how to "play" with money. On a more domestic level, this card can foretell workable, though often difficult, partnerships.

Three of Pentacles: The Three of Pentacles appearing in a spread often represents someone who is working hard in life to build up a business of some sort. It can represent a very creative period for the querent in which any hard work and planning are paying off or are about to. With this, the querent can pay close attention to the enjoyable and productive aspects of work and deal with the creative sides to it that the querent loves. A material venture may well show rewards but this may only be a temporary solution. Hopefully, with hard work and effort it will develop into more permanent rewards.

Four of Pentacles: The Four of Pentacles often foretells a period of financial security. This often follows a period where the querent has not felt secure on the financial scene or has experienced much financial pressure. The financial security is often the result of a successful venture or project. When this card appears in a spread, it is perhaps now time for the querent to appreciate all that he or she has achieved so far. The querent may well feel confident to move forward in life and achieve the things that are so desired. The card can also indicate a return to better physical health after a period of being unwell. It is very favourable. However, the card can also indicate that the querent should try to learn to take risks on the financial or business level as there is an element that the querent is holding on too tightly to things – such fear of losing things may mean no loss, but there may also be no gain.

Five of Pentacles: When the Five of Pentacles appears in a spread it can foretell financial problems or loss. The querent may be experiencing much difficulty on the financial scene and this may be creating negative fears, anxieties and worries. The querent may well be fearing that he or she will lose everything that has been worked hard for. However, the card often only indicates these negative feelings towards financial insecurity rather then the actual loss of something. The querent should instead focus on ways to put things right rather than constantly worrying about the negatives of their situation. The querent should be aware that there is a way around any problems and that faith in the self can be restored by making the right choices.

Six of Pentacles: The Six of Pentacles appearing in a spread often indicates a situation of generosity involving finance. This may be the querent who helps others with money or substance or it may be the querent who seeks help from others. On the other hand, the Six of Pentacles can indicate that the querent may be asked for advice on a financial level because he or she has reached a period of success and security. It may be the querent himself or herself who needs the advice from someone of a successful position. This card can also indicate the arrival of unexpected cash from an unexpected source.

Seven of Pentacles: The Seven of Pentacles can indicate that hard work is finally paying off for the querent. There is a feeling with this card that the querent is experiencing a sense of achievement but there is still work to be done. However, with true commitment to everything that is important and belief in abilities, the querent can expect to get what is desired. The card suggests growth and expansion of some sort. However, continued effort and dedication are needed if desired results are to be realised in the future. The Seven of Pentacles can sometimes mean a difficult decision and the querent may be wondering whether to continue with a project or business that has already been built up or to move on to something else.

Eight of Pentacles: The Eight of Pentacles in a spread often indicates that the querent will soon have an opportunity to express his or her talents with the promise of a reward involving finance. The querent may soon have the good fortune to have success with any venture or project he or she undertakes and from this will come a sense of value on both emotional and material levels. The Eight of Pentacles can indicate a period in which the querent can just enjoy whatever makes him or her happy. This can involve the enrolment on a course of study, the development of a hobby or even a new career direction.

Nine of Pentacles: When the Nine of Pentacles appears in a spread there is often a sense that the querent has made good judgements and decisions regarding business and finance. Therefore, these areas of the querent's life are starting to pay off. There may then follow a period of leisure and relaxation within the querent's life. The card can indicate a welcome relief from the concerns of business, finance, family arguments, credit cards, bank loans and so on. There may be a sense that the querent can just feel comfortable with himself or herself. The result will be that others will seek the pleasure and enjoyment of the querent's company. The card strongly indicates that the querent has a strong sense of identity.

Ten of Pentacles: The Ten of Pentacles in a spread can indicate ongoing contentment, security, happiness and material fulfilment. There is a sense within the querent's life that something has been well-established, something of great value and permanence that can be handed down to others who the querent perhaps cares very deeply about. This can involve a very successful business or a property. It can even involve something of a more personal and artistic nature, such as a book that others will find very useful and valuable. Either way, whatever will be passed on there is a sense that the querent can feel content in the knowledge that he or she can offer something of value in the future.

Page of Pentacles: The Page of Pentacles is usually a harbinger of excellent news. This can involve financial issues, competitions, property or rewards for hard work or good deeds done. The Page of Pentacles symbolises a hard-working and responsible youth who has very creative ideas and theories. Therefore, the card can indicate in a reading that the querent needs to find these qualities to deal with any financial, business or domestic problems. The card represents that the key to success to protect your future is to embrace very careful management and gentle care of things. The card can also indicate that money will come in small amounts which should be saved and nurtured rather than seen as insignificant and wasted on things that are not really needed.

Knight of Pentacles: The Knight of Pentacles can indicate the coming or perhaps ongoing of matters concerning business affairs, money, property or practical solutions to things. The knight symbolises the endurance, dedication and patience that is needed to make progress within life. The querent is on the right path for this but at a steady and measured pace. The Knight of Pentacles may symbolise someone who comes to the querent. This someone may well embody all of the qualities that are symbolised by the Knight of Pentacles and be able to advise the querent appropriately. He may well not be very creative, but he is honest, trustworthy, steadfast and loyal.

Queen of Pentacles: The Queen of Pentacles can indicate those qualities of a very down-to-earth woman who is known for her nurturing and generous personality as well as her wisdom regarding finance, business, practicality, sensuality and value of the physical body. Often the card is telling the querent to embrace these qualities for himself or herself in order to enrich life and to achieve security on the financial, business or domestic levels. The Queen of Pentacles may symbolise someone who comes to the querent. This person, usually a woman, will come to help the querent and guide him or her appropriately. This person will help the querent to bring forward all the qualities associated with the Queen of Pentacles for a brighter and more positive future.

King of Pentacles: The King of Pentacles can indicate those qualities of a very successful businessman or perhaps a leader of some sort. He is a realist who embraces and thrives on the practicalities of life. He is earthy, experienced, steadfast, reliable, grounded, trustworthy, resourceful and a very good planner for things of great importance. In a spread, the King of Pentacles can be an indication that the querent needs to embrace these qualities. The King of Pentacles may symbolise someone, usually a man, who comes to the querent. This person who comes to the querent is very strong-willed and may help the querent to manifest all the qualities associated with the King of Pentacles so as to develop confidence for material things desired in life. This strong-willed person may have the solutions to long-standing issues of a material nature.

The Minor Arcana: Wands

Wands, or Staffs, of the Minor Arcana correspond to the element of air and the direction of the east. In some tarot decks, however, wands relate to the element of fire. Their season is spring and their zodiac signs are Aquarius, Gemini and Libra. They relate to everyday events associated with the element of air, such as the human mind, new beginnings, swiftness, legal matters, communication, reason, mental power, visions and wisdom. This is the part of the tarot deck that relates to how we think and perceive things. Here are the fourteen tarot cards of the Wands and some brief discussions on them:

Ace of Wands: The Ace of Wands relates to that creative, masculine and artistic part of the self. The card indicates that the querent is on a very creative period of life that will probably be successful. The querent may well feel very restless as he or she continues with the creative idea or project. There is a pursuit of a vision when this card shows up in a spread after feelings of dissatisfaction with the present circumstances of life. The querent may well want to change current circumstances as he or she embarks on a new adventure. He or she may well feel that hopes and dreams are now possible as old feelings become a distant memory.

Two of Wands: often indicates some sort of creative partnership that will bring much thoughtfulness and management. Often, this partnership will result in creative ideas or theories that will soon come to fruition in some way. Often, the querent will benefit financially from their creative skills when this card appears and material stability will be realised. There will be a belief in oneself for the querent with this card and efforts will be rewarded. All it takes is for the querent to keep trying despite any problems. With this card there is a sense that the creative potential will be revealed in the future.

Three of Wands: When this card appears in a reading there is a feeling that the querent is thinking about starting some sort of creative project. It indicates that the time is right to start artistic pursuits and for expressing new ideas and theories. The Three of Wands often indicates money coming to the querent as their confidence in their creative side increases. There is a feeling with this card of high enthusiasm, optimism and potential regarding projects. But the querent must realise that there is still hard work ahead for the creative ideas to fully come to fruition. Good foundations and satisfaction are implied with this card.

Four of Wands: With the Four of Wands appearing in a spread, there is a sense that the querent is reaping the benefits of a creative project. There is a sense that the querent is consolidating all their achievements. The querent may feel that a move to a different home or style of life is in order. The querent may be wanting to broaden their horizons and just enjoy the company of much-loved friends and family. There is a sense with this card that the querent has experienced early fruit with a creative project and that he or she has every right to celebrate and relax. However, this early fruit is only the beginning as the ship must sail on in order for the final goal to be accomplished.

Five of Wands: The Five of Wands often indicates that the querent is being tested to the limit. There are people around the querent who are causing conflict and the querent is trying their very best to manipulate others to ensure calmness and tranquillity. When this card appears it may be time for the querent to not focus on the past success or think that problems will resolve of their own accord, but rather take action. The querent should be meticulous around areas of life that are important. Although there may be much battle that the querent has to face, making the right decisions will lead to what is wanted out of life. Compromises must be made but also personal integrity will also need to be maintained.

Six of Wands: The Six of Wands appearing in a reading can often indicate triumph over outward obstacles. There is a feeling with this card that the querent has worked very hard to maintain peace and tranquillity and so he or she should be very proud. The Six of Wands often indicates that there is some very good news on the way with regards to law or career. A rewarding contract, a new qualification or a promotion in employment may be coming for the querent. The querent may well be in line for public acclaim and acknowledgement. The hard work put into things that are important will be realised.

Seven of Wands: like the Five of Wands, often indicates struggle and heavy challenges. But from this negativity there is potential for great possibility if the querent overcomes it. Much wisdom and lessons from life may well be achieved. The card often indicates that the querent's great powers to overcome any negativity will be rewarded after much struggle. The card can indicate the stiff competition and the struggle to overcome other people's creative ideas. There is a feeling with this card that the querent is doing everything possible to achieve in a very competitive world.

Eight of Wands: When the Eight of Wands appears in a spread it is often an indication of excellent news. There may well be great opportunities and journeys coming to the querent, helping him or her to gain much wisdom and get forward in life. The talents, gifts and creativity of the querent are realised and other people will respect his or her true worth. This should be appreciated by the querent so that he or she can build upon future ambitions. Imagination flows when this card appears in a reading and travel is sometimes implied.

Nine of Wands: The Nine of Wands often appears when the querent has been working very hard in life to the point of exhaustion for a creative project but there is one final challenge to overcome. There is a feeling with this card that the querent should never give up and do what it takes to overcome this final challenge. He or she will find the strength to overcome this challenge if the goal is so important to the querent. The querent must keep on keeping on regardless of any obstacles or outward challenges. After all, why stop now after coming so far?

Ten of Wands: When the Ten of Wands appears in a reading there is often a sense that the querent has taken on too much in life and is feeling overloaded and oppressed with stress, worry and tension. The responsibilities of the querent may well lay heavy on the querent's mind and there is a sense that he or she simply wants to escape. The creativity and potential of the querent may well have become overburdened with too many worldly concerns. The child-like qualities of the querent to be daring and take risks in life may be somewhat lost. If this card shows up in a reading perhaps it is time for the querent to refresh their thinking so that a new creative period can begin.

Page of Wands: The Page of Wands often comes in a reading when the querent needs to pay urgent and particular attention to detail with the creative projects that are of great importance. It can also mean that people around the querent are all talk with little action. The querent may need to check any details first before taking action. The Page of Wands can often represent someone within the querent's life who is very inventive and creative, yet easily bored with little action or intention. However, much wisdom can be gained from this person. This person may create ideas within the querent's mind for a very bright future.

Knight of Wands: When the Knight of Wands appears in a spread it may well be time to take real action regarding matters of business and creative ideas or theories. Perhaps the querent has been thinking about something that needs to be done and it may well be time to just do it rather than wasting time dwelling on it. The Knight of Wands often indicates things that will now move fast and the coming results of long-awaited decisions. The Knight of Wands may symbolise someone within the querent's life who embodies all the qualities of the card who comes to give advice about things that need to be done. Excitement, new journeys, freedom, expedition and adventure are implied when this card appears in a reading.

Queen of Wands: The Queen of Wands symbolises a very creative, well-balanced, nurturing, imaginative, warm, loyal and consisting woman. She is very intuitive and understanding to people who she cares very deeply about. If she shows up in a reading it may well be time for the querent to embrace these qualities if he or she wants to get far in life. The Queen of Wands may be urging the querent to do what it takes to meet any needs, but also take particular attention to care for those who are of great importance. The Queen of Wands may appear in a tarot reading to symbolise a person who embodies all the qualities associated with the card. This person, usually a magnetic and sincere woman, can offer great wisdom to the querent.

King of Wands: The King of Wands symbolises a very protective father figure with great authority, loyalty and emotional maturity. He often has many friends and associates as well as very close family connections. He is approachable but not too domineering. He often appears in a spread when the querent needs to learn how to handle others with reserves of charm, strength and compassion. The card can symbolise a need to initiate new ideas and theories to further matters of great importance. The querent may well need to learn how to evoke the creative spirit within in order for things of importance to manifest. The King of Wands in a reading may symbolise someone, usually a very intelligent and imaginative man, within the querent's life who comes to offer great wisdom about how to get far in life.

The Minor Arcana: Swords

The Swords, or Daggers, relate to the element of fire. In some tarot decks, however, they relate to the element of air. This often creates confusion but I always associate Swords with fire in the tarot cards. "Wand", as one definition, means "wind" which represents intelligence and communication. Wands are often made of wood which comes from trees. Trees need air to breathe. Although there are many similarities with the elements of air and fire, to me, swords always represent the fiery force of willpower and the challenges of life. In a sword fight, sparks can be created which is another reason why many Witches associate swords with the element of fire. The season of these tarot cards is summer and their zodiac signs are Aries, Leo and Sagittarius. They relate to everyday events associated with the element of fire, such as strength, victory, responsibilities, enthusiasm, encouragement, confidence, sexual potency, stimulation and transformation. Here are the fourteen tarot cards of the Swords and some brief discussions on them:

Ace of Swords: often indicates great victory and success regarding projects that have been worked on. This is the result of the querent's enthusiasm and driving forces to do well in life. The card can indicate that everything that the querent has worked hard for is about to take him or her by storm and there may well be a need to keep the mental stability to cope with the fast pace. There may be some conflicts on the way but the creative potential and viewpoint will inevitably emerge with great fiery energy. This card always reminds me of the emergence of summer, a time that symbolises when we become aware of our responsibilities.

Two of Swords: The Two of Swords can represent that some sort of balance is needed within the querent's life. There may well be a need to consider the position in which the querent has been placed with another person, whether a business partner or a romantic one. There is potential for much success with this partnership but the querent must work wisely with the other person, using reason and fairness. Being too emotional around this situation may not be appropriate right now. The partnership may well be a very tense and unpredictable one so the querent may need to use creativity to solve any problems.

Three of Swords: When the Three of Swords appears in a reading it can often indicate some sort of heartbreak. This can involve the breakdown of a romantic relationship, a friendship, a business or anything else of great importance to the querent. If this card appears, it is time for the querent to not blame himself or herself too much and to learn how to move on in life. The querent should realise that self-delusion must not continue. With any destruction there are always new possibilities in the future. The only way to really reach new things is through battles and the turbulences of life.

Four of Swords: The Four of Swords often comes in a reading as welcome relief after a period of much conflict, stress and tension. It can symbolise a period when the querent has some time to recuperate and heal wounds after a complete, exhausting period that has taken up too much time, energy and strength. The Four of Swords often appears in a reading when the querent is recovering from an illness. With the fiery energy and creative potential within, the querent can overcome any problems.

Five of Swords: When the Five of Swords appears in a reading it can indicate that the querent is working very hard on a current project that is resulting in very few benefits. There is a sense that the querent is working on a goal that is unattainable. Often, the querent should just accept defeat and simply learn how to move on in life from it. The querent should not let pride get in the way from other creative potentials in life. He or she should not let a punishing schedule to overtake other things of importance. Often, the most wisest and courageous thing to do in life is to simply walk away. The querent should realise that we can only work within the confines of our own individual abilities.

Six of Swords: When the Six of Swords appears in a reading there is a sense that some order is needed within the querent's life. This can help the querent to solve any harsh problems. Often, this card appears when the querent needs to distance himself or herself from worrying and troublesome situations or perhaps people who cause hardship. Therefore, travel is sometimes implied with the appearance of this card. There is still a lot of hard work to come for the querent but the distancing will allow him or her to recharge and recuperate. During this distancing of the querent, there will be time for him or her to think about what needs to be done for future success. Self-respect and dignity will be retained as the storm moves on.

Seven of Swords: The Seven of Swords often comes in a reading when the querent is experiencing feelings of mistrust around difficult situations regarding a particular and dangerous person. The querent may well need to be aware that he or she will have to use their fiery energy and creative tactics to overcome the opponent. There is a sense that the querent will need to be very clever and cunning to win the game. There is a very important message that comes with this card: fight very hard for what is yours and don't let anyone or anything get in the way of your future success. Although the querent may have a sense of falsehood around their situation, there are sometimes when life needs it.

Eight of Swords: The Eight of Swords often heralds a time of much conflict, heartbreak and hardship. There may well be a feeling that the querent has little means or compulsion to seek advice or overcome any problems. This can be the result of too much heartache or abuse of some sort. The message of this card is to use the fiery energy to clarify any thoughts, seek help where possible and release any negativity so that healing can begin. If the querent does not act now the troubles will continue. Facing the realities of a bad situation is what is needed right now within the querent's life.

Nine of Swords: Unfortunately, this card is often a very bad omen of much stress and hardship within the querent's life. There is a sense that the querent is feeling like he or she is the victim of other people's negativity. The card can also indicate an ongoing illness. Resilience is very low and the querent may feel that he or she does not have the ability to get through the troubles of life. What is important for the querent right now is to use whatever reserves of energy that are present to get through any problems. Guilt may well be the root of any negativity within the querent's life right now.

Ten of Swords: The Ten of Swords in a reading often indicates the dramatic ending of a very stressful time. There may have been much hardship within the querent's life and the ending of a bad situation seems inevitable. This can involve a relationship of some sort or business. The querent will gain much experience from any bad situations of life and should be open to the creative possibilities of the future despite any pain or anxiety.

Page of Swords: The Page of Swords often appears in a reading as a positive omen. The querent may well be eager to learn about the responsibilities of life. Progress and wisdom are implied with this card for the querent. With this wisdom, the querent will learn how to be a good judge of character. The card may be urging the querent to muster his or her wits in order to stay ahead of any negative situations. There is much creative potential and independence applied in a reading when this card shows up for the querent. The card can symbolise someone within the querent's life who embodies all the qualities of the Page of Swords. This person, usually a young man, can help to spark the creative potential within the querent.

Knight of Swords: When the Knight of Swords appears in a reading there may well be very hard challenges coming to the querent. It symbolises the coming of battles that are unavoidable if success and progress are to be made. Alternatively, the Knight of Swords can indicate someone who comes to the querent to help to embrace the qualities of progression, enthusiasm and creativity. This person, usually a hot-tempered and volatile male, may hurdle into the querent's life and then disappear just as quickly. There are many changes and upheavals applied to a reading involving this card.

Queen of Swords: The Queen of Swords represents a very charming, creative, warm and protective woman. She has amazing wit and she loves to praise and challenge people. When the Queen of Swords appears in a reading it may well be time for the querent to embrace these qualities in order for life to move forward and for future success. Faith in abilities and confidence are needed right now for the querent. The querent may well need to defend matters of a very personal or emotional nature. The Queen of Swords can symbolise a very strong and confident person within the querent's life, usually a woman, who embodies all the qualities of the card. This person may come to the querent to act as a catalyst for the necessities of life to do with the element of fire.

King of Swords: The King of Swords symbolises a very fiery, quick-witted, competitive and ambitious man. He is strongly business-orientated and has strong associations with leadership and responsibility. He symbolises someone who we can turn to for the things that are needed in life. He is good at helping us to solve any major issues that life often throws at us. When the King of Swords appears in a spread it may well be time for the querent to embrace these qualities in order for life to progress forward in the way that is desired by the querent. The querent may well need to protect things around him or her in the everyday mundane world. The King of Swords can symbolise a very strong-willed person within the querent's life, usually a man, who embodies all the qualities of the King of Swords. This person can encourage great wisdom and determination within the querent's life for future success and comfort.

The Minor Arcana: Cups

The Cups, or Goblets, of the Minor Arcana correspond to the element of water and the direction of the west. Their season is autumn and their zodiac signs are Cancer, Pisces and Scorpio. They relate to the day-to-day events associated with the element of water, such as love, affection, friendship, marriage, emotions, empathy, motherhood, pleasure and psychic sensitivity. They are associated with all emotional matters basically and all things of a very watery nature. Here are the fourteen tarot cards of the Cups and some brief discussions on them:

Ace of Cups: When the Ace of Cups appears in a spread it is time for the querent to express that deep, sensitive and emotional side around an important situation. Perhaps there is a situation that needs particular care and attention. The card often symbolises pregnancy or the beginnings of a relationship in which the querent will fall passionately in love. The card can also symbolise the querent's need to express creativity, artistic pursuits, love, friendship and affection around an important situation. The card often implies reconciliation around a troublesome or overwhelming relationship. The querent may well feel the need to start again around a relationship that has caused much heartache and depression.

Two of Cups: When the Two of Cups appears in a reading there is often a feeling of commitment with the querent on emotional matters. Perhaps the querent wants to enter a marriage and after much contemplation he or she feels ready to do so. There is a feeling of harmony with this card as partnerships and friendships show their rewards. There may have been much difficulty in a relationship but this will soon be overcome as reconciliation is reached. Often, this card appears in a reading when the querent is in an emotional relationship with their business partner.

Three of Cups: The Three of Cups in a reading often implies the querent's feelings around a growing relationship. Perhaps the querent has worked hard to make a relationship flourish and the rewards will soon become apparent. The card can also imply something of a very emotional nature that the querent has worked hard for that will show early success. The card in a reading can also signify that some sort of healing is needed around matters very close to the heart. There may well need to be recovery and rejuvenation around matters that are very close to the querent. This card is also a symbol of celebration and social events. So there may be a wedding or christening that the querent is preparing for. Emotional fulfilment is implied with this card.

Four of Cups: When this card appears in a reading it may well be the time for the querent to look at their situation with truth, rather than seeing the world through rose-tinted glasses. Perhaps the querent is enjoying the benefits of something very close to the heart but dissatisfaction is starting to come forward within the querent's mind. The card often implies that romance may well need to be rediscovered in order to progress forward. There is a sense of boredom when this card appears which can eventually lead to very serious unhappiness. Perhaps the querent has been trying too hard in a relationship and he or she is thinking about moving on. The card implies unexpected and unresolved issues in matters very close to the heart.

Five of Cups: The Five of Cups can unfortunately imply unhappiness and dissatisfaction in a relationship that has been worked hard for. There may well have been some sort of break-up with someone who means a lot to the querent. There is a sense that the querent may well understand that he or she cannot go on with these feelings as the realisation that hurt can't be healed with any regrets. When this card appears in a tarot reading perhaps it is time for the querent to focus on what remains rather than thinking about anything lost.

The card implies betrayal and final endings regarding things of a very emotional nature. Often, there is a feeling with the querent that not everything of an emotional nature has truly been lost and things can be recovered if the querent is willing to work for what he or she wants.

Six of Cups: When the Six of Cups appears in a reading there is a feeling with the querent that everything worked for in the past is flowing into the present and this can give the querent a feeling that he or she can plan for things of an emotional nature in the future. The personal history of the querent is often realised with this card and from this can come great rewards as the querent is able to make the right decisions in life. There is a sense with this card that the querent has a renewed sense of direction in life with regards of a very emotional nature. When this card appears in a tarot reading old memories very close to the heart resurface and the querent may well feel the need to get in touch with old friends and family who the querent has had no contact with for some time. Security regarding past dreams is implied when this card appears in a reading.

Seven of Cups: When the Seven of Cups appears in a reading there is a sense of great potential and creativity regarding a matter of a very emotional nature. Perhaps the querent has been working on something very close to the heart and the importance of achieving a cherished dream surrounds him or her. When this card appears perhaps it is time for the querent to only accept offers that will lead to emotional fulfilment and not the undoing of anything that has been worked hard for. There is a sense of confusion when this card appears but the querent should always trust his or her instincts. Challenge and knowing one's own limits are implied with this card.

Eight of Cups: The Eight of Cups appearing in a reading can indicate a sudden change on an emotional level. There may well be a feeling that the querent has to let go of a cherished relationship in order to be more secure in the future. Although this can be painful and traumatic, the decisions made on an emotional level will be best if the querent wants to move forward in life. The truth of a very emotional and difficult situation must be faced when this card appears in a reading and the querent must learn to let go. This card often implies mourning and depression but in the long run this will only strengthen the querent emotionally.

Nine of Cups: When the Nine of Cups appears in a reading there may well be new friends and associates coming to the querent. The card implies excitement regarding matters of an emotional nature. There is a sense that the querent has a good sense of humour that will attract many new and exciting people. These people will inspire the querent to get far in life regarding matters of communication and expression. There is a sense that creativity will be enhanced when this card appears in a tarot reading. When the Nine of Cups appears in a reading there may well be good health and security coming to the querent, perhaps after a period of not knowing. A cherished dream that the querent has worked hard for is often implied when this card comes up in a reading. Emotional pleasure and fulfilment are strongly implied with this beautiful card.

Ten of Cups: The Ten of Cups appearing in a reading indicates completion, contentment and emotional fulfilment. The past achievements of a very emotional nature are realised as the querent now understands how hard he or she has been working. The card appearing in a reading can indicate much emotional fulfilment with friends, family and associates. There is a feeling with the querent that peace and tranquillity are long-lasting as the confidence of the querent grows and matures. The querent can now simply sit back and enjoy the benefits. When the Ten of Cups appears in a reading now is the time for the querent to enjoy the company of others and the benefits of group activities. There is a sense of contentment with this card in matters very strongly associated with the heart.

Page of Cups: The Page of Cups represents a very emotional, intuitive and vital man who is governed by his feelings. When this card appears in a reading it can indicate the birth of new ideas and theories regarding matters of a very emotional nature. The querent may well have a very youthful attitude regarding things very close to the heart. However, there is a sense of insecurity and there may well be a lot to be learned. At this time within the querent's life, there may well be a need to seek emotional guidance from people who are very important. There is also a renewed sense in the capability to love with this card. The card can also indicate the birth of a child. The Page of Cups in a reading can also indicate a person, usually an emotional male with a very youthful attitude, who comes to the querent as a guide on matters to do with the heart.

Knight of Cups: The Knight of Cups in a reading can indicate the onset of relationships that will mean a great deal to the querent. There is a sense that the querent needs to express his or her power to explore the romantic dimension of love and emotion. The card may appear in a reading when the querent has recently had a proposal of marriage. The querent may well be going through a period of falling in love and he or she is eager to express deep emotions. The Knight of Cups can also indicate the proposal of something very artistic and creative that will be very fulfilling on an emotional level. The Knight of Cups can symbolise a very emotional and sensitive youth, usually a man, who comes to the querent to help bring forth the wonderful dimension of love and romance.

Queen of Cups: The Queen of Cups symbolises the Goddess's very emotional, maternal and compassionate side. It can symbolise someone within the querent's life who embodies all of these qualities, often a mother or mothering figure. This person can bring emotional healing with ease for the querent. This very intuitive person is someone who the querent can turn to for emotional support and stability. She looks upon the querent with very loving and emotional energies. When the Queen of Cups appears in a reading perhaps it is now time for the querent to take notice of the deep, hidden messages of dreams and intuition. The card implies the deepening of the spiritual self and the awakening of intuition and psychic abilities.

King of Cups: The King of Cups symbolises the emotional, compassionate and sensitive side of the God. It can symbolise someone within the querent's life who embodies all of these qualities, often a father or fathering figure. This is a person who can heal emotions and matters of the heart with ease. As with the Queen of Cups, the King of Cups can symbolise someone who the querent can turn to for emotional support and stability. The King of Cups can symbolise that the querent needs to embrace that authority figure within with quiet confidence as the potential of great achievements are realised. The potential for matters of business, intuition and artistic talent often surround the querent when this card appears in a reading. The mastering of deep emotions are implied with this card.

Bibliography

Alexander, Brooks and Jeffrey B. Russell, *A New History of Witchcraft: Sorcerers, Heretics & Pagans*, Thames & Hudson Ltd, 2007.

Aten, James, *The Truth About Wicca and Witchcraft: Finding Your True Power*, 2008.

Baker, Marina, *Spells for Teenage Witches*, Kyle Cathie Ltd, 2000.

Bowes, Susan, *The Wiccan Handbook: A Practical Guide to Creating Magic and Mystery*, Godsfield Press Ltd, 2002.

Buckland, Raymond, *Buckland's Complete Book of Witchcraft*, Llewellyn, Revised and Expanded Edition, 2002.

Buckland, Raymond, *The Tree: The Complete Book of Saxon Witchcraft*, Samuel Weiser, Inc., 1974.

Carr-Gomm, Philip and Richard Heygate, *The Book of English Magic*, John Murray Publishers, 2010.

Clucas, Douglas and Philip, *Guide to Dreams: A Comprehensive Guide to Dreams and Dream Symbolism*, Parragon, 2012.

Crisp, Tony, *Your Dream Interpreter*, Cico Books Ltd, 2004.

Cunningham, Scott and David Harrington, *The Magical Household*, Llewellyn, 2001.

Cunningham, Scott, *Cunningham's Encyclopedia of Magical Herbs*, Llewellyn, Expanded and Revised Edition, 2002.

Cunningham, Scott, *Divination for Beginners: Reading the Past, Present & Future*, Llewellyn, 2003.

Cunningham, Scott, *Earth, Air, Fire & Water: More Techniques of Natural Magic*, Llewellyn, 1997.

Cunningham, Scott, *Earth Power: Techniques of Natural Magic*, Llewellyn, 2016.

Cunningham, Scott, *Living Wicca: A further Guide for the Solitary Practitioner*, Llewellyn, 2000.

Cunningham, Scott, *Magical Herbalism: The Secret Craft of the Wise*, Llewellyn, 2003.

Cunningham, Scott, *The Complete Book of Incense, Oils & Brews*, Llewellyn, 2019.

Cunningham, Scott, *Wicca: A guide for the Solitary Practitioner*, Llewellyn, 2011.

Dean, Liz, *The Art of Tarot: A complete Guide to Using Tarot Cards and their Meanings*, Cico Books, 2004.

Dee, Jonathan, *Runes: Reading, Casting and Divination*, Kerswell Books Ltd, 2010.

Dee, Jonathan, *Tarot: An Illustrated Guide*, Silverdale Books, 2004.

Dell, Christopher, *The Occult, Witchcraft & Magic: An Illustrated History*, Thames & Hudson Ltd, 2016.

Eason, Cassandra, *A Complete Guide to Fairies & Magical Beings*, Piatkus Books, 2011.

Ellis, Jeanette, *Forbidden Rites: Your Complete Introduction to Traditional Witchcraft*, O Books, 2009.

Farmer PHD, Steven D., *Animal Spirit Guides: An Easy-to-Use Handbook for Identifying and Understanding Your Power Animals and Animal Spirit Helpers*, Hay House, 2006.

Farrar, Janet and Stewart, *A Witches' Bible: The Complete Witches' Handbook*, Robert Hale Ltd, 1981, 1984.

Filan, Kenaz, *The New Orleans Voodoo Handbook*, Destiny Books, 2011.

Gallagher, Ann-Marie, *The Wicca Bible: The Definitive Guide to Magic and the Craft*, Godsfield Press Ltd, 2005.

Gallagher, Ann-Marie, *Wicca for Everyday Living: The Definitive Guide to Magic and the Craft*, Octopus Bounty Books, 2015.

Gardner, Gerald B., *Witchcraft Today*, 1954.

Gemondo, Millie and Trish MacGregor, *Animal Totems: The Power and Prophecy of Your Animal Guides*, Fair Winds Press, 2004.

Green, Marian, *How to be a White Witch: A Book of Transformation, Spells & Magic*, Hermes House, Anness Publishing, 2001, 2003.

Greene, Liz and Juliet Sharman-Burke, *The Mythic Tarot*, Rider Books, 2001.

Greenwood, Dr. Susan, *Witchcraft: A History: A Study of Magic and Necromancy Through the Ages, with 340 Illustrations*, Lorenz Books, Anness Publishing Ltd, 2013.

Grist, Tony and Aileen, *The Illustrated Guide to Witchcraft: The Secrets of Wicca and Paganism Revealed*, Godsfield Press Ltd, 2000.

Holland, Eileen, *The Wicca Handbook*, Robert Hale Ltd, 2009.

Horne, Fiona, *Witch: A Magickal Journey: A Hip Guide to Modern Witchcraft*, Thorsons, HarperCollins Publishers Ltd, 2000.

Hurrell, Karen and Brenda Ralph Lewis, *A History of the Unexplained*, Flame Tree Publishing, 2003.

Hutton, Ronald, *The Triumph of the Moon: A History of Modern Pagan Witchcraft*, Oxford University Press, 1999.

Illes, Judika, *The Element Encyclopedia of Witchcraft: The Complete A-Z for the Entire Magical World*, HarperElement, HarperCollins Publishers Ltd, 2005.

Jennings, Pete, *Pagan Paths: A Guide to Wicca, Druidry, Asatru, Shamanism and Other Pagan Practices*, Rider Books, 2002.

Johnstone, Michael, *The Ultimate Encyclopedia of Spells*, Eagle Editions Ltd, 2004.

LaVey, Anton S., *The Satanic Bible*, Avon Books, HarperCollins Publishers Ltd, 1969.

Lilly, Simon and Sue, *The Essential Crystal Handbook*, Duncan Baird Publishers, 2006.

MacCulloch, Diarmaid, *A History of Christianity*, Penguin Books Ltd, 2010.

Markale, Jean, *The Pagan Mysteries of Halloween*, Inner Traditions International, 2001.

Melville, Francis, *The Book of Alchemy*, Quantum Publishing, 2013.

Miller, Gustavus Hindman, *10, 000 Dreams and their Traditional Meanings*, W. Foulsham & Co, 1995.

Moura, Ann (Aoumiel), *Green Witchcraft: Folk Magic, Fairy Lore & Herb Craft*, Llewellyn, 2002.

Murray, Margaret A., *The Witch Cult in Western Europe*, Oxford University Press, 1921.

Nature's Medicines, The Reader's Digest Association Ltd, 2003.

O'Hara, Gwydion, *Pagan Ways: Finding your Spirituality in Nature*, Llewellyn, 2013.

Parker, Julia and Derek, *Guide to Astrology*, Dorling Kindersley Ltd, 2000.

Patterson, Rachel, *Kitchen Witchcraft: Crafts of a Kitchen Witch*, Moon Books, 2013.

Philip, Neil and Philip Wilkinson, *Mythology (Eyewitness Companions)*, Dorling Kindersley Ltd, 2007.

Podlech, Dieter, *Herbs and Healing Plants of Britain & Europe*, HarperCollins Publishers Ltd, 1996.

Poets' Premiere, Arrival Press, 1997.

Ravenwolf, Silver, *Silver Ravenwolf's Teen Witch Kit*, Llewellyn, 2000.

Ravenwolf, Silver, *Solitary Witch: The Ultimate Book of Shadows for the New Generation*, Llewellyn, 2007.

Silverwind, Selene, *The Witch's Journal: Charms, Spells, Potions and Enchantments*, Apple Press, 2009, 2011, 2012, 2013.

Smith, Diane, *Wicca and Witchcraft for Dummies*, John Wiley & Sons, 2005.

Starhawk, *The Pagan Book of Living and Dying: Practical Rituals, Prayers, and Meditations on Crossing Over*, HarperCollins Publishers Ltd, 1997.

St. Clair, Marisa, *Sun & Moon Signs: An Astrological Guide to Love, Career & Destiny*, Brown Packaging Books Ltd, 1999.

Struthers, Jane, *Tarot for Life and Love: Using the Tarot to get the Most out of Relationships*, Silverdale Books, 2004.

Struthers, Jane, *The Psychic's Bible: The Definitive Guide to Developing Your Psychic Skills*, Godsfield Press Ltd, 2007.

Valiente, Doreen, *An ABC of Witchcraft Past and Present*, The Crowood Press Ltd, 2016.

Valiente, Doreen, *Natural Magic*, The Crowood Press Ltd, 2016.

Valiente, Doreen, *The Charge of the Goddess*, The Doreen Valiente Foundation in association with The Centre for Pagan Studies, Expanded Edition, 2014.

West, Kate, *The Real Witches' Coven: The Definitive Guide to Forming Your Own Wiccan Group*, HarperCollins Publishers Ltd, 2003.

Wilkinson, Philip, *Religions (Eyewitness Companions)*, Dorling Kindersley Ltd, 2008.

Extended Contents

Introduction	7
Part One: About Witchcraft	13
Chapter One: Witchcraft Past and Present	14
The Ancient Roots of Witchcraft	14
The Pagan Persecutions and the Witch Hunts	17
The Golden Dawning of a New Era	23
What Then is Modern Witchcraft?	25
Witchcraft and Magic	28
The Wiccan Rede	28
Witchcraft Traditions	34
Chapter Two: The Ultimate Deity	37
Mysteries of the Goddess	39
Mysteries of the God	41
The Green Man	43
Gods and Goddesses	44
Chapter Three: The Elements	52
Element of Earth	53
Element of Air	55
Element of Fire	57
Element of Water	60
Elemental Spirits	62
Chapter Four: The Wheel of the Year	64
Yule: December 20th-23rd	65
Imbolc: February 1st-2nd	67
Eostar: March 20th-23rd	69
Beltane: April 30th to May 1st	71
Litha: June 20th-23rd	73
Lughnasadh: July 31st to August 1st	75
Mabon: September 20th-23rd	77
Samhain: October 31st to November 1st	78

Chapter Five: Witchcraft Rites	82
Naming or Wiccaning Rites	83
Coming of Age Rites	84
Initiation	85
Self-Initiation	87
Craft Names	90
Handfasting Rites	91
The Great Rite	93
Elderhood Rites	93
Death Rites	94
Chapter Six: Tools of the Trade	97
Superstitions	98
Athame	100
Bell	100
Bolline	101
Book of Shadows	101
Bowls	103
Broomstick	103
Candles	105
Cauldron	106
Censer	109
Chalice	110
Cords	110
Crystal Ball	111
Deity Images	112
Necklace	112
Pentacle	113
Scourge	116
Sword	116
Wand	117
Chapter Seven: The Altar and Sacred Space	120
Sacred Space	120
Altar Types	122
Placing the Altar	123
Arranging the Tools on the Altar	124

A Guide to Colours 127

Part Two: Spellcraft 133
Chapter Eight: Casting Spells 134
Low Magic and High Magic 135
White Magic and Black Magic 137
The Witches' Pyramid 138
Meditation 140
Visualisation 141
Spells and the Moon 142
Spells and the Sun 144
Spells and the Zodiac 146
Spells and the Seasons 148
Spells and the Four Winds 149
Spells and Correspondences 150
Spells and Herbs 151
Spells and Runic Magic 153
Spells and Poppets 158
Spells and Witch-Bottles 159
Spells, Amulets and Talismans 160
Spell Materials and a Magical Pantry 161
Robes or Skyclad? 161
Performing High Magic 163
General Preparation 163
Purification of Self 164
Consecration of the Altar and Tools 166
Purification of the Sacred Space 169
Casting of the Magic Circle 171
Invocation of the Elements 173
Invocation of Deities 175
Raising the Power 177
Fulfilment of Purpose 179
Earthing the Power 180
Thanksgiving and Farewell to Deities 181
Thanksgiving and Farewell to the Elements 182
Breaking the Magic Circle 183

Chapter Nine: Love Spells	185
Correspondences for Love Spells	187
Magical Ways to Attract Love	189
A Full Moon Love Spell	192
Chapter Ten: Money Spells	194
Correspondences for Money Spells	196
Magical Ways to Attract Money	197
A Runic Money Spell	201
Chapter Eleven: Healing Spells	204
Magical Ways to Promote Healing	208
A Water Healing Spell	213
Chapter Twelve: Success Spells	216
Magical Ways to Attract Success	219
A Fire Success Spell	222
Chapter Thirteen: Protection Spells	225
Correspondences for Protection Spells	227
Magical Ways to Aid Protection	229
An All-Purpose Poppet Protection Spell	234
Casting the spell:	235
Chapter Fourteen: Fertility Spells	237
Correspondences for Fertility Spells	239
Magical Ways to Aid Fertility	240
A Full Moon Fertility Spell	244
Casting the spell:	244
Part Three: Occult Aspects and Correspondences	247
Chapter Fifteen: Astrology	248
The Twelve Signs of the Zodiac	249
The Astrological Birth Chart	255
The Heavenly Bodies	256
Jupiter	257
Mars	259

Mercury	261
Moon	264
Moon Esbats	267
Neptune	271
Pluto	272
Saturn	274
Sun	277
Uranus	280
Venus	281
Chapter Sixteen: Herbal Lore	285
Witches and Trees	287
Herbs and the Moon	288
A Witch's Herbal	289
Chapter Seventeen: Crystals, Stones and Metals	314
Witches and Alchemy	316
A Guide to Specific Crystals, Stones and Metals	318
Chapter Eighteen: Animal Kingdom	343
The Witch's Familiar	345
A Guide to Specific Animals and Mythical Beasts	347
Chapter Nineteen: Dreams and Dream Work	391
Dreams and the Moon	393
Astral Travel	394
Universal Dream Symbolism	395
Chapter Twenty: Divination	427
Mediumship	429
The Art of Scrying	430
A Simple Scrying Ritual	431
The Art of the Tarot	433
The Major Arcana	436
The Minor Arcana: Pentacles	444
The Minor Arcana: Wands	448

The Minor Arcana: Swords 452
The Minor Arcana: Cups 457
Bibliography 463

www.ingramcontent.com/pod-product-compliance
Lightning Source LLC
Chambersburg PA
CBHW070949160426
43193CB00012B/1812